The Mirror of
SOCRATES

The Mirror of SOCRATES

Twelve Essays of a Reader on World Literature

TIBOR SCHATTELES

ARCHWAY
PUBLISHING

Archway Publishing books may be ordered through booksellers or by contacting:

Archway Publishing
1663 Liberty Drive
Bloomington, IN 47403
www.archwaypublishing.com
1-(888)-242-5904

Because of the dynamic nature of the Internet, any web addresses or links contained in this book may have changed since publication and may no longer be valid. The views expressed in this work are solely those of the author and do not necessarily reflect the views of the publisher, and the publisher hereby disclaims any responsibility for them.

Any people depicted in stock imagery provided by Thinkstock are models, and such images are being used for illustrative purposes only.
Certain stock imagery © Thinkstock.

ISBN: 978-1-4808-0552-1 (sc)
ISBN: 978-1-4808-0553-8 (e)

Library of Congress Control Number: 2014904642

Printed in the United States of America

Archway Publishing rev. date: 03/31/2014

These are simple exercises of a reader who also wants to communicate with other readers. I wrote these essays as part of a humble trial to imitate Montaigne, who said in his essay about reading books:

> «*Je ne fay point de doute qu'il ne m'advienne souvent de parler de choses qui sont mieus traictées ches les maistres du mestier, et plus veritablement. ... Ce sont icy mes fantasies, par lesquelles je ne tache point à donner à connoistre les choses, mais moy .... Je ne cherche aux livres qu'à m'y donner du plaisir par un honneste amusement.*", Montaigne, *Essais, Livre 2, Ch. X.*["I have no doubt that I quite frequently talk about things which may be better treated by the masters of the trade, and with more competence. ... These are only my fancies by which I don't try to pretend to know these things, but rather to know myself. ... I don't ask from books to offer me anything but the pleasure of an honest entertainment."]

And many books gave me indeed an *honnest amusement* which was enriched by the pleasure of discussing them with my dear wife Agnes. But I would also like to share my ideas with other readers, and, maybe, with some of those *maistres du mestier* with whom I often disagree. We may engage in discussions considering, in most cases, a second reading of the works analyzed.

These essays are based on notes made during many years of "first reading" and, after my retirement from the Canadian Federal Civil Service, I decided to organize them in one volume according to the principles developed in Introductions I and II. However, this book is not meant to be a "treatise" but rather a testimony of my reading enjoyment and an invitation to share it.

CONTENTS

INTRODUCTION I
Of Mimesis: the Eternal Debate

- Notes of a Hesitant Peripatetic -

The Ancients and the Rest of Us

The reader, certainly the attentive and discerning reader of Aristotle's Poetics and Plato's Republic, specifically the latter's books III and X, could remain with an obsession throughout his reading life: the urge to measure all his readings against the two, partly conflicting and partly complementary, theories of poetry. The compelling, if not always convincing peroration of Socrates against (many) poets *as imitators*, and poetry in general, calls for being either approved or rejected - (always in an elaborate argument) - never neglected, never again ignored. And if your conscience is bad, for having yielded to the "honeyed Muse" - and how difficult it is to resist her! "Do not you yourself feel her magic, and especially when Homer is her interpreter?" (Republic X,607,c) - then you resort to Aristotle for consolation. Most obviously to the Poetics, because immediately offering itself as a gentle antidote to the austere preaching of Socrates. Though the Stagirite's writings on logic could supply the instruments for the delightfully nasty exercise of collecting and exposing the plethora of fallacies in which Socrates/Plato indulge, they are not relieving the burden of guilt for having yielded to Feeling.

When reading just casually the *Poetics*, one cannot escape the impression that it was meant to counter the "book X" of the Republic, and to clear up as well the numerous contradictions in which Plato gets entangled when

1

discussing poetry in so many parts of his work. But this, in itself, wouldn't satisfy since the difference between the two great philosophers seems to consist only in a basic value judgment: Aristotle took the negative statements of Socrates about the *function* of art or poetry and, so to say, multiplied them by a factor of (-1). (All considered, this was quite a performance if you think that he had no clue of negative numbers.) Consequently it is as if you would have to make a *choice* between the delights offered by the "honeyed muse" and the austerity of the philosophers supposed to rule over the postulated Platonic commonwealth. No relief, such as an objective *criterion of choice,* seems to be offered by Aristotle. His major complements to whatever is to be found in book X of the Republic refer essentially to the *construction and functioning* of the poetic work, and the assessment of its characteristics as extant in Greek theater and epic up to his time. Essential to his contribution is the emphasis he places on those components which, if properly developed, will best serve the ultimate purpose of the poet when reaching and moving his public.

But what is the poet's purpose?

Socrates:

> "Listen and reflect. I think you know that the very best of us, when we hear Homer or some other of the makers of tragedy imitating one of the heroes who is in grief, and is delivering a long tirade in his lamentations or chanting or beating his breast, feel pleasure, and abandon ourselves and *accompany the representation with sympathy and eagerness, and we praise as an excellent poet the one who most strongly affects us in this way.*" [Republic X, 605, d).

This is a negative echo of a widely held view of poetry, which a forerunner of poetic theory, also an opponent of Socrates, has gracefully formulated in the words I need to quote:

> "Into those who hear it comes a fearful fright and tearful pity and mournful longing, and at the successes and failures of others' affairs and persons, the mind suffers, through speeches, a suffering of its own." [*Gorgias of Leontini: Encomium of Helen,* 9]

This is what is common to "the very best of us" and the not so good ones as well. The difference is purported to consists in the fact that the former live their own life under the stern control of Reason, and abandon themselves to the Irrational only in theater or when reading poetry and, of course, before having been warned by Socrates:

> "If you would reflect that the part of the soul that in our own misfortunes, was forcibly restrained [by reason] and that has hungered for tears and a good cry and satisfaction...then relaxes its guard over the plaintive part, inasmuch as this is contemplating the woes of others, and it is no shame to it to praise and pity another who, claiming to be a good man, abandons himself to excess in his grief, but it thinks this vicarious pleasure is so much clear gain, and would not consent to forfeit it by disdaining the poem altogether."
> [Republic X, 606, b]

Thus, it is the imitation of the meaner characters and tempers by which the poet so often appeals to the meaner, i.e. emotional and dark part of our nature.

What can Aristotle say *against* this? Whatever his answer, it is not deduced, in every respect, from a different definition of poetry. He only changes the value qualification of Socrates' assessment though never naming his opponent. Neither will he argue against the hero "who is in grief, and is delivering a long tirade in his lamentations" thereby causing us, even "the very best among us", "to praise and pity another, who claiming to be a good man, abandons himself to excess." In fact, if this pathetic hero sprang from the mind of Homer or Sophocles, he is likely to be recognized as "a higher type of character" - as we are assured in the third chapter of the Poetics. And the poet's purpose is in fact to communicate the kind of emotions for the spread of which Socrates/Plato will ban him from their Republic.

Aristotle:

> "And since the pleasure which the poet should afford is that which comes from pity and fear through *mimesis*, it is evident that this quality must be impressed upon the incidents" [Poetics, XIV, 3].

In the tragedy and the epic poem as well. And nothing is wrong with what Socrates so disdainfully calls "feeding fat the emotion of pity": this is the *catharsis*, the purgation of the soul, for the achievement of which, Aristotle sends us to theater! And much of his Poetics is concerned with the modalities to achieve this purgation.

If we agree with all three of them, Socrates, Plato and as it so often seems, also Aristotle, that *poetry* acts upon our feelings and senses, and affects our reason by their mediation, then what remains is to choose between whether this is good or bad. And if so, as always with value judgments, we would have to decide whether our choice is compatible with the set of our other values. If we may already have chosen the principles on which to build the ideal Republic (*our* ideal Republic), then the good or bad of Art, particularly poetry, will have to be measured on their scale. And if it does not measure up - banned it be from *our* Republic!

Thus what if *knowledge* about the world as perceived by our senses and thereby *learning* about it are recognized as legitimate aspirations in *our* Republic? Then we have to see whether the poet and artist can bring forth such. But can he? Indeed, asks Socrates:

> "...is Homer reported while he lived to have been a guide in education to men who took pleasure in associating with him and transmitted to posterity a certain Homeric way of life just as Pythagoras was himself especially honored for this, and his successors even to this day...?"[Republic X, 600, a-b]

The answer, as expected, is "no". But is this a proof that poetry can fulfill the desire of learning only in that limited sense promoted in the III-rd book which condemns "imitational" art? It certainly is not - except that we are to establish what can be learned, what learning is. And here the peculiar Socratic approach does not give much credit to poetry. Learning for Socrates means helping knowledge dormant in our soul to emerge with the help of a wise teacher - like him. And this knowledge is *not* about the world perceived by our senses! The world of our senses is only a pale and ephemeral reflection of the "Real World" which wise men aspire to *know*. But it is this shadow-like world which is imitated by art and poetry, thereby making even thicker and more impenetrable that screen which separates Truth from our understanding.

Consequently, we are again facing a choice: we either dismiss any possibility of knowledge other than that of the eternal Realities, dismissing thus art/poetry by implication - or we follow Aristotle. This we can also do without engaging in a lengthy debate, never to be decided. (And better switch later to Kant for a pragmatically comfortable solution).

For *Aristotle*, "the pleasure felt in things imitated" springs from a natural inclination of any human being:

> "to learn gives the liveliest pleasure, not only to philosophers but to men in general, whose capacity, however, of learning is more limited. Thus the reason why men enjoy seeing a likeness is that in contemplating it they find themselves learning and inferring..." [Poetic, ch.IV, 4]. And in another place: "Since learning and wondering are pleasant, it follows that such things as acts of imitation must be pleasant - for instance painting, sculpture, poetry - and every product of skillful imitation; the latter, even if the object imitated is not pleasant;" [Rhetoric, 1371 b, 4-8.]

But then, *Socrates* would ask: why imitate things which *are* given anyway? Learning is discovering, yet imitating the things extant is tantamount with taking

> "a mirror and carry it about everywhere. You will speedily produce the sun and all the things in the sky, and speedily the earth and yourself and the other animals and implements and plants and all the objects of which we just now spoke", [Republic X, 596, e).

Hence: what does the mirror add to what we may perceive, and thus learn about, directly?

Still, the mirror parable of Socrates wouldn't work all that well against the following two major objections of Aristotle:

> (1) "For if you happen not to have seen the original, the pleasure will be due not to the imitation as such, but the execution, the coloring, or some such other cause." [Poetics IV,5]

(2) "Objects which in themselves we view with pain, we delight in contemplating when reproduced with minute fidelity: such as the forms of the most ignoble animals and of dead bodies." [Poetics IV,3]

It is interesting that this discussion about poetry and art between the two Greek sages - who were separated by almost three generations, yet still continuing their debate even in our day - is fought with the very devices of poetry, namely parables, allegories and metaphors. Socrates himself, when promoting his argument against poetry, uses the tricks of the poet when borrowing metaphors from the art of image making. After all, he was the son of a sculptor. The difficulties of transition from these so particular examples, such as the mirror metaphor, to poetry, are not even considered: since if both - the imagery of Socrates' philosophizing and that of poetry in general - are but particular forms of imitation, why should something we say about the one not be relevant to the other? Well it is, but not all the way; and even if it were, what would then be the *raison d'être* of poetry apart from being a pedagogic device? If we peel off the film of artistry covering an instructive statement, do we not prove the futility of such "imitation"? Or do we not prove, with Socrates, *ipso facto*, that we are ready to sink basic facts of knowledge and recognition in the mire of aesthetic pleasure and the indulgence of joy, passion and pity? Remember the terrible charge of Socrates against poetic wisdom:

"So mighty is the spell that those adornments naturally exercise, though when they are stripped bare of their musical coloring and taken by themselves, I think you know what sort of a showing these sayings of the poets make. For you, I believe, have observed them"(Republic X, 601,b).

Not really a compliment to poets and their sayings. But then: why did Socrates need a parable? Perhaps because his audience was addicted to this kind of communication of which it might be cured with gradually diminishing dosage. Does anything remain, to Aristotle and everybody else, but to *proclaim* artistic pleasure to be good, vindicating thus all "those adornments" and the "musical coloring" as well? Or, maybe the Stagirite could have used against this effusion of parables employed to contest poetry, the example of a

Socrates who engages himself in poetry calling it philosophizing. Just remember book VII of Plato's Republic in which poetic artistry is used in that most beautiful parable of the cave. It was, of course, in order to impress upon his audience - *impress* I say, since *proof* it was not! - the difference between some "real" world, buried since ever in our unaware souls, and the world of shadows it casts on the only wall we can see in that metaphoric cave in which we are all captives, shadows which produce our contradiction-ridden perceptions of an elusive "Reality". Was this not teaching by poetic imagery by one who claims to disdain it? Yet Aristotle, the Father of Logic, knew quite well that resorting to such argument would have meant the crime of a grave fallacy: by *ignoratio elenchi*, the question about what the plus in art is, would have continued to beg for a plausible answer. *Ignoratio elenchi* together with *petitio principi* issued as a consequence of yielding to Man's nastier inclination towards arguing *ad hominem* was not Aristotle's way of conveying an idea! [Though Socrates never shied away from such - while neither used yet this classificatory terminology.]

If the appropriate objects had been available in his time, Aristotle could have replied, that carrying about mirrors is not the only form of imitation. There are microscopes which magnify the apparently invisible; telescopes which bring nigh the un-reachable - and as they approach the physical world, so the devices of the poet can reveal human nature and picture the human condition.

Choice and Insight

Fiddling on the optical metaphor we may get the insight which justifies poetic imitation. It is not only the microscope and the telescope which help us beyond Socrates' mirror, but it is also the *camera obscura*. "Photography is not art because it just simply imitates and reproduces" - have you ever heard this? Of course you did, just as you heard expressions of distaste when the "moving camera" allegory is used. Well, in what follows, I would argue that just as the mirror of Socrates helped to obscure the true purpose of mimesis, photography should help us understand it - up to a point.

Any imitation is a choice; and so is photography, as any earlier pictorial imitation. It doesn't simply project three-dimensional objects into a two-dimensional plane but, because this type of space requires such, makes also a choice: the angle, the closeness, the detail are not "the" object pictured, but the artist's own view of the World. Thereby it shows that the choices are the photographer's, not of the beholder's of the ready picture. Also the novel, the drama, the poem, result from a choice in which the reader/viewer does not participate; it is not the reader/viewer who chooses where that mirror of Socrates is to be carried. When you look into a microscope, a telescope or take your own photographs, it is *you* who makes the choice; when you behold a picture, attend a play, read a story - you are transferred into a world chosen by somebody else; but, possibly, chosen as a fragment of the same external world within which you may also have free choices. Except that the artist has substituted his freedom to yours: the purpose was to convey you something which was not assumed to be known to you. Or was it not the purpose to move you? - to pity the hero or poke fun at him? But then again: "who to pity?" is answered by a choice. Some are to be pitied in some context; in other context you may hate them or laugh at them - which is another choice.

Art chooses to reveal by focusing. Yet so does science. And Lucretius puts art in the service of spreading science. What can art do beyond telling us *De rerum natura* in meters? If, as Socrates would, "we will strip bare" Lucretius' didactic poem of its "musical coloring" and take it "by itself" it would remain the inventory of the knowledge of his time, that part of it we would call today scientific, with some focus on this or that - but we may not have needed the metrical rendition. It may very well be, as Aristotle said in another work, that poetic rhythm would even distract our comprehension of subjects which by their nature require discussion in prose:

> "The metrical form destroys the hearer's trust by its artificial appearance, and at the same time diverts his attention, making him watch for metrical recurrences". [Rhetoric, 1408 b, 22-25].

As for the poets who do not propagate science, "you know what sort of showing" their "sayings" make "when stripped bare of their musical coloring and taken by themselves". Still what they focus upon is the living of their experiences which does not lend itself to the conceptual rigor of science. To best understand this, let us compare the work of the scientist to that of the artist, the difference between conveying the results of *experiments* and of transmitting an *experience* (for which the German *Erlebnis* - the event lived - is probably a better term).

The scientist chooses the phenomenon to be reproduced; it is a choice between what to stabilize or neutralize in the laboratory, and what to let loose. The result, if best described, is unambiguously termed: you may agree or disagree with the generalization, you may object against the way the trial was set, but you not only know what the scientist was talking about, you may as well test the experience by repeating it (!) according to the described conditions, and arrive at a result which verifies or falsifies the scientist's contention. Never forget: the scientific experiment once *described* can be repeated.

What is the difference between a repeated experience and a play offered for the thousandth time on stage to an ever enthusiastic public? First of all that you cannot falsify its statement - it doesn't *state*! It conveys a chosen *experience*, in which you may or may not participate through empathy. The public of the literary work has something in common with the heroes. There is no 'electron' or 'molecule' or 'gene' sitting around and watching the "performance" in the laboratory; and if they were, what would they care about the results? But the "experiment" of the actors in the tale or on the stage may be your own compressed in an alembic! And that surely would interest you. It is the *parable* of the "You" one cannot make *statements* about. Because, you wouldn't really need the poetic work if you were able to reduce the experience to precise statements. It is the hallmark of bad poetry, futile one indeed, when we can translate it without a rest which cannot be *stated*. It is that *rest* we are interested in. Yet while we cannot completely reduce the parable to statements, we can, nevertheless, make statements about parables; also parables can be told about parables.

To return now to the earlier used metaphor: the picture infringes upon your freedom of choice. Some of it, anyways. But this is exactly the learning by the artist's choice: learning-by-being-taught means gaining awareness of what, in freedom, we may have missed by inadvertence or ignored on purpose. But this is not the end of your freedom. You behold the picture and you reach for a magnifier. Then you glide it on the picture, directed by your attention and get "distorted" relationships between what is framed and what is excluded by the rim of the glass - and new pictures emerge. Thus it is when you read several times the same novel, or see again and again the same play: you move around inside the closed frame.

The Superiority of Drama
(or the Dramatic)

The metaphor employed above may be modern, but very much in keeping with the Aristotelian side of the argument: the importance of focusing is fundamental in the Poetics in which tragedy is deemed superior to epic poetry. "Focusing", of course, is a term neither used in the Poetics nor employed elsewhere by the great man of Stagira. Still, the concept behind the word is definable with the help of the argument which assigns to tragedy the top place in the hierarchy of forms of literary representation; and we could easily extend this argument to drama generally, whether tragic or otherwise. The superiority of dramatic poetry, if I understood Aristotle well, consists in the concentration of the plot on a unified action. It is that "unity of action", as set up in the dramatic plot, which distinguishes the play from epic poetry:

> "As, therefore, in the other imitative arts, the imitation is one when
> *the object imitated is one*, so the plot, being an of action, must imitate
> one action and imitation that a whole, the structural union of the
> parts being such that, if any one of them is displaced or removed,
> the whole will be disjointed and disturbed". [Poetics VIII,4].

Since things and actions to be imitated exist not alone, by themselves, their extraction from the continuity of things and stream of events in order to be transformed into a *unity by mimesis*, is a choice. And Aristotle views this as being best achieved in most - not all! - cases by the dramatic plot, by its representation of action and not necessarily by the fact that it is performed on stage. Tough the *spectacle* is not altogether dismissed. We are told that emotions

> "may be aroused by spectacular means; but they may also result
> from the inner structure of the piece, *which is the better way, and
> indicates a superior poet.*" [ibid. XIV, 1].

It is the structure of the plot, the *Mythos*, which brings about the effect, and it

> "ought to be constructed so that, even without the aid of the eye,
> he who hears the tale told will thrill with horror and melt to pity

at what takes place..." [ibid] "... The Spectacle has, indeed, an emotional attraction of its own, but, of all the parts, it is the least artistic, and connected least with the art of poetry. For the power of Tragedy, we may be sure, is felt even apart from representation and actors. Besides, the production of spectacular effects depends more on the art of the stage machinist than on that of the poet." [ibid. VI, 19]

In which case what remains as the major merit of tragedy/drama is its superior ability to concentrate. But, could not any other literary form develop devices of achieving the same results expressed in the catch-phrase "unity of plot?" This possibility, in fact actuality, is granted by Aristotle but only as an exception. Homer - who else? - is the exception:

"But Homer, as in all else he is of surpassing merit, here too - whether from art or natural genius - seems to have happily discerned the truth, ... he made the Odyssey, and likewise the Iliad, to centre round an action that in our sense of the word is one." [ibid. VIII, 3]

It is thus the "arrangement of incidents", the sequence of their emergence in a necessary flow which is handled better by tragedy - and Homer.

Focusing on things we cannot put words upon: penetrating in the depth of human nature, beyond the muddled talk of the psychologizer, revealing alternative patterns of interaction in the impenetrably dense network of social relations - this is what drama is instrumental to. Not simply *imitating*, but choosing the angle of the mirror, *focusing*, reflecting in the mirror. This induces to participate in the experience which cannot be translated into a discourse of minimal ambiguity as attempted by science. The poet of drama sets up an "experiment" on the stage, I would call it a "focused imitation" of something in Nature (e.g. the Nature of Man) in order to generate *experience by empathy*, the only way of learning about things not amenable to experiment, and which cannot be described by words with precise meaning.

Dramatization of Literature

What seemed to be an indicator of superiority, characteristic of the drama (and Homer), was in fact the target pursued by literary creation, first of all by story telling, throughout its history: the transformation of sequences of stories, accidentally connected by a frame story, into necessary sequences of actions and speech, as in the modern novel, is the *history of dramatization of epic literature*. From the accidental insertion of stories within the vaguely connected novel of Apuleius to the terse unity of the best novels of Balzac, Stendhal and, of course, Flaubert, a well studied history of plot unification illustrates the yet much less well understood fact that all this is a convergence towards Aristotle's standards applied, beyond tragedy, to all poetry. Tragedy, as discussed by Aristotle, will remain thus but an exemplary paradigm: what in early times made tragedy superior to all other forms of poetry, becomes slowly the own of several other forms of story communication. Reading again all the books we ever read, now by Aristotelian standards, and comparing them with alternative readings, will reveal those unnoticed treasures which help us gain insight into the human nature beyond what can be conceptually stated, with or without pity and terror. This, however, requires an additional form of mimesis: that of the reader.

INTRODUCTION II
The Reader's Mimesis

After Socrates, the legitimacy of artistic *mimesis* has seldom been questioned in any substantive argument. The question was rather: who imitates *what* and *how*, and not *whether* to imitate. Yet the prevailing answers defined and interpreted artistic imitation from the point of view of the artist's or the poet's own relation to the thing imitated. After all, the Work itself was the product of the artist's Mimesis. For the viewer, listener, reader - passivity was implied; for them somebody else's choice was there to be accepted or rejected. But, are we only passive receivers when confronted with the artwork? Is only he who carries around the Mirror, Socrates' mirror that is, actively choosing and focusing? Can we do anything beyond simply receiving the reflected image? These questions were already hovering in the background of philosophical discussions in the time of Plato, but were more explicitly raised, in a variety of formulations, in the para-philosophical literature of Hellenistic vintage. A most revealing instance is communicated by Philostratos of Lemnos in his fiction-like recounting of the travels of *Apollonius of Tyana*, which includes, in a frame of colorfully - and thereby readably - distorted historic facts, a wealth of charming parables, alternating with philosophical discussions, as well as an assortment of plain nonsense.

The Lesson of Philostratos

The section to be discussed is a dialogue between Apollonius himself and his travel companion Damis concerning imitation, particularly painting. With the suggestive power which is any good parable's own, we are induced

13

to sense the possibility of effectively transcending our status of passive recipients of an artwork. While indicating a positive acceptance of artistic imitation, Apollonius makes a clear distinction between *the skill to imitate* and the ability to *think the imitated object*:

> "Then, O Damis, the mimetic art is twofold, and we may regard the one kind as an employment of the hands and mind and producing imitations, whereas the other kind consists in making likenesses with the mind alone".

But Damis would not agree to such a radical distinction:

> "'Not twofold,' replied Damis, 'for we ought to regard the former as the more perfect and more complete kind being anyhow painting, and a faculty of making likenesses with the help of both mind and hand; but we must regard the other kind [imitating with mind alone] as a department of that, since its possessor perceives and imitates with the mind, without having the delineative faculty, and would never use his hand in depicting its objects.'"

> "'Then,' said the other, 'we are both of us, Damis, agreed that *man owes his mimetic faculty to nature, but his power of painting to art*.'"
> [Book II, Chapter XXII]

The explication conveyed through this dialogue implies that not only the artist, the master of a particular *techne*, is in the possession of the faculty of imitation. His imitative work would be worthless if the *mind* of the viewer wouldn't be able to perform the same imitative act when receiving the artwork:

> "And for this reason I should say that those who look at works of painting and drawing require a mimetic faculty; for no one could appreciate or admire a picture of a horse or of a bull, unless he had formed an idea of the creature represented."

The value of an imitation is thus to be judged according to the ability of the viewer "to do the same" as the artist, but only in thought. This would then be the *mimesis* of the art receiver, in this particular case, the beholder of a painting. At least it is a first step in the viewer's imitation, since he may be able to go beyond that, and *imitate the artist's constructive venture itself.* "Going beyond" could certainly be more important as soon as we have to do with imitations which are less straightforward than the "picture of a horse or of a bull". From this point on, however, two lines of interpretation can be developed, both present in the disquisitions of Apollonius; the first expounded in more detail, the second just outlined *in nuce*.

First, we have the traditional attempt to stress the purportedly manifest message of the imitation, as well as the search for hidden meanings. Thus, when arriving in Nineveh, Apollonius saw

> "an idol set up in barbarous aspect, and it was, they say, Io, the daughter of Inachus. ... He [Apollonius] was staying there and forming wiser conclusions about the image than could the priests and prophets." [Book I, Chapter. XIX.]

We never learn from the text what those "wiser conclusions" were. It remains a mystery whether they were translated into parabolic wisdom, as often encountered in this remarkable book, or expounded as hermeneutical exegesis. We may, perhaps, discount the latter, if we believe the confessions of Apollonius about his knowledge of all languages without ever having learned any of them:

> "You need not wonder at my knowing all human languages; for, to tell you the truth, I also understand all secrets of human silence."

This virtue is particularly valuable when that silence comprehension is not mistranslated into words. Of course, many an interpreter of texts and artworks, from the author of the Barnabas letter to Martin Heidegger and his disciples, were deprived of such excellence. But our sophist Philostratos, in his *Imagines*, did not go beyond the meaningfully speakable, recommending even the avoidance of the anecdotic splicing of art interpretation with chatter about the lives of artists, an overrated practice which plagued the study and understanding of the arts in his days as in ours:

> "The present discussion ... is not to deal with painters nor yet with their lives; rather we propose to describe examples of paintings in the form of addresses which we have composed for the young, that by this means they may learn to interpret paintings and to appreciate what is esteemed in them." [Book I., Introduction.]

But there is a *second* kind of "making likenesses with the mind alone" and indeed "without having the delineative faculty" of the artist. It is the *production of mental equivalents of the artist's "delineative faculty" itself*, an exercise to be performed by those who receive the product of this faculty. This is the concern of the present exercise which discusses the *imitative faculties of the reader*, though employing examples from other arts as paradigms of interpretation.

Imitating the Imitated and the Imitator

We may approach the artwork in two ways. One is the way of science which communicates its findings in (so we desire) clearly stated propositions. These statements may be true or not; accepted (verified) or falsified. Yet scientific results can (should) be translated into clearly definable terms; at least so we aspire.

Of course, we may do the same thing for the work of art or poetry in a variety of contexts: linguistic, psychological, sociological etc. All these, however, refer to the work of art or poetry as a source of indirect information about something quite often alien to its own purpose. The work serves in this case as a document or, perhaps in a roundabout fashion, as an object of scientific experimentation. Of the same class are studies pertaining to the artist's life as, perhaps, relevant to the subject of "how artists get an idea to produce a work" under such and such circumstances. However interesting such studies may be, they are extraneous to the work itself; in such investigations the work of art becomes an object like anything physicists or astronomers are studying, except that it will prove to be - in this context! - much less interesting than the mechanics of molecules or the movement of galaxies. The work of art - or literature, if worthy of consideration, is a lot more than an auxiliary for indefinite "sciences" such as psychology or sociology, and reaches beyond its often assigned degrading role of a pretext for anecdotic recreation.

The alternative to be chosen is that of Mimesis. *Imitating* the art work? Yes. Not copying it but mentally imitating the process which brings it about, i.e. mentally "simulating" the technical process of creation *implicit in the accomplished work*. The necessity of such imitation has its origin in the assumption that the art/literary work carries more than what can be clearly stated. The *understanding* is not meant to happen by simple, passive contemplation or, God forbid, mediated by hermeneutic adulteration. Neither is meant the use of that elusive something designated by the semantically atrocious term: "deconstruction". The latter is anyway nothing but an attempt to translate into purportedly meaningful statements that what cannot be stated, thus an exercise in burying the artwork in pseudo-statements. (This should be discussed later. Here the positive and not the polemical should be of our concern.)

The mimesis we mean is the one stressed by Philostratos. Of course, as earlier quoted, we ought to know that

> "... those who look at works of painting and drawing require a mimetic faculty;"

But then we also are told that

> "... man owes his mimetic faculty to nature"

quite independently of whether he possesses or not any kind of "delineative faculty". And, we should add, this *mimetic faculty* employs techniques just as the *delineative faculty*, and in many respects very similar ones indeed. In other words it mentally imitates the *delineative process* itself. This point shall be stressed by examples the order of which, itself, is meant to convey what is difficult (impossible?) to convey by conceptual discourse.

The *raison d'être* of art consists in the fact that the artwork is the conveyer of something which is beyond what can be meaningfully, *completely*, stated. This is best shown in music, the first of the examples to be discussed, which offers the extreme case of that which cannot be translated into meaningful speech. Further, the argument will return to painting, as an explanatory paradigm, thus bringing us a few steps closer to the literary adventure. And a warning should be added: this is not a discussion about "how music/painting should be understood". It is rather an exercise in which we try to recall the most common facts about our access-path to these arts, putting the stress on the *imitative element* in our own approach. Thereby we may come close to gain, by analogy, an understanding of what we call the *reader's mimesis*.

What Cannot be Stated: Music

Take any particular piece of music. What does it "say"? Well, it may not be very difficult to find a music critic who will quickly oblige with some sort of an answer. But then, when asking how his sentences *follow* from the sounds constituting the mentioned composition, you (and he) may be at a loss if he will fail to remain silent. No statement can follow from sounds. We know that; yet most of us indulge, occasionally, in trying to verbally express our subjective impressions with the claim of characterizing that what we have listened to.

How is this different from "speaking science"? The things a scientist talks about may be real or imagined. But the language he uses - words, sentences, symbols, formulae - can partly be "pinned" on those things (real or imagined) and partly deduced by logical consecution from the former. We know what the scientist talks about whenever he uses words "on things". Or, if we don't know what it is about we can learn it unambiguously. But can we put a *sound* or any musical phrase on a "feeling" or an "idea"? Perhaps each of us can do this separately, but then how do we communicate it to one another? And then: how do I translate my "feelings"?

The composer when composing may think about anything real or just fancied. But the language he uses - sounds according to their scale, harmonic principles, etc. translated into scores - cannot be connected in any fashion to things or clear and distinct concepts. We may get close to what he does by studying music, i.e. its technical language. But then we find out how the composer masters the sounds, not how he relates to them, not "what he wants to say" by them. It is quite likely that there may be many technically and historically different ways of expressing the same thing. But then how do we retrace the relationship and translate it into statements? We certainly don't. Yet we may still have an access to the "message". This could happen by the mimesis of the listener: he will *imitate* the music - without the composer's "delineative faculty" - in several phases, either in an orderly sequence or, perhaps, by skipping some phases. Such imitation may proceed, e.g., by stages:

- Listening, i.e. directly developing affinities with the composition; but then the

- study of technicalities is to follow along with their *mental imitation*, which helps to

- relive the creative process of somebody else when listening to and/or reading his music.

Do we thus arrive to something? Well, at least to the pleasure of doing it. He who is sufficiently lucky to "intuit" the composer may reach far. But then there is the intervention of the instrumental interpreter of music when, once again, the word will be absent and technical "imitation" will communicate the composition. When the Word intervenes, as in the Opera, then the music becomes, at least partly, a language convention; it is the composer's musical mimesis of a text which limits our freedom, that freedom which music without "words" may give us.

The merely suggestive character of these remarks should now be completed with a short discussion of an art which, unlike music, *admits a limited meaningful verbal translation of its contents*. It is, once again, *painting*.

The Metaphor of Painting

Throughout the history of literature *painting* was a frequently recurring *metaphor of poetry interpretation*. Well, not only painting but any other form of two-dimensional imitation of three-dimensional objects in the world of our elementary perception. The archetype of this metaphor is the mirror of Socrates: it reflects in two dimensions whatever is given as the world experienced as being three dimensional. From this to painting proper there is only a small step. Aristotle made this step when justifying poetic imitation in his *Poetics*, and Philostratus has most ably used it in the above quoted history. Later Horace offered examples for the various uses of the metaphor in his *Ars Poetica*. When claiming that *ut pictura poesis*, he proposed a wide application of this symbol, ranging from the criticism leveled upon various odd aberrations produced in the name of *poesis* - as in the first lines of his poem about poetry; to the manners of viewing the work - as in the section from which the above words were quoted. So, given the distinguished lineage of the subject, nobody has to be embarrassed by raising it up again. Only this time an attempt will be made to spell out all its practical implications in connection with the parallelism of approaches to poetic and pictorial works.

The Lesson of the Painter and the Poet

Let's walk into a museum and try to translate in words some of the paintings we see. The *prima faciæ* physical perception is easily translatable, with no advanced information or study, even before reading the titles which in many cases go beyond the strictly visible. Thus we may assess that: "this is a man on a crucifix"; "this is a woman with a child in her arms"; "this is the left profile of a man with a crooked nose, wearing a red cap"; "on this picture there is a scene [we know, of course, how imprecise the word 'scene' is] with about eight characters, among them three light clothed diaphanous young women"; "on this picture a winged personage [conventionally designated as 'angel'] is kneeling in front of a lady in a gracious, elegant attitude [already a problem: what is 'gracious' or 'elegant'?], while in the rear, a landscape is visible through an open window" [and we may go about detailing the landscape]; etc. etc. We used mostly terms which will not be questioned by anybody beholding the same paintings; and we may go into great detail in this procedure. But thereby we limited our translation to the narrowly meaningful and thus (almost) totally useless from the point of view of that something which we may call, or rather suggest being, "artistic experience". We may add a little more by describing colors, forms etc. again in very general, convention hallowed terms, and therefore, once again, with a very limited range. If we now continue by stating that the crucified man is surrounded by paintings of scenes then, unless we have exogenous literary information (such as the Gospels), the only thing we can do by *verbal translation* is to count the characters, describe their attires and attitudes, etc. The rest is strictly our intimate experience of what we so hazily call and deeply feel as Beauty, which we may *express* in equally hazy terms (as your favorite art critic would gladly do); but whatever we manage to translate remains ambiguous, to say the least. (Not so for the person to whom the painting is a religious symbol because he is already beyond the physically visible and verbally translatable: his access to the painting is determined by its conventional significance which follows from more than the verbal record of the optically perceivable). Thus, beyond music, the untranslatable, we find that painting, sculpture, etc. may be given verbal expression in a very limited way. Just let us see how far we may go.

In common parlance we may be able to communicate what we see in very simple terms and perhaps with a measure of precision. Say, for example, about the young ladies we saw on that above mentioned painting that they are "aerial" or "charming" or "gracious" or "diaphanous", and we will surely find somebody who may associate with these terms lacking precision, the same type of emotion as ourselves. Such may not always be completely useless, though far it may never lead. Thus consider that there still remains room for *verbal imitation* of the pictorial art work, namely that of the poet. It could be qualified as an *imitation of an imitation* which leads the beholder beyond the simple optical registration, guided by somebody who does *not* resort to conceptual explication. Countless examples, of unequal value, could be quoted from literature. As a paradigm we may choose a very fine one, namely Robert Browning's *Fra Lippo Lippi*. The choice is not random. Lippi's purported confession, if its fragments are rearranged as a discourse, will reveal the complete process of what we may perceive as a *poetic "imitation" of the genesis of a work of art*, and discover also the limitations of this type of imitation. One may start with a section, well beyond the middle of the poem, when the painter argues against those who echo the Socratic indictment of imitation, and who profess that

> "... His [God's] works
> "Are here already; nature is complete:
> "Suppose you reproduce her - (which you can't)
> "There is no advantage."

It no doubt reminds us the words of Socrates that such imitation is tantamount to taking

> "a mirror and carry it about everywhere. You will speedily produce the sun and all the things in the sky, and speedily the earth

and yourself and the other animals and implements and plants and all the objects of which we just now spoke" [Plato: Republic X, 596, e].

This will not lead you to anything new, least the "Truth" you are searching for. Browning's answer, instead, echoes Aristotle [Poetics, 1448b, 5-20]:

"... don't you mark? we're made so that we love
"First when we see them painted, things we have passed
"Perhaps a hundred times nor cared to see;
"And so they are better, painted - better to us,
"Which is the same thing. Art was given for that."

And to add the poet's/painter's belief:

"God uses us to help each other so,
"Lending our minds out."

The Knowledge which goes into the work is of two parts. The first is life's experience, the things un-translatable into conceptual discourse. In the case of Lippi:

"... when a boy starves in the streets
"Eight years together, as my fortune was,
"Watching folk's faces to know who will fling
"The bit of half-stripped grape-bunch he desires,
"And who will curse or kick him for his pains, -
"Which gentleman, processional and fine,
"Holding a candle to the Sacrament,
"Will wink and let him lift a plate and catch
"The droppings of the wax to sell again.."

These conditions then enlighten us:

"Why, soul and sense of him grow sharp alike,
"He learns the looks of things ..."

And the first results come forth:

"I had a store of such remarks, be sure,
"Which, after I found leisure, turned to use.
"I drew men's faces on my copy books,
"Scrawled them within the antiphonary's marge."

Here the poet *imitates the painter's insight* but *not yet his work*. Is it possible to go beyond what is said so far? When the artist paints, and the poet imitates him, poetically, the verbal reproduction of the things seen is similar in content to the "protocol statements" or "elementary statements", as the ones listed at the beginning of this section, and designated here with expressions borrowed from the Vienna School of philosophers or Wittgenstein. It does reproduce only the rudiments of the process of bringing about the work, while the description of the result is that gentle, kindly spoken rendition of the plainly visible, to move those who already developed emotional sensitivity for the spoken *Word* beyond the *Thing* beheld. Yet they will recall only the obvious or the facts stressed by convention:

"First, every sort of monk, the black and white
"I drew them, fat and lean: then folk at church,
"From good old gossips waiting to confess
"Their cribs of barrel-droppings, candle-ends, -
"To the breathless fellow at the altar-foot
"Fresh from his murder, safe and sitting there
"With the little children round him in a row
"Of admiration, half of his beard and half
"For that white anger of his victim's son
"Shaking a fist at him with one fierce arm,
"Signing himself with the other because of Christ..."

How much farther can we go on this way? So far we passed through the following stages of reckoning with the art work:

1) Verbal description of the things in which we employ, as Apollonius would say, our own "mimetic faculty"; but this mimetic

faculty offers us access only to as much as we have previously perceived with our own mind. It does not imply anything about the *recognition which is generated by the experience of "delineation"* which we haven't yet imitated. Because we have no prior experience of it!

2) The poet may lead us a step farther when stirring our empathy for the artist's experience which lent him the vision yet still not the *techne*, the only thing verbally translatable, to be thus imitated.

And when the poet establishes communication between us and the work of art, then we just moved from one set of conceptually inexpressible experiences to another one, the one to be studied later, yet not before pointing to a deeper layer of our *possible* imitative participation in painting. The first hint should come from yet another work of master poetry - in prose: an instance from Proust's *chef d'oeuvre,* specifically its fifth part, *La Prisonnière.*

Literary and Technical Imitation of the Pictorially Imitated

It is the story of the experience of the writer Bergotte, an important character in the novel, with Vermeer's "*The View of Delft*". As we read in the story, the painting was lent out by the museum in The Hague to be displayed at a Dutch exhibition in Paris. A sick Bergotte came to see the display in spite of his doctor's advice, because

> «... *un critique ayant écrit que dans la Vue de Delft de Ver Meer ... tableau qu'il adorait et croyait connaître très bien, un petit pan de mur jaune (qu'il ne se rappelait pas) était si bien peint qu'il était, si on regardait seul, comme une précieuse oeuvre d'art chinoise* ...» ["a critic has written that in the *View of Delft* by Ver Meer ... a painting he adored and thought to know very well, there was a little yellow wall section (which he didn't recall) so well pained that if viewed separately it looked like a most precious Chinese artwork."]

and he wanted to see and *experience* it again. Bergotte made thus additional discoveries:

«... *grâce à l'article du critique, il remarqua pour la première fois des petits personnages en bleu, que le sable était rose, et enfin la précieuse matière du tout petit pan de mur jaune.*» ["thanks to the critic's article he noticed for the first time tiny blue characters, that the sand was pink, and finally the precious matter of that very little yellow wall section."]

Once again we read about an attempt to verbally communicate something of what was made visible by the painter. The *critique* in the story was, of course, more honest than some of his colleagues. He was talking only about quasi-technical details. But the *literary imitation of the pictorially imitated* could not go farther without running the risk of becoming a technical treatise on painting. Such treatise, however, can be specific about one or another work only in terms of the verbally translatable aspects of what we have encountered in Philostratos as the *delineative faculty*.

Learning about the "Delineative Faculty"

Consequently, as discussed earlier, words hit a limit when trying to reproduce the particular, individual aspects of any given work of art: the *personality* of the artwork is not translatable in scientific words, which are deprived of personality. When reaching that frontier, the verbal road bifurcates: either blah-blah or parable. The latter, however, becomes a new art form, a new form of imitation, i.e. imitating the artistic imitation by yet another artistic, literary, imitation; and we discuss it where it belongs: literature. To understand how the reader "imitates" that, let us dwell first upon the technical part of painting, its simulation by the beholder.

We always start, naturally, by simply viewing any work. A great step ahead in *mentally imitating the painter's labor* is made by learning about the *techniques* of the painter and not, Heaven forbid, about "what he wanted to express". Learning about colors, paints, drawing, perspective, light and its effects, proportions and masses ... etc. etc., either by formal study or "by training the eye" in the museum, is the best way to imitate the painter. Why? Because this is the only way to mentally reproduce the manner in which another person, perhaps a great artist, produced the object to which we are in search of an approach. Thus we may imitate the artist's work and share in his effort and - who knows?

- his joy. Though there is no discourse by which we could translate his recognition and joy into ours.

Everything in the technical process - not the talent! not the thoughts of the artist! - can be imitated mentally, because the rules of the *craft*, the *techne*, can be indeed translated into words. Thus the viewing "imitator" may put himself in the state of mind of the artist and - may be! - partake in his experience. Any other "explanation", "interpretation", "reading" is sterile verbiage. We *may* state non-technical things about the artwork; but as far as this usually goes, it will degrade the work of art to the rank of a futile exercise. However, what may be stated in plain, clear, meaningful sentences, are the construction principles of the work, and by this approach we may learn about the artist's activity and get ready to mentally partake in his experience.

Imitating the Poetic Imitation

While meaningful speech is word-locked, words themselves are free; they may *indicate* (i.e. *allude to, suggest* etc., but not unambiguously *designate*) that which we are supposed to be silent about; they may also conjure (by association) experiences we had and want others to partake in. Such experiences occur within given *circumstances*. As these circumstances are given we may describe them meaningfully; we must not be silent about them. The multiplicity of events, materially identifiable situations and actions which the words can meaningfully describe, create the *experimental* conditions for the human *experience*, that experience which itself cannot be translated into scientific discourse, but which may be suggested by a poem, a play or a story.

[An example, a rather sordid one, is offered by the stories of Hemingway. He wrote numbers of stories in which the action was built-up to a one-step-from-death situation; be it under the glittering snow of the Kilimanjaro, or across a river, in the trees, lurking for the game. These were the *circumstances of an experience* which may only have been suggested. Because the experience proper was that of the author who shot himself, after which he did not communicate anything anymore.]

Thus not only music, painting and other non-verbal "imitative" arts find their *raison d'être* in the push beyond the limits of the speakable, but the art of language, Literature, itself. We all know that the simple telling of a story or relating of an experience is in itself not yet a literary work; and that it becomes such only by some "tricks". Some of these can be typified, some others not. The rules of prosody may refer to one class of such "tricks"; yet even these don't constitute a closed set. New membership is always admissible - with clear identification of the members. Yet the unlimited treasure of ways of verbal representation of things, people, their actions, states of mind etc. cannot be typified *for the use of the reader*. The scientific researcher may be justified in doing classifications. All science begins with such but, in the case of literature, the reader's profit from the exercise will often be altogether limited. His imitative transcending of that which is expressible in scientific discourse is to proceed in a different fashion. First, he will have to renounce any attempt to *state* anything beyond what is *in the work*. Otherwise he may push himself into a hermeneutic quagmire. Yet he can still *say* a lot, reaching beyond what can and has been - usefully - typified by the literary scholar. This is about the way, the infinity of ways, a story, an anecdote, a tragic/comic occurrence has been molded into a literary work. Doing this we may relive the production of the work and enjoy a second reading. How? No rules can be given. But the few exercises included in the following essays may testify for an enjoyable way of *imitative reading* which I recommend as an antidote against many a fashionable pretentious nonsense. Thus we proceed to some exercises in reading "essential" works, some of them of the classical heritage of Western literature. The essays to follow intend to be exercises in *imitative reading*. This will, partly, mean a return to older approaches, some as old as the ancient philosophers', some others being nurtured on the lessons of such great, yet "out-of-fashion" scholars of the literary adventure as Albert Thibaudet and Erich Auerbach, or even Georg Brandes - to mention only a few of those whom I so highly respect. Thus the choice of readings and the leaning on past achievement will purpose the introduction, through exemplary cases, in the *reader's imitation*.

NOTE to INTRODUCTION II
A Few Nasty Remarks on the Verbal
Translation of Paintings

How far can you go in explaining "what the artist intended to communicate"? Let us review a couple of examples. Several years ago I enjoyed a retrospective exhibition of the works of Cezanne. Among the many beautiful paintings there was a canvas representing a *"young girl at the piano"*. It could have been any nice little girl playing anything and the painting would still have been beautiful. To the painter himself it represented, naturally, something from his personal experience. So he mentioned it in a remark added to the title, which reads: *"Ouverture to Tannhäuser"*. Does this really mean something? Because I had the distinct impression that she was playing *"Malbrough s'en va-t-en guerre"*. When I first saw it. A second time I had the impression that she was rather playing *"Für Elise"*. After all, I had great trouble understanding how the little girl could have tinkled Wagner's music with her little fingers.

Well, the artist can be forgiven, and his memories do not carry any obligation for the viewer. Neither do the following profound remarks added by an erudite museum curator to a Picasso painting titled: *Woman seated in an armchair,* dated 24.06.39 and exhibited in Montreal, 1995. Here is the text meant to benefit the puzzled viewer:

> "The elegant features of Picasso's mistress, Dora Maar, were subject to increasingly alarming deformations in his paintings of 1939.
> Both painter and model are said to have been profoundly disturbed by contemporary events and their anxiety is perhaps reflected here in crude application of paint, the distorted, angular forms and the tense pose of Dora Maar gripping the arms of her chair."

Now you know at least where the "crude application of paint" is coming from. In this respect another painter, the one who so much angered Don Quixote, was a lot more precise. We remember, of course, that

> ".. Orbaneja, the painter of Úbeda, who when asked what he was painting, answered: whatever may come out of it. Once he was painting a cock so miserably that it was necessary to write bellow it 'This is a cock'" [DQ, v.II, Ch.III]

I am sure Picasso did not skip this chapter. And what we ought to know is not so much "what a painting represents", but rather what we can understand of that which is represented by investigating the art, the τεχνη of representation.

ESSAY NO.1

Aristotle's Poetics: Limits and Relevance

- Concerning the "Unities": from Aristotle to Shakespeare -

"But the Unities have for me, at least, a perpetual fascination. I believe
they will be found highly desirable for the drama of the future. For one
thing, we want more concentration."

T. S. Eliot

A Reader's Confessions

There was a time when, at least in some parts of the world, literary education
even on high school level included also the basic principles of Aristotle's
Poetics. This time included also my own school years. Though Aristotle was
not really the norm recommended to be followed, his poetic doctrine – edited a little according to Boileau - was studied as a measure to relate to; which
means that when literary forms were analyzed, they were defined as either
illustrating or contradicting the principles set down in the "*Poetics*". Not that
major literary doctrines, from Horace to Corneille to Lessing, were neglected, but they were measured always against the classical text of the Stagirite.
And so it happens that being brought up in respect for the great philosopher
he continues to nestle in the back of my mind, from were he keeps exerting
control over my choices as a helpful yet stern teacher, but often also as a rather uncomfortable intruder. Still, whenever I considered emancipating from
this tutorship, I perceived him as quite irritating. There is, of course, a gentle

and considerate way of emancipation (or cop-out) from such guardianship which pays Aristotle and his literary theories the due respect by proclaiming their validity limited, yet still applying in our days, while admitting his contribution as having paramount pertinence only for the poetry of some remote past. Well, how narrow or wide are then the limits within which Aristotle's Poetics could still bear relevance in our days? Because, though he constantly interferes with our readings claiming to be, if not fully accepted, at least considered and only then, if at all, qualified or rejected. And I don't really mind to engage in such an exercise which I could easily accommodate with Descartes' wise advice to first take shelter in a however humble philosophical hut before having completed the design of a more palatial system of understanding. So I will try to first ascertain how resistant the Aristotelian "hut" is, and what security it is still able to provide, before carving out, from past readings, the elements for a more comprehensive design.

The modern reader - by which I mean the reader since the late Renaissance - as well as the critic, had and still have trouble with several important theses in the "Poetics". Some of these propositions have been simply dismissed as wrong or obsolete or by that they were "not really meant". Thus the "three unities" - of action, space and time - as a norm to be followed by the dramatic poet, were said to have only been read-into the "Poetics" by fellows such as Giulio Cesare Scaliger (1484-1558) and later canonized by French literary doctrinaires, the latter receiving also the blessing of Richelieu, moved by whatever odd *raison d'état*. Further, the dismissal by Aristotle of acting and stage managing as a secondary matter, which has very little to add to the relevance of the plot, is said to apply mainly to the theatre *as known to him* but not to writing for the stage in all times. And then there are the theses about the unity of the work of epic poetry and the problem of the unbalancing burden of episodes. I subjected all these propositions, not once but very often and deliberately, to a reading and theatre going test, to a subjective experience that is. Since the tests were subjective, they produced no general theoretical propositions. Such results could have been accomplished, perhaps, by the academic or professional litterateur. I, however, was out for enjoyment and have repeatedly discovered the pleasure of approaching literary works from different theoretical angles.

One trick I employed was to confront the arguments not of scholars but of the poets themselves, poets separated in time or space, applying contradictory principles and calling in as witness their own poetical achievements. Is there a difference between the way poets and scholars deliberate on the topic of poetics? One answer seems to be obvious: the poet is able to quote his creative experience, alien to even the most erudite authority. This should be granted. But here the focus will not be on the sources of knowledge but rather the medium by which it is conveyed. Poets, of course, notwithstanding their intimate experience, may resort to the same vehicle of scholarly dissertation as any professor or just literary critic. That their discourse may be written in the fine verses of Horace's epistle on the "*Ars poetica*" or Alexander Pope's "Essay on Criticism" (or in the bad verses of several others), would not make for the dissimilarity to be emphasized. The point to be made is that since the late Renaissance and to our century, poets often braided their own *ars poetica* into some of their poetic work. The most important yet also most neglected example to be quoted is that of Shakespeare. He may not have been the first, but certainly the best among the early users of this trick. Therefore let us invite him, and his great contemporary, Cervantes - two masters separated in space, of course, and unknown to each other - and let them debate the issue of the "unities".

In fact these two distinguished examples are not an exception in the age we commonly call the late Renaissance. But then, what exactly was the purpose of such an exercise? One possible goal could have been to educate their public for the reception of an innovation. Because, unlike theoretical works, plays and stories are not written for scholars or nosy amateurs who also read erudite disquisitions. They are addressed to the "general public". Yet this public may have only limited access to the literary artwork when the innovative poet attempts to transcend the frontiers of unmediated receptive intuition or any hallowed custom. Therefore some poets must have thought it useful to smuggle theory into the poetic text itself thus expanding the reader's or viewer's own range of reception. Yet, again, it may be that the poet simply thought to promote some innovation against the opposition of a section of the more sophisticated part of their public. To convey the argument within the poetic work itself, as Shakespeare did (in the example to be discussed), could have been just a matter of personality. Another contemporary, Lope de Vega, an author in the very next class of excellence, wrote instead a rather casual, but worthwhile and revealing discourse on the *"Arte nuevo de hacer comedias en este tiempo"*, or "The New Art of Writing Comedies in our Age", purporting to be an apology for his departures from the classical canon. Typically, it was addressed to a learned society and not to the general public whom he believed to already well understand his unorthodox manner of "writing comedies". It is likely, however, that while both, Lope *and* Shakespeare, aimed at the educated, (Shakespeare was often criticized for his ignorance of Latin), the English poet was addressing everybody attending his plays. Is it still of some interest to us? The forthcoming argument implies an answer in the affirmative.

The Aristotelian "Yoke"

Aristotle *did* imply the unities, though it is not quite clear whether always as a stringent norm or just as part of the assessment of the state of poetic/dramatic arts. That the *unity of action* was viewed as a basic norm, follows from the critical disapproval of works composed of stringed-up and barely related episodes. For the *unity of time* we learn that "tragedy endeavors, as far as possible, to confine itself to a single revolution of the sun, or but slightly to exceed this limit; whereas the epic action has no limits of time" (*Poetics*, V.4-5) [All subsequent quotations from the "Poetics" are in the translation of S.H.Butcher.]. And though nothing is explicitly stated about the *unity of space*, the elementary intuitive association of space with time makes it anyway difficult to imagine a big deal of traveling during one theatre performance [or more liberally: "a single revolution of the sun"] if the unity of time is to be respected. Since, as we are told by Crites, a character in Dryden's *"Of Dramatic Poesy"*,

> "... a greater distance will bear no proportion to the shortness of time which is allotted, in acting, to pass from one .. [scene] .. to another; for the observation of this the French are to be most commended."

(Never mind that in Aeschylus' *Eumenides*, Orestes starts out in Delphi and pops up later in Athens. He may have taken the day-tour option and thus created one of those exceptions which stress the rule. And this was well before a more "sloppy" writer, Euripides, made Theseus traffic between Athens and Thebes, to the posthumous reproach of Eugenius, another purported friend of

Dryden.) So a statement about the unity of space was in fact redundant once the unity of time was postulated. At least if we apply some tolerance; since the time/space continuity was never perfect.

The unities were meant as a focusing device which was to guarantee that particular attribute of the dramatic work which, by Aristotle, made it superior to other poetic output, namely the quality to concentrate on *action*. Transcending the unities meant for everybody a huge leap beyond the immediate, the elementary-intuitive, and it might have required a major intellectual effort. At the same time, the respect of the three restrictive principles assured *comfortable receptive passivity* for the member of the public who was not compelled to the strain of *substituting thinking for direct intuition* - something Shakespeare was to request from him very explicitly. Whether the first intellectual effort to transcend naive perception was indeed so great, remains an open question. It may not have been all that easy, considering the centuries required for such a big leap forward. We should recall that well after Shakespeare yet another friend of the already quoted Dryden called "unnatural" all space and time incongruities on the stage. This may hardly have been an isolated opinion or way of perception and it was probably more widespread among the average theatre goer, who had no idea of Aristotle or the Greeks. And should "the French ... be most commended" it might have been because they, as represented by Boileau, so well understood the public's mode of perception:

«*Qu'en un lieu, en un jour, un seul fait accompli*
Tienne jusqu'à la fin le théatre rempli»
[That in one place, in one day, a single action performed,
Will keep the theatre filled.]

[Boileau. *Art poétique*, III]

It is probably this common viewer meant by Boileau whom also Cervantes defends when criticizing some of his contemporaries for having sinned against the "unities" - changing thereby the approach of the public. Cervantes probably expressed the amazement of the less sophisticated theatre-goer when asking through the good priest of Don Quixote's parish:

"What greater non-sense can you think of in the context of our subject [i.e. the three unities] than having a baby in diapers walking on the stage in the first scene of the first act and then seeing him again in the second scene as an accomplished bearded man" (Don Quixote, part I, ch.XLVIII).

Does all this not contradict the wise

"opinion of Tully, that comedy be a mirror of human life, a sample of customs, an image of truth"?

And if there was any "greater non-sense" than the one quoted, here it is:

"I have seen comedies in which the first act started in Europe, the second took place in Asia and ended with the third in Africa; and had the play had a fourth act too, this one would have been placed in America".

[It is significant that the acts in some of these plays are called "jornadas" which shares the etymology of the French "journée" as well as the English "journey" suggesting in itself space/time mutations.] Seventy or eighty years later, a defender of the unities in Dryden's colloquy, echoes this quotation of Cervantes:

"... for one spot of ground, which the stage should represent, we are sometimes in more countries than the map can show us".

And yet it is not likely that he quotes the great Spanish master. It is only that this type of objection was hovering all over, and Shakespeare could not ignore it.

For a long, long time, there were many for whom it was not clear at all why the good curate of Cervantes should be wrong, and why should William Shakespeare and Lope be right, and why some insist that it were so unproblematic to jump over time and space while reclining comfortably on our seats in the theatre. The solution to the problem is not all that simple: while Shakespeare was probably right, the curate was not all the way wrong. We may not get more by abandoning the unities, only something else.

The Dramatic Principle

Initially, all dramatic and epic works abided by a more general principle of which the "unities" were only a particular application to the conditions of the stage. The principle has not been stated as a norm, at least never before Aristotle, but has been spontaneously applied by the poets. It called for respect of our immediate, naive, "uncultured" perception of things in a time/space continuum; or, put differently: it considered our difficulty - when unwarned and uneducated for the particular purpose - to make sense of things which we do not immediately perceive in the time/space continuum. But the stories to be told either in the theatre or in the epic work intended to say more, to convey experiences of longer time periods and wider space tracts than coverable by the time and space of a performance or the readings (public recitings in antiquity!) of a book. Therefore the art of building a play, an epopee or a novel had to find a method to bridge the gap between the immediate, elementary perception of the spectator/reader, with the wide scope of the story to be told. The different modes of solving this bridge-building problem may have lead to the historic separation between dramatic and epic which in Homer still did not exist and which proceeded only slowly after him.

The dramatic solution, in early times, went through the "unities". Histories covering a long sequence of events in time, occurring in many places of the world, may still have been presented. But a public uneducated for more than naive time/space perception had to see all this on a narrow stage where relevant events of the past or of faraway where not *enacted* but *narrated* by the choir; and two reciprocally relevant occurrences were not given in two scenes or acts, which by the physical necessities of a play had to be *subsequent* (even if they occurred simultaneously), but a "messenger" or some other story conveyer was to fulfill the task of connecting them. *The public was not to contribute;* it could only receive passively, irrespective of education and degree of intellectual or moral satisfaction.

The epic solution, on the other hand, was able to insure the same time/space continuum because it did not shackle the spectator's fantasy to the stage scaffold and the play time. Even so, flash-backs and simultaneities were not easy to handle: for many centuries, from Homer to Cervantes and indeed Goethe and Gogol, so many story-tellers had to make travelers of their heroes in order to insure that the continuum of time and space is kept as close as possible to the reader's intuition.

[Before the 18th century there were only very few major works which could be subsumed to the class of "novels" and in which the hero should not have been a traveler. Typically, it was women who were to have "stories" during which they were sitting at home. But even in these cases their own story was about waiting for somebody on a trip, and her thoughts, relevant to her "interior life", were about some adventurous traveler. - This requires a detailed discussion not to be inserted here, and will be treated in another essay.]

The price was often the weak focus, while strong focus was exactly the thing theatre provided, wherefore it earned high marks from Aristotle.

In the antique theatre and its late imitations there was always a tension between the unity of action and the necessity to respect passive intuition. One could (and why should not somebody?) write a history of theatre from the point of view of experiments, tricks, trials and failures to get around, get rid of, or simply abolish this tension. Solving the problem required not simply new procedures of representation, but new *techniques of reception*, the rearing of a special kind of intuition, completed by learning about new elements sensitive to new influences. The purpose was to preserve the unified action and abandon, while still within the physical limits of the stage, the other two strictures, and this with the help of the *public as contributor*. At an occasion, in Henry V, Shakespeare extended an invitation to his public to participate in the reconstruction of a story - and it seems that most critics failed to understand what he aimed at. Let now this be mended, and from the quoted particular case we shall try to extract a more general lesson. We may also read the fragments to be discussed as pieces from which to re-compose Shakespeare's own, implicit, Ars Poetica. [N.B. In Shakespeare's work we can find scattered references of a similar character - a worthwhile subject for researchers - but only the ones to be discussed here form, so to say, a consistent set.]

A Lesson from Shakespeare

"The life of King Henry the Fifth" is quite a unique play in this respect, where the poet, beside the life of the King, gives us clear "stage instructions", or rather "gallery instructions", to the public, helping it to overcome the inherited (inborn?) urge to perceive everything in an unbroken continuum of space and time. These instructions are conveyed by the much discussed and mostly misread chorus sections. If carefully read, these sections will prove to be *a systematic argument in favor of the unity-transcending approach* and not - not at all! - apologies for "the inadequacy of the medium", as formulated by Gary Taylor who, otherwise, seems to be one of the very few to appreciate them at their true worth. A typical case of misreading is that of Mark van Doren who writes that "The prologues are the first sign of Shakespeare's imperfect dramatic faith. Their verse is wonderful but it has to be, for it is doing the work which the play ought to be doing, it is a substitute for scene and action". This rather odd statement is an epitome of a large class of opinions on the subject. In the subsequent argument we would rather say that the controversial chorus insertions convey "imperatives to imaginative effort ... which overcomes the inertia of time and space" (Gary Taylor). Shakespeare's verses bear a systematic argument, as it is to be shown, in step with the polemics and discussions in his time. Let us first review them before expanding the discussion to related fields which may also provide explanatory analogies.

Each act is introduced by the Chorus as Prologue; and the Chorus returns also to close the play. Well, nothing new about this - except that this time, unlike in the antique drama, *the chorus does not only complete the tale,* to which now it adds very little, *but explains the way the play has to be looked at.* The invocation, of course, sounds familiar:

> "O! for a Muse of fire that would ascend
> "The brightest heaven of invention;" [1.1-2]

Yet beyond begging the Muse for inspiration Shakespeare moves directly to the argument. The story ought to cover a big piece of geography, and it assumes

> "A kingdom for a stage..." [1.3]

which means a clear *abandonment of the unity of space.* But how can it happen

> "On this unworthy scaffold to bring forth
> "So great an object: can this cockpit hold

"The vasty fields of France?" [1.10-12]

Certainly not. Very little indeed could we

"cram in this wooden O"! [1.13]

The viewer will have trouble transcending the physical limits of the unworthy scaffold. Therefore he is warned that there are tiny symbols on the limited stage representing mighty things it normally cannot enclose in their actual magnitude. To associate these tiny things, which stand as

"...ciphers to this great accompt" [1.17]

representing those mighty things outside, the author has to enlist his public's fantasy: by the "cyphers" which

"On your imaginary forces work", [1.18]

and consequently make you feel right in the middle of "the vasty fields of France", if required. Thus *you are expected to have "imaginary forces" when going to the theatre, beyond those of the poet.* Also instructions are given about how you may use those "imaginary forces", or rather, what you should imagine:

> "Suppose within the girdle of these walls
> "Are now confined two mighty monarchies,
> "Whose high upreared and abutting fronts
> "The perilous ocean parts asunder;
> *"Piece out our imperfections with your thoughts".*
>
> [1.19-23]

So King Henry goes to France, wins at Agincourt, marries the fair princess of the French, everybody roaming fast between London, Southampton and France - and all this in a couple of hours *with the help of you* sitting on the rotten wooden benches of the "O", which otherwise is the foundation of a rather tenuous "unity of space". And your help is always counted on:

In Act II

"...to Southampton:
There is the playhouse now, there must you sit" [2.35-36]

After having been warned that your contribution is absolutely required:

"Linger your patience on, and we'll digest
"*Th'abuse of distance..*" [2.31-32]

Which doesn't mean at all that you will not stay in the same "wooden O". Then:

In Act III

"... Suppose you have seen
"The well-appointed King at Hampton/[Dover] piers
"Embark his royalty..."[3.3-5]

and if you want to make any sense out of what is going on in the harbor, it is required that you

"... play with your fancies .. '[3.7]

and also

"... work, work your thoughts..." [3.25]

Because moving in space/time always means physical perception organized according to that kantian *nacheinander* and *nebeneinander*. Since what is space and time if not THINGS organized *nacheinander* and *nebeneinander*? [Joyce understood this well in his Ulysses, though not his commentators.] Consequently when jumping over such a frame of reference you ought, nevertheless, to *think* the things in it. Thus if you think of the

"... well-appointed king at Dover piers
"Embark his royalty ..."[3.4-5]

that will require from you to go to such detail as to fancy

"Upon the hempen tackle ship-boys climbing."[3.8]

as well. The urge is clear at the end of the third act's chorus introduction:

"... Still be kind,
And *eke out our performance with your mind*"

[3.34-35]

Act IV invites a short excursus. In it there is no direct apology for the "*little room confining mighty men*" and for the "*small time*" in which they ought to perform their great deeds. Instead, we get the beautifully suggestive description of the faraway, unseen, stage when

"Fire answers fire, and through their paly flames
"Each battle sees the other's umbered face,
"Steed threatens steed, in high and boastful neighs
"Piercing the night's dull ear ...[etc.]" [4.8-11]

That is about what the "Messenger" of a Greek play might have said (e.g. in the *Persians* of Aeschylus), though no example so rich in verbal picturing is known to be quoted as a paragon. The monumental beauty of this prologue in Act IV should have made it totally useless for Sir Olivier or anybody else to drive so many real steeds over the movie screen. But then, not everybody knows about the beauty of the Verb, getting satisfied only

"With four or five most vile and ragged foils,
"Right ill-disposed in brawl ridiculous."[4.50-51]

"much disgracing... the name of Agincourt". Because, as well known to Lisideus [once again in Dryden' *Dramatic Poesy*], even as much

"renders our stage ..[into] .. theatres where they fight prizes. For what is more ridiculous than to represent an army with a drum and five men behind it"?

Lisideus also knows, and the last quoted chorus section is a superb proof, that

> "there are *many* actions which can never be imitated to a just height".

since

> "the words of a good writer, which describe lively, will make a deeper impression of belief in us than all the actor can insinuate into us...".

In Act V

First:

> "...Now we bear the King
> "Towards Calais..." [5.6-7]

Yet soon after we

> "... *behold,*
> "*In the quick forge and working hours of thought*[!]
> "How London does pour out her citizens" [5.22-24]

who are supposed to receive

> "The conquering Caesar". [5.28]

Yet King Henry got business again, nimbly jumping over time and space, and we are getting new instructions:

> "...to France
> "There must *we* bring him",

where he will marry princess Katherine, who in the meanwhile is enjoying her English immersion classes to help her qualify for the bonus. This is doubtless the end of the "unity of space". And of the *unity of time* as well, as programmatically stated in the Prologue:

> "For 'tis *your thoughts* [!] that now must deck our Kings,
> "Carry them here and there, *jumping o'er time,*
> "*Turning the accomplishment of many years*
> "*Into an hour-glass - for the which supply*
> "*Admit me chorus to this history.*" [28-31]

All the six chorus insets, if put together in proper arrangement, would make for a nice little essay on the relation between public and the theatre, which aims at transcending both physical limits and the most immediate forms of continuity-related time/space intuitions. And all this without the strain of scholarly engagement, just so, by the way, while watching the show.

No passionate criticism but friendly excuse is conveying the instructions, such as does the chorus introducing <u>Act V</u>:

> "Vouchsafe to those that have not read the story
> "That I may prompt them: and of such as have
> "*I humbly pray them to admit th'excuse*
> "Of time, of numbers, and due course of things,
> "Which cannot in their huge and proper life
> "*Be presented here.*" [5.1-6]

They cannot, of course. Not in a direct fashion. And to account indirectly for *"time, numbers, and due course of things"*, when they are but suggested, requires the enlisting of the viewers' contribution. As art developed, art in general, and in particular the art of poetry, epic and dramatic, so the demand on the receiving public's contribution increased. Yet we have to distinguish between the demand on the reader's/viewer's memory and the demand on his elementary intuition. It is a difference between knowing from learning, tradition or hearsay who were Ulysses or Orestes, Oedipus or Xerxes, and yet another one of making sense of their acting on a stage or in a story in a way conflicting with our primitive-intuitive perception of the world. And in this latter sense every major break requires a considerable conscious effort which will be forgotten (the effort, not its result!) as soon as the new way of perceiving is accepted, thus becoming "elementary" on its turn.

We follow here the development of *two interlaced processes*, namely that of the *breaking up of the "unities"*, which had so far a natural appeal to elementary intuition, and *the developing contribution of the public*. We can clearly see that such development goes far beyond what Aristotle explicitly or implicitly represents as "functioning" principles for the dramatic work. He never meant to discuss the public's role assumed to be the passive part in the arts game. It is an *active public*, as emerging in the Renaissance and as it still exists in our day, which was meant to gain added insight by partaking in the "liveliest pleasure not only to philosophers but to men in general". (Poetics, Ch.4).

Had the early public of "Henry the V-th" been that of our own century, then the chorus would have been unemployed and the play had to live and impress on its own. [Try to consider the following: 1. This play can be played in our days without the help of the chorus - with a great loss for its beautiful poetry; yet: 2. No Greek play can dispense with the chorus if it is to make sense.]. Whatever its virtues or shortcomings, it certainly is a unified play by our, already reformed, perception of the stage event. But in his time, which was also that of the quoted Cervantes, it required still polemic standing, possibly against some doctrinaire opposition and in support of what the public, in fact, has already started to learn. Two things seem to be clear:

1) Today the play makes perfect sense to us, without the theory proposed as an alternative to the classical approach, filtered through the verses of the chorus.

2) There are several other Shakespeare plays built in the same discontinuous fashion, understood and enjoyed in his own time, yet having absolutely no "how to" instructions to the public.

So why here, in "Henry V"? One plausible hypothesis is that part of the public may still have been uneasy with such "crazy, modern experiments"; uneasy as were for quite a long time, even after Shakespeare, many sophisticated critics. An analogy in the next chapter of this exercise should offer, perhaps, a key to the understanding of the problem. Because one thing is obvious: the chorus portions are a clear, however musically clad, exposition of a new poetic doctrine.

All considered: why was it so difficult to overcome the problems of un-mediated intuition?

Answering this question may be easier by using a more recent form of art, cinematography, as a witness. Some of us may still recall our first childhood experience at the movies which could help understand the incongruities between elementary intuition and the artwork's construction, very similar in nature to those difficulties which Shakespeare's public may have had to face at times. Of course, to most of us, going to the movies - an ever more depressing and perverse experience - is a simple exercise, not requiring the viewer to sew together the time and space fragments of which a play is composed. This just "comes about" in our mind. Neither does it seem that the early movie goer, often a theatre amateur, had any major problems with time/space/action unity. However, he was called upon to make another type of contribution, namely to piece together sliced-up images of the kind never to be seen in "life", something the theatre stage wouldn't have him do. Now, instead of quoting some worthy and learned theories of the *Gestalt* school, or of the fine, but technically difficult achievements of Jean Piaget, I prefer to quote a story from a book on movie aesthetics by Bela Balázs, the *excursus* intending to suggest, by way of an analogy, what Shakespeare really meant when urging his public to make a mental effort and piece together something which might still have appeared disjoined, at least for some viewers.

A Lesson from the Movies

It happened in the early twenties in Moscow, were the Hungarian political exile Béla Balázs was living and working. Some friends of his have employed, for housekeeping service, a country girl from Siberia. She was intelligent, went through a complete elementary school education, but has never seen a movie in the countryside where she grew up. On a holiday, her employers decided to send her to the movie where a fashionable comedy was being offered, and which the big-city public thought to be extremely funny. After the show the girl returned in a gloomy mood, deeply shaken. Inquired about the movie, she proclaimed it, without any hesitation, as "frightening": "I saw how they tore people to pieces. The head, the feet, the hands everything was thrown around". Was this indeed what happened in the fashionable comedy? Balázs explains:

"We know that in that Hollywood movie theatre in which Griffith has presented for the first time ever detail pictures in close-up, the public burst into panic when smiled at by an immense 'chopped-off' head. We are now more aware how complicated the process in our conscience was which lead us to learn how to make [certain] visual associations.

"The task consists in gathering in our conscience, into a unified and continuously evolving scene, the pictures decomposed in their elements as they appear in a continuous sequence; and this ought to happen without us being aware of the complicated process. After all, the sequence of separated instances of an action, happen simultaneously in reality and are elements of a continuous action." [Béla Balázs:*Der Film, Werden und Wesen einer neuen Kunst*, Globus, Wien 1950, p.24-25]

Simultaneity decomposed in sequences, sequences told as if simultaneously happening, or even in changed order ("flash-backs") - all these tricks employed to *choose by focusing* from the imitable, require, in order to make sense, a contribution from the viewer and reader. Both historically interlaced processes, the breaking up of the unity appealing to primitive intuition and the developing contribution of the public, go beyond what Aristotle has described as rules of functioning for the poetic work. Yet they have been pursued because they originate in that desire for insight which "gives the liveliest pleasure not only to philosophers but to men in general" and which seems to require also the collaboration of the public as called upon by the Chorus in Henry the V-th:

"...eke out performance with your mind".

An *essay*, in its old meaning as given by Montaigne, should be a *trial* of our own ideas, their consistency and validity. Well, reexamining my old peripatetic ideas (prejudices?), I was bugged down by the ever puzzling "unity" problem so often thought to have been "solved" or, at least, "overcome". What was, and for several authors of more recent times continues to be important about the classical rules, is the fact of their being an early developed application of a more general, and eternally valid dramatic/mimetic principle. This meta-principle is that of *poignancy*, the vehicle by which the literary work conveys more than its verbal discourse. Acting is another instrument which leads us beyond the text satisfying that very same principle of emotional intensity; something to be discussed in what follows considering its positive and negative aspects. But writing itself takes forms, other than poetry proper, in which the more general principle overcomes the limits of the stage and of the, well, Unities. These should be examined in what follows, while still considering the Aristotelian standard.

PARERGA

related to
Aristotle's Poetics: Limits and Relevance

- Concerning the "Unities": from Aristotle to Shakespeare -

1) A Lesson from Aeschylus

Be it as it may, we have to return to the question initially implied: how much did we gain in the understanding of human motives and actions on the stage because theater has "improved" beyond the classical rules? How much did we gain by the "new ways" which have replaced the antique chorus and the perennial "messengers", thus modifying the perception of the public? Parallel reading of ancient and modern masters could offer some enlightenment. This may not be easy, given the widely different field of stories from which the subjects have been chosen. Thus, e.g. almost all Greek tragedies are mythology combined with unascertainable history. Yet reaching back to the oldest of the great tragedy writers, Aeschylus, we will find an interesting example. It is his "Persians" we should choose, because it happens to be almost the only historic play in early Greek literature which does not originate in ancient mythology, and thus comparable on at least one important account to the Shakespearean play we have discussed.

The "Life of King Henry V" is the history of his battles and victories. It was a story

> "In *little room confining mighty men,*
> "Mangling by starts the full course of their glory.

"*Small time*, but in that small most greatly lived
"This star of England".

The story of King Xerxes of the "Persians" is the history of his battles and his defeat. A continuous confrontation of "mighty men". But how much could Aeschylus confine in the "little room" of his "Persians"? True, in the "small time" of the play's progress the drama was "greatly lived". But only because much of it is told us by the chorus and a messenger rather than performed by the actors; unlike in "Henry V", in which we get the heroes in "the full course of their glory" while the chorus helps us only to sort out the continuum from the "mangling of their starts" without completing the story itself. In the "Persians" the scene is throughout the royal palace in Susa to which a tomb of Darius is to be "crammed". Yet we learn not only about the anxieties of the queen-mother Atossa and the senate acting(!) as chorus, but also

- how Xerxes went to war,
- how he was defeated (news by a messenger),
- how his advancing soldiers behaved (meanly), and
- how much different it was under King Darius

who, by dispatching his ghost, helps us to a flash-back, complete with re-telling an early prophecy of doom. Is the thus structured story a "primitive" play? Does it in any way move less (by "pity and fear" or otherwise) or enlighten us less than any play which abandoned the "unities"? It may certainly be worth examining whether that superiority of the drama plot which, according to Aristotle, can hardly be improved by "spectacular means", is not still better insured by the devices employed by Aeschylus. For once, it seems to be that theater, after Lope and Shakespeare, lends itself to more abuse by the spectacle monger who may have been granted an extra opportunity, often interpreted by him as a license, to impudently overwhelm the poetic work with exhibitionist corruption. Yet, again, that minimum of histrionic contribution if added to the story, could, perhaps, lead to something beyond the experience of terror and compassion. It is that other purpose of poetry mentioned by Aristotle which the revolution of the Renaissance has helped promote, precisely by abandoning the stage-unity condition:

"...the reason why men enjoy seeing a likeness is that in contemplating it they find themselves learning and inferring" (Poetics, IV.5).

This has justified Shakespeare who took a(n implicit) stand in the "unities" debate. And understanding of how the new ways came forth, on a slower pace, and with wise prudence, also from across the Channel:

> «*Il est facile aux spéculatifs d'être sévères, mais, s'il voulaient donner dix, ou douze poèmes de cette nature au public, ils élargiraient peut-être les règles, encore plus que je ne fais, sitôt qu'ils auraient reconnu par l'expérience, quelle contrainte apporte leur exactitude, et combien de belles choses elles bannit de notre théâtre.*» (Corneille: Discours des trois unités.) ["It is easy to be stern for those who are devoted [only] to speculation. But if they were to [try to] give to the public ten or a dozen of poems of this nature, they themselves would, perhaps, relax these rules, and even more so than I have done, as soon as they will come to realize, by their own experience, how restraining their exactitude is, and how many beautiful things they banish from our theater.."]

If we would try to break up the "Persians" - without any iconoclastic purpose! - into a time/space mosaic, fancying how this might have been done by a later dramatic poet, we might get a clue about that plus in "learning and inferring".

2) Apropos Shakespeare's Lesson

It may be so, indeed, that the ancient rules were more apt to make the concentration and the *poignance* of the poetic work more effective, as long as intuitive perception was not reeducated. But, at the same time, they became canonized, so that learned sophistication would accept them in exclusivity. The breakthrough in Spain and England of the "new way of writing comedies", as we know it not only from Shakespeare but several of his immediate predecessors, may not have come about by such built-in didactic discourse as to be found in Henry the V. It may be that all those severally condemned vulgar theatrical tricks could claim the merit of having promoted the New. Yet for the learned, it was still barbarous. It is interesting to mention that this very "barbarity" of the stage procedure was viewed by their proponents as a merit. As Alexander Pope's ambiguous wit illustrated some such view:

> "..Critique-learning flourished most in France:
> The rules a nation, born to serve, obeys;
> And Boileau still in right of Horace sways.
> But we, brave Britons, foreign laws despised,
> And kept unconquered and uncivilized;
> Fierce for the liberties of wit, and bold,
> We still defied the Romans, as of old."
>
> [*An Essay on Criticism*, 712-718]

This opinion long prevailed along with the persuasion that the denial of the antique rules meant also "the liberty of wit". And though the Spaniards were hardly as fierce fighters for liberty as the Britons fancied to be, particularly when *they* were still ruling the waves, they also yielded to the vulgar taste. But, then again, was not the "vulgar" perception closer to the ancient rules, because closer to elementary intuition? Very likely yes. But the *vulgus* was swayed by the tricks of the stage, while more sophisticated exercises, such as Shakespeare's or, later, the discussants' in Dryden's boat on the Thames, were meant to break the resistance of the educated. As in earlier times Dante had to plead in *Latin* with the Latinist erudites for the *vulgari eloquentia*, already flourishing in Sicilian, Provençal or Aragonese poetry, so now Shakespeare had to plead in favor of yet another form of poetic expression to which the "rabble" - but not the chosen few - already adapted their perception.

3) The Dramatic Strain in Literature

- Of Something Forgotten by Aristotle -

According to Aristotle, the superiority of dramatic poetry consists not in the simple fact of a story being offered on the stage, but in the *plot's* efficacy in focusing or targeting. This is what was understood to distinguish it from the prevailing forms of epic poetry. But then we may still have to seek a justifying explanation for the histrionic translation of the plot. No doubt, theatre came about as a ritual performed for the benefit, not of readers but of the multitude of illiterate viewers. True again that the early Greek rhapsod was the sole performer, or rather *reciter* of the plot, and that multi-actor performances expanded their scope as literacy and learning also spread - however modestly. But then it is also true that *stage theatre* fast evolved into a ritualistic requirement of the literate, and remained in our days a consumption article mainly for those who read more than the "low brow", video, TV, and rock concert addicted part of society's rank and file. In our days, theatre going continues to satisfy those long acquired ritual needs. But is this all to it? It was argued in the previous essay, as will be in some of the following disquisitions, that positive word-setting is seldom, if at all, possible on things art has to reveal. If so then also the *contemplation* of the theatric recognition itself may ask for the assistance of a parable.

Actors and Plots

I tried to elaborate on the above point in a conversation with a friend, and I was using a parable borrowed from a very "modern" author:

> <u>Me</u>: In a charming and wise story, Jorge Luis Borges ...
> <u>He</u>: Sorry, stop here! What is "charming" and "wise"?
> <u>Me</u>: Well, we probably agree that when I claim that something might charm you, this means that you will be put in a state of mind which ...
> <u>He</u>: Hold it! What exactly is a "state of mind"?

I certainly was cornered. But, on the other hand I wanted to prove (in fact: *suggest!*) my point with a story. So, whether the story was charming or wise - (and I better had forgotten about wisdom) - I should have left the emotive, may be *indicative*, but not *expressible* reception, to be my friend's business. This time I will try to *re*-tell the story, more prudently, in a stern, "documentary" and austere manner; more than that should be granted to its author, who does it so much better - and whose quoted (and other) work is hereby recommended. Here is an abstract tailored according to the requirements of this discussion, hence, not exactly following the author's own presentation...

J.L. Borges tells the story of a conversation Averroes had with some learned and traveled friends on the subject of what words can or cannot convey. This happened at a time when the great Cordovan philosopher was deeply absorbed in the translation of Aristotle's Poetics, and bewildered by some expressions in the text for which he couldn't find an Arabic equivalent. Such were the terms "tragedy" and "comedy". One of the friends in the circle was Abulcasim Al-Ashari who was said to have traveled to China:

> "His detractors, with the peculiar logic of hatred, swore he had never set foot in China and that in the temples of that land he blasphemed the name of Allah."

But in this company his stories were attentively listened to. He recounted that in the city of Sin Calan [we call it probably Canton], friendly Moslem merchants took him to a big building which surrounded a big yard, furnished roundabout with numerous "cabinets and balconies" in which people were sitting, eating and drinking, and most importantly watching some other people doing strange things on an elevated "terrace":

> "The persons on the terrace were playing the drum and the lute, save for some fifteen or twenty (with crimson colored masks) who were praying, singing and conversing. They suffered prison, but no one could see the jail; they traveled on horseback, but no one could see the horse; they fought, but the swords were of reed; they died and then stood up again."

To the learned company this sounded at first like an exhibition of madmen. But Abulcasim elaborated:

> "Let us imagine that someone *performs a story instead of telling it.*" [And we could wonder whether Averroes would have found the word for "perform", which Abulcasim seems to have luckily discovered.] "Let that story be the one about the sleepers of Ephesus. We see them retire into a cavern, we see them pray and sleep, we see them sleep with their eyes open, we see them grow as they sleep, we see them awaken after three hundred years, we see them give

the merchant an ancient coin, we see them awaken with the dog. Something like this was shown to us that afternoon by the people of the terrace."

And when the host asked whether they were speaking, the answer was in the affirmative. This was just a new puzzle to the host:

"In that case twenty persons are unnecessary. One single speaker can tell anything no matter how complicated it might be." [The quotations are from the English edition of a selection by Donald A. Yates and James E. Irby, *"Labyrinths"*, 1964]

One thing is clear to us, the readers, and of lesser importance to the discussion: the listeners had some trouble accommodating the strange phenomenon in the store of their experiences. We, however, are helped by this little [fragment of a] story to go back to the root of the problem here examined, since the story as told would suggest us the naive first impression of a theatre experience of which all of us are deprived. Let us slightly modify the contribution of Abulcasim and suppose that his answer to the question of the host was in the negative. It is clear from the description he gives of what those people on the *terrace* were doing, that speech was not an absolute requirement. While, had speech been involved, one reader would have been sufficient; or, in the case of many *mimes*, the text could have been redundant. They could have prayed, sung or even conversed with gestures. We know about dance and pantomime, of course. So we arrived to no less than two, instead of one question as earlier: (1) what can the acting add to what may be clearly said by a reader, and (2) what can words add to the play performed by a mime; where it is to be recalled we mean the use of words other than making *statements*, such as in a legal, a scientific, a philosophical essay or treatise, a political pamphlet, or anything which purports to make a complete statement within the realm of the *logos*, and nothing more. It may sound silly to have such scruples, because it is adopted as a self-evident truth that plays are a *necessary* synthesis of both, words and acting. Except that, going back to Aristotle, we still know that the plot is fulfilling its role, almost completely, when being only read. Provided, of course, that it is a good plot. (And some aspects of the quality of *goodness* will be analyzed in subsequent essays.) For once, when we read the text, it is always the same text; what is not in it, what I experience as a reader is *my* contribution. Yet when we see the same play performed by two different actors under two different stage directors, we *may* have two very different experiences. We gave up our freedom, as always when the mind yields to the eye. And this is what Aristotle may not have realized. When we read, our experience goes only through our own mind; in every additional representation of the same play, however, somebody else's contribution is filtered through our mind. Re-enacting life, in a verbally un-translatable form may be thus the unexplained and unexplainable plus.

ESSAY NO. 2

The Mirror of Socrates Carried by the Travelling Hero

"..né dolcezza di figlio, né la pieta
del vechio padre, né'l debito amore
lo qual dovea Penelopè far lieta,
vincer potero dentro a me l'ardore
ch'i' ebbi a devenir del mondo esperto
e de li vizi umani e del valore;

———

Considerate la vostra semenza:
fatti non foste a viver come bruti,
ma per seguir virtute e canoscenza."
(Dante, *Inferno*,XXVI,94-9;118-120)

"Nor fondness for my son, nor reverence
For my old father, nor the due affection
Which joyous would have made Penelope,
Could overcome within me the desire
I had to be experienced of the world,
And of the vice and virtue of mankind;

———

Consider ye the seed from which you sprang;

Ye were not made to live like unto brutes,
But for pursuit of virtue and of knowledge."
(translation of Longfellow)

Not much honor bestows Socrates upon *artists as imitators*: they are said to be deprived of the ability to reproduce even only a faint image of those *Ideas* which are alone worthy of our cognitive endeavour, because alone endowed with the attribute of *Reality*. Indeed, the humblest of craftsmen using his mechanical skills may come closer to some of these abstract entities of which the world, as we experience it, is nothing but a pale, contradiction fraught, confusing reflection. Poets, when regarded as just another class of imitators, are not granted any exceptional status either: "For it is phantoms, not *Realities*, that they produce" [Plato: Republic X, 599a], because, as "everyone can see, they are [just] a tribe of imitators" [Timaeus, 19d]. What they do is tantamount to what you yourself could achieve "*if you should choose to take a mirror and carry it out everywhere*" [596e] thus reproducing, or *imitating*, nothing but the already existing, those vaguely perceivable shadows of the ideal "Reality". Yet, this is exactly what the major heroes of epic literature were doing almost literally. From as early as the times of Homer up to the XVIII century, epic poets were always sending their heroes on a journey with the apparent purpose, even if not explicitly stated, to carry around a mirror reflecting people and things in their time. Exceptions - *major and worthwhile exceptions*(!) - were few, while glorious illustrations of the rule abound.

Odysseus, of course, was a traveler, and so was Virgil's Aeneas; the golden ass of Apuleius moved from place to place thus encountering many adventures, and so did the heroes of chivalry romances, who were deliberately seeking them, as well as the many characters of *Orlando Furioso* engaged in a true geographic orgy. *Don Quixote* followed in their steps, and *Lazarillo, Gil Blas and Simplicissimus* did the same, though in a less gentlemanly manner, as was revealed to the Spanish, French and German readers of their respective times. And *Pantagruel*? He was also sent on a trip by Rabelais, and moved from isle to isle discovering many spots on this round world while copiously amusing the readers. The same was offered later by Swift's *Gulliver*, Defoe's *Robinson*, and, in a more realistic manner, by Fielding's *Tom Jones*.

These "long-stories" of adventures in travel, or travel-war-travel, in real or imaginary lands, being often elaborate frame stories enclosing numerous short stories, were and still are rich troves for whoever seeks reading enjoyment. But as the casual reader could sample at his leisure among the discovered gems, the reading and learning poets understood that many of the stories, pulled out of their traveling complex, are worthy of a special treatment, of analytical scrutiny, so to say. The Greek drama is a major and still unparalleled instance of this analytical decomposition of a long trail of legends spread in fictitious space. It may be, of course, and it very likely is so, that the long-story called *Greek epos* is itself the assembly of earlier, partly independent, stories. But their collection with the accent on their *expansion in space* is what remained predominant and what offered also to poets of following centuries the bag from which to pick the subject of their plays corseted into those "three unities". In the Hebrew tradition, the short story, as well as the parable, testify for the same attempt of condensed recounting of stories plucked off their main thread expanded in a continuous historic *and* spatial context. *Ruth, Esther,* several of the *Apocrypha* are the main examples. Yet, beyond theatre and the short tale, no form of story telling could impose itself for so many centuries as a major competitor of the traveling hero's adventures. Major epic was for a long, long time moving in a real or imaginary *space*, its heroes cutting through obstacles with the sword or their wits, thus transforming Socrates' scornful dismissal of art into an able metaphor of storytelling and World cognition.

The Fourth "Unity": the Traveling Hero

One cannot do justice to all the great examples crowding around the edge of the pen and claiming a well deserved citation. Still some of these instances are more compelling than others, mostly for their *explanatory power of the here discussed literary phenomenon.* Their allegorical representative is Dante's (and later Tennyson's) version of Ulysses, whom we know from Homer to have been of "nimble wits", and who discovered in himself the urge of voyage *"per seguir virtute e canoscenza"*, or "for the pursuit of virtue and of knowledge", which in his case - so the Dante version - proved to be stronger than homesickness or filial duty. When, echoing Dante, Tennyson says that Ulysses was

".. yearning in desire

"To follow knowledge like a sinking star
"Beyond the utmost bound of human thought.",

he implies, in fact, the motive of many a storyteller to send his hero to a literary adventure in the known space. The urge to collect experiences in "the world, and of vice and virtue of mankind" was the ultimate subject of the various story-mosaics unified in and by the dominant character moving in space and carrying that allegorical mirror. *The unity of the hero* was not considered by Aristotle. But the hero could unify many experiences when traveling in pursuit of virtue and fame, or just driven by the Devil or hunted by indigence. And when the world of mortals proved to be too limited, then the hero went to encounter the shadows of the Underworld. Ulysses did it, and Aeneas, and Lukian provided us with some rudiments of a travel guide for this our world when coming on a trip from the underworld. Dante's main voyage was in such a realm, which is beyond immediate human experience, but reflective of it, making him the ultimate *"esperto e de li vizi umani e del valore"* or "expert of the vices and virtues of mankind". And when one man's adventures were felt to have hit the limits of information on human failings and valour, then a soul was put to travel from body to body to collect the experiences of many, such as we read in *El siglo pitagorico y vida de Don Gregorio Guadaña* of Antonio Enriquez Gomez. Was not the author himself a soul hiding alternatively in many "bodies" to escape the rigors of the Holy Office?

The wealth of human images, the variety of events and experiences were more or less loosely connected as encounters of a hero randomly erring or deliberately pursuing an aim by overcoming towering obstacles. Such characters, if confined to a very small area, seem to have had very little opportunity to become the subject of a longer narration by the art of earlier writers. The physical localization, or anyways narrow geographic delimitation of the *long story* and its transformation into the modern novel, started only in the XVIII century and was perfected in the XIX, ironically in the time when traveling became easier and, certainly, faster. Or may be because of it? After all how much can happen on a railway trip from, say, Paris to Berlin? Maybe a lot, but only in the same sense in which "something of importance" may happen in a single city, house or even a room - as the modern novel has taught us. Aeneas' itinerary from Ilium to Latium can nowadays be covered comfortably in a Mediterranean cruise of only ten days, as eventless as a few days' driving from *parador* to *parador* covering the space of Don Quixote's sallies so rich in adventures. And to realize how eventless can be a fast trip across the American continent, just remember - since many have already forgotten - Jack Kerouac's "On the road". Unfortunately, many have forgotten also Steinbeck's "Grapes of Wrath", from which we could find out how sadly eventful and rich in discoveries a crisscrossing of America could be also in a precarious, wobbly truck. The "space adventure" still survives but, as to be seen, with a new character, and having lost its predominance in novel writing.

Therefore, it may sound as an exaggeration that epic in space was out *because* of the advent of fast means of transportation. But we surely see that few major novels were built around a continuum of experiences gathered by a traveling hero ever since the invention of the steam locomotive. Among the novels illustrating the transition from the "old" epic to the "new" one, I mean among those of major consequence, one should mention Gogol's "Dead Souls"; a "travel story" from those days when the steam locomotive went about conquering the world. We recall Chichicov traveling in "the sort of carriage in which bachelors ride", within a short radius, from country estate to country estate, to pursue the crooked business of acquiring non-existing bondage serves, the purported number of which would entitle him to a mortgage on some equally imaginary estate somewhere in the endless Russian Empire. The techniques of these deals are relevant only to the extent that they justify the hero's moves who, while collecting his "dead souls", experiences a variety of adventures, and offers occasion for similar experiences of others, exploits which are assembled by Gogol in one single novel: *the story of an anti-Don Quixote with a rather cheerful countenance.*

Of course, the novel *in* travel, the novel of a traveler or even the novel of a warrior-traveler, is not necessarily out. However, this time, travel is no more the pretext-frame uniting relatively isolated events in order to compose episode mosaics of ingenious artistry; it is a *unique* story moving in space, such as, to some extent, Moby Dick. Also Fabrice del Dongo fled his parental home to encounter adventures on his tortuous way through Switzerland, France and Italy, until ending his days in the *Chartreuse de Parme*. It was much in keeping with Stendhal's view of what a novel might be, very close to Socrates' assessment but(!) with a positive sign appended:

«.. un roman est un miroir qui se promène sur une grande route. Tantôt il reflète à vos yeux l'azur des cieux, tantôt la fange des bourbiers de la route.» [*Le Rouge et le noir*] ["A novel is a mirror walking along a highway. Sometime it reflects the azure glare of the sky, [while] some other time it reflects the slushy mud of the road."]

And, to be sure, Stendhal *commends* the carrier of the mirror for imitating that *"fange des bourbiers".* Unlike Socrates who sees the wayfaring speculum as an instrument of futility. But this hero of Stendhal's marked the end of the *great* novel-in-and-by-travel. In this case, moving in space from adventure to adventure was just one of the many ways in which life was lived, and no more the required, dominant, pretext-frame, to unite into a long story an array of tales. It was the age of, well, Balzac.

I am afraid that all this is too general to delineate the essential difference (or one of several essential differences) between the modern novel, as it slowly emerged in the XVIII century, and the previous period's epic, in which travel was the frame of the hero's mirror meant to reflect the wealth of pictures encountered during his journeys. Mirrors are not focused as lenses, and do not analyze like prisms. A mirror set on a spot, in a given angle, reflects the same image if the viewer is confined to the lectern; it has to be turned around or has to be moved so we could recognize, if we are longsighted enough, a variety of moving pictures. A prism can decompose the light emanated by the issuing object - but of course the literary equivalents of it have first to be invented.

Not to further abuse this optical metaphor - blame it on Socrates! - I would try to outline, by giving paradigmatic employment to some better known examples, the characteristic differences between stories-in-travel as we have known them from earlier literature, and the ones in the modern novel. The former were predominant in long-story telling for over two and a half millennia, the latter - just another kind of story among many. This inquiry is in keeping with the general purpose of these essays, which is the *identification of various narrative structures, tricks, patterns etc. within the reading exercise, so as to enhance the delight of reading by simulating an implied/ assumed working procedure of the author.* All this by strictly avoiding to probe for intentions, purported messages etc. of the author, an exercise so dear to so many literary critics. Atop the short list of examples we put Don Quixote. But not because it were "the first modern novel" as so often said. To give any sense to this claim, a definition of "modern" would be required first, which we do not have. And then, do we really need one for a casual colloquialism as this, even if countless times repeated? Formulations of this kind serve only one purpose, namely to discharge the analyst from the duty of precise inquiry. Instead of this, peeking over the shoulder of the author will be the exercise pursued here; in the pieces actually written we may discover patterns which reveal something about the artistry of composition while still enjoying its result.

These few exercises will start with the major work of Cervantes, being then completed with a look at a couple of more recent, apparently - and in many respects *actually* - very different travel stories, stressing the relevance of these very differences. *This is a reader's adventure in discovery* with no claim of scientific generalization. It should compare, rather, with a gourmet's sampling from a box of fine chocolate.

[An apology is due here for not having always resisted the trap of generalizations. There are several worthy exceptions to the claim - hereby qualified - that all major story telling works before the XVIII century were about wayfaring characters. Generality is not to be viewed as exclusivity. Whatever was exception from "travel" did already carry the intimate, the moral and "psychological", but only in a minor fashion. Perhaps the only major exception in antiquity was the Book of Job. Yet this is to be examined later and in yet another context.]

The Case of Cervantes

"Most happy and blissful [*venturosos*] were those times in which that most audacious knight Don Quixote de la Mancha was born; since due to his so honorable determination to try to revive and to give back to the world, the lost and almost dead order of the knights errant, we can enjoy now, in this our age so wanting in cheerful entertainment, not only the sweetness of his true story, but also those stories and episodes of which at least some are as pleasing, skilful and true as the main story itself." [Chapter 28, vol.I].

The same is true today, four centuries later. This work of Cervantes is something we may call a collection of experiences. He created one of the last *very great* frame novels of a traveling hero, (not - please! - "the first modern novel"), full with lovely stories of various adventures, enwrapped in the flood of *bons môts* generously dispensed by Sancho as well as by the worthy knight, while at the same time supplying technical innovations, to be used in the new novels, by "decomposing" the old genre. "Don Quixote" already displays the difference between the various ways of story telling, a subject worth to be discussed in some detail. At the same time Cervantes develops, with great mastery, *new ways of short story telling and consistent novel outlines* which are independent of the hero's continuous errantry. We shall try to identify the technicalities (*as they worked out to be,* with little knowledge about *intentions*) and enjoy participating in a plausible way of composing such stories.

As above stated, this novel may be viewed as a long series of experiments, i.e. the creation of artificial situations with the help of the hero's madness, situations which reveal realities and truths. In the whole story everything is "as if normal", except for Don Quixote and his chivalry. It so worked out that a fool's adventures reveal aspects of the "normal" world which others may not directly experience. DQ is thus the catalyst of revealing events: you need a fool to show you the truth, and enjoy, at the same time, the turns and shifts of the narration; a worthwhile pleasure in itself. Is it social and moral criticism? If it is, it is *ipso facto;* the intention is irrelevant. We delve in the wealth of stories for their own sake; the learning and understanding is implicit and of greater value than the obvious, "revealing" stories with a doctrinaire edge.

Let us start with an attempt to construct a typology of the stories in DQ from the point of view of the mirror metaphor.

The Stories within *Don Quixote*

At first, the variety, indeed *richness,* of choice of stories within the frame of "Don Quixote", would appear to have caused, even to Cervantes, that proverbial *embarras.* However, the author of our book found a quite easy way to overcome his and the reader's difficulties in handling the wealth, but not by diminishing the surfeit with the chisel of the aesthetizing artist [who, often, has only few stories to tell]. He, rather, offers us, as reported in the third chapter of the second volume, an amusing discussion on literary theory *à propos* the purported publication of a first volume of Don Quixote's adventures. By introducing this discussion, the profusion of episodes, which the aesthetic purist might have seen as a burden, is presented as a perfectly integrated part of the larger story itself. How? By the simple trick of offering yet another opportunity for the main hero to reveal himself - this time as a worthy scholar. As in other instances within the general narrative, here too, our hero goes into field on the platonic side, while Carrasco, the Salamanca boy, holds it with the peripatetics. Thereby the "problem" became, in fact, part of the adventure itself.

Thus our smart author puts none other than Don Quixote to protest the manners of the book's previous edition saying that:

> "... I can't see what moved the author to commit himself to *novellas* and other outlandish stories, when he had so much to write about my own adventures." [Chapter 3, volume II]

But he was really not all that concerned given that the *bachiller* Carrasco offered him enough consolation when reporting on the adventures recorded in the book, as well as the good reception by people of various tastes and interests:

> "In this respect ... there are as many opinions as there are tastes: some prefer the adventure with the windmills, which your grace thought to be briareuses or giants; others enjoy the story with the windmills; there are those who favor the description of the two armies which then turned out to be two flocks of sheep; and again those who are amused by the story with the dead man carried to Segovia for burial; one told me that of all stories he liked most the one with the liberation of the galley slaves; yet another one assured me that none equals the story with the Benedictine 'giants' and the fight with the brave Biscayan." [ibid.]

These examples are not to be taken as a representative sample of *all* stories incorporated in the larger novel of DQ; yet they are typical for the majority of *stories which reflect the hero's character.* But then there are the *stories which are primarily reflections, in the hero's mirror, of the world in which he moves.* And the manner in which these more complex subjects are introduced by Cervantes, is also exemplary for the progress towards a new art of story telling.

There are many ways to classify the stories embedded in the larger history of the ingenious Manchan, most, of course, arbitrary, as classifications go. But whimsical as they may seem to be, they are normally carried out on the basis of a set of common characteristics perceived, at least by some of us, to be relevant. One such cluster can be assembled according to whose mirror is involved, or what images the interference of several mirrors bring about. And then *we, each of us readers, may even compose our own little anthology of good stories offering the pleasure similar to the one enjoyed by the readers quoted in the bachiller's account* [or, more likely, by that fellow who samples delicacies from a box of fine chocolate - a metaphor no less compelling, if the reader's point of view is considered, than the mirror of Socrates]. This, quite apart from the insight we thereby gain in the fascinating intricacies of Cervantes' manners of narration. Hence I propose to dwell upon the following classes of stories, completed in the next section with the discussion of some relevant examples:

(1) The stories where *the hero reveals himself in his own decisions and actions,* while all other actors are either passive sufferers of his actions, or its obstacles. Some of the examples quoted by *bachiller* Carrasco are of this category. (E.g. the windmills, the two "armies" turned out to be flocks of sheep, etc.) But there are several others, especially in the second volume. All these are, of course, a fool's hilarious exploits.

(2) The stories where the reaction of some other actors is prevalent; these characters could be activated by Don Quixote, i.e. prompted to action as a response to his own moves. All examples on the list of Carrasco belong either here or in the previous category. For types of human reaction (and meanness) the case of the flogged and then "liberated" country boy, as well as that of the actually liberated galley slaves - particularly that of Gines de Pasomonte - may be quoted as very pertinent. The list is, of course, much longer.

(3) The feats and adventures of *independently active characters,* unprovoked by the main hero in any direct fashion. These appear in

stories which may stand on their own, prefiguring the more complicated *short story* to come - and of which Cervantes was already
an accomplished master, as revealed by his *Novelas ejemplares* or,
most particularly, the *Coloquio de los perros*. Enlightening examples are provided by the story of Grisostomo and Marcela (vol. I,
Ch.X ff.) and that of the marriage of the rich Camacho (vol. II, Ch.
XX-XXI).

(4) There is also a more complicated class of stories in which
Don Quixote *and* Sancho are active participants but not necessarily initiators. Example: the longer account of Don Quixote
meeting (in vol II, Ch. XXX ff.) the *bella cazadora* who, along
with her *duque,* go in on the chivalry game, and when Sancho becomes, at last, "Governor" of an "island". Here we discover - and
this should be examined in more detail - *the net-knitting pattern of
a master novel.*

(5) Development of complicated novelistic sub-plots, being more
daring literary enterprises. E.g. the story of mixed-up lovers in vol.
I. Ch. XXIII. ff.

Members of class (4) and (5) could qualify for an independent small
novel, the difference being that in the latter group our main heroes are, so to
say, episodic characters.

For the amateur of short formulations with a mnemonic purpose, the stories of the listed classes can be characterized as follows:

(1) The main hero is *active,* while all the others are *passive* sufferers.

(2) The main hero is *active,* but (re)*active* are also those whom he
provokes.

(3) The main hero is *passive* (mostly) and remains most of the time
uninvolved, *active* being other characters who don't care for him
and are independent of him or his initiatives.

(4) The main hero is originally *passive* but later becomes *involved* in the endeavours of the originally *active* characters.

(5) The story which can be told *independently of the main hero;* the latter is involved only for the sake of the larger novel.

And when the "mirror" metaphor is to be considered, the listed classes tell us the about following:

(1) The shape, polish, biases and stains on the mirror of the main hero[es].

(2) The shape, polish, biases and stains on the mirror(s) of the other participants, but only as the pictures in their mirrors are reflected in those of the central heroes'.

(3) & (4) That which can be seen in the mirrors of Don Quixote and Sancho, what we are now able to interpret since we often rehearse our knowledge about their "shape, polish, biases and stains" [(1)].

There is in the novel, as we will recall of course, one single inset story which could be taken as class in itself:

(5) The *"Curioso impertinente"*.

The relative merits of the listed classes depend entirely on the *sampling reader's pleasure*. Yet, by doing the sampling, we may also identify the seeds of that modern novel which so often is associated with *Don Quixote*. Let us examine a few examples chosen according to the above, perhaps fancifully, listed classes.

[It is up to the reader of these notes to follow the subsequent process of example sampling or to jump to the section on Gogol's "Dead souls". Though, it may be, as I hope, that the spectrum of instances to be quoted, and which are understood as archetypes, will properly delineate the path of transition from the adventure-in-travel type of story to the modern novel.]

The "Active" Don Quixote

For class (1):

Don Quixote asserts his personality in taking on "evil" whenever he encounters it. We could engage in a game of separating all such stories, and then uniting them into a single set. The result would be a remarkable portrait of the knight himself, without that alleged "pollution" which the illegitimate intrusion of other stories may have caused. All stories in the class have a very similar pattern though they reflect a great wealth of color and imagery. The structure is simple and can be reduced to a few obvious phases:

(1) - Don Quixote, after every failed adventure, proceeds *on the road*, the road being his *raison d'être*.

(2) - Along the route, "Evil" shows up in some disguise: "giants" appearing as windmills; "sorcerers" who are but Benedictine monks; "Death" itself; lions - in a cage; etc.

Consider one of the most brilliant examples, the one taken from v. I, Ch. XVIII, where two herds of sheep covered by a thick cloud of dust are taken by the intrepid knight to be two armies, believers fighting non-believers, whom he was able to characterize with maximum precision:

"God help us! how many provinces he was able to name, how many nations to enumerate, assigning each their fitting attributes, with a marvelous presence of spirit, being entirely captivated and spellbound by the lies he read in his books."

(3) - Don Quixote makes moves to engage Evil's agents in a fight, which always, as in the case of the mentioned herds of sheep, aims at

"... helping the frail and those in distress" [... *ayudar a los menestro-sos y desvalidos*]

(4) - Some, mainly Sancho, will advise him to give up the adventure, often foretelling a frightful outcome.

(5) - Against all advice, Don Quixote engages in the fight; or, anyways, gets ready to do so. The non-believer sheep were thus also to be attacked by the brave champion of noble causes, who

"... rode in the midst of the sheep and went about to pierce them with so much audacity and fierceness as if he were to confront his own mortal enemies."

(6) The outcomes are expected in suspense by the reader, not because the failure of the fantastic fighter would be in doubt - by the standards of what we call *normal* people - but because the *forms of the outcome* cannot be foreseen. In the particular, quoted example it was not very surprising:

"The shepherds and the ranchers, who escorted the flocks, shouted that he may desist from doing this. However, realizing that their pleas were futile, they grabbed their slings and began to salute [Don Quixote's] ears with fist size stones".

(7) - The outcomes in the many similarly structured stories, which together portray our hero and depict his world, are often explained away by Don Quixote as being the baleful work of sorcerers. And he did this so well that Sancho came to the conclusion that

"Your honor would make a better preacher than a knight errant."

But, as we find out, the two callings are not so far apart, since:

"Knights errant know everything and ought to know everything, said Don Quixote; in past centuries there were knights who were

able to give a speech or a sermon in the middle of a military camp
as if they had graduated the University of Paris."

And this is an achievement which anybody who is familiar with the rhetoric abilities of Sorbonne alumni could duly appreciate. Thus the continuation
and repetition of similar adventures is perfectly justified - but would not make
in itself a coherent novel. These small stories are amusing intermezzos in the
web of a more complicated system of stories of which several layers are to be
identified according to the above listing. So we arrive now to the stories which
could be illustrations

For class (2):

Don Quixote is not only acting but also provoking the revealing action
of others. The stories which are engendered by such interaction are different
from those of the first class in that they include the core of one or several independent narrations. They may, of course, display some resemblance with the
sequence pattern of the "class 1" stories but, thanks to the vigorous involvement of third characters, they are free of the mechanically repetitious structure. By collecting a sample of these stories, so much more exciting than those
of the previous bundle, we will find that even though

- the same two characters are invariably present and active in each
of them, only

- the active presence of third characters assures in each case a new,
unexpected development.

We understand, of course, that no particular excitement can be induced
by reading in an arbitrarily composed anthology of short stories the account
of a confrontation with sheep, when we previously read, in the same collection, the report of a fight with windmills which was unfolding according to
a similar pattern. However, when reading in sequence these stories followed
by such as that of the liberation of the galley slaves, we will appreciate the
freshness due to the increased diversity of the characters associated to the
unifying main heroes, and the changing pattern their exploits impress upon
the recount.

We may try now the example of the liberation of galley slaves in v.I, Ch.XXII:

> "Says the Arab and Manchan author Cide Hamete Benengeli in this most serious, uplifting, minute, sweet and purely invented story that ... Don Quixote lifted his eyes and saw approaching on the road about a dozen men on foot, stringed up by their neck on a long iron chain as beads on a rosary, and all of them handcuffed."

Not considering Sancho's explanations that these were prisoners to be punished on the galleys for their crimes, Don Quixote saw only human beings "lead against their will and not voluntarily", and instantly realized that

> "... this is a case where my calling is relevant: to fight abuse and help the wretched."

But here he did not proceed to action [as the pattern of the "class I" stories would require] but rather insisted that he may be told by each and every one of the prisoners the cause of his disgrace. This was, of course, the occasion to introduce a picturesque lot of crooks, along with an interesting sample from the vocabulary of the contemporary underworld. Among the characters presented, two are of particular importance; one, because he offered the lofty champion the opportunity to expound a hitherto not revealed chapter of his political philosophy, the other because of his role also in some future adventure.

Concerning the first personage, a very sad and subdued individual, Don Quixote was told by one of the guards that he was a "procurer and sorcerer/witch", *un alcahuete y hechicero*. The former qualification was slightly distressing to our hero because:

> "... for having been nothing more than a procurer he would not deserve to have to row in the galleys, but rather should command them and be their general. Since nothing compares to the job of a procurer; this being a most subtle and absolutely necessary office in any well ordered commonwealth, and it should be entrusted to none but wellborn people. And they should be supervised and

tested for ability, as it is the practice in other public offices. Also their number should be limited and made public as that of brokers on the exchange (*corredores de lonja*). In this manner much harm will be avoided which is caused when this office is entrusted to silly and uneducated individuals, such as women of doubtful character, or all kind of jokers and rascals with little experience, who are unable to distinguish between right and left whenever an important decision is to be made."

Therefore the poor fellow should be excused, the more so since he denied having been a sorcerer, that is a man practicing an art which, as Don Quixote explains us, has no real substance anyways.

This bright intermezzo is then followed by several other "confessions" culminating in that of an individual whom the guards characterize as "a great talker and a rather able master of Latin" and who thought that

> "..it is getting boring the way you [Don Quixote] delve in the lives of others. However, if you want to know about my life, you may know that I am Gines de Pasamonte whose life story has been written by these very fingers of mine."

No doubt that the champion of justice and defender of the oppressed, a great reader himself (not the last reason of my great love for him), became instantly interested in this fettered literary gentleman who modestly confessed that his autobiography

> "is so good that the *Lazarillo de Tormes* and all the other works of the same variety, written or to be written in the future, are nothing compared to it."

We learn that this work is not yet finished, since

> "How could it be finished ... when my life did not come yet to an end?"

And this is very important, because we will meet him again in the second volume, Chapter XXVII, where his story, as told so far, will be intermeshed with the web of the entire novel. The story of Pasamonte could, of course, continue beyond what we read about him as a wandering artist in the second volume, since so does his life. Thus we do have here, picked from the picturesque sample of convicts encountered by Don Quixote on the road, a relatively independent story, the sprout of a novel of the kind we were just reading, yet, possibly more concentrated, with a more unified action. Such stories stand *completely on their own,* some as perfect *novellas,* some others as outlines of novels. The latter we subsume to Class (3):

The "Passive" Knight Errant

In this category of stories, the hero will not end up with a beating but rather as a peacemaker, accepted and respected as such. The recounting has also in these cases a typical structure, but unlike in class (1), and very much in keeping with the main attribute of tales discussed in the previous section, they can exist *on their own.* More specifically, in this genre of tales the two permanent protagonists are nothing but frame characters. Their intervention completes their own, more comprehensive story, but does not add anything essential to the appeal of the particular inlaid narration.

We recognize also here a particular common structure, given by a three-phase unfolding of the recount:

(1) the knight and his page encounter on their travel somebody who tells them about something of importance to happen sometime soon and somewhere close by;

(2) Don Quixote and Sancho will be lead to *assist at* but not to *participate in* the occurrence, thus the adventure itself, without them, will be *the* story of interest;

(3) the outcome of the plot is likewise completely independent, and Don Quixote intervenes only as a wise judge - to help along the continuation of his own adventurous story.

We may quote two of these independent *novellas* which, as most of the others in the same class, have something to do with the unavoidable theme of love. This, at least, brings them close to the otherwise uninvolved Manchan who is himself a lover, as well as fighter and dedicated reader, and who braids with passionate delight the threads of love themes - his own love, that is - whenever the occasion arises. Probably a quotation about his own amorous dedication could help us understand his interest in the intrigue of the various inlaid accounts of love schemes. It happened, as reported in v.I, Ch.XVI, when the gallant knight rested in the barn of a shoddy inn:

> "This marvelous quietness, as well as the fancies which our knight always derived from the many episodes related in the books that caused his misadventures, induced in him the weirdest hallucination one could possibly think of. So he envisioned that he arrived to a famous castle (since, as we know, castles were all those inns in which he found shelter), and that the daughter of the innkeeper was the daughter of the lord of the castle, a lady who, overwhelmed by his gentleness, fell in love with him and expressed her desire to lay by him for awhile, without the knowledge of her parents. And while taking for absolutely true this self-invented fantasy, he started making himself thoughts about the dangers to which his integrity may be exposed, yet he vowed to commit no infidelity against his lady Dulcinea del Toboso even if Queen Ginevra herself, attended by her Dame Quintañona, were to tempt him."

A man of honor, true to himself, will always be on the side of those faithful to their vows and so we understand his restraint - rarely shown in other circumstances - in the stories we shall examine. The first is told in volume I, Chapters XI-XIV.

One evening Don Quixote and Sancho arrive to the hut of some goatherds who grant them friendly reception, shelter and food. Later another fellow, known to the goatherds, arrives, and tells them about the death of one Grisostomo. We learn that Grisostomo was the very intelligent son of a wealthy peasant, who studied at university and returned very knowledgeable, particularly in "the science of the stars". Such knowledge gave him the ability to predict the weather and thereby to advise his father about the right mix of plants to be grown in every season, thus father and son becoming very rich. This young man who, among others, was also "a great chap when it came to composing songs" was to be buried next day, and everybody, the goatherds and their guests, prepared to attend the funeral. Lovesickness killed the poor fellow, and we are further told how it all happened. There was in the village another rich peasant called Gulliermo who had a most beautiful daughter, Marcela. Every young man was in love with her, and so was Grisostomo. Yet she avoided them all, left the village, joined the shepherdesses and lived with them on the hills, not caring about her numerous suitors. She did not yield to the entreaties of Grisostomo either, who engaged also his considerable poetic talent in the service of his love. Everybody blamed Marcela for her cruelty and for the death of Grisostomo, who was characterized by a friend in his funeral oration as follows:

> "This body, honorable assembly ..., was the vessel containing a soul which Heaven has endowed with its richest gifts. This is the body of Grisostomo whose genius was unique, who was incomparable in his nobility, unparalleled in gentleness, unequalled in friendship, magnanimous beyond compare, serious yet unpresumptuous, cheerful yet without vulgarity, and, finally, the first in all virtues and second to none in his despondency."

During the funeral, the public's feelings turned hostile towards Marcela, especially after a friend read aloud the poetic laments of Grisostomo. This friend saved the manuscripts of the deceased in spite of the latter's last wish to have them destroyed, a breach perfectly acceptable by any moral standard since even

> "Caesar Augustus could not permit that [similar] provisions in the testament of the divine Mantuan should be executed."

Grisostomo being as important to his friend as Virgil was to Augustus, it was only normal that his literary bequest should be preserved.

But, towards the end of the funeral, we were to learn another side of the story. While friend Vivaldo was about to start the reading of yet another manuscript he refused to commit to the flames

> "he was prevented [to do so] by a miraculous apparition (since an apparition it was indeed) which suddenly emerged atop the

rock under which the grave was dug. It was the shepherdess Marcela looking even more beautiful than proclaimed by her fame".

Now an almost feminist Marcela went about telling the assembled mourners her side of the story, explaining that she came to defend herself against the accusations of cruelty:

"With my God-given natural understanding I know that everything pretty is loveable; but I don't understand why somebody beloved for her beauty must love him who loves her."

No obligation follows from being loved, she argues, and then

"True love ... must be free and not compelled. ... I was born free and in order to be able to live in freedom I have chosen the loneliness of the pastures. The trees of these mountains are my friends, and the clear water of these brooks is my mirror; I communicate my thoughts and my beauty with the trees and the waters. I am a faraway fire, and a resting sword. If someone fell in love with me I made him sober-up with my words. And if desires were fed by hopes, these were never given by me either to Grisostomo or to anybody else. Thus we might say that he was killed by his stubbornness rather than by my cruelty."

"I live independently and have no desire to become dependent. ... These mountains are the limits of my desires; and when I go beyond them it is only to contemplate the beauty of the sky. Such a hike leads my soul back to its origins."

And she left. Some, aroused by her beauty, wanted to follow her but were stopped by a warning from Don Quixote who realized that

"... this was a good opportunity to prove the purpose of his chivalry, namely to gave protection to maidens in danger."

To true lovers he also gave protection, much in the same fashion, as we could find out when reading about the wedding of the rich Camacho in chapters XIX-XXI of the second volume, a story so much more cheerful. And though Occam's razor is not to be applied when good stories are shortly recounted, the investigation should continue by skipping this one and moving to yet another class of our stories.

The "Real" Novel of Don Quixote

Class (4)

This class carries particular relevance for the understanding of the art of Cervantes. Here is a relevant example.

It was once again according to the pattern of most encounters of the traveling hero that

> "one day, at sunset, while coming out from a forest, Don Quixote sighted people at the end of a green meadow, and approaching them realized that these were hunters of higher standing. When coming even nearer he saw a distinguished lady riding a white palfrey with green trims and a silver saddle." (v.II, Ch. XXX)

This was not a provocative encounter - so far, strangely enough, Evil never showed up in the guise of a beautiful lady - and Don Quixote sent Sancho to communicate to the *bella cazadora* his homage and admiration. The Lady was not only beautiful but also intelligent and a good sport. She soon realized that the two fellows are none others than the ones she read about in that already published first part of the story. Deciding to participate in Don Quixote's game of chivalry she gave the appropriate instructions to her retinue and received the full participation of the equally well informed Duke, her husband. Her good humored approach, which nevertheless commanded composure also during that burlesque accident when Sancho fell from his *burro* and the knight from Rocinante, was expressed in her appreciation of Sancho's rather peculiar drollness. She attested that:

> "I appreciate Sancho the more for his fun which is a sign of his intelligence. Since humor and wit are not attributes of awkward

minds, as you know too well, mister Don Quixote. And given that the good Sancho is endowed with humor and wit I affirm him as intelligent." (v.II, Ch.XXX)

Had Don Quixote ever had some doubts about his calling, they were dispelled now by the Duke's invitation:

"The Knight of the Lions may come to one of my castles, the one right hereabouts where he will be received as due to a person of such high distinction, and as we, the Duchess and myself, always receive knights errant when they visit us." (v.II, Ch.XXX)

And everybody joined in the game, except the Duke's chaplain

"a somber clergyman of the type who are overseeing the households of the nobility; one of those characters who not being of noble ancestry are unable to instruct those who are; who would like to downsize the grandness of the grandees so that it may match the narrowness of their own mind; who, trying to teach moderation to those whom they advise, achieve only to make them feel miserable." (v.II, Ch.XXXI)

But Don Quixote who experienced

"his first day in which he was fully convinced to be not an imagined but a real knight errant"

was ready to confront the mean *togado,* the frocked one, dismissing him and his caviling remarks by stating that

"the weapon of the frocked ones are the same as those of women, which is their tongue." (v.II, Ch.XXXII)

(The shepherdess Marcela would surely have had some reservations concerning this remark. But even as chivalrous a person as the Manchan could be excused for a slip of his tongue when challenged by meanness while the respect for religion - not to speak of the regards due to the *Santo Officio* - keeps him from reacting more bluntly to the petty remarks of "the frocked one".)

And from this point on we do not have anymore one of those independent tales for which Don Quixote and his page offer only a mirror. Now both our heroes are part of a complicated story in which everybody is involved, even Dulcinea who was to be delivered from the spell cast upon her by those evil *encantadores*. And on top of all this, Sancho will become, at last, the governor of an island where his wisdom conveying loquacity (worthy itself of our studious attention) enlightens and entertains the reader as well as the participants, well trained and organized by the duke and duchess. Now, comparing this exemplary story with those of the previous classes will make clear its new and particular character.

Manners of Reading Don Quixote.

The difference between the reader of a novel and the viewer of a play consists in the degrees of their freedom when receiving the work. In the seat of the theatre you are a captive; you are not given the time to think *during performance* about too many alternatives, or to consider the possible destiny of the characters, mentally reproducing or *imitating* their thoughts. All you may be given is to wait in suspense after alternatives of possible outcomes were made obvious in the dramatic process. The reader, instead, may stop, reflect, and rearrange the ideas, his as well as those of the characters. He is not compelled to follow the pace of the novel, the epos, or any other type of literary output destined primarily for reading. So he may, to some extent, play the author. This possibility is generously offered by writers like Cervantes. If we classified the components of the novel [- and don't forget: many other classifications, by different criteria, are equally conceivable and legitimate, possibly also relevant -] it was because we desired to have a choice among the types of lectures we fancy.

Suppose we want a novel on a fellow like the erring knight called Don Quixote. Let's then pick some stories from the categories 1, 2, and 4, and we will be able to have a perfectly "round" traveling novel in the old fashion - its satiric version, of course. One or other - not all! - of the episodes in classes 1 and 2 may be dropped without damaging the structure, that *unity* which is given by the mirror carrying hero. But stories of class 4 will be the real backbone of the novel, the previous ones being only the trimming. Nevertheless, the movement in space will be as indispensable as in the Odyssey or the "real" chivalry romances. And again, our taste for *intimate experiences* will be satisfied by stories in classes 3 and 5.

Why should we separate the last groups? Well, we must not. It is however a *game of discovery* in which fine short stories, which the author could as well have offered us separately, emerge to view. It is not illegitimate in the literary art to have the same hero acting in a variety of separate stories. However, the most important thing is the fact that by a clear separation of the traveling hero's novel from the rest of the jewels in the book, we will understand what we gained in more recent travel story artistry - and what we *may have* lost by the death of the fine old ones. To make sure that nothing is lost, let's read it as often as possible. Never mind that some fellows are still writing novels, in most cases for reasons we may have trouble to comprehend.

Gogol's Counterpoint to Don Quixote

If I were able to formulate a theorem about where the traveling hero ends as a dominating character, then by doing so, the subsequent disquisition would be the requisite demonstration. But, in spite of all my efforts, I am unable to formulate a terse *proposition* on the subject. Still, I will try to continue to elaborate, based on private reading experience, a set of criteria in order to offer them as a guide in the choice of tidbits which testify for the newly emerging forms of epic, emerging that is from the "traveling" variety.

Cervantes started out with the time honored technique of putting the traveling hero to work so that he produces essentially all, or most, stories of the longer *opus*. Yet he broke through the combination pattern in a way others did not succeed. What he achieved was still not *a single unified story in which all episodes are organically connected to the main line of the narration* and, as Aristotle would have had it, without redundant episodes from the point of view of the entire construction. But he offered us a huge, colorful brick-box, a *Baukasten,* with which we can play constructing various subsets of consistent, entertaining and - never underestimate Cervantes! - enlightening stories. The great novel later to emerge is a solid, unified construction, with essentially indispensable episodes. Dispensable ones, as in the earlier epics, could be always justified with the spatial change of the scene. But once the novel became a unified structure, even its travel (or, if you want it: "picaresque") version will be unified, with an indecomposable texture. Example: "The Dead Souls", the major counterpoint to "Don Quixote" - two hundred years later.

As long as the poet did what Socrates reproached him, namely take a mirror (one single mirror!), and walk around with it in the world in the guise of his hero, more complex situations could not be revealed. It was always the author or his main hero who were the exclusive carriers of the mirror. Everybody was reflected in *their* mirror; a rather limited, even if mobile, vantage point. The most significant *others,* those who turned the mirror towards Don Quixote, instead of but being seen by us in the knight's mirror, were the parish priest and the barber, and later, to some extent, the duke and his charming and frolicsome wife, the *bella cazadora.* Yet the "Dead Souls" started with reflections in the mirrors of those "others". We first "gaze" into the mirror of two peasants idling around the village tavern and noticing the appearance of the anti-hero Chichicov's carriage:

"Look there ... look at that wheel! Think it'd hold out as far as Moscow?
"It'll make it ...
"And what about Kazan? I say it won't make it."
"It won't make it - the other agreed"

So we already learned a lot about the stage - it was obviously closer to Moscow than Kazan - as well as the carriage, sort of a Rocinante among carriages, well before the main character would put the surrounding little world in action, while traveling in it. His subsequent travel experiences may have had a similar pattern, but they were required, without exception, for the unity of the story. Our rather cynical crook-errant will now carry *his* mirror, but many more *autonomous characters* will have their own; the whole story will be now a play of reciprocally reflected images. What is most interesting for this inquiry is the fact that Gogol reveals the long-story's difficulty of emancipating from the travel pattern whenever theorizing about his "poetics" in the middle of chapters (just as Cervantes did). Let us start with a few points to help our recollection.

Chichikov shows up in a nameless town, inquires about serfs, subjects of landowners in this quasi-feudal system, offering to buy up the dead ones among them. The plan of his scheme is difficult to understand when postulating the legal context of capitalism where the individual is free - yes, often also free of those all determining "means of production". It amounts to the following. The landowner must pay taxes also after his dead serfs until the next census when their passing away will be reported and recorded. Therefore it was quite convenient to sell them to somebody willing to pay a price and, as it seems, take the fiscal burden upon himself. Why should somebody do that? In order to mortgage them to the Imperial Treasury ... and disappear with the money. Chichikov thought it through very carefully for all possible inconveniences:

> "True, there's a snag that peasants aren't usually bought or mortgaged without land. Yes, but then I can buy 'em for resettlement. Today one can get land in Kherson and Tabriz provinces free. Just like that: help yourself so long as you bring people there to settle! ... And if they wish to inspect the serfs, well then I'll present 'em with an inspection certificate signed by the rural police inspector. As to the name of the village, it might be called Chichikovka, say, or else, using my Christian name, Pavlovka."

We get from the author this so flawless presentation of the scheme only as a short recapitulation at the end of the novel, after its essentials have been slowly revealed as the story unfolded. It was most important for the construction of the plot, that we, the readers, should take cognizance of the unfolding events in the same order as the characters in the story, ignorant throughout of Chichkov's main motive. We were not to know very much more than they, except that we were assumed to be a trifle more intelligent. And from here on, for about half of the novel, the adventures of Chichikov will have a simple cyclical character. After having collected the essential information while in the town, he went about to travel around in the county (not very different in size from that of Don Quixote in the first volume), moving from one landowner to the other, by the following program:

(1) Outing from the inn or the last station.

(2) Friendly reception by some landowner.

(3) Proposal of the deal, in fashions varying with the type of the landowners; remarkable portraits which make the revealing difference between each of these cyclical stories. Negotiations. The essential purpose is never revealed and nobody inquires about it; what is of interest to everybody is the money.

(4) A satisfied Chichikov leaves or, as in one instance, an unsatisfied one escapes to avoid the police - though without a reason for fear. Yet.

In introducing the novel, Gogol reveals why it is so difficult to break away from the traveling pattern when the travel itself may not be so important. It is because travel implied in early ages some sort of heroism, even if only that of playing continuously the lottery of changing sceneries. It gave the traveler a grander image which did not require much analytical virtuosity. But is it easier to present such characters? Gogol writes:

> "It is much easier to paint a character of grand dimensions. You just have to splash the colours onto canvas - fiery black eyes, beetling brows, a furrowed forehead, a cloak, black or flame-red, flung over the shoulder, and there you have it. But gentlemen like Manilov, of whom the world is full, who look very much alike but, on a second look, turn out to have many very subtle peculiarities - these are terribly difficult to portray. You have to concentrate hard to bring out all the fine, almost imperceptible traits and, in general, you have to pry very deep, however practiced an observer you may be."

This was purportedly the explanation of the difficulty describing Manilov, the first seller of dead souls visited by Chichikov. But it also may give us a clue why the thus described task was tackled in the past almost only by either the playwright or the short story teller, with a limited scope and high degree of concentration. A longer, complicated intrigue would have required the same degree of concentration for which techniques developed very slowly. So it seems. But Gogol managed to successfully produce such for the representation of a still traveling *"character of grand dimensions"*, a caricature to be sure, and yet *"to bring out all the fine, almost imperceptible traits"* of a host of characters, without any trace of schematizing. It is one of the last great novels of a traveling hero, and possibly the first grand synthesis of the "old" and "new" type of "long-story".

Had "Chichikov, quite pleased with himself ... rolling along the highroad", collected characteristic picaresque adventures - for heroic ones he was unfit, of course - he may still have given us a good assortment of stories. But Gogol mastered a new art by now. His traveling hero has a different approach to what he encounters: he is supposed to learn and, implicitly, teach. Says Gogol (in Chapter 6):

> "Long ago, during my youth, in the days of my childhood which have flashed by and vanished irretrievably, I felt a joyful anticipation on approaching a place for the first time. No matter whether it was a village, a town, or some suburb - *my keen young eye always discovered much that was fascinating there.* ... I would stare at the unfamiliar cut of a coat ... I would watch an infantry officer walking along, swept by destiny from God-knows-what corner of the country to the backwoods boredom of this small district centre ... or a merchant wearing fur jacket, dashing by in a light carriage ... *And then in my mind's eye, I would follow all these people into their lonely lives.*"

He further tells us that these times are gone by. Yet he uses Chichicov as a spy to find exactly all those things which excited him in his youth. Since this is what the novel is all about. Its focus is on

> "all those things that an indifferent eye fails to notice - all the slimy marsh of petty occurrences into which we sink, all the multitude of splintered everyday characters who swarm along the drab, often painful road of life ..."

And the author

> "shows them clearly in relief, thanks to the power of his merciless chisel..."

Because, says Gogol

> "Supernatural powers have ordained that I should walk hand in
> hand with my odd heroes, observing the life that flows majestically
> past me, conveying it through laughter, which the world can hear,
> while seeing it myself through tears it never suspects."

So we have here outlined a program of gaining and transmitting insights
extracted from the encounters of the traveling odd character. They may not
be very pleasant to those who would prefer the author depict a grander, more
beautiful world. But this is so because they don't appreciate the recognition
we gain from

> "... microscopes, revealing the movement of unseen creatures, [and
> which] are just as wonderful as telescopes, which give us a new
> view of the sun."

And while Gogol is wedging his literary-theoretical disquisitions in the
flow of the tale (just as Cervantes), we recognize the foundation of the new
novel. It consists in the refinement of those "microscopic" methods by the
writer who will gradually dispense with the traveling hero carrying a mirror,
or if you please, a telescope, and still arrest our attention all the while we are
reading a long book.

Yet, if beyond the superficial contacts of the traveler, we concentrate on
the minute (those "microscopical") characteristics of all things encountered,
on *"all the slimy marsh of petty occurrences into which we sink, all the multitude of
splintered everyday characters who swarm along the drab, often painful road of life"*,
than the infinitely entangled networks of human relations will come to light.
Therefore Chichicov will have to yield part of his role to those whom he was
supposed to just "mirror". By Chapter 8 somebody else went on a trip: mother
Koroboshka, the lady landowner who sold Chichikov her dead souls, came to
town. Her suspicion awoke a little late but early enough to activate a new set of
characters, ladies in the first place:

> "'It's really quite odd', the lady-delightful-in-every-respect said.
> 'What on earth could those dead souls mean?'"

The wildest theories were submitted. The scale of the local nobility's fantasy ranged from stories about Chichicov going after the hand of the governor's daughter, to the suspicion that he is none other than the exiled Napoleon in disguise. Never mind that the connection with the dead souls was only tenuously outlined. The world of mysteries does not require logical rigor. But the colorful fare of rumors and tales (including one on a captain Kopeikin disguised as Chichikov, a grand *novella*-torso of the "Overcoat" class) offered exactly "all those things that an indifferent eye fails to notice". The treasure included episodes - tightly fitting into the structure! - from the conversations of two ladies of the local "society" (Maupassant himself could have been proud of producing such), or the death of a stunned prosecutor revealing unexpected truths:

> "...it was discovered that the deceased had a soul although, out of modesty, he had never given any evidence of having one."

Chichikov had to get out of the way. But he was to travel again. Except that the second part of his travels is not known to us. But travel it was with its mystery, which fascinated Gogol:

> "There is so much allure, wonder, fascination in the very word *road* and how wonderful the actual road is."

And Chichicov was to take advantage of it:

> "There's still a good distance to go for the light-carriage-of-the-kind-used-by-bachelors, occupied by a middle aged gentleman and his servants..."

And so the characteristics of the old and new novel met. The great spaces-covering story blended with the characteristics of the new novel: the thinking and not only acting hero, sensing the diverse human relations in the surroundings. The carriers of the *speculum* stop; complicated "optical" games emerge which could be played without the feverish collection of experiences scattered in the wide world.

Rudiments of a Synthesis

Apart from entertaining us, Don Quixote also teaches us something about why the traveling hero is often so much more interesting than others. Of course he does it in an indirect fashion dissertating about the use of erring knights as the only hope for so many afflicted people around the world. Because these people would in vain seek help

> "*a las casas de los letrados, ni a la de los sacristanes de las aldeas, ni al caballero que nunca a acertado a salir de los tèrminos de su lugar, ni al perezoso cortesano que antes buscas nuevas para referirlas y contarlas, que procura hacer obras y hazañas para que otros las cuenten y las escriban*" ["in the houses of learned men, or at the sextons of village parishes, or from those knights who never venture beyond the edges of their estate, or from the slothful courtier who would gather gossips to recount and spread rather than engage in actions and works which then others would recount and write about.]

And to him who engages in the hopeless exercise of teaching the world of better, it will also reveal more about it than the scholarly *letrado* in his study, the *sacristan* whose horizon is limited by the walls of the parish vestry, the listless *caballero* who never ventures beyond the confines of his fief, or the idle *cortesano* never being able to do anything but peddling gossips.

One could endlessly theorize about the cause, reasons, justifications of the long-lasting prevalence of stories in spatial unfolding. Much of the benefits of such enquiry flow from the joy of recounting and discovering of juicy details, while searching for an answer. The empathic exercise is itself a serene intellectual relief in this our age of standardized package tours: when reading these works we participate in adventures which send us beyond the fences and walls of otherwise inaccessible microcosmic compartments. But then, what was for a long time prevalent, if not exclusive, privilege of drama and poetry, became the subject matter of the novel *qua* novel. The *social* and *psychological* was revealed in coherent plots transcending the practice of just assembling pictures unified only by their mirror carrying hero. And by now, even the traveling hero of a "social" and "psychological" novel, when on the road, collected insights not adventures. Movement in space offered different discoveries. In the Odyssey or Don Quixote, the Golden Ass or Gulliver's Travels, or even the Dead Souls, it is the actions of the hero which reveal the World to the reader. Now, the World will have to settle for the back seat. The new travel adventure discovers the hero's interior life.

All this is, once again, very short of being a theory, but the examples should illustrate the patterns of transition. How to choose them? Of course, Leopold Bloom is now sent on a "trip" by Joyce, simulating an "Odyssey" in and around the city of Dublin. But we don't learn only about his encounters; we, the readers, get now an intimate view of his thoughts. *His* thoughts *for himself.* Not only what is uttered and spoken in communication with others. The thoughts of the hero have taken over from his acts and deeds. The book lover participates now in the *mental processing* (excuse my industrial metaphor) of the wandering hero's experience, whether it is exciting and colorful as in the case of Leopold Bloom and Stephen Dedalus, or, as in many other instances, just imposing boredom on the diligent reader (mostly of the English tongue) who will dutifully dull-away, stooping over his book, submitting to oppressive fashions.

The remarkable example offered by Joyce's book will be addressed in a different context. Here two exemplary cases will be shortly reviewed, epitomizing the manner in which the traveling and introspecting hero were blended. We borrow the examples from Anton Chekhov and Italo Svevo, respectively.

Late Echoes: Chekhov

The "meeting" seems to have been extended in time well after the "new" novel's complete development. One fine example in the Russian literature, to be briefly mentioned here as an instructive comparison, is Chekhov's *The Steppe: the Story of a Journey*. It grew out of the same earth as Gogol's stories, yet it is not light-hearted and satirical as *The Dead Souls,* though it shares with the latter not only [part of] the landscape, but also the mode of story telling. Except that the main character does not engage in anything which may qualify as *action* but is rather a mirror - close to literally *a mirror* - of the actions of others. It is about the travel adventures of a little boy from the country, Yegorushka, who went to town, to be enrolled in a better school. We read that he left his village and his loving mother:

"Early one morning in July [in] a shabby covered chaise, one of those antediluvian chaises without springs in which no one travels in Russia nowadays, except merchant's clerks, dealers and the less well-to-do among priests..."

His two main travel companions in this precarious cart, worse than Chichikov's, were exactly fitting the above requirements. They were Yegorushka's uncle Ivan Ivanovitch Kuzmitchov, a merchant of rather modest station, and their parish priest, Father Christopher, who tried to make ends meet by engaging "part time" in the wool trade. And Yegorushka will see and "reflect" a cross-section of Russia's rural society, yet from a more humble perspective than Chichikov's, namely that of a simple country boy. But it may be that therefore the picture composed by the young traveler's experience was richer and sharper. Among Yegorushka's travel companions father Christopher was by far the most interesting, being very much the type of travel-story protagonist:

"In all the numerous enterprises he had undertaken in his day what attracted him was not so much business itself, but the bustle and the contact with other people involved in every undertaking. Thus in the present expedition he was not so much interested in wool, in Varlamov [a rich wool merchant on whom most everybody depended], and in prices, as in the long journey, the conversations on the way, the sleeping under a chaise, and the meals at odd times ..."

Exactly the type for a *Story of a Journey*. And then he was also a man of learning. Though he forgot a lot of what he studied at the seminary, and what he knew in those glorious days when the bishop himself conversed with him in Latin, father Christopher still entertained high respect for scholarship urging his young travel companion to dedicate himself to it. But only "what God has blessed":

"Take example ... the holy Apostles spoke in all languages, so you study languages. Basil the Great studied mathematics and philosophy - so you study them; St. Nestor wrote history - so you study and write history. Take example from the saints."

And then came the inevitable innkeeper, the Jew Moisey Moisevitch, and his brother Solomon, who freely dispensed his own brand of bitter wisdom. Father Christopher addressed him as "Solomon the wise" while "making the sign of the cross over his mouth". And this is a sample of their conversation:

> "'... You see [said Solomon], I am a menial, I am my brother's servant; my brother is the servant of the visitors; the visitors are Varlamov's servants; and if I had ten millions, Varlamov would be my servant.'
>
> "'Why would he be your servant?'
>
> "'Why, because there isn't a gentleman or millionaire who isn't ready to lick the hand of a scabby Jew for the sake of making a kopeck.'"

This was that very same Solomon who burned all the money he inherited from his father in the stove, to stay poor and be free to have any opinion. Thus the first Jew whom Yegorushka met was one ... who burned money in the stove. And more strange and colorful characters were to be braided into the travel story. So he attended a group of waggoners - carrying wool for Varlamov - at their austere dinner, and listened to their conversation and

> "gathered that all his new acquaintances, in spite off the differences of their ages and their characters, had one point in common which made them all alike: they were all people with a splendid past and a very poor present."

But he also met somebody whose present and presence was splendid indeed. It was *the Countess Dranitsy* who, like everybody else, was also trying to contact the rich and rude Varlamov, an irrelevant circumstance for the young boy:

> "'how beautiful she is' thought Yegorushka, [while once again on the road] remembering her face and smile."

"His drowsy brain refused ordinary thoughts, was in a cloud and retained only fantastic fairy tale images, which have the advantage of springing into the brain of themselves without any effort on the part of the thinker..."

Those thoughts which "spring into the brain of themselves without any effort on the part of the thinker", we are now accustomed to call "stream of consciousness". And they are "streaming" indeed into Yegorushka's consciousness since they are of the same stuff as all things he encounters. They hover over things, and when you travel against them, so to say, they stream through your brain. (Remember the *ether wind* from the physics class? Yet physicists assure us that it doesn't really exist. But this one does. You have only to travel to realize its existence.) These thoughts become now the new stuff of which travel heroes are kneaded. Their experiences are experiences of the thinking receiver of impressions. Such one was Yegorushka who

"looked about him, and could not make out where the strange song came from. Then as he listened he began to fancy that the grass was singing; in its song withered and half-dead, it was without words, but plaintively and passionately, urging that it was not to blame, that the sun was burning it for no fault of its own; it urged that it ardently longed to live, that it was young and might have been beautiful but for the heat and the drought."

Thus, while on the trip, it turned out that Yegorushka was a poet, but only for himself. This is so on the road:

"You drive on for an hour, for a second [...] And then in the churring of insects, in the sinister figures [you meet], in the ancient borrows, in the blue sky, in the moonlight, in the flight of the nightbird, in everything you see and hear, triumphant beauty, youth, the fullness of power, and the passionate thirst for life begin to be apparent; *the soul responds to the call of her lovely austere fatherland, and longs to fly over the steppes with the nightbird.*"

And so Yegorushka was an early example whose consciousness, just as that of Gogol, registers

> "all those things that an indifferent eye fails to notice - all the slimy marsh of petty occurrences into which we sink".

The particular trend set by Chekhov - the rediscovery of the *sentimental traveler* - has an interesting follower, or perhaps, imitator.

The Version of Italo Svevo.

Un corto viaggio sentimentale [A Short Sentimental Journey] is just a torso. May be it was intended to become a novel but remained unfinished and was published in this form well after the death of the author. Of the manuscript as available in printing, the first part, about two thirds of the short text, is a piece which one could offer as a school example (that German *Schulbeispiel*) for what was claimed in the above three paragraphs. The remainder flattens into a rather poor sort of picaresque, dotted with psychoanalytic sham. Maybe, had the novel been finished, we would have gotten something else. It was not to be. But those mentioned available two thirds of the manuscript are worth the inquiry: it is of the best of Svevo's output.

The story is about *signor* Giacomo Aghios traveling by train from Milano to Trieste. No more Rocinante or wobbly carriage. We first meet him at the Milano train station where his wife bids him farewell, and then observe him, as he observes others, in the railway car and later, in transit, in Venice. It is a study about *why travel is a discovery*. But the discovery is now, once again, different, though still in travel. The difference is perhaps best *expressed* by a little girl traveling with her family who, while sitting at the carriage window, complains about not being able to see anything.

> "'But what do you want to see?' asks the mother. 'Can't you see everything?'"
> "The little girl burst into tears: 'I can't see the train'"

Chekhov's Yegorushka wasn't very happy either at the beginning of the trip, before his great discoveries:

"How stifling and oppressive it was! The chaise raced along, while Yegorushka saw always the same - the sky, the plain, the low hills."

This was to change later because the boy was intelligent and observant, but the little girl was bored, and her well thought remarks were taken as a joke by the cruel grownups. Yet while everybody in the compartment had a good laugh, Aghios was moved:

"The pleasure of traveling had been quite different if she had been able to see the big train with its engine progressing across the countryside as a fast and silent serpent. To see the country, the train, and oneself at the same time. This would have been a true journey."

It was the first train trip of the little country girl who, as disclosed by the mother, was talking for fifteen days about nothing but the expected journey. Still her problem was not so childish. If the heroes of past stories carried that Socratic mirror in the world, they were not able to show us simultaneously themselves, others, *and* the "World". Positions and vantage points had to be frequently changed to reveal something. But they were sailing, riding horses, chariots, or simply walking endless roads, so they could sometime change their perspective. The train does not offer thus many insights. *Signor* Aghios knew as much:

"He was like the little girl. [For him] the true journey would have been in a stagecoach and along natural roads (this is how he called the roads free of iron), and crossing inhabited places, with stop-overs not at rail stations, which in Italy never reflect the image of the town to which they are the gate, but in front of a local joint, integral part of that town, for repair and to change horses. Not even by automobile could the road, the towns, the people be so closely experienced."

No doubt such advantages were enjoyed by Chichicov, or at least his inventor Gogol as well as Yegorushka. But locked-up in the compartment of the railcar, Mr. Aghios could still engage in something we may call a series of *adventures of thought,* of the kind mentioned as "streams of consciousness"

- by those who read William James, as well, and mostly, by those who never heard of him. And the impressions are just streaming along, sparked by either a charming young lady or a nasty but stiffly polite young man, when the eternal love theme emerges inscribed into new coordinates. Because neither the old fight for a heart to be conquered, nor the eternal dedication to an unattainable Beatrice or Laura - or Dulcinea, of course - would fit within the narrow confines of a *coupé*. A tuft of curly hair shifted from the eye uncovering the winsome face of a lady, or the discrete appearance under the seat of "*un piedino in aria*", a little foot in the air, proved to be a gold mine of thoughts about feminine beauty:

> "Because a woman, when she is beautiful, offers very much to the stranger and to everybody, and first of all a feeling of gentleness. ... It is enough to live isolated for several months in a strange country where they speak an incomprehensible language, where they avoid you fearing that you might be a thief or a murderer, and then, at once, to discover your intimate connection with them all, your belonging to that country, your right to citizenship, in the very moment when your sight chances upon a shining eye, a nervous little foot, or unusually colored and trimmed hair."

The chances to discover such a "land" of enriching and gratifying impressions is no doubt greater when you travel than otherwise. Indeed, any attempt to transcend the world of superficial impressions could ruin everything:

> "Because if the exchange of glances were to be followed by words, one would run the risk of being projected out of the ideal country into the most dangerous bush land."

Speak one does also when on a trip, but not about and around the unspeakable. Indeed, many things which one does not dare to mention in conventional surroundings would much easier leave the lips during "the great freedom of travel". So it was also with Giacomo Aghios, who, after all

> "*ci si trovava nella grande libertà del viaggio*".
> ["enjoyed now the great freedom of travel."]

The type of travel experience is not one of fight but of careless liberation. It was hovering above "life", addressing it in passive contemplation:

> "He did not suspect anymore how life may be ... he enjoyed it by forgetting about it."

He engaged a conversation with "the normal man" who, normal as he was, quickly came to jokingly ask:

> "May be you are a poet in disguise?"

The stranger hit a sensitive point:

> "[Aghios] looked inside himself with curiosity. He saw himself as a man who desired so many forbidden things, yet deprived himself of these, realizing that they are prohibited. Still he permitted the desire to survive."

And many of these, some quite uncanny, claimed a share of his thoughts during this trip, while enjoying "the great freedom of travel", when everybody can afford to be a poet. So we discover with our hero a young blond man sleeping in a corner seat. But then:

> "As soon as the train left Mestre, the *biondino* in his nook moved, stretched his arms, as if emerging from a deep dream, and murmured quite clearly: 'How beautiful can dreams be! What a shame that we have to wake up!'"

This was the fellow with whom Aghios was to have an unpleasant adventure in that last, uninteresting, third part of the incomplete story. Here he revealed a dimension of the *grande libertà del viaggio* which is part of the adventure in discovery. Later, when in Venice, sitting in the same *gondola* and getting better acquainted, the young man introduced himself:

> "'Funny! I am also Giacomo. Giacomo Bacis. The name reveals my Friulano origin. Am I right if I think, yours too?'

"'No, No!' answered *signor* Aghios with a heartfelt laughter. 'My race is much older than the Celtic one'
"'Greek?' asked Bacis with admiration.
"*Signor* Aghios nodded. 'It's comfortable' he said 'to belong to another race. It is as if you were always on a journey. Your thinking remains free. And thus when things are viewed from an Italian point of view, I disagree. And I disagree with the Greek way of looking at things as well. The last Greek with whom I am in a consensus is Socrates.'
"'I am one of those *Friulani* who speak two languages and a dialect' said Bacis. 'So I am also on a journey.'"

He won quickly the sympathy of his older travel companion, who thought:

"How intelligent is my new friend. He understood right away the theory which defines the traveler as an exceptional character, whereas I had to put in almost 60 years to develop such a simple principle."

The "secret" of the travel romance is thus discovered in an unfinished literary work, thereby becoming almost a symbol for the destiny of the genre.

The character of the traveler is formed by his freedom; and freedom was the element of past heroes. This was no more the case with the heroes of the new novel. They disclosed inside connections, dependencies, and lost the lightness which made them float above things. All those who sought adventure in travel, did so to be free. All the breed of Don Quixotes were thus travelers. And all travelers have the potential of being like Giacomo Aghios or, that other "Greek" among yet other "Italians", Leopold Bloom, wandering on the streets of Dublin. But their story is now to be told in a different manner. Because trains travel so much faster. Not to speak of airplanes.

The Reader's Adventures

If you read the adventures you are part of them. Why so eager to participate? The answer may be found, perhaps, in a very, very short note of Kafka concerning "*The truth about Sancho Panza*". There we read:

"Sancho Panza never bragged about it but he succeeded to distract his Devil, whom he later called 'Don Quixote', from nagging him, by feeding the fellow, throughout the years, with lots of books about chivalry and bandits. The trick worked so well that 'Don Quixote' engaged in the most foolhardy adventures. These, however, were totally harmless because they were lacking any clear aim, which Sancho Panza would have offered otherwise. Thus Sancho Panza, a free man, followed Don Quixote in his adventures in a relaxed manner, possibly also out of some concern for his responsibility. Thereby he enjoyed great and useful entertainment until his end."

And so, to keep him distracted, we feed with stories our own devil, the one which nestles within all of us. Because if, should that happen, we will fail to supply him with appropriate reading stuff, he may awaken and go about plaguing us to death. And he himself may also suffer, because he is not really that dreaded Devil. He is one of the type we are accustomed to call a "poor devil", perhaps the hidden side of our own personality who, sometimes, speaks so smartly *"que el mesmo Satanas no las podria decir mejores"* or "that Satan himself wouldn't be able to say it better", but who is also often only too helpless to care for himself. Therefore we look after him like Sancho after his own devil, since we know what he knew:

> *"... somos de un mismo lugar, he comido su pan, quierole bien, es agradecido, diome sus pollinos y, sobre todo, yo soy fiel, y asi, es imposible que nos pueda apartar otro que el de la pala y azadon".*
> ["we are from the same place, I was eating his bread, I rather like him, he is grateful, he lends me his mules and, above all, I am loyal, and thus nobody could separate us but the one with the spade and the shovel."

PARERGA

related to
"The Mirror of Socrates Carried by the Traveling Hero"

The pleasure of reading a good story can be enhanced by figuring out the author's ways, and by identifying the building blocks he used to construct his work, thus partaking in the joy of composition. This would be an adventure in the "how" of the literary enterprise, some results of which are outlined in these essays. Yet, irrespective of our concentration on the "how", we are never freed from the question about the "why". Of course the philosophical, sociological, political or personal motivations of the author could be interesting on their own. They have been avoided here on grounds amply argued for, mainly in the introductory essays. But the "why" of the choice of form may prove to be just another aspect of the "how". And while sampling from travel-framed stories, the question about the reason why earlier "long stories" are mostly spread out in space has frequently returned. So: why? The sociological historian of literature may have an easy task here. He will argue - indeed "he" often argued in the past - that in societies preceding the one we call "bourgeois", the common man/woman was simply not considered to be worthy of the talents of great authors/poets. They were rather meaning to satisfy the myth-making needs and ambitions of some powerful Maecenas yet also to offer the simple man a feast of the grand and unusual. At first one would be inclined to agree without objection, recalling also that, as far as theatre was concerned, Aristotle himself thought the ordinary man to be worthy only of comedies. Now, while all this is never to be completely denied, it still does not explain why that "common man" was still *always* present in *short* (!) stories, parables, legends, fables etc. And when there was to be said something more longish about him, well it was again on the road.

From the "Golden Ass" to Lazarillo or Simplicissimus. The explanation is not to be given here. However, appended to the main essay on *Socrates' mirror* and its list of instances, a few additional cases should be quoted revealing the divide between travel-framed epic and the "modern" novel. It is about marginal cases, where the two forms meet on their common frontier. And also a few references are given to past discussion of the here employed relevant metaphor.

(1) Of Lawrence Sterne, Denis Diderot and Italo Svevo

The story of a "*Corto Viaggio sentimentale*" by Italo Svevo is avowedly in debt to Lawrence Sterne's "*Sentimental Journey through France and Italy by Mr. Yorick*", for its title as well as for the choice of the subject. It is an homage paid to the 18th century English writer by the 20th century Italian novelist. It could be stuff for interesting, pleasant and blessedly useless speculation whether the influence of Sterne's parody of literary travelogues is or is not related to many an author's propensity to yield to the temptation of spatial fabulation. The fact is that at least one major "travel" related classical work is said to owe its existence to the suggestive power of the *Sentimental Journey*, namely Diderot's *Jacques le Fataliste*. This has been countless times repeated in erudite writings about Diderot and the more humble manuals of French literature as well, but few mention the much more important fact that it was Diderot's *Neveu de Rameau* which projected Stern's satyric approach into the same medium but not as a story-on-the-road. Instead, Svevo's fine little *novella* torso, of lesser purport in the history of literature, and of only secondary importance in its author's oeuvre, was meant to be a variation on the same fundamental theme. Svevo may have sympathized with the idea of a *sentimental traveler*, a type added by Sterne to the typological inventory of the more distinguished wayfarers of his time, and tried to re-create him in a 20th century environment. But it should be reminded that an interesting *non-travel* variation on Sterne's theme could reveal something about the art of increasing the reflective depth of "Socrates' mirror" while reducing the radius of its deployment. It could, indeed, reveal the path of transition to new forms of novel. This can be done by citing some features shared by the *Sentimental Journey* with the *Neveu de Rameau* - rather than *Jacques le Fataliste*. First, recall Sterne's classification of travelers, an exercise not without educational employment, and then his notion about the purpose of travel:

> "It is sufficient for my reader, if he has been a traveler himself, that with study and reflection hereupon he may be able to determine his own place and rank in the catalogue - it will be one step towards knowing himself."

Yet the doubts about any positive use of travel, as jokingly disclosed by Sterne, include also some positive thoughts about the problem discussed in the essay on the mirror-carrying hero. First the doubts:

> "But there is no nation under heaven abounding with more variety of learning - where the sciences may be more fitly woo'd, or more surely won than here [in England] - where art is encouraged, and will so soon rise high - where Nature (take her all together) has so little to answer for - and, to close all, where there is more wit and variety of character to feed the mind with. - Where then, my dear countrymen, are you going?".

Well, it was perhaps "to feed the mind" with even more "wit and variety of character" to be then presented within a story of traveling adventures. Since it is obvious that

> "An English man does not travel to see English men"

only, even though his country may have all those above cited virtues.

So the sentimental traveler asserts himself in spite of his doubts. It is this type of wayfarer for whom also Svevo had an obvious sympathy, not least due to the charm of Yorick's discrete eroticism (which, *because* of its discretion, proves to be of great relief to him who is familiar with the gratuitous *grossièrtés* in Tristram Shandy). Yet there is an essential difference of approach between the two unfinished works. Sterne's is an alternative to the travel books of his age which chronicle the voyages of a new breed of gentlemanly travelers who, in most cases, do not get high marks from him. An example of his scorn for such writings is expressed in relation to the travel reports of a distinguished contemporary who

> "... with an immense fortune, made the whole tour; going from Rome to Naples - from Naples to Venice - from Venice to Vienna - to Dresden, to Berlin, without one generous connection or pleasurable anecdote to tell of; but he had travel'd straight on looking neither to his right nor to his left, lest Love and Pity should seduce him out of his road."

As far as it goes beyond the simple stocktaking, slipping into the fictional, Sterne's work is still part of the old tradition; a torso of its kind, yet with a hero of different social background. And it is not understood differently by the author himself:

> "'Tis going, I own, like the Knight of the Woeful Countenance [!],
> in quest of melancholy adventures - but I know not how it is, but *I
> am never so perfectly conscious of the existence of a soul within me, as
> when I am entangled in them.*"

It is also a hint, a suggestion - not an explanation - as to what moved the authors of the grand epic works: it is likely that all those authors were "never so perfectly conscious of the existence of a soul" *also in their heroes* but when sending them to explore a slice, even if only a thin slice, of the globe, *per seguir virtute e canoscenza*, by causing them to get *entangled* in as many "melancholy adventures" as possible. Just as the Knight of the Woeful Countenance. It is yet another testimony about the choice of travel as a medium of discovery; the discovery not of strange lands but rather of human souls. *Why* is it easier on the road? No answer. Yet this seems to have been the fact for so long a time.

Of course, *A Sentimental Journey* is not "grand epics". It is rather a sketchbook for fine ... short stories. Or, indeed, more than that, since we recognize in it occasional anecdotic elements of which other authors - whether by Sterne's suggestion or by coincidental concern - made the seed of interesting new stories. A couple of examples from the book should illustrate the point. Thus, here is Mister Yorick in Paris making his cunning entry into the jungle of high society, "*yearning in desire to follow knowledge*" (though less tragically then

Tennyson's Ulysses), and always prepared to flatter those who had the power to open him the gates. Thus:

> "Mons. P**** the farmer-general was just as inquisitive about our taxes. - They were very considerable, he heard - If we knew but how to collect them, said I, making him a low bow.
> "I could never have been invited to Mons. P*****'s concerts upon any other terms.
> "I had been misrepresented to Madame de Q*** as an *esprit* - Madame de Q*** was an *esprit* herself; she burnt with impatience to see me, and hear me talk. I had not taken my seat, before I saw she did not care a *sous* whether I had any wit or not - I was let in, to be convinced she had. - I call heaven to witness I never opened the door of my lips. ..."

And when he succeeded to flatter a quite attractive Madame de V*** in the unlikely circumstance of a theological discussion, during which Mister Yorick so ably controlled his delicate inclinations, the result was the desired one:

> "I declare I had the credit all over Paris of unperverting Madame de V***. - She affirmed to Mons. D*** and the Abbé M***, that in one half hour I had said more for revealed religion, than all their Encyclopedia had said against it - I was listed directly into Madame de V***'s *Coterie* ..."

It is the ingredient which enters the composition of such characters as Diderot's *Neveu de Rameau*, who, though a lot more vulgar than Yorick, knew well the essentials of the art of discovering the hidden facets of the *société* of his time. So he knew that

> «*c'est qu'il y a baiser le cul au simple, et baiser le cul au figuré*»

or as we may translate, or rather "render it into English", while blushing a little:

"there are two ways of kissing an ass: by doing it just plainly or only figuratively."

And such art was then transformed into a tiny novelistic masterpiece. The recipe, well, one version of it, reads as follows:

«*Supposez la dispute enagée et la victoire incertaine: Je me lève, et déployant mon tonnèrre, je dis: Cela est comme mademoiselle l'assure. C'est là ce qui s'appelle juger. Je le donne en cent à tous nos beaux esprits. L'expression est de génie. Mais il ne faut pas toujours approuver de la mème manière. On serait monotone. On aurait l'air faux. On deviendrait insipide. On ne se sauve de la que par le jugement de la fécondité; il faut savoir préparer et placer ces tons majeurs et péremptoires, saisir l'occasion et le moment; ... [j'ai] ... une manière de contourner l'épine du dos, de hausser ou de baisser les épaules, d'étendre les doigts, d'incliner la tête, de fermer les yeux, et d'être stupéfait, comme si j'avais entendu descendre du ciel une voix angélique et divine. C'est là ce que flatte.*" ["Think of me engaged in a dispute while the victory is still uncertain: I stand up, unleash my thunder, and say: This is exactly as *mademoiselle* is telling us. This is what I call judgment. This is way above anything our *beaux esprits* may be able to say. It reveals genius. - But one should not express approval always in the same manner. One would become monotonous and it may look as if faked. And one could also become dull. One could be saved only by the judgment of proficiency: one has to know how to prepare and how to direct those lofty and peremptory speeches, how to seize the occasion and the moment; ... [I have] ... my way of bending my spine, to raise or lower my shoulders, to stretch my fingers, to bow my head, to close my eyes, to be stupefied as if I had heard an angelic or divine voice from heaven. This is what flatters."

But this is still only the surgical *method* of dissecting the body social. The *result* will be exposed later in the new novel. Perhaps by Balzac. Until then experience was still collected on the road, the last refuge of Mister Yorick, who got an upset stomach while perfecting the method as later exposed by the *Neveu de Rameau:*

> "For three weeks together, I was of every man's opinion I met. - *Pardi! Ce Mons. Yorick a autant d'esprit que nous autres. - Il raison bien,* said another. -*C'est un bon enfant,* said a third. - And at this price I could have eaten and drank and been merry all the days of my life at Paris; but it was a dishonest *reckoning* - I grew ashamed of it - it was the gain of a slave - every sentiment of honour revolted against it - the higher I got, the more was I forced upon my beggarly system - the better the *Coterie* - the more children of Art - I languish'd for those of Nature: and one night, after a most vile prostitution of myself to half a dozen of different people, I grew sick - went to bed - order'd La Fleur to get me horses in the morning to set out for Italy."

We don't know what happened there. We know, however, that the method continued/continues to be employed. The *Corto Viaggio sentimentale* is an example.

In a different fashion we may say that Sterne's travel story was the beginning of a new strain of a literary genre. In the ages old tradition it was the *hero's actions* which provoked the World to reveal itself. Now, ever since the XVIII century, the *hero's thoughts* gain in importance being provoked by his actions and his contact with the world. *Mister Yorick's Sentimental Journey* is the travel version of this approach; it is one way of developing the intimate. In this sense the trip is just one way of doing the same thing in a limited space as the *Neveu de Rameau.* The action "in space" is now substituted by movement in a limited space, to get the characters' reasoned reactions to the world in the *salons* of Paris, the cafes of the *Palais Royal* or, as in the case of Svevo, in a passenger car of the Italian Railways.

This latter case reminds of another example from modern Italian literature. It is *Il fu Matia Pascal* [The Late Matia Pascal] by Luigi Pirandello. He also travels, but always as somebody else. Because he is dead. Or rather believed to be so, and therefore he cannot travel as himself. Not fitting the above category of "mingled approaches" it is a good pretext for several investigations. One is that of stories about substituted personalities, such as *The Golden Ass,* or traveling souls, such as that of *Gregorio Guadaña* by Antonio Enríquez Gomez; and of course the entire Pirandello genre where most everybody is, most of the time, somebody else.

(2) The Mirror Metaphor of Stendhal and ... Joyce

The mirror metaphor has had a destiny similar to many other sayings of Socrates/Plato about art in general and poetry in particular: it was warmly embraced by those who were meant to be dismissed by it. It is astounding how poets, as well as litterateurs of all description, fall in love with philosophers who despise them. If it were only for the metaphor of a mirror carried about reflecting the already existing "world of shadows", as perceived by our senses, then this entire section in Plato's *Republic* wouldn't be worth to be mentioned as something particularly interesting *for the poet.* Yet it is interesting rather by its hostility to poets and artists. The stress on the mirror's/artist's/poet's inability to achieve and convey cognition of the *Realities,* thus making "imitative" poetry a trifling, indeed futile exercise, is the essential content of the Socratic message. Not much is to be improved on it, which does not mean that there have never been brave men and women to take up the challenge. Yet it is clear: by the dogma of platonic idealism, reflection of perceptions is not a source of that insight and cognition with which some poets would like to flatter themselves. However, it is non-, indeed anti-platonic philosophies, the lots of them, many not in a very high esteem with artist and poets, which recognize perception as the primitive source of knowledge, and it is these doctrines for whom the performance of the poet is, or rather can be, yet another form of cognition. Notwithstanding the otherwise great differences between these philosophies! But if you understand that what is in our mind is constructed of the data of our perception - as absorbed by our *a priori* mental reception frame (I am a Kantian, you know!) - then the mirror metaphor will gain a positive meaning. In such case also the much debated difference between "realistic" and "romantic" story-telling will prove to be something else then the radical opposition of the "mirror" to "subjective invention" or legitimate poetic folly. The discussion will then focus on the distinction according to subjective choices of *what is mirrored!* But then it becomes also a matter of choice of subject and *techne,* while "reflection" will still be with us.

Thus the mirror, when seen as a device by which common eyesight can be expanded, oriented, perhaps concentrated, will loose its function as a metaphor of *a* particular artistic approach. It will once again prove to be nothing but just an older and more widely used metaphor of intelligent human perception, along with the more recently developed optical accessories such as telescopes or microscopes. Gogol knew about them, as shown. And Stendhal repeatedly returned to them. And he thereby unwittingly fed a burgeoning critical literature debating the existence or non-existence, in his work, of a basic inconsistency between what is *realistic*, mirror-dependent, and what is to be seen as *romantic* or purely invented. The philosophical paucity of some of these writings exposes itself also in the way in which the problem of reality/perception is treated. Thus we read references to the mirror metaphor as either pure non-sense or relevant only to "realistic" story-telling. Now, polemics should be avoided here, as elsewhere in these essays. Instead the "mirror", as it appears in Stendhal's work, will be rehabilitated as a discriminator. Because metaphors, when used by great writers, such as Stendhal, may bear significance beyond the critical blahblah.

The relevant quotations will be advanced according to their implication within the logical frame of this short discussion and not in the chronological order of Stendhal's work. The best known instance, of course, is the one already partially quoted and now to be quoted more completely from *Le Rouge et le Noir:*

> «*Eh monsieur, un roman est un miroir qui se promène sur une grande route. Tantôt il reflète à vos yeux l'azur des cieux, tantôt la fange des bourbier de la route. Et l'homme qui porte le miroir dans sa hotte sera par vous accusé d'être immoral! Son miroir montre la fange, et vous accusez le miroir! Accusez bien plutôt le grande chemin où est le bourbier, et plus encore l'inspecteur des routes qui laisse l'eau croupir et le bourbier se former.*» ["Well, sir, a novel is a mirror walking along a highway. Sometime it reflects the azure glare of the sky, [while] some other time it reflects the slushy mud of the road. And you accuse of immorality the man who carries that mirror on his back! His mirror shows the slush, and you accuse the mirror! You should rather accuse the road where the mud is gathered, or indeed the

road inspector who has tolerated the accumulation of water and the formation of the mud."]

This is the "moving mirror", the metaphor we could also employ in reference to the epos, the *chanson de geste*, the picaresque novel or, indeed, to Stendhal's own work akin to the former in many respects. The association has often been made quite explicitly by Stendhal himself, and recognized frequently and with good reason. Thus Maurice Bardèche (*Stendhal romancier*) makes it clear *à propos* the relation between the metaphor of the mirror walking along a highway:

«*Son récit suit la grand route, et les rencontres viennent l'une après l'autre, et aussi auberges, les passants, les moments de bonheur. Le romancier se borne à noter les impressions du promeneur. Si les romans de Stendhal ressemblent à quelque chose, c'est aux romans picaresques.*» ["His story follows the road, and thus encounters follow one another, just like roadside inns, passing travelers, as well as moments of happiness. The novelist just limits himself to marking down the impressions of the passerby. [Therefore] if Stendhal's novels may be compared to anything, then to the picaresque novel."]

And again:

«*la structure du roman stendhalien reflète l'enchevêtrement du roman picaresque.*» ["the structure of the Stendhalian novel reflects the entanglement of the picaresque novel."]

But then the new novel, as emerging in the XVIII century, knows of a different type of mirror. It is the static one which is mentioned in the preface to *Armance*, Stendhal's first novel, in the defense of the authors of a satiric comedy:

«*Ils ont présenté un miroir au public; est-ce leur faute si des gens laids ont passé devant le miroir? De quel parti est un miroir?*" ["They showed the public a mirror; is it their fault if ugly people walk by in front of the mirror? With whom is a mirror siding?"]

This quotation signals the transition in the art of realistic "long-story" telling. It refers to a different mirror; this one does not move in space. It is the *characters* which pass review in front of it. True, in the quoted instance, it alludes to a play where the unity of space may still apply as of old. But it is meant to defend a novel's new approach which is no more *un miroir qui se promène sur une grande route*. It is a novel in which the *time* required for the story to unfold is no more an accident of *space*. It is the clear start of a process in which space becomes just an accident of time. And it is only fair to say that the much neglected *Armance* is itself an, however modest, example of this development. (This novel would deserve, of course, more studious attention, and the reader, so far influenced by the academic neglect of the work, could find in it dispersed text fragments of uncommon beauty and elegance. If, of course, that reader will forget about biographic and gossip details and the psychoanalytic junk stuck to the novel by some sort of "literary scholarship".)

The process of transition can be followed all over the European literary landscape. In Goethe's *Bildungsroman*, the endless *Wilhelm Meister*, the report of wanderings in space is still the requisite conveyor of the tale about how a brave young man passes his apprenticeship while moving from adventure to adventure. That these are no more adventures of the sword makes a difference only as far as the subject is concerned, not the writer's method of constructing it. But in the family novels of the late XIX and early XX century *space* becomes, as said above, an accident of time. The characters do not travel anymore to *collect* quite disparate adventures to be displayed in a not always very stout frame. It is rather a *unified story* of a hero or, indeed, a whole family, where time is the medium, and space just its necessary attribute. They parade in front of mirrors, such as the *Buddenbrooks* of Thomas Mann, the *Thibaults* of Roger Martin du Gard, the *Forsytes* of Galsworthy, or the *Artamanovs* of Gorki. The applicable examples are, of course, more numerous. These titles are listed only as a clear contrast, and not necessarily as paragons in which the new novel proves itself at its best. It shows that while the characters are not always sedentary, their majority assembles around the mirror rather than hauls it about.

But then mirrors are not all that neutral, whether perambulated or just steadying on a spot. Neither is impartial any of those other optical instruments offering instances of variation on the Socratian theme, such as telescopes. Stendhal knew it as revealed in yet another instance of playing with a variant of the metaphor. It is in *Henry Brulard* were, examining Molière's *Ecole des Femmes,* he refers to the bias of such instruments as the source of artistic creation:

> « *Tous les faits qui forment la vie de Chrysale sont remplacés chez moi par du romanesque. Je crois que cette tache dans mon télescope a été utile pour mes personnages de roman, il y a une sorte de bassesse bourgeoise qu'ils ne peuvent avoir ..* » ["All the facts which constitute Chrysale's life are replaced [in my work] by the *romanesque*. I believe that this stain on my telescope was useful to the characters in my novels; there is some sort of bourgeois meanness which they can't have .."]

Little doubt that the romantic stain in Stendhal's telescope puts a stress on points which may never be revealed by instantaneous perception.

Now, there are various stains and different damages to mirrors, telescopes, etc. An example will be offered by another, more recent case of the road-mirror association. It is Joyce's *Ulysses*. (Though we may forget about the analogies, forwarded by erudite critics, between every movement of Leopold Bloom in Dublin and those of the ancient navigator.) Here is a relevant quotation from the first chapter:

> "Stately, plump Buck Mulligan came from the stairhead, bearing a bowl of lather on which a *mirror* and a razor lay crossed."

It will prove to be a mirror of consequence. A bit farther we read:

> "He swept the mirror a half circle in the air to flash the tidings abroad in sunlight now radiant on the sea. ...
> "` - Look at yourself, he said, you dreadful bard.`
> "Stephen bent forward and peered at the mirror held out to him, cleft by a crooked crack, hair on end. .... It is a symbol of Irish art. *The cracked looking glass of a servant.*"

What follows is the wanderings of Leopold Bloom and Steven Dedalus in the city of Dublin, each carrying about his own *cracked looking glass* [as to be discussed in essay No.9]. All *looking glasses* are either cracked or, in the more fortunate cases, stained. This makes them reveal aspects of the world which simple and direct perception may never discover. This makes the work of the epic and imitative poet an instrument of knowledge.

(3) Transcending the Traveling Hero

The history of epic literature may be - and has been - written from many points of view. The historic context, biographic implications, psychological, sociological or ethical relevance, are all legitimate criteria of the historic examination of literary works, just as the emphasis on technical aspects which may enhance the studious reader's pleasure and understanding. It may require the employment of all of these standards to understand any author's choice of the frame within which he parades his characters. We are familiar, of course, with the discussions about the *three unities* of the dramatic work as originating in the readings and misreading of Aristotle's *Poetics*. We also know that the "unities" asserted themselves for a long time, whether spontaneously or by the author's deliberation. Whichever be the case, once the decision was taken that the work is to cover action which unfolds "in one revolution of the sun", not much movement in space was to be covered - if the paramount requirement for the *unity of action* were to be respected. Now the epic work was able, of course, to expand in space which, naturally, implied also the abandonment of the time limitation. Any kind of travel takes time. However, the opposite is not true: advancement in time does not necessarily require expansion in space. E.g. a psychological novel may not require it at all. Yet the subordination of the spatial expansion of a story to historic time, appeared very slowly. Its earlier roots are probably found in the subservient role which women had in classical epics and early societies. They did seldom "travel" in the sense of seeking and encountering adventures. The exception of adventurous women in Ariosto's romance (mock epos?), as well as in a few more writings, will not contradict the conclusion we could draw from the rule. Penelope was sitting at home and waiting, as most women, providing thus the opportunity of an insight into the human condition essentially different from the one offered by a collection of adventures on the road. And not to forget: the first major psychological novel in the modern sense of the word was Boccaccio's *Elegia di madonna Fiammetta*. To be sure, she also intended to go on a short trip after her unfaithful lover; but it was subordinated to the "action" of time-spread lovesickness. Pretty similar was the literary approach to a, rather limited, world by Mme. de La Fayette when three centuries later she wrote the *Princesse de Clèves*. The quoted examples can be multiplied. We know, of course, about the very prominent role of English lady authors as pioneers of the modern psychological novel. It may be worthwhile to explore the role of the *passive woman*, as author and main character as well, in developing of the art of modern novel. This is meant in reference to that "convenient vantage point" [*behaglicher Standpunkt*] attributed to women by Robert Musil, an issue to be discussed in yet another context.

ESSAY NO. 3

Paragons of Suspense and Peripeteia: a few Exemplary Cases

[1] Of Oedipus and Hamlet

We read in Aristotle that the "reversal of the situation", the *peripeteia* (περιπετεια), and the "recognition", the anagnorisis (αναγνωρισιζ) are "the most powerful elements of emotional interest" (Poetics XI, 1450a). In the particular case of tragedy, perhaps unduly emphasized by Aristotle over other forms of drama, the emotional culmination of the plot is that unexpected turn of events, the peripeteia, which leads to the hero's fall. Such change in fortune yields "recognition ... change from ignorance to knowledge" (1452a) of the unexpected and sorrowful. And the author, the good author that is, wishing to captivate his readership or audience, will carefully construct his story so as to enhance the expectation of a peripeteia or/by recognition. It is an essential device of literary creation to generate and amplify the expectation and, thereby, to increase also the impact of the recognition. Let us compare the manner in which it performed in the paragons of classical Greek and renaissance tragedy. The reader of this essay has, of course, knowledge of these two masterpieces.

Types of Expectation

There are three kinds of expectations by which we relate to a story, whether performed on stage or in a piece of reading.

The *first kind* is open ended and in most cases without causing anxiety: you certainly expect something not heard or read before when you open a book for the first time. You may be thrilled or disappointed at the end, but when you start reading your expectations are open ended. When the story, while unfolding, generates more than one, but still only a few, clearly definable outcome possibilities, that is when expectations cease to be open ended, then we have something we came to call *suspense*, using a term often employed by courts and lawyers in earlier times. This is the *second kind* of expectation. The simplest among the rich variety of suspense situations is the one we are now used to call a "cliff-hanger", and which is referred to here because of its clear-cut character rather than its presence in tragedy proper. The expression is likely familiar to movie goers and is suggestive of a situation, in many cases anything but tragic, in which a fellow hanging from a cliff, could end up only in either of the two situations: falling into the precipice, or being saved in the last minute by some lucky circumstance or, perhaps, by somebody's heroic intervention. (I can only hope that the great classics of dramatic poetry will forgive us when we can't help but remember in this context none other than Buster Keaton, who is anything but a "tragic hero".) The viewer's excitement comes from the *suspense* which lasts, of course, until the cliffhanger comes to a tragic or redeeming end. And this excitement itself comes from the clearly spelled out alternatives for a solution. Never mind the various meanings of "suspense" in past and current usage, such as the legal one; here it refers strictly to the expectation of a reversal "from ignorance to knowledge". In other words it means that a choice has been made from a set of possible solutions.

Even if the choices in a suspense situation are more numerous than two and not always clearly spelled out, as in the paradigmatic cases to be discussed, the excitement comes from their small number and the fact that the possible outcomes may be definable without either of them having to occur with unavoidable necessity. Thus this suspense is different from the first kind of expectation in that its outcome is not open ended but reduced to a distinct number of logically *possible* yet not *necessary* consequences.

The cliffhanger - in the above proposed usage! - is a simple, indeed very simple, yet intuitively appealing illustration of the *second kind* of expectation. Suspense, either in such plain or in more complicated forms was introduced very early in the art of storytelling and originated always in alternatives easy to spell out and limited in number, thus recognizable by readership or audience. This example does not exhaust the variety of "second kind" cases which may be granted more attention in the subsequent discussion. Here, yielding to some extent to our elementary urge to classify things, we should make the following distinction between suspenses within the "second kind": in one subclass we put the varieties of cliff-hangers where the "what will happen" is the relevant question; in the other, the "who done it" type of stories. *Oedipus the King* is the most pertinent classical example for the latter.

A *third kind* of expectation is not always easy to segregate from the previous one and is entertained by the more sophisticated reader/spectator. In this case, the definable alternatives, though perfectly compatible in a logical sense with the story as told, are not equally valid in a literary sense; it may be that one, or more, of the logically available alternatives would yield an *uninteresting* outcome. In this case your expectation is reduced to those possibilities which "make sense" for a good story. Of course, the reader may be betrayed, finding that the author has chosen the dull outcome. The story may also lose excitement when it turns out that of two or more alternatives, only one is *storyworthy*. So the story may still be beautiful but the suspense is gone. Or it may shift from the story to the author: is he a good or a dull one?

Of the three kinds of expectation, the second is the most interesting from a literary point of view. It remains, of course, a matter for the psychologist to establish why people get excited by a suspense situation. However, for the reader it is interesting when it is worthwhile. No doubt, some excitement in stories is desired, we want it; but because we want it and enjoy it, suspense may become a vehicle by which to convey more than the tingle. The discovery of the variety of human characters may be done through stories charged with the kind of titillation we are inclined to associate only with a literature of lesser standing. Yet some of the greatest classical works of world literature are "thrillers", though never classified as such. Their higher quality comes from the degree of suspense refinement, and much of the message which emerges from it and the recognition we experience, is due to the able manipulation of the *excitement of choice*.

Theory will not lead us very far beyond this taxonomic enunciation. So let us read once again some major pieces of world literature, specifically tragedy (for a start), and try to get more learning out of them, while keeping in mind the framework offered by the general principles stated above.

Oedipus the King

"Oedipus the King" can be viewed as the prototype of a thriller of the "who done it" class. Well, let's make it a bit milder: it is not a thriller *per se* but it is the first major case of application of very sophisticated and highly concentrated suspense techniques in the history of literature. It is also a paradigm of lasting relevance for that particular way of story rendition in which anxiety and suspense enhance the compassion and participation of the public. That it is compressed in space and unfolds "within one revolution of the sun" as it behooves a classical tragedy, helps; yet the procedure remained essentially unchanged in drama as in all other literary forms to our day.

Another highly distinguishing characteristic of the play is to be emphasized now, and illustrated by the forthcoming discussion. It is an example of implicit logico-geometric story construction, something seldom stressed by either litterateurs or classicists. Thereby it is perhaps more Greek than many other ancient plays. In the times of Sophocles the art of formally rigorous presentation and solution of a problem, in a story or otherwise, was still in its early stages. Yet the construction principles of the play betray a state of mind which will culminate in geometry, the greatest achievement of the Hellenic spirit.

Warning: this is not to be an "interpretation" of the play. It is meant to be just an attempt to reveal *what is actually in it.* I do not risk the adulteration of story or text in an attempt to uncover purported hidden meanings. In the forthcoming exercise the purpose is more modest. It will be achieved by "moving the magnifier" over the play thus emphasizing an important agent of our literary and theatrical enjoyment. A play or a story is like any creation of God or Man: looked upon from different angles it will offer our sight a corresponding variety of aspects and insights. So we should now try to move a little around the play and search for less explored angles. The *suspense in Sophocles* proves to be important in many respects, not least *as an exemplary case for the understanding of how this device acts upon us if employed in any literary work.*

The Author's Story and Ours

Whether it is a novel or a play, the author and the reader/spectator relate differently to it. The author knows from the beginning how the story will end. That gives him also the freedom to choose between the ways of telling it, the freedom to select from possible manners to lead us to that end we, the readers, know nothing about. We know, of course, that one and the same story can be told in very different fashions without changing even only a single little detail in what actually happened. And one among the many choices the author may have is that of a "thrilling" rendition. The handling of the art of suspense is one possible way to achieve that. One and the same story has an array of "real" sequences in its own "historic time", which is the order of events as they happened in "reality". Still, their arrangement and re-arrangement in the recounting of all of it will make the story "exciting" or not.

Let us first retell the story of Oedipus as it "actually happened" and as Sophocles has known it when starting to write, and then compare it to what we can read in the text or see in the theatre. Each phase of this summary will get a number; each numbered component of this summary is to be viewed as some sort of a building block; the play will come about by a rearrangement of these building blocks - without any one remaining unused. Here is the "real" story, (it is the "reality" of Sophocles), the succession of events which "occurred" before any chronicler or story teller has reported them:

(1) Once upon a time, in the city state of Thebes reigned king Laius. His queen, Jocasta, bore him a son.

1.1) As it was the custom, Apollo's oracle was enquired about the son's future. The seer had not much good to foretell: the son was to kill his father and marry his mother. Parricide and incest was to be his lot! King and queen thought that only the death of the child could belie the oracle. But since neither king nor queen wanted to take upon themselves the sin of child slaying,

1.2) they handed the child to a servant, a shepherd, directing him to abandon the little boy to his destiny in the wilderness, with riveted feet.

1.3) However, the compassionate shepherd preferred to entrust the child to the care of a fellow shepherd, this one from Corinth. Without explanation! - and without disclosing his deed to his masters.

(2) The Corinthian shepherd brought the boy to his childless masters, king Polybios and the queen Merope, who adopted him. They called the boy Oedipus (i.e. swollen-foot, because of the rivets).

2.1) Oedipus will believe for a long time that he is indeed the son of Polybios and Merope.

(3) The oracle tells the now grown-up prince Oedipus of Corinth, that he will kill his father and marry his mother.

3.1) Oedipus flees Corinth to avoid any possibility of having the prophesy fulfilled, not knowing that Polybios and Merope were not his real parents.

(4) At the same time, King Laius of Thebes goes on a trip with his retinue, purportedly on a pilgrimage. Somewhere on a road Laius and Oedipus meet. Neither recognizes the other.

4.1) A misunderstanding sparks a fight and Oedipus kills Laius, his father. N.b.: he doesn't know whom he killed.

4.2) Messengers returning from the sight of the fight with the news of Laius' death, claim that highwaymen slew the King. They honestly believe it to be so.

(5) In the meanwhile, i.e. in the absence of Laius, Thebes is challenged by the ferocious Sphinx. Freedom from death will be granted only if somebody will solve a riddle proposed by the Sphinx. So far all whose wits were challenged by the monster failed - and died.

(6) Oedipus arrives in Thebes, accepts the challenge of the Sphinx and solves the riddle. The city is free.

6.1) Celebrated as a hero, unwitting Oedipus marries the widowed and equally unaware queen Jocasta, his mother. They will have two sons and two daughters.

7) After fifteen years of happy reign a terrible pestilence and famine is plaguing the city.

Thus we arrived to the point where the play starts. We have now to distinguish between three types of awareness of the contents of the story so far told, according to different involvements with it.

The author. he knows everything in all the details and it is his choice what, how much, in what order and with what emphasis the above recounted events shall be included in the forthcoming play.

The public knows nothing so far and will learn only what the author has chosen to tell in what follows. Of course, it cannot be assumed that all the ancient Greek spectators, even those attending the first performance, were unaware of the legend behind the story. But the play is written - as we will find out rereading it - under the assumption of the spectator's ignorance. This assumption was more justified than classical scholars are ready to admit, as will be shown in an appended note. Until then we postulate a spectator who sees and hears for the first time about the story of Oedipus. (No doubt the spectators of later times often loose the dramatic effect because they are "too educated" and "knowing" the play's prehistory from school or at least the playbill.)

The agents of/in the story. While the author knows everything and the spectator knows (purportedly) nothing, all agents know something which is less than everything. Each knows his/her side of the story unawares of the others' or how it fits together with the picture and information of the others.

During the play the agents will discover the connection of their respective stories; this will be the tragedy - and the recognition. At the same time the spectators will find out about the same connection by also learning the prehistory of the play which they so far ignored; this will be the viewers' dramatic experience. And while the play is unfolding, *the knowledge of agents and spectators converges to the knowledge of the author.* All this goes through a cascade of suspenses; every suspense comes about by a puzzle and the suspense is over when the puzzle is solved.

The phases of the dramatic development of the story will now be marked with Roman numerals to which the numbers of the prehistory's corresponding phases will be associated in the order in which they are discovered by the spectator. Let's now "read" the play:

(I) Equivalent to 7 above (Eq.7) which is the end of the story *qua* history: Pestilence plagues the city.

(II) The people, i.e. the chorus, implores Oedipus, the husband of queen Jocasta, to save them and reminds him of Eq.5 and Eq.6:

"Art thou not he who coming to the town
of Cadmus freed us from the tax we paid
to the fell songstress? [35] ......

"....O Oedipus, our peerless king,
All we thy votaries beseech thee, find
Some succour, whether by a voice from heaven
Whispered, or haply known by human wit." [39-43]

Thus we find out something that we, the public, are assumed not to have known but the people of the city know: sometime, in the past, Oedipus has saved the city from some enchantress and is assumed to be able to perform once again such feat. So far he receives Creon, Jocasta's brother, returning from Delphi with the oracle's message:

"... Phoebus bids us straitly extirpate
A fell pollution that infests the land,
And no more harbour an inveterate sore." [96-98]

Further we find out the implication: Laius, the once king of Thebes, was killed (Eq.4.2 and Eq.4.1)

"and now the god's command is plain:
Punish his takers-off, whoe'er they be." [106-7]

We do not know who the killer of Laius is; nor does Oedipus or the people of Thebes represented by the chorus. Oedipus initiates now an investigation:

calls in the local prophet Teiresias. The choice is most appropriate as the chorus assures us, since

> "if any man sees eye to eye
> with our lord Phoebus, 'tis our prophet, lord Teiresias." [284-5]

But Teiresias first refuses to impart his knowledge:

> "... my voice will ne'er reveal my miseries - or thine." [328-9]

Yet he soon becomes more explicit:

> "Thou art the man, Thou the accursed polluter of this land." [352-3]

And later:

> "... this man whom thou hast sought to arrest
> With threats and warrants this long while, the wretch
> Who murdered Laius - the man is here.
> He passes for an alien in the land
> But soon shall prove a Theban, native born." [451-5]

So far the accusations have not yet been proven, and chorus (as well as the public) need not believe them:

> "Are they true, are they false? I know not and bridle my tongue
> for fear,
> Fluttered with vague surmise; nor present nor future is clear." [487-9]

says the chorus and thereby the *first suspense element* is being introduced.

(III) A conflict is slowly building up between Oedipus and Creon, the former accusing the latter of attempting to deprive him of the throne and therefore feeding stories to Teiresias. This only strengthens our uninformed doubts as above expressed by the chorus.

Jocasta joins Oedipus and Creon on the stage and counters the accusations of the "rascally soothsayer" by claiming that

"no man hath scot or lot in the prophetic art" [708-9]

Were it otherwise, Laius would have been killed by his own son and not, as she thinks it was obvious, by some highwayman - and she proceeds to recount the oracle of her son whom Laius and herself have abandoned and is thought by her to be dead. So we are at Eq.2 of the "real" story. We, the ignorant spectators, wouldn't yet have much to doubt about. Not so Oedipus:

"What memories, what wild tumult of the soul
Came o'er me, lady, as I heard thee speak!" [726-7]

and we, the spectators, still don't know what it could be. In due course, urged by Jocasta, he tells the story of his own oracle, the one he was told when still prince of Corinth - Eq.3. It shall be retained that there is no clear cut logically necessary reason for believing that the two oracles, though identical in substance, refer to the same person.

The Structure of Suspense

Before continuing to follow the process of recognition, we have to stop and take stock of the problems we face as students of the play, and as readers/ spectators.

These two roles are not quite identical. *As students* we realize that the play starts at Eq.7, and as it proceeds it reveals (in reverse order) elements of the "true" background story. The correspondence between the components of the play and of the story, so far reviewed, can be exhibited in the following table:

Play	Story
(I)	Eq.7
(II)	Eq.5 and Eq.6
(III)	Eq.4 and parts of Eq.2 and Eq.3.

So far our knowledge as readers/spectators converges to the knowledge which agents already have. As the play unfolds, we get a stream of new information. Not so the agents: until "building block" (III) of the play, they do not learn anything positively new. But public and agents alike share now the same anxieties. These follow from the two unsolved ambiguities:

The first: There are two similar oracles, one told to Laius about his son and one told to Oedipus (still believed to be from Corinth). Do the two oracles refer to the same person or not? We do not know the answer; nor does Oedipus.

The second: Did Oedipus kill Laius? Or did he kill somebody else while Laius was murdered by an unknown highwayman.

Given these two unresolved questions clearly spelled out in the play, spectator and agents arrived to a point where they have a choice between four possible explanations which are logically equally compatible with what they discovered so far but of which, naturally, only one can be true. These are:

1) Oedipus is indeed a Corinthian, and he also killed a stranger (Laius was killed by other than Oedipus) and the two oracles refer to two different persons.

2) Oedipus did kill Laius but the two oracles, though similar in substance referred to two different persons. (Oedipus is not a parricide and is not incestuous.)

3) Oedipus killed a stranger (Laius was killed by other than Oedipus) but the two oracles refer indeed to the same person, thus to Oedipus. (After all, maybe, oracles are not always right.)

4) Oedipus killed Laius and both oracles meant him.

The spectator's agony consists in the fact that there is no logical necessity for either outcome: the solution is left in *suspense* because all possible outcomes, of which there are only four, are equally compatible with what he knows so far. A good thriller - and such is Oedipus King - is told, in its first part, as an accumulation of equally likely outcomes of which, up to a very advanced point, no logically necessary choice can be made.

How are these four possibilities to be seen from the point of view of developing a tragedy? Here the *third kind of expectation* comes into play.

Case 1 implies that Teiresias is wrong and that there is some substance in Oedipus' accusation against Creon. Hence the tragedy ought to develop as a conflict between the two while modern illuminists and ancient Greek blasphemers will be vindicated: oracles and prophecies aren't worth anything; or, as Jocasta put it, "no man possesses the secret of divination". And yet an interesting play could be constructed on the power conflict which developed between Creon and Oedipus in which "truth" is confronted with "falsehood", i.e. insinuations, inventions etc. .

Case 2 also grants a point to illuminists but would make the oracles a useless episodic burden on the play. Thus the more sophisticated reader or spectator, who would expect from Sophocles a good and exciting play, will consider only *cases 1), 3) and 4)* as premises of a great drama or tragedy. And this is sufficient for real good excitement, especially when you agonize between believing or not in divinations. Thus the play has to continue and answer the two questions:

- who killed Laius?

- how do the two oracles, with all their consequences, relate to one another?

We are back now at the play.

Solutions of Suspense

(IV) A messenger from Corinth comes with the news that Polybios is dead. Jocasta seems vindicated:

"Ye god-sent oracles, where stand you now!
This is the man whom Oedipus long shunned,
I dread to prove his murderer; and now
He dies in the nature's course, not by his hand." [946-9]

All of a sudden it seems that the oracles are eliminated and, because we know how a good tragedy is to be structured - don't we? - we can expect a rather dull play to follow. But we are saved: the messenger from Corinth happens to be the shepherd who gave Oedipus to Polybios. When Oedipus enters the stage the messenger also explains him the origins of his name - all this is Eq.2. Jocasta is struck with fear and tries to prevent any further investigation, but Oedipus insists on his research. A *second major suspense* is then expressed by the chorus:

> "Why, Oedipus, why stung with passionate grief
> Hath the queen thus departed?" [1073-4]

(V) The shepherd who gave the child to the Corinthian is called; tormented confrontation and Eq.1 is disclosed to everybody.

(VI) A tragic Oedipus leaves etc. etc.

The convergence is perfect: agents as well as spectators learn all the author knew from the very beginning. And we establish now the final relationship between the story's "building blocks" and the play: the order of the story is reversed in the process of recognition and peripeteia:

Play	Story
(I)	Eq.7
(II)	Eq.5 and Eq.6
(III)	Eq.4 and parts of Eq.2 and Eq.3.
(IV)	Eq.2
(V)	Eq.1

And still, some small pieces from one or two building blocks remained outside. For some of us, at least. We should arrive to this by way of the subsequent *excursus*.

Of Drama and Geometry

I yield to the temptation of an analogy. The perfect frame for the geometric, or more generally, mathematical beauty of *Oidipos Tyrannos* is based on its respect of the three unities which also permits the massive concentration of an extremely complicated history covering the lifetime of its actors. The reader/spectator experiences the convergence of the actors' knowledge to the truth in history (i.e. the knowledge of the author) as an elegant demonstration. Yet "mathematically elegant" as it may be, the excellence of this (of any good) play is to be understood by both: (1) the difference between the sequences of its unfolding and the dramatic process of a rigorous demonstration *more geometrico*, and (2) the features they share as well.

In geometry the adopted ritual of a demonstration begins with the statement of a theorem which is then followed by the demonstration proper. So if the proposition is correct, i.e. when it is indeed a theorem, then the triumphant *quod erat demonstrandum* will not conclude an unexpected outcome: no surprise will be in the serene pleasure of understanding. There will be, however, more tension in the act of driving *ad absurdum* an incorrect proposition first thought to be a correct one. This will be akin to a *peripeteia*. The most important difference between truth-emergence in geometry, respectively drama, consists in the introduction of *suspense* in the plot, thus supplying both the pleasure of recognition *and* the thrill of emotional participation. We can understand the way this comes about by contrasting the recognition in Oedipus with that in a demonstration. And it is good to stress that the interest here is not in *what* we recognize but in the *process* of recognition. Because the "what" is *general truth* in the case of geometry, and only a very *particular discovery* in the case of drama/tragedy. If anything general is to follow from it, it is the result of the reader's contemplative contribution - free and not rigorously bound, as in geometry. Yet there is something significantly common between the plot of a play and the carrying out of a proof: it is the participation in the process.

It is still by contrasting the two ways of recognition that the function of suspense-tension can be best understood. In the case of Oedipus, we have four implicit propositions coming up at a certain point of the play, about *what happened to Laius* and *who Oedipus is,* and the reader/spectator experiences thus the agony of being unable to choose the true one, because none of the alternatives is necessary *more geometrico*. The four are all compatible with whatever is known at some point - but that is all, and not enough. Only Sophocles (and the silent Teiresias) knows the truth; we and the agents of the play ignore it yet. Simply stating the truth and then bringing in the witnesses would do in a court testimony for the prosecution. But there we don't participate in the agony of the accused, accomplices, victims and judges. Such comes about only by keeping the truth from us: not even the prosecution is to air a suspicion. (In the play the prosecution is implicit, anyway.)

The geometric approach would be different. In the case of Oedipos Tyrannos it is Teiresias who could make the statement:

> "Proposition: The man who married queen Jocasta [and who claims to be the son of the King of Corinth] is Jocasta's son."

That may not have relieved the anxiety in the expectation of a proof, but could have reduced considerably the tension on the path of recognition. It would now be incumbent upon Teiresias to carry out the proof. And such proof will have to be based on coherent facts, since oracular revelations have already been dismissed by Jocasta and, partly, by the chorus. Otherwise, the earlier suspense would be substituted by a new one: is the revelation true or not? The proof could have been similar to that we have in the play, but our agonizing doubts would be appeased by Teiresias' statement. Oedipus may still hope for an error in the seer's assessment, but the most to remain for us is the appreciation of the beauty of the "demonstration". No agony, some suspense of course, but no emotion.

Yet there is an essential common feature between the Sophoclean and the Euclidean. And this is the construction of the argument. Let us recall the fact that at some point we have spelled out four logically possible alternatives for an outcome: *quintum non datur*. Each of them is a potential "theorem". For either of them to become the truth, some missing propositions have to be supplied. And here they are:

> Corinthian shepherd: The boy given to me by a Theban shepherd grew up as the son of Polybios and Merope.

> Theban shepherd: I gave the son of Laius and Jocasta to this Corinthian shepherd.

Oedipus as well as Jocasta can only recognize that they are incestuous. This is now proven beyond doubt. Not *beyond reasonable doubt* as in a Court, but by solid logical rigor. No guessing, no prophecy, no "psychic" brain wave. Oedipus and ourselves, and everybody else, we all know now that the two oracles referred to the same person. Did they tell the truth? Well, as far as the incestuous marriage is concerned the truth and the oracle coincide. And what about Laius' death? There is still no proof; it may be true by implication and because we believe in oracles. In order to be true that Laius was indeed killed by Oedipus, we would need an additional *postulate* which states: oracles are always right. But had everybody, author, agents of the story and the public, firmly believed in the truth of this proposition, then the entire dramatic development would have been futile. Thus, after 2400 years we still don't know who killed Laius, and we are still in suspense as to whether Case 3) or Case 4) is the true "theorem". But then, Euclid affirmed himself when Sophocles was already an old man. And after Euclid few wrote plays as well as Sophocles. And just by the way: it may very well be that the suspense of the ancient Greek spectator was over with the non-logical conclusion that "given so many coincidences, it may still be that oracles are, at least some times, right".

The Case of Hamlet

As Oedipus is the perfect classical play, something we have to recognize not by Aristotle's authority but by the strength of his argument, so is Hamlet the paragon of modern theatre after the fall of the "unities". The use of suspense technique in Hamlet is characteristic for the "new" play writing. In Oedipus, the stage being confined to the steps of the palace and the square in front of it, and the time limited to exactly as much as we read on the clock from the beginning to the end of the performance, every other implication of the story, covering a long stretch in physical time, has to be revealed by the alternating narrations of the actors; and all these stories converge to one major moment of suspense. In "The tragedy of Hamlet, Prince of Denmark" with the story breaking through the unities, there is not one central moment of suspense, but rather a sequence of such, constituting the phases of play. One of these suspense-sequences should offer an example for the discussion.

First, we have the appearance of the spook, the ghost of the King of Denmark, whom we do not yet know to have been assassinated. Nor do the agents in the play know it. The tense expectation is shared by actors and spectators: no one knows the cause of the appearance. Horatio proposes:

"... by my advice
"Let us impart what we have seen tonight

"Unto young Hamlet; for, upon my life,
"This spirit, dumb to us, will speak to him." (I.1, 173-176)

But Hamlet's own suspicion sends first to the sin of his mother:

"... O most wicked speed! To post
"With such dexterity to incestuous sheets!
"It is not, nor it cannot come to good.
"But break, my heart, for I must hold my tongue. [I,2. 156-158]

No suspense yet; only that open ended expectation (of the first kind).

Did Horatio, Hamlet's friend, have some premonition? We don't know. But Hamlet, after learning about the appearance of his father's ghost, seems to have some, and will confirm it in scene 2:

"My father's spirit - in arms! All is not well;
"I doubt some foul play. Would the night were come" (I.2, 255-256)

And later comes the ghost's revelation:

"Brief let me be. Sleeping within mine orchard,
"My custom always in the afternoon,
"Upon my secure hour thy uncle stole
"With juice of cursed hebenon in a vial
"And in the porches of mine ear did pour
"The leperous distillment ... " (I.5, 59-64)

"Thus was I, sleeping, by a brother's hand
"Of life, of crown, of queen at once dispatch'd." (I.5, 74-75)

This solves the first suspense completely, yet creates the theme of a tragedy. The thus created *suspense* issue seems to be the expectation of the vengeance and the possible outcome of such attempt. But then this would make a rather simple story, tragic or not. Instead, a *new element of suspense* is introduced. As Jocasta (and Oedipus) entertain ambiguous doubts about the oracular statements of Teiresias, so Hamlet has his own doubts:

"... The spirit that I have seen
"May be a devil: and the devil hath power
"T'assume a pleasing shape, yea, and perhaps
"Out of my weakness and my melancholy,
"As he is very potent with such spirits,
"Abuses me to damn me." (II.2, (593-599)

Thus Hamlet did not reject altogether the ghost's revelations yet neither did he free himself from his tormenting doubts. These doubts are ours as well and we expect an opportunity to test the truthfulness of the ghost's story. After all, the ghost may still have been only a devil assuming a pleasing shape. The introduction in the plot of itinerant actors offers the occasion for a test; their stage simulation of a royal fratricide will become the test. Like Oedipus, now Hamlet takes upon himself the role of the investigator suggesting to the players a purposely re-tailored version of their story and warned:

"... The play's the thing
"Wherein I'll catch the conscience of the King". (II.2, 600-601)

So we are now at the *second major suspense*: the seed of doubt is sown [we see the play for the first time!] and wait for the play-in-the-play to provide the solution. However, the process of convergence to the truth is not continuous. First it is Rosencrantz and Guildenstern who introduce the players, but then it is they themselves who will be the source of a new, the *third suspense;* before solving any given suspense, already the next suspense is introduced. Careful rereading should show us that if any expectation were to follow only after the previous one is solved, the play would fall apart forfeiting its *unity of action.* So we discover here a new variety of the dominant Aristotelian unity which works by keeping tension alive during a lengthy story built with the abandonment of the other two "unities". [Then it is the tragedy of Ophelia, grafted upon that of Hamlet which has a structure for an independent tragedy.]

We leave thus the second act being "in suspense" about the outcome of Hamlet's "controlled experiment". The result, in Act III, is now to come from the performance of the play, called by Hamlet "The Mouse-trap". *It* is to reveal the King's guilt and dispel our and Hamlet's doubts. Everything in that Act III is only heightening our tense expectation until the King, caught in the "mouse-trap", betrays himself by his own behavior, and Hamlet can confidently state:

"O good Horatio, I'll take the ghost's word for a thousand pound."
(III. 2, 280-281)

In the next scene we, *the public* - nobody else! - receive also the confession of the King:

"O, my offence is rank, it smells to heaven;
"It has the primal eldest curse upon't -
"A brother's murder." (III. 3, 36-38)

but not before he prepares that above mentioned third suspense, namely to dispatch Hamlet to England in the company of Rosencrantz and Guildenstern. In the meanwhile we expect Hamlet's reaction: will he avenge his father's death or not, before being sent to England? First he avoids killing the king kneeling in prayer, not because he is such a philosophical doubter as commentators make him out to be, but because a man murdered while praying is swiftly sent to Heaven. Yet soon he will kill the wrong man inadvertently. The King knows that: "It had been so with us had we been there", behind the arras, in the queen's chamber. No vengeance now, and Hamlet is sent to England with Rosencrantz and Guildenstern. He knows not why. We [only we, the spectators, nobody else!] are told by the king, who counts on the meanness of the English vassal, to execute what has been ordered

"... By letters congruing to that effect,
"The present death of Hamlet". (IV. 3, 67-68)

The riddle of this suspense is: what will happen to Hamlet? Two elements reinforce the state of tension. One refers directly to the outcome of the previous suspense. It would be a shallow end of the previous suspense if Hamlet were to abandon forever his vengeance. Then Fortinbras walks through the stage with his soldiers reminding a listless Hamlet his duty following from the discovery in the play:

"How all occasion do inform against me,
"And spur my dull revenge!" (IV. 4, 32-33)

If Fortinbras can go to war for a worthless piece of land then how to justify idleness when having a real cause?

"... I do not know
"Why yet I live and say 'This thing's to do';
"Sith I have cause and will and strength and means
"To do it." (IV. 4, 43-46)

The frame of a third suspense is now completely defined. Here are the alternative outcomes:

(i) the king contrives to kill Hamlet (sending him to England);
(ii) Hamlet nurtures "bloody thoughts" against the king (though *en route* to England).

Who will succeed?

This suspense is not yet solved when preparations are already made for the next, the fourth one. Laertes appears to inquire about the mysterious - so it seems to him - death of his father, just before the third suspense is moved closer to solution by the pirate-sailor bringing letters from Hamlet. Thus we know that Hamlet will not be executed in England, but a new suspense is already introduced:

(i) Laertes vows that "my revenge will come";
(ii) The king contrives a new "device, under which he [Hamlet] shall not choose but fall".

Then, *suspense No. 3* is solved:

(iii) Hamlet returns to translate in deeds his "bloody thoughts".

Further the plot of the king and Laertes add to the suspense and causes the solution with the death of all three plus the queen.

The choice of the above repeated series of moments is meant to reveal the essential dissimilarity between the Shakespearean and classical method to keep anxious yet indefinite anticipations alive throughout the unfolding of the drama. Once the "unities" were abandoned, and the stage action was to cover a longer sequence of "real" actions which occurred in a longer stretch of "real" time, the dramatic tension was to be secured by the concatenation of interdependent suspense situations. Not simply one after another! That would have made for a collection of individual plays, however related between them by their heroes. It was rather *the sequential generation of a new suspense situation every time before the previous puzzle was solved,* which made the difference.

[2] The Dramatic Story Telling

Tragedy, as we are told by Aristotle, is "imitation by means of action" and deemed to be superior to other forms of poetry, including the epopee. It seems to be this *action,* the imitated movement of life, carrying, and carried by the spoken words of the dramatic poet, which guides the reader/viewer towards the insights purportedly offered by the play. But the action-simulation of dramatic poetry does not characterize also that particular form of "poetic imitation which is narrative in form", though its "plot manifestly ought, as in tragedy, to be constructed on dramatic principles" (Aristotle, Poetics, XXIII,1). If any sense is to be made of this, then the "speech + action" union in the theatrical work is to have some "speech + description-of-action" union as its epic counterpart. Yet the principles of the *action to be staged* and the *action to be narrated* have to be essentially the same - the latter having not to be confounded with "historical composition". Homer is praised by Aristotle for having achieved the highest possible degree of perfection in contriving massive epic works in a manner to fit the requirements which otherwise only the finest tragedies have matched. At the same time he seems to grant much poorer marks to other narrators, and with good reason. No wonder, since it is very difficult indeed to balance the direct speech of the actors - something which prevails in tragedy and is condemned by Socrates/Plato as amounting to *mimesis* - with the narration *stricto sensu,* including also elements of physical description meant to be a substitute for the stage setting. Few authors, between Homer and the XIX century, have been able to reedit that high degree of fusion between narration and dramatic speech, which is the excellence of the Iliad. In the meanwhile, however, several avenues have been explored in view of perfecting the art of blending *stage describing* and *action narrating* with speech proper in accordance with the different requirements formulated by Aristotle. We could say without exaggeration (so I hope) that the progress made throughout many centuries in the art of story telling consists in the refinement of the narrative methods so as to satisfy each of the "*dramatic principles*" which "*the plot ought manifestly*" conform to. This includes, of course, action representation and the implicit requirement of stage description.

One major direction of the history of story telling is thus the development of its dramatization. Awareness of this development could perhaps enhance the pure and simple enjoyment of a tale or a novel, and make the "learning through imitation" it offers, richer, fuller, more intensive. Reading a work under this recognition should offer thus new pleasures by the mental *imitation of the imitator*. Sampling examples for a few of the Aristotelian requirements should convey, with the help of the chosen parables, that understanding which cannot be communicated by conceptual analysis.

Peripeteia and Suspense: Acting and Telling

The demands on the poetic work, and the receptive faculties of readers and viewers, have probably never changed essentially. These demands were meant to be satisfied by the poetry of the early bards as well as those of the later dramatic poets; no less by the movie makers of our days. What changed in time were the media by which this demand was satisfied and the reception instruments commanded by members of the public or the various sections of it. As far as literature is concerned, a decisive difference was made by the increase in the number of the literate, and then, the increase in the number of those who had the means affording the multiplied texts. The way of conveying a story (or of teaching, for that matter) in an illiterate society, as that of Homer, was by singing, reciting or recounting, often in relatively small convivial companies. Ritualistic festivals served the purpose of making the same accessible to the large masses to which later free theatre was offered by Pericles (as Plutarch tells us). This called for short, concentrated, unified actions, and the appropriate new style of presentation of the same matter which earlier was spread by word of mouth. Later again, the expansion of literacy offered access to the written word to a greater number of individuals. Only this time, in the early ages of popular literacy, that particular type of literature which was spread through copies of the written texts, addressed still only a chosen few. All classes attended the Greek theatre of the Golden Age, but not all classes had access to the written word. The new, the *written* literature addressed the same human emotions but also a different, more cultured, mind. *Reading* meant first of all that the *reader*, unlike the theatre-goer, could decide freely about his time for literary enjoyment: he could choose when to start, when to stop to muse over a line in the text, and when to return to consider yet again a section read earlier. And he could put aside the book and continue reading at some later time. All this did not prevent him from having the same expectations, at occasions transformed in suspense, as if he were sitting in the theatre in anxious anticipation. But the story could cover more time and, most importantly, the reader could afford more time to spend in reading descriptions imitative of the real world. Such representations offered to the educated a more complete depiction of things which in the theatre were produced only by means of clumsy improvisations and not always convincing gestures. Thus, with the change of media and the potential of reception, the earlier purpose of the theatre could be transferred also to *the readable*.

None of the techniques which achieved the effect of dramatization of the narrative text came about by spontaneous generation. Their potential is to be found in the most ancient monuments of literature and, probably, the elementary receptive capacities of human nature as well. But the activation of these primary potentials so as to become actual techniques of dramatic discourse was a long process likely still to continue. And an important path in this history was the evolution of *suspense*, the state before that tragic or redeeming *peripeteia* which makes the reading of stories a pleasurable exercise. We should remember once again Aristotle's conclusion to his most subtle psychological analysis of the receiving public:

> "Dramatic turns of fortune and hairbreadth escapes from perils are pleasant, because we feel all such things are wonderful." [Rhetoric, 11th Chapter, 1371b]

The following examples gathered in a rather unlikely company should illustrate three significant phases in the process of narration dramatization.

As in the previous note referring to tragedy, it may be repeated that the *converging evolution of the knowledge* of the readers, that of the story's agents, and the implicit dramatic discourse between these two classes of recognition, is at the roots of any reading pleasure. The subsequent examples are chosen according to the degree of complication of this discourse in a suspense situation, each example, however arbitrarily chosen, reflecting a phase in the development of the rhetoric of suspense creation. <u>First</u> we have the simple case of the *reader in suspense.* Which may imply, though not necessarily, the <u>second</u> case considered, when some or all actors of the story are also in suspense, a situation recognized by the reader as well. A <u>third</u>, more advanced form of suspense conveyance is the interplay of suspenses between the story's agents and the reader.

An Example from the Bible

The binding of Isaac (Gen. XXII) is an oldest instance of a story with suspense. Abraham, following God's command, travels to the place where he is to offer his and his wife's, Sarah's only son, as sacrifice to the Almighty. The story is unfolding with deliberate detail in spite of the shortness it shares with most other narrations in the Pentateuch. No phase of the process initiated by Heavenly Command is skipped:

> "3. And Abraham rose early in the morning, and saddled his ass, and took two of his young men with him, and his son Isaac; and he cleaved the wood for the burnt offering, and rose up, and went unto the place which God had told him..."

And the first reader of the story, in knowledge of the terrible command, is now anxiously waiting for whatever is to happen. Could he not been told right away what the twelfth verse will reveal? Simple that would have been anyway and the reader would have *known* or *learned* about the power and ultimate goodness of God and the righteous yet meek submissiveness of Abraham. (Abraham is not a tragic hero who falls battling against God's design. He is an obedient survivor by God's grace.) All this could be indeed known and learned because it could be simply, plainly said. But this was not enough, because the Book's purpose is to offer participation, communing, *experiencing* of

135

the secondary, unspeakable content of the message. And slow heightening of the narrative's tension is the means to such end:

> "6. And Abraham took the wood of the burnt offering, and laid it upon Isaac his son; and he took in his hand the fire and his knife; and they went both of them together."

The son and the father with the knife! And they exchanged kind words about God who "will provide Himself with the lamb for a burnt offering" and "so they went both of them together". And then - no blasphemy meant! - verse 9. reads like instructions for a cliff-hanger in a movie thriller's scenario:

> - "And they came to the place which God told him of; *and*
> - "Abraham built the altar there; *and*
> - "laid the wood in order; *and*
> - "bound Isaac his son; *and*
> - "laid him on the altar on the wood".

And the tension reaches a climax when:

> - "...Abraham stretched forth his hand, and took the knife to slay his son".

And we know now the hand is lifted, the fist clenching the deadly tool ready to fall and fulfill the terrible yet Holly Command. But an angel of the Lord changed the outcome when "he said: lay not thy hand upon the lad, neither do thou any thing unto him". Because He is shown to be terrible only in his tests and trials, not his ultimate resolutions. With the righteous, of course.

The weapon lifted, ready to hit, then - stop! [in the movie technique it is "cut!"...]; it is a device which was never lost for the art of story rendition. It proved to be an instrument of rich potentials to be used especially since the Renaissance when, what was understood as Aristotle's teaching about dramatic construction, retained its character as a holy doctrine only in Richelieu's Académie. The stage and the story book were spreading enjoyment and enlightenment by means of suspense, in uncountable and unclassifiable variety.

Don Quixote

Remember the Ingenious Hidalgo? Undeterred by pain and suffering, he relentlessly pursued glory on the highways of Castile, not glory for its own sake, but glory by fighting injustice in the service of the *sin par y fermosa*, the incomparably beautiful Dulcinea del Toboso. He encounters one day a small travel company, consisting of two friars on mules, followed by an elegant coach surrounded by several horsemen and trailed by two peasant lads. Would not every sign confirm the hidalgo's conjecture that:

> *"esta ha de ser la más famosa aventura que se haya visto; porque aquellos bultos negros que allí parecen deben de ser, y son, sin duda, algunos encantadores que llevan hurtada alguna princesa en aquel coche, y es menester deshacer este tuerto a todo mi poderío"?* (I. Ch. VIII) ["...this could be the most famous adventure ever heard of, because those two black chaps which are approaching must be and are, beyond doubt, two sorcerers who are concealing in that carriage an abducted princess; and I will engage with all my strength to unmake their iniquity"?]

Sancho's forewarning that "this will be worse than the wind mills" didn't help, and the valiant man of Mancha, after having been unable to persuade them to "liberate" the "abducted princess", rode against the two "sorcerers" from Saint Benedict's order, pulling one off his mule, frightening the other into flight and then stopping at the coach door where he proclaimed "free" the traveling lady. When addressing her as *"la vuestra fermosura"* [or *hermosura* in some modern editions] and asking nothing less than that she and her retinue go straight to Toboso and bring the glorious news of her liberation to the matchless Dulcinea, he is rudely and ungratefully confronted by a shield bearer type riding a rather wobbly mule. Insults were exchanged, swords unsheathed and the two brave champions were ready to engage in a fierce armed showdown:

> *"Venía, pues, como se ha dicho, don Quijote contra el cauto vizcaino, con la espada en alto, con determinación de abrirle por medio, y el vizcaino le aguardaba asimismo levantada la espada y aforado con su almohada, y todos los circunstantes estaban temerosos y colgados de*

lo que había de suceder de aquellos tamaños golpes con que se amenaz-
aban." (ibid.) ["And so, as said, Don Quixote went against the alert
Biscayan, with his sword lifted up high, determined to strike and
cleave him in two; while the Biscayan awaited him likewise bran-
dishing his sword and shielding himself with a blanket. All the bystanders were now waiting, in dread and suspense [*colgados*!!], for
what was to result from those dreadful blows with which they were
threatening each other."]

No wonder that the lady in the carriage, just as her maids, were hoping
to avert the worst by making vows and promising offerings to all the so numerous holy places in Spain, while all of them being *colgados*, i.e. hung up,
suspended, in suspense. A double spectacle thus: we, the readers, are offered
the suspense "show" of an impending battle, while at the same time some
of the actors in the story are also in a horrified expectation. This, of course,
doubles the reader's excitement, who is now also *colgado* in the expectation
of the outcome for the other set of spectators who are participants at the
same time.

"*Pero está el daño de todo esto que en este punto y término deja pen-*
diente el autor desta historia esta batalla, disculpándose que no halló
más escrito destas hazañas de don Quijote de las que deja referidas."
(ibid.) ["But unfortunately, right on this place and at this time the
author of the story had to interrupt the fight with the excuse that
he didn't find anything more about the deeds of Don Quixote than
he has so far said".]

Quite a peculiar interruption. Had the *roman fleuve* already been invented, the reader could have waited - in suspense, of course - till the next sequence was printed and issued. But here it is clearly stated that the "second
author", who is Cervantes, and who purports to only re-tell the first history,
is in trouble. So here we are with two mounted champions facing each other
with drawn swords, the weapons cutting the air, advancing towards ... Cut!
End of chapter.

Luckily, Cervantes, browsing on the Toledo market chanced upon an
Arabic manuscript and instantly found also a *Morisco* to translate it.

> *"Y no fue muy dificultoso hallar intérprete semejante, pues aunque le*
> *buscara de otra mejor y más antigua lengua, le hallara."*(I. Ch. IX)
> ["It was not too difficult to find such an interpreter, 'cause had you
> searched you could have found there also translators of a finer and
> more ancient language".]

And while we are reading about this interesting occurrence we are still
kept *colgados*, waiting for the picture to continue to move again, to find out
whatever will happen to the two men whose swords are arrested in the air. But
the newly found text, finally, informs us: the suspense is over and the outcome
better then expected. Sancho was wrong; it was *not* worse than with the wind
mills! Of the two, the Biscayan attacked first with untold furry.

> *"Mas la buena suerte, que para mayores cosas le tenia guardado, torció*
> *la espada de su contrarío, de modo que, aunque le acertó en el hombro*
> *izquierdo, no le hizo otro daño que dezarmarle todo aquel lado, lleván-*
> *dole, de camino, gran parte de la celada, con la mitad de la oreja.*(ibid)
> ["But Fortune which kept him [Don Quixote] available for greater
> deeds, turned aside the sword of his antagonist, such that, though
> hitting his left shoulder, it didn't cause more harm than unarming
> him on the same side by cutting off a good portion of his helmet
> and half of his ear ..."]

Bad as this was, it did not prevent the recovered and furiously attacking
brave champion of Mancha to finally inflict a disgraceful defeat on the foolhardy Biscayan. And so the suspense ends as the "incredible battle between
the *gallardo vizcaino* and the *valente manchego*" came to a resolution.

It was earlier claimed that the fight with the Biscayan has a double element
of suspense in that not only the reader is tensely awaiting the outcome, with
the excitement heightened by the interrupted manuscript, but the personages in the story are also *colgados*. However, the most interesting aspect of the
example chosen as a paradigm is the union between action-description and
suspense; more precisely the introduction of suspense by way of action-description. *Now, the extension of the suspense-tension from the reader to the persons
in the story*, opens additional possibilities of dramatization. The quest of the
storyteller to overcome those shortcomings of his art which were emphasized

by Aristotle and said to consist in its failure to represent *action*, has reached a new height. Telling the story as a web of suspenses, with everybody in the tale participating, brings into the plot the element of continuing action, a main novelistic element developed by the great story-tellers of the late Renaissance, Cervantes leading among them. The perfection of the method has, however, a later date. The subsequent example should illustrate it.

Goethe's *Novelle*

The master example chosen is the short story of Goethe, plainly called "*Novelle*". It is based on a perfect system of interwoven suspense situations to be reviewed in what follows.

The beautiful young princess and her uncle, the wise old prince, are riding out to enjoy the beauty of the landscape. They are assisted by a young courtier, Honorio, who renounced to participate in the young prince's hunt in order to serve and be close to the much admired first lady of the Principality, relishing in that bitter-sweet feeling which a beautiful, never-to-be-fulfilled dream gives. The young lady obtains from her uncle the concession of a ride through the neighboring town where the annual fair takes place, in spite of the old man's reluctance, originating in the oft retold dismal incident of a fire, many years ago, during such an event. The visit on the market place was a joyful event, the princess reveled in the sight of the rich supply of wares and

> "*das Volk schaute mit Freuden die junge Dame, und auf so viel lächeln-*
> *den Gesichtern zeigte sich das entscheidene Behagen, zu sehen, das die*
> *erste Frau im Lande auch die schönste und anmutigste sei*". "the people
> watched joyfully the young lady, and one could notice on as many
> smiling faces the positive satisfaction of seeing that the first lady of
> the land was also the most beautiful and the most graceful.]"

An idyllic picture which could proudly adorn the walls of the *Rathskeller* in any better town, especially as it is completed, by the taste of the early eighteen hundreds, with the cages of wild animals, a tiger and a lion, tended by a swarthy little child. And thus continues the story: the distinguished company rides down the vale, then up the slope, and stops to admire the views, when all of a sudden, Honorio notices smoke emerging from the market. The fair was once again in flames. And while the frightened company was now negotiating its way back to the castle, the tiger, escaped from its burning prison, emerged from a bush, appearing in all the ferocity it so far displayed only on the poster hanging above the cage set up in the market. This is now the starting point of the first suspense component of the story:

- the tiger jumps against the hypnotized princess;
- the frightened Honorio calls her to escape;
- the princess flees: "*sie wandte das Pferd um, dem steilen Berg zu, wo sie herabgekommen waren*" or "she turned the horse about, directing it towards the steep mountain slope which they earlier descended";
- the tiger follows her;

and there are now two in *suspense*, the reader and Honorio. Only the former may not be so frightened since he might have a hunch that Goethe cannot be so callous as to permit the most beautiful lady of the land to be torn to pieces by a wild beast. But Honorio, who has no idea that he is only the invention of a great poet, is tense, and transmits some of his tension to the reader and then

- jumps on the "stage", faces the monster, pulls his pistol, charges and ... misses; the danger grows while
- the tiger runs uphill pursuing the lady

and the reader, obviously, roots for her while

- "*sie sprengte, was das Pferd vermochte, die steile, steinige Strecke hinan, kaum fürchtend, dass ein zartes Geschöpf, solcher Anstrengung ungewohnt, sie nicht aushalten werde.*" ["she rode uphill on the stony slope, as fast as the horse could, not fearing that the frail creature, unused to such strain, may not be able to endure."]
- Then the horse stumbles and falls. But the beautiful lady, fit and brave, jumps on her feet.
- The tiger continues to catch up with her, while Honorio, unswerving, pursues the beast.

And we read in tension what happened further. When on the crest of the hill, the young knight shoots again, this time hitting the head of the tiger. The subsequent romantic exchange between the princess and Honorio is interrupted by the lament of the suddenly emerging gypsy woman and her black eyed, black curled little boy, holding a flute, on which, as we will learn later, he played "a melody, which was none, a sequence of sounds without a rule, and probably therefore so soul touching". And then: the lion! A peasant discovered the beast, and the prince, newly arrived with his hunting party, made arrangements to find, encircle and kill the escaped animal. The gypsy family imploring him to spare the lion, leaving it to the little boy, playing the flute, to induce the escapee to return into the gentle captivity at his loving masters. This marks the new starting point for a slowly mounting tension with a string of suspense moments. What follows is again the perfect description for a movie setting: Mother and little son, accompanied by a servant of the prince (rifle in hand), descend the slope towards the lion's hiding place. They move along just as a camera would, what they see is recorded and we see with them: the ravine which is at the start of the way to the castle; here the hunters gather brushwood for a fire; yet there is no need for it, as the Gypsy woman says, because everything will happen with goodness; then sitting atop a wall, a dreaming Honorio with his double barreled rifle is addressed by the woman: "handsome young man, you slew my tiger, yet I curse you not; spare my lion, good young man, and I will bless you..."; the servant of the prince leads them along some crumbling walls, facing the entry to a hole to which the lion is supposed to be lured, and from this point on the child goes it alone:

- the child descends slowly from the wall;
- we first see the child appearing and then disappearing;
- the child's disappearance is followed by
- the fading of the flute's sound followed by
- portentous silence.

The reader knows about the *suspense of all the actors in the story* except the child's mother. The reader's suspense is now the suspense transmitted by both the action and most everybody in the story. The tension is on until, the *denouement*:

*"Endlich hörte man die Flöte wieder, das Kind trat aus der Höhle her-
vor mit glänzenden Augen, der Löwe hinter ihm drein, aber langsam,
und, wie es schien, mit einiger beschwerde. Er zeigte hie und da Lust,
sich niederzulegen, doch der Knabe führte ihn im Halbkreise durch die
wenig entblätterten, buntbelaubten Bäume, bis er endlich in den letz-
ten Strahlen der Sonne, die sie durch eine Ruinenlücke hereinsandte,
wie verklärt niedersetzte und sein beschwichtigendes Lied abermals
begann..."*

["Finally, one could hear again the flute while the child stepped out
of the cave with shining eyes, with the lion following at slow pace,
and as it seems with some difficulty. From time to time the lion
showed the desire to lay down, yet the kid lead the beast in a half
circle around the leafy, colorful trees until, lit by the last rays of sun
flashing through the holes of some ruins, the little boy sat down
starting anew his serene song ..."

And we are relieved; aren't we?

The Lion and Don Quixote

We are relieved because the end was happy. Yet a happy end was not the
only one plausibly implicit in its antecedents. It was just one of the possible
yet not necessary outcomes. And we were in an uneasy suspense because an
equally implicit alternative would not have been all that fortunate. Knowing
how fierce lions can be, we may have thought of only two possible, presumably
obvious, consequences. Could any other possibility have been considered by a
thoughtful reader? A little consideration would lead us to an answer in the affirmative. Yet would any additional alternative be *story worthy*? It can turn out
to be. We know this from Cervantes. So let me refresh the reader's memories.

One day Don Quixote, erring on the roads of Castile, met a distinguished
gentleman in a green cloak - therefore also remembered as *el caballero del verde
gaban*, the gentlemen of the green garb. Don Diego Miranda by his real name,
was a very learned gentleman - he owned no less than six dozen books! - but
was unhappy seeing that his only son was given to the vanity of poetry. We
learn about the young man from Don Diego, that he

*"será de edad de diez y ocho años; los seis ha estado en Salamanca,
aprendiendo las lenguas latina y griega, y cuando quise que pasase a
estudiar otras ciencias, halléle tan embebido en la de la poesia (si es
que se pude llamar ciencia) que no es possible hacerle arrostrar la de la
leyes.."* [II, ch.XVI] ["was eighteen of age; that he stayed six years
in Salamanca studying Greek and Latin, and when he was about to
switch to the study of other sciences, he found himself so deeply
immersed in that of poetry (if we may call that a science) that it
became impossible to make him study law.."]

The ingenious knight sided with the young man and poetry in general.
And in the following adventure he also demonstrated that poetry, indeed, is
anything but a science. In this respect he proved Don Diego right yet he also
granted a positive recognition to the art of fine writing. At the same time he
revealed the useful, but very limited relevance of classificatory exercises as initiated by Aristotle and adumbrated in this humble essay.

Thus while Don Quixote and Don Diego pursued their erudite discussion,
something happened on the road which can illustrate the above made considerations: a strange looking cart, garnished with the flags of the King, came
their way. DQ, who naturally saw the beginning of a new adventure, was ready
for a confrontation. And the reader had once again an *open ended* choice of expectations until the number of outcome possibilities were narrowed down by
additional information. It turned out that the wagon was carrying two caged
lions being a gift offered by the governor of Oran to the king of Spain. Apart
from the fierce beasts only two men were in the cart: the carter himself and
the keeper of the lions, the *leonero*. The men introduced themselves as such,
but DQ could not be misled by such a much too simple and obvious story.
He firmly believed to face yet another devious scheme plotted against him by
those ubiquitous *encantadores*. It was *they* who were now dispatching lions to
provoke and test him! But the ingenious hidalgo who could not be misled and
who, as always, was once again ready for a fight, addressed the lion keeper with
the following words:

*"Apeaos, buen hombre, y pues sois el leonero, abrid esas jaulas y ech-
ademe esas bestias fuera: que en mitad desta campaña les daré a
conocer quién es don Quijote de la Mancha, a despecho y pesar de los*

encadadores que me los envian." [II, ch. XVII] ["Come down good man, and since you are the *leonero*, open those cages and turn those beasts out: and in the middle of this field I will let them know who don Quixote de la Mancha is, in spite and against all those *encantadores* who sent them to me."]

The hidalgo could not be resisted and the *leonero* gave in, but not before Sancho and Don Diego took cover. And so the adventure starts. Or almost, because the role of Rocinante was still to be decided. And we learn that

> "*En el espacio que tardó el leonore en abrir la jaula primera estuvo considerando don Quixote si sería bien la batalla antes a pie que a caballo, y, en fin, se determinó de hacerla a pie, temiendo que Rocinante se espantara con la vista de los leones.*" [ibid.] ["While it took some time for the *leonero* to open the cage, don Quixote was considering whether it were better to take up the fight on foot or rather mounted. He finally decided that it is better to do it on foot being worried that Rocinante may get frightened when seeing the lions."]

This is good judgment but also the source of a new suspense. Since it is obvious that the reader himself remains *colgado*, i.e. in suspense: what will now happen? And the reader's apprehensions are shared by the author who inserts into the flow of the narration his own considerations expressing the same concern:

> "*Tú a pie, tú solo, tú intrépido, tú magnánimo, con sola espada, y no de las del perrillo cortadoras, con un escudo no de muy luciente y limpio acero, estás aguardando y atendiendo los dos más fieros leones que jamás criaron las africanas selvas. Tus mismos hechos sean los que te alaben, valeroso manchego; que yo los dejo aqui en su punto, por faltarme palabras con que encantarlos.*" [ibid.] ["You on foot, you alone, you the intrepid and the magnanimous, with nothing but your sword, which is not one made by a famous armorer, you with just a shield which is not made of shiny and polished steel, you stay here in wait for the two most ferocious lions ever engendered by the African wilderness. It is your own deeds which will have to praise you,

valiant *Manchego*; 'cause I will have to stop here since I can't find the proper words to praise them."]

We now see the *leonero* opening the cage of the first lion. And the wild beast? Well, the lion

> "*abrió luego la boca y bostezó muy despacio, y con casi dos palmos de lengua que sacco fuera se despulvereó los ojos y se lavo el rostro; hecho esto, sacó la cabeza fuera de la jaula y miró a todas partes con los ojos hechos brasas ...*" [ibid.] ["opened his mouth and yawned very slowly putting out his two palms long tongue with which he then licked his eyes and washed his face; this done, he stuck out his head looking in all directions with glowing eyes ..."]

But Don Quixote was not to be frightened. Both seemed to be ready for a showdown, as also the reader would expect.

> "*Pero el generoso león, más comedido que arrogante, no haciendo caso de niñerías ni de bravatas, después de haber mirado aúna y otra parte, como se ha dicho, volvió las espaldas y enseño sus traseras partes a don Quijote, y con gran flema y remanso se volvió a echar en la jaula.*" [ibid.] ["However, the generous lion, more restrained than arrogant, having no intention to engage in childish bravados, after staring in all directions, as stated, turned around and showed his hind parts to don Quixote, and then, with calm and nonchalance, jumped back into his cage."]

And we are even more relieved than in the case of Goethe's *Novelle*, because thereby the ingenious hidalgo was preserved for several even more exciting adventures to the reader's pleasure. Also Cervantes may have proven wrong the Stagirite who thought that tragedy is the highest form of poetry.

Appendix
to the Essay on
"Suspense and Peripeteia"

Of Suspense and the Knowledge and Ignorance
of the Ancient Theatre Spectator.

Every suspense situation in a literary work assumes the *a priori* ignorance by the reader/spectator of essential aspects in the narrative. Since ignorance spurs interest, authors were often [though not necessarily] avoiding the direct or "linear" rendition of their tale, preferring to implant into the web of the recite various elements breeding anxious expectation. Indeed, if the reader/spectator "knew" something for sure, it was his expectation that the author will prove himself to be a good one by packing the plot, even if based on a "known" story, with unforeseen elements. Otherwise why read the book or buy the ticket to the show? - or make Pericles pay for it. But how ignorant is/was the ancient Greek reader or spectator? And what, if any, is the function of devising a suspense situation when the tale, in its simple, straightforward version, is known to the public? It is often assumed that the general public of the classical Greek theatre in ancient Hellas was quite knowledgeable about everything offered on those ritualistic biannual festivals. Now, it is of course hardly questionable that a significant section of the populace had indeed some idea about the subject of the plays presenting stories from Greek mythology. Yet the naive and cursory information of the public did not blot out the type of "ignorance" which is implicitly postulated by the framer of a good plot. This being given, as it is to be shown, the construction of suspense situations was not only possible but also necessary to make the vaguely "informed" ancient viewer interested.

It is interesting to note that many admirers, as well detractors, of the antique theatre base their various and contradictory explanations of the Greek theatre phenomenon, on the assumption that the ancient Greeks were well informed about what they were supposed to be offered during those major spectacular events. The admirers, respectful and erudite, are trying to solve a contradiction: if the public was knowledgeable, why was the "suspense" needed in the first place? After all, how can it be true that they knew everything while, at the same time, the author was still toiling on his

> "literary works on whose phrases he spends hours, twisting them
> this way and that, pasting them together and pulling them apart"

as characterized, so spitefully, by Socrates [Plato: Phaedrus, 278e]. Both cannot be true. There are various *types* of answers to the puzzle, here only mentioned as examples. Some authors simply neglect the suspense issue, and we can read in amazement in some scholarly "Study of Sophoclean Drama" that Oedipus is a "linear" story. Other authors venture a semantic pirouette around the problem. Thus, in an appendix to his beautiful Aeschylus translations, Paul Roche writes that "the thrill of anticipation, the gradual unfolding of inevitable disaster, took the place of suspense". While this may have been the case for part of the public, it seems that the differentiation between "the thrill of anticipation" and "suspense" as two, purportedly different concepts, is more an attempt to save the myth of a certain "ancient Greek" who never really existed, rather then explain the phenomenon under scrutiny.

To discuss this issue in somewhat more detail a classical case of detraction of the great ancient writers, as well as their public, would offer a good starting point. So let us quote the peroration of Eugenius in Dryden's *Of Dramatic Poesy:*

> "Next, for the plot ...; it has already been judiciously observed by
> a late writer, that in their tragedies it was only some tale derived
> from Thebes or Troy, or at least something that happened in those
> two ages; which was worn so threadbare by the pens of all the epic
> poets, and even by tradition itself of the talkative Greeklings (as
> Ben Jonson calls them), that before it came upon the stage, it was
> already known to all the audience: and the people, so soon as ever

they heard the name of Oedipus, knew as well as the poet, that he had killed his father by mistake, before the play, and committed incest with his mother, before the play ... [p.141] etc."

This is a classical instance of an oft repeated opinion - sometimes by academic scholars - which is as erroneous as it is vicious in the rendition of "Eugenius", and charged with the upstart's malicious haughtiness expressed with the pretence of some assumed "common sense". At first reading it may sound convincing; maybe because some secondary remarks of Eugenius, here not addressed, are correct. But a careful examination will reveal the argument's flimsy construction.

To begin with, we may distinguish three degrees of knowledge and information in the Greek audience - paralleled by any audience in any place and at any time - and examine the corresponding relevance of a classical play.

First, it should be clear without any special study, that any and every ancient Greek would have had first to receive his "tale derived from Thebes or Troy" from somewhere, well before realizing that it already "was worn threadbare by the pens of all the epic poets, and even by tradition itself". One major media of communication was the theatre itself. Every play, story, traditional tale, was heard (more seldom read) by somebody, somewhere, sometime for the *first time.* Now, in an illiterate society, the wandering bard's performance just as that on the theatre stage was a first source. For a newborn Greek, everything was new. Also the story of the Trojan war.

Second, there was no established canon of the history or mythology of the ancient Greeks, nor did anybody pretend such to exist. Consequently nobody was at any time in the possession of the *true* story. Proof are the variants in which the "same" tale from Troy or Thebes was rendered by different poets, sometimes with most surprisingly diverging ends and solutions. Thus the Greek who was no more "newborn", as far as the lore of his people was concerned, while being a regular at the theatre festivals, was always entitled to expect something new - to improve his knowledge about his heritage. And, naturally, to re-live the drama at the performance, to heighten his thoughts and cleanse his soul.

Thus we may differentiate between elements of suspense or "thrill of anticipation", according to whether they addressed the Greek of the first or second level of enlightenment.

And *third*, there is always the knowledgeable spectator or reader for whom *the art of rendition of a story* is a source of pleasure and a focus of his interest.

We do not and cannot know what was in the mind of the ancient Greek authors when devising their plots. Nor do we have a clear idea about what exactly the "average ancient Greek" knew. What *we* know for sure is what is written in the plays which survived. And their structure, as we find it, is compatible with a viewer expecting to discover things unknown. This viewer may have been on any of the above enumerated three levels of enlightenment. Yet the most perfect play would have had to satisfy all of the three classes of viewers. And by this criterion *Oidipos Tyrannos* is unquestionably the most accomplished work: for the first-time viewer or reader it offers a tense backward reconstitution of a story with a beautiful structure engendering "discoveries"; for the one who knew the general gist of the tale, the details of presenting it will be the discovery; and finally, for the savvy member of the public, it will always be interesting to discover how the author edited the story to best satisfy the "thrill of anticipation" of the people in both the previous classes. To which it may be added that none of those tales "derived from Thebes or Troy, or at least something that happened in those two ages", has been rendered in the same fashion by two different authors, while the seemingly arbitrary additions were meant to serve the "thrill". No factually established truth or canon was in the way, and doubtless, "the talkative Greeklings" made sure that none such should come about. They may have known a lot about who Orestes was, but then they still may have experienced the "thrill of anticipation" to find out how Electra was to recognize him. And the three great classics gave him three different answers, none unworthy of the "thrill". Or did they always know everything about Helen? Well, those who first got their story from Homer's Iliad must surely have been surprised to find out the version of Stesichorus, which is probably similar to what Herodotus tells us when reproducing the story of an Egyptian priest, according to which the beautiful wife of Menelaus never reached Troy but was safely sheltered in the land of the Nile. To others it must have been an equally great surprise to find out, while watching the performance of Euripides' "Helen", that Menelaus chanced upon her in Egypt while believing - as many Greeks in the theatre - that she was captive in some grot.

And Iphigenie? Did she perish sacrificed in Aulis or lived, not so happily ever after, in Tauris? A big, fat book can be written just quoting examples of this kind presenting so many interesting variants of the ancient legends. And it will not require hermeneutic abuse to show that all the variations were conveyed to enhance the thrill of anticipation which brings people to the theatre.

Was it any different later, say in the days of Shakespeare? Were not the majority of the great poet's stories originating in the history books, in Celtic and classical mythology, or in those rather frivolous Italian story books? Will you proclaim Shakespeare a bore because you know the history of the kings of England or because you have read your Italian Renaissance stories "worn so threadbare" by the pens of many a poet, writer or chronicler?

ESSAY NO.4

Apparatus and Experiments in Balzac's Laboratory

- Notes on a few Significant Examples -

Styles and periods in the history of literature can be and have been defined according to various criteria, yet most such exercises would yield a consensus regarding the later part of the XVIII and the first half of the XIX century as a watershed in the history of epic literature. Balzac's *oeuvre* is, of course, a major example of the accomplishments of the *new novel* which emerged in that period. Or so it is viewed by many, though by far not all historians and analysts of literature.

Some of these widely known interpretations could guide the reader to the discovery of valuable elements in a literary work which may not be immediately revealed by casual reading. Yet many critics, who are not always employing the standard of objectivity, are often bypassing essential aspects in Balzac's art of plot crafting, and therefore prove to be of very little help to the reader. Thus the accusation of "vulgarity", coming from Sainte-Beuve, bears little relevance to the art of the great storyteller. And when Turgenev dismissed him as yet another "anthropologist", he may just prompt us to consider the following question: what is a great novel if not an inquiry into human life beyond the natural confines of *scientific* anthropology, psychology, sociology and philosophical ethics? Since what is essentially new in the modern novel is its ability to transcend, with the help of its new technical apparatus, the epistemological and linguistic confines of such sciences. Of course, the novelist's purported intention may be *only* to tell us a very good story, for which – if the story id good indeed – we owe him gratitude. But by what objective criterion/criteria is the writer's probe into the real world's *comédie humaine* to be dismissed?

Discussing such issue would lead us ultimately to the fruitless exercise of choosing a set of subjects purported to be "legitimate" in novelistic literature. After all is it not clear that the legitimacy of the subject, whichever that be, has to prove itself (also) by the art of presentation or of story crafting? And in the few examples to be subsequently discussed, Balzac's technical virtuosity is perfectly revealed. At least when applying the analytical criterion chosen in these essays which is: who carries the "mirror of Socrates", or rather the mirror dismissed by Socrates, and how he employs it.

It was argued in previous essays that, since early times, the "long story" of any kind, epopee or novel, could not dispense with the hero (or heroes) whose adventures were unfolding in a *wide space* during the *long time* of the story. Such character was carrying the mirror for the *duration* of the tale *in the wide space* of his adventures. His exploits, his ability to collect relevant experiences - reflections in the mirror, that is - was to supply the substance of the *long story*. But in the XVIII century the radius of the mirror narrowed down to an ever smaller area, while its sharpness increased. The mirror of the poet-imitator, so deeply loathed by Socrates, was now shifted around to change its angle, rather than carried about to reflect events acted out in segments of wide spaces, thus offering the tiles for novel mosaics. And, though there is still a lot of traveling in the novels of Balzac, the essential is not encountered on the road itself. There are fixed points of departure and destination, precisely defined poles, where the stage of the main story is located, and where sharp insight is gained by the hero *and* the reader. And the examples chosen from Balzac will illustrate the thus fully accomplished transition to the "new" novel. The instances reviewed may not necessarily be paradigmatic for the entire oeuvre of Balzac, but they are - so I believe - a paragon for the new art of storytelling. The here employed metaphor of a laboratory is most appropriate since it points to the concentration on what we may call perfectly managed *experimental situations*, as earlier encountered only on the theatre stage, yet with a wider scope.

The Exemplary Characters

«*Quand, à Paris, vous rencontrez un type, ce n'est plus un homme, c'est un spectacle! Ce n'est plus un moment de la vie mais une existence, plusieurs existences.*»

[When in Paris, you meet a character, he is no more a man, but a show! He is
not simply a moment in life, but an 'existence', several 'existences'.]

The man you meet in Paris is a concentrate of potentials; there is no
single predetermined path for his future. Only the past is unique. It is the
past which limits even God's almightiness, according to Albertus Magnus:
He may choose any future but He can't go back on the past which becomes
unique when once chosen and spent. However, the threads of anybody's potential futures form a dense knot enveloped in the apparent shape of any *type
que vous rencontrez à Paris.* Unknotting any or several of his possible futures
is the kind of experiment which is performed in a writer's laboratory. How
is it done?

There are different ways. Traditional story-telling relates essentially the
"past": it is about a unique, however tortuous, historic trajectory. Each point
on such a trajectory could have been the start of an infinity of branching-out
exercises, yet only one set of lines, however sinuously concatenated uniting
the points of the path "actually" pursued, will be mapped by the story. It is the
path which reveals the hero; and the obstacles he encounters tell us about others; and it is the outcome of the tale which reveals a given human landscape.
Only *one* of the many potential human landscapes will emerge, as related to
the given frame of reference which is the unique, "actually happened", story of
the hero, the trajectory followed by him. The hero is a Hero because he is the
Measure to which everything and everybody relates. He, through his story,
teaches us about a part of the World we either did not experience directly or, if
having had some experience with it, wouldn't be able to translate it into clear
concepts. Through him, we find the only way to transcend the *limits of the
meaningfully expressible.*

The history of storytelling is unfolding in two main directions: it is the
history of expanding these limits as well as that of the multiplication of the
avenues which transcend them. And as far as the traditional recounting is concerned, i.e. the telling of stories which are verisimilar to contemporaries, Balzac
achieved the supreme mastery in both directions. The *Comédie Humaine,* and
all its satellite works, are a tremendous achievement in singling out the most
potential laden points from which a human trajectory is to set out. In them
Balzac performs the complex exercise of unknotting those *plusieurs éxistences*

to which any point on a thread is germane, thus discovering that each and every one *"est un spectacle!"*, and rendering them as such to the reader.

Purportedly, the *Comédie Humane* purposed to offer a gallery of characters of its time in various social contexts, but, in the process, Balzac hit upon the limits of simple narration. Storytelling arrived to the watershed which divides what was to become known as romanticism and realism. The former drowned the unspeakable in verbiage or diluted it in myths, old or invented ones, with metaphoric pretences. Realism instead, developed new techniques of breaking down the spectrum of human lives into its psychological and social components, enriching by insight the knowledge conveyed by the philosopher or historian. Without competing with them! Therefore, among the so many techniques employed by Balzac, attention should be paid here to what one may call *human and social spectroscopy*, the art of using the main character as an instrument for social and psychological analysis. Two major characters should exemplify the method in the discussion to follow.

Few of Balzac's heroes are neglected by scholars of literature, yet there is always something new to be discovered about them. Unlike many other literary characters, Balzac's personae are part of a world which we can easily join in fantasy. And while never participating in their exploits, the reader may always gossip about or, indeed, "with" them. However frightening, disgusting or lurid some may be, we can get absorbed in their world, the world of the *Comédie humaine*, because it is so verisimilar. Though their time, or more exactly the time of their "world" - i.e. not of the characters *qua* types - is long gone by, we may still taste the pleasure which Balzac and some of his friends have enjoyed when gossiping about their progress. The two characters chosen to illustrate Balzac's method are relevant not only to his work but also to a chapter in the history of literature structured according to the standard provided by the mirror metaphor. The choice of examples may appear to some as either arbitrary, in one case, or just unduly concessive to plebeian taste, in the second. The selection of the main character of a rarely read small work, treated by some as of subordinate importance, may appear arbitrary. This, however, is not what I believe. The second choice could be interpreted as acquiescence with popular taste, since it concentrates on a character appearing in works popular also with the less refined reader, including the only moderately literate moviegoer. It is not to be denied that subjective elements, more than considerations of popularity, entered in this selection. But, however the choice from many equally qualified works may have come about, the ultimate purpose was to extract what is methodologically relevant. Thus the examples may reflect personal fancy, though without ignoring the point which the discussion is meant to illustrate.

The first example chosen is *Gobseck*. In this story the "hero" is employed as an analytic reactive as well as a catalyst. Or, to use the chosen metaphor, we see Gobseck as a "mirror" with a very narrow radius of movement yet a very sharp reflective power. So we take an angular look into this sharp mirror. The second example is the better known *Vautrin*, a character appearing in several novels, and acting often as *Diabolus ex machina*; also as the Devil constructing apparatuses, so to say, in order to perform *controlled experiments*. This is the function of the Devil. He was always an experimenter, whether he appeared as the *Shatan* of Job or the *Mephistopheles* of Faust. Vautrin, as type, is among the best known actors of the *Comédie Humaine,* yet viewed mainly as a "character", a human type with specific moral connotations. In this context the accent will be on his experimental techniques, not always overlooked in the past, but especially emphasized here.

The approach to be exemplified requires a particular definition of the personae involved. There is, of course the writer and the reader; the former knows "everything" before starting to write, the latter is ignorant of everything when he starts reading. But the characters in the story are of two different classes themselves. There are those who act upon others so that these reveal themselves. Without this first category, the second would not come into action. The first type is like a scientist who manipulates his object of enquiry. To some extent it's these characters who, so to say, invent the second group for the benefit of the reader.

Gobseck the "non-Hero" and Experimenter

> «*Le bonheur consiste ou en émotions fortes qui usent la vie, ou en occupations réglées qui en font une mécanique anglaise fonctionnant par temps réguliers. Au-dessus de ces bonheures, il existe une curiosité, prétendu noble, de connaître les secrets de la nature ou d'obtenir une certaine imitation de ses effets. N'est-ce pas, en deux mots, l'Art ou la Science, la Passion ou le Calme?*"*[p.82]* [Happiness consists either in strong emotions which consume your life, or in organized occupations which make your life an English mechanism working regularly. Beyond this happiness, there is also the purportedly noble curiosity to

discover the secrets of nature or to obtain some imitation of their effects. Is
this not, in two words, the Art and the Science, the Passion or the Calm?"]

The "non-hero" is a person whose life could be the stuff for an old time
narration - yet is not used as such. Think of Gobseck. His life. Well:

> «*Sa mère l'avait embarqué dés l'âge de dix ans en qualité de mousse
> pour les possessions hollandaises dans les grands Indes, où il avait
> roulé pendant vingt années. Aussi les rides de son front jaunâtre gar-
> daient-elles les secrets d'événements horribles, de terreurs soudaines, de
> hasards inespérés, de traverses romanesques, de joies infinies: la faim
> supportée, l'amour foulé aux pieds, la fortune compromise, perdue, re-
> trouvée, la vie maintes fois en danger, et sauvée peut-être par ces déter-
> minations dont la rapide urgence excuse la cruauté*». [p.79] [When
> he was ten years of age, his mother put him on a ship as a cabin boy
> to go to the Dutch colonies in Greater India, where he wandered
> about during the next twenty years. The wrinkles of his yellowish
> forehead were hiding the secrets of horrible events, sudden dreads,
> unexpected risks, romantic misfortunes, and endless joys; the hun-
> ger he supported, the failed love affairs, the wealth lost, then found
> again, the life often endangered and then saved, perhaps by his de-
> termination, the cruelty of which may be excused by the instant
> necessity.]

What a formidable stuff not for one novel but for a cycle. (Try to think
what Stevenson or Conrad might have made out of it.) But we don't get anything of that kind. These few lines serve only to explain his part in the Grand
Design of Balzac: somehow, somewhere, Gobseck became rich and due to his
wealth, he will now be able to watch the world as a show from angles inaccessible to others. And yet you are still invited - by Balzac - to Gobseck's *loge*.

It is irrelevant whether Gobseck was originally meant to be part of the
larger gallery of the *Comédie humaine*. As we know the story, it stands on its
own as a most perfect short novel and as an example of how the limits of
the explainable can be expanded. Here you have a man, a usurer, immeasur-
ably rich, yet making no use of his amassed wealth for anything "money can
buy", such as all those vanities for which Balzac's other heroes are craving

and ruining themselves. To all of them money is the desired *means* to achieve whatever purpose. Even the frugal and miserly Père Goriot sees the purpose for his money in the pleasures and worldly brilliance of his ungrateful daughters. Not so Gobseck:

> *"Il abhorrait ses héritiers et ne concevait pas que sa fortune pût jamais être possédée par d'autres que lui, même après sa mort".[p.79]* [He hated his heirs and could not conceive that his fortune could be owned by others than himself, even after his death.]

No purpose of the usual kind is revealed by Gobseck, either for himself or for his money. The money was not to be used as *means* to be spent but as a *potential* to be kept; not as an element to disappear in the process in which it participates, but as a reactive and catalyst which reveals things other than itself.

Gobseck, by the power of his money, the money by all desired, is able to satisfy a single great passion, the only one he confessed: *knowledge* of his customers as they really are behind the screen of their hypocritical acting. They all need him, they all come to him, and they all reveal - for the want of his gold - all those traits of their character which are normally shrouded in the blanket of conventions. He himself is impenetrable. So are mirrors; they reflect, and are not reflected - except by yet other mirrors. It would be easy to construct an explanation for Gobseck's motives. But if it is to be more than only an anthropological, sociological, psychological or even plain ideological footnote to a usurer's life, than it has to be revealed *in action*. But what if he cannot be put into a plausible act? The romantic would simply try it with an un-plausible one. Not so Balzac. For him persons who do not reflect themselves ought to reflect somebody else. Reflecting others is a function of a mirror. Yet a mirror truncates, it shows things from a constant angle. Still, it sharpens the images by concentration. Hence the discovery of a new device: *the personage or hero whose only raison d'être is to reflect others.* One is sincere to ones mirror; out of need, not love. You may hate your mirror but you need it - to reveal what is to be covered up. This is why at the door of the usurer the make-up fades. The simple fact of knocking on his door reveals a person, exposes him, because

«*Aucune personne ayant quelque crédit à la banque, ne vient dans ma boutique, où le premier pas fait de ma porte à mon bureau dénonce un désespoir...*» [p.80] [No person having some credit at the bank would come to my boutique, where the first step at the door of my office betrays despair.]

And the temptation is there for Balzac to slip into the usurer's explanation - whose story is retold by his former notary - on conventional lines:

«*Je suis là comme un vengeur, j'apparais comme un remord*».[p.84] [I am there as an avenger, I appear as a remorse.]

Is this his, Gobseck's, explanation? How to prove that any vengeance is implied indeed or any remorse provoking intended? In fact it is not even intended: "...je suis *comme*..." and "...j'apparais *comme*..." is *ipso facto* but not by causal explanation. The temptation of the conventional narration is cut short: "*Laissons les hypothèses*" and Gobseck goes about "confessing", revealing of himself only a few but essential things:

«*...toutes les passions humaines agrandies par le jeu de vos intérêts sociaux viennent parader devant moi qui vis dans le calme. Puis, vôtre curiosité scientifique, espèce de lutte où l'homme a toujours le dessous, je la remplace par la pénétration de tous les ressorts qui font mouvoir l'Humanité. En un mot, je possède le monde sans fatigue...* [p.82-83]

_____

Croyez-vous que ce ne soit rien que de pénétrer ainsi dans les plus secrets replis du coeur humain, d'épouser la vie des autres, et de la voir à nu?»[p.88] [... all human passions amplified by your social interests are parading in front of me who lives in calm. Then, your scientific curiosity, sort of a fight in which man always remains below, is replaced by my penetration into all those means by which humanity is moved. In one word, I own the world without an effort. ... Do you believe that it is nothing to penetrate in this manner the secret places of the human heart, to associate with the life of others and to see it naked?]

And denude them he does, their heart and soul, more even than taking usury. While, one morning, making the round of his debtors whose payment was due, each short encounter with a victim reveals to Gobseck more about the sordid truth concealed behind the convention supported brilliance of their deportment, than any long story. A typical example: Arriving at noon to the countess, one of those prodigal daughters who assumed the debts of her young lover, Gobseck finds her in bed, after an obstreperous night, unable to pay. The unexpected arrival of the count, creates a moment of tense suspense: the countess lies to her husband that Gobseck is her "supplier"; the usurer, with a slight, calculated gesture, hiding behind the count, shows to the lady the paper corner of his *billet de change;* the frightened woman pulls an expensive, richly gem laden ring from her finger, slipping it stealthily to Gobseck who leaves satisfied; at the entrance he meets the beau who caused the debts of the countess and reads the future on his face:

> «*ce joli monsieur blond, froid, joueur sans âme, se ruinera, la ruinera, ruinera le mari, ruinera les enfants, mangera leurs dots et causera plus de ravage à travers les salons que n'en causerait une batterie d'obusier dans un régiment."*[p.87] [this good looking, blond, cool gentleman, a gambler without a soul, will ruin himself, will ruin her, will ruin her husband, will ruin the children, will eat up their dowry, and will cause more havoc across the salons than even a battery of small canons would be able to cause.]

These remarks are almost useless: the reader can infer them based on the peculiar prismatic decomposition of Parisian high life - in about two pages! The *composition* of the great novels has here its opposite version, the *decomposition* of the same. In the major epic works of the time, Balzac's in the first place, the author holds the mirror reflecting a complicated action thus *composing* the novel, while the reader "looks into the mirror" askew, so to say. Here, however, a "mirror" divulges its own impressions with the analytic sharpness afforded by its particular polish.

After a few pages of masterly sketches of the high society types, we see Gobseck going towards the rue Montmartre where, instead of "*cette comtesse qui, déja tombée dans la lettre de change, va rouler jusqu'au fond des âbimes du vice*",[p.88] [this countess who already fell deeply in debt and will now roll deep down to the abyss of vice,]

he finds Virtue herself, a working class girl, honest, clean (n.b. she was in the bath when he called earlier in the day) and extremely hard working in order to be able to put her brother through school; so much so that the miser was about to offer her a reduced interest, but then he changed his mind:

"*me mettant en garde contre mes idées généreuses, car j'ai souvent eu l'occasion d'observer que quand la bienfaisance ne nuit pas au bienfaiteur, elle tue l'obligé*" [protecting myself from generous ideas, because I often had the occasion to see that whenever the good deed doesn't harm him who does it, it just kills the beneficiary].

Fany Malvant is there for the contrast and nothing more, except that she married later the purported story-teller, the advocate Derville. (We don't even know what guarantee did Gobseck get from her for his loan. Why did he lend her money at all if not for the sake of the story?)

And the parade goes on. One after another the victims show up in the cage of Gobseck, where the structure of pretences, of which they are made, is falling apart. First Maxime de Trailles, the lover of the countess: "*anneau brillant qui pourrait unir le bagne à la haute société*", that is "a glittering ring which could unite the prison with high society". In the life outside Gobseck's laboratory, were the reactive Gold is breaking down every artificial compound, he may be the chap who "*se connait en chevaux, en chapeaux, en tableaux*" ["is knowledgeable of horses, hats, paintings"] wherefore "*toutes les femmes raffolent de lui*" ["all women are passionately fond of him"]. However, when crossing the threshold of the moneylender, at every step, he sheds one after another those shells of hypocritical pretence which are his everyday guise; and from the inside off each cast-off shell, an ever smaller de Trailles steps forth; like those Russian dolls, except that the diminishing inside is not simply reduced scale identical with the one cast off, but increasingly monstrous. The arrogant, disdainful aristocrat diminishes into a vulgar bargainer, then shrinks further to a mean sycophant and finally, facing the stone-steady laconic money sponge, recoils into the soft spineless role of a mean pimp, who threatens with suicide as a last trick to get his lady accept Gobseck's conditions. Neither lengthy psychological explanations nor the sifting through the web of a long story was required to point on so many layers of human nature. It is this refinement of the technique of experimenting with humans, of decomposing them, which made Balzac's storytelling path breaking.

"Gobseck" seems to be just simply a fine story, yet its quality originates with the highly refined employment of what was suggested to be an *"experimental technique"*. Its distinction consists in the fact that the poet/author departs from simply imitating reality. He rather *creates situations*. It is the transition from the poet who *reproduces experiences*, even if by using the metaphor of fictitious characters and their adventures, to the one who *engineers experiments which generate experience* to be conveyed to the reader. This is implicit in Gobseck, but it can be done quite explicitly by introducing a character, such as Vautrin, who is a master experimenter himself.

Vautrin

> *Je suis l'auteur, tu seras le drame.*
> [I am the author you will be the drama].

Remember? Once upon a time there was a pharmacist in the lower town of Angoulême, by the name of Chardon. He had a son, Lucien, who was a poet. Talented, to be sure, yet furnished with an oversupply of that pernicious stuff which is a necessary ingredient for both doom and glory: *ésprit*. So he dreamed of that glory and the things which go with it, money and love. The last he already achieved as a gift of a local noblewoman who had a taste for his charm and poetry; but the rest had still to be conquered. In Paris - where else? - where lots of glory and money were just waiting to be scooped up by whoever knows where and how to. In the Paris of the dreams of his provincial Madame de Bargeton, *née* Nègrepelisse. One day they both left for the City of Light. It looked like, and both set out believing it to be, an elopement - yet it was not to be. The lady was quickly sucked up - courtesy of her aristocratic relatives - in the vertigo of Parisian life, and the poor little *poétrieau* of Angoulême was dropped. Determination follows disappointment: Lucien Chardon's fight for literary fame begins. First he sweats on the manuscript of his novel *L'archer de Louis IX*, then stumbles through the traps of Paris literary life, sells himself as a journalist, engages in a new *grand amour* with the actress Coralie and reaches the inevitable doom of him who is marked to be a tragic hero. Or almost! Only Coralie dies - not Lucien. Ruined, sick and *sans sous*, he returns to Angoulême to the care of his beloved sister Eve and his faithful brother-in-law David Séchard. It would have been fitful for Lucien to die too. But then he wouldn't have been ready for a second round, which starts right towards the end of the *"Illusions Perdues"*.

There are countless ways of losing illusions, and the flames of failure which devour those false hopes will cast their cruel and revealing light on more hidden resorts of the mechanism which first traps the *ingénue*. So Lucien has to resurrect and show us a new hidden side of the world. Yet this can no more be achieved by the earlier method of telling the story of the tragic hero who falls when fighting and trying to trick the will of the fallen angels holding sway over the Parisian witches' Sabbath. In a first phase, he faces the Devil's legions but never gets behind their lines. And if *he* does not, how could *we* see what is going on there? Well, Lucien Chardon may not, but such insight may be gained by his reincarnation carrying also a new name:

> *"une Ordonnance du Roi m'a rendu celui de mes ancêtres maternels, les Rubempré"* [an Order of the King has granted me the name of my maternal ancestors, the Rubemprés].

And Lucien (Lucien II), now purportedly a nobleman, is introduced behind the lines of the Hell's host by the Devil himself: Vautrin. We know, of course, this man's story, his several changes of identity, and his appearance in the life of Lucien purportedly as a Spanish priest, the one whose death he engineered to expropriate his identity. The story *qua* story has its own merits. But now, Carlos Herrera, as we got to know him along with Lucien, becomes the stage director of Lucien's real tragedy. Considering his false identity, we have to be aware of some traits which set him apart from other characters with a borrowed, or stolen, personality. He himself, as a fake person, would be perfect stuff for an interesting story, yet Balzac never "finished" such, using him only as a staging instrument: he put Vautrin-Collin-Herrera on stage only to use him as stage director. The revealing potentials of his own counterfeit personalities are never fully explored. The art of fully representing such alternating personalities developed only slowly in the history of literature, and had to wait for Pirandello to achieve its perfection. Here the "transformed" person does not have his own novel; he was meant to be the catalyst of the novel(s) of others. What we are told about him after Lucien's tragedy, is his role:

> «*Jacques Collin, espèce de colonne vertébrale qui, par son horrible influence, relie pour ainsi dire LE PÈRE GORIOT à ILLUSIONS PERDUES, et ILLUSIONS PERDUES à cette ÉTUDE*» [SM, p.533]

> [Jacques Collin, sort of a backbone who, by his horrible influence connects, so to say, the '*Pere Goriot*' with the '*Illusions Perdues*', and the '*Illusions Perdues*' with this study].

Now, *cette étude* is not only the *Splendeur et Misère des Courtisanes,* but also that added, complicated, story of another criminal, Théodore Calvi, worth itself a discussion, but to be avoided here. Now we are interested only in Vautrin as revealing himself in the "laboratory" as an "experimenter".

Preparing an Experiment

Let's take now the two books, the "*Illusions Perdues*" [IP] and the "*Splendeur et Misère des Courtisanes*" [SM] and read them again. But not one after the other, as if the second were the continuation of the first - which it purportedly is; but simultaneously, to understand two sides of the same world by two methods of story construction. This you can afford when you read the books for a second time. Even if not completely. Because now you offer yourself the delight of studying some of the author's tricks.

We begin with Lucien I: he has a *narrated* story. Lucien II has a *manipulated* story. What is important is not simply that Vautrin is "manipulating". World literature can provide a remarkable sample of manipulating and manipulated couples, many quite interesting in their own right. But here the entire "laboratory" is manipulated - and we want to see how. A new Lucien steps in to meet partly the same personages, whose defenses he couldn't penetrate in the earlier story. His presence is to provoke their reactions, to spur them to act and bring forth hitherto hidden aspects of their world. But the experiment may be foiled by secondary intrusions. Therefore Vautrin stabilizes the disturbing variables - as if a scientist in a laboratory. [It may be added that the *Illusions perdues* is also, partly, the story of manipulation, yet in a less obvious fashion than the *Splendeur et misère*. The common features of the two novels, relevant to the "manipulation" aspect, will be outlined in the conclusion of this essay.]

In awareness of the fact that *an experiment is being performed,* we may take a look at the results recorded by selecting an example. The instance to be quoted is about the manner in which a parallel depiction of two aspects of the same world is instrumented; once from outside, and a second time by the main character placing a mirror behind the screen through which our and the hero's gaze couldn't peek at first.

Lucien's two appearances at the Opera should illustrate this point. First in the *Illusions Perdues* we have the young poet's awkward entrance to the *loge* where he was supposed to be induced by Mme Bargeton. We see him as

> «.. *un saint Jean de procession, bien gileté, bien cravaté, mais un peu gêné dans cette espèce d'étui où il se trouvait pour la première fois. Suivant la recommandation de madame Bargeton, il demanda la loge des Premiers Gentilshommes de la Chambre. A l'aspect d'un homme dont l'élégance le faisait ressembler à un premier garçon de noces, le Contrôleur le pria de montrer son coupon.*» [p.146 - IP] [...a Saint John of processions, well dressed, but a little embarrassed in this wrapping in which he found himself for the first time. Following the advice of madame Bargeton, he asked for the box of the upper class gentlemen of the Chamber. Seeing a man whose elegance made him look like a first best man on a wedding, the Controller asked him to show his ticket.]

After a moment of embarrassment, for not being recognized by the just arriving marquise d'Êspard, which earned him an ironic remark by the same *Contrôleur* of tickets, he was finally saved by Madame Louise Bargeton. But while we see him humiliated, Lucien will also recognize a new Madame Bargeton:

> «*Louise était restée la même. Le voisinage d'une femme à la mode, de la marquise d'Êspard, cette madame de Bargeton de Paris lui nuisait*

tant; la brillante Parisienne faisait si bien ressortir les imperfections de la femme de province, que Lucien, doublement éclairé par le beau monde de cette pompeuse salle et par cette femme éminente, vit enfin la pauvre Anaïs de Nègrepelisse la femme réelle, la femme que les gens de Paris voyent: une femme grande sèche, couperosée, fanée, plus que rousse, anguleuse, guindée, précieuse, prétentieuse, provinciale dans son parler, mal arrangée sur tout!» [p.147 - IP] [Louise remaind the same. The vicinity of a fashionable lady, the marquise d'Espard, this Madame Bargeton of Paris, harmed very much (the real) Madame de Bargeton; the brilliant Parisian lady made even more evident the imperfections of that provincial woman, so that Lucien, enlightened by the elegant public of that pompous hall and the distinguished lady, saw at last the true Anais de Negrepelisse, as the Parisians have seen her: a big dry woman, with blotched face, reddish, bony, stiff, affected, pretentious, provincial in her speech, and above all in bad order.]

No doubt it was to be expected that the ambitious Lucien

«honteux d'avoir aimé cet os de seiche, se promit de profiter du premier accès de vertu de sa Louise pour la quitter.» [p.147 - IP] [ashamed to have loved that odd fish-bone, promised to himself to profit of the first access of virtue of his Louise to leave her.]

This, however, did not lead to any major change. The conditions of Vautrin's experiment had to be changed, as above emphasized, for the *new Lucien* to appear *in the same environment* and reveal its secrets. It was after the "conditioning» that

«en 1824, au dernier bal de l'Opéra, plusieurs masques furent frappés de la beauté d'un jeune homme qui se promenait dans les corridors et dans le foyer, avec l'allure des gens en quête d'une femme retenue au logis par des circonstances imprévues. ... Le jeune dandy était si bien absorbé par son inquiète recherche qu'il ne s'apercevait de son succès». [ibid.] [in 1824, at the last ball of the Opera, several characters were stunned by the beauty of a young man who walked along the lobby

and the foyer as if searching for a lady who may have been forced to stay home by unforeseen circumstances ... The young dandy was so absorbed by his anxious search that he could not notice his success.]

The few who remembered him from his first appearance were simply muted by some sharp remarks of Lucien II. Vautrin did his job with others. The disturbing variables had to be stabilized. Most importantly a warning went to the ubiquitous de Rastignac, who inclined to alert everybody about de Rubempré's first incarnation, trying to spoil the game. He was to be neutralized by Vautrin:

«...*sachez, pour votre sûreté personnelle, que si vous ne vous comportez pas avec Lucien comme un frère que vous aimeriez, vous êtes dans nos mains sans que nous soyons dans les vôtres*». [... you should know, for your own safety, that if you will not behave with Lucien as he were your own brother whom you love, then you are in our hands without us being in yours.]

He was no more of disturbing consequence, but rather collaborated with Vautrin in letting Lucien II unfold in the new environment. And so Rastignac, when warned by a friend about the new Lucien, dutifully replied:

«*Il vaut mieux s'en fair un ami, car il est redoutable*». [p.123] [It is better to make him a friend because he is frightening.]

The contrast of the two approaches extends also to the way Lucien's lovers are respectively chosen in the two hypostases. In the *Illusions perdues* it is the actress Coralie. She just "occurred" to him. From outside. She was the pretext of a spontaneously surfaced experience to introduce the poor provincial poet into the peripheries of a world he until then only dreamed about.

«*Coralie offrait le type de la figure juive, ce long visage ovale d'un ton d'ivoire blond, à bouche rouge comme une grenade ... un regard languissant où scintillaient à propos les ardeur du désert.*» [p.255 - IP] [Coralie displayed the image of a Jewess; a long oval face of a blond-ivory tone, red lips like a pomegranate ... a languishing and twinkling look as if adapted to the heat of the desert.]

And if you should not have known where else to find all these characteristics, it was Coralie herself who displayed that

«*gorge chantée par le Cantique des Cantiques.*» [throat song by the Canticle of Canticles.]

The reader will not be surprised to find that all this being given, Lucien

«*Lucien en voyant cette créature jouant pour lui seul ... mit l'amour sensuel au-dessus de l'amour pur, la jouissance au-dessus du désire, et le démon de la luxure lui souffla d'atroce pensée. 'J'ignore tout de l'amour qui se roule dans la bonne chère, dans le vin, dans les joies de la matière, se dit-il. J'ai plus encore vécu par la Pensée que par le Fait. Un homme qui veut tout peindre doit tout connaître. Voici mon premier souper fastueux, ma première orgie avec un monde étrange'.*»[p.255 - IP] [... placed now sensual love above pure love, enjoyment above desire, while the demon of lust suggested him atrocious ideas. He told to himself: 'I still ignore everything about love associated with good living, wine and the material pleasures. I lived mostly in ideas rather than in actuality. A man who wants to paint everything has also to know everything. Here you have now my first pompous supper, my first orgy with a strange world.]

Thus Coralie was the casual, however important experience. An uncontrolled experience. An experience which eventuated spontaneously and hence did not lead very far. The tragic end of Coralie pulled her off the stage, and Lucien **I** was to be reshaped as Lucien **II**. Once this happened, a passion with a passionate girlfriend was required - but this time the girl was to be kept under control. No spontaneous love affair! The object of Lucien's love was now Esther, a prostitute, once again Jewish like Coralie, [narrow choices were offered to poor Lucien], who first had to be "conditioned", then kept under tight control. She was to be prepared for baptism, to be made into a "Magdalene" in a convent where, purportedly, her faith was to be strengthened, but in fact only to enhance her desire for Lucien. Esther is presented as "the portrait which Titian would have liked to paint", because:

> «*Esther venait de ce berceau du genre humain, la patrie de la beauté: sa mère était juive. Les Juifs, quoique si souvent dégradés par leur contact avec les autres peuples, offrent parmi leur nombreux tribus des filons où s'est conservé le type sublime des beautés asiatiques.*» [p.87 - SM] [Esther came from that cradle of the human race which was the birthplace of beauty: her mother was Jewish. The Jews, however demeaned by their contact with other nations, included within their many tribes those veins which have conserved the sublime type of Asiatic beauty.]

And she was perfectly conditioned for the plot of Vautrin-Herrera:

> «*Le changement devint si complet que, à sa première visite, Herrera fut surpris, lui que rien au monde ne paraissait devoir surprendre...*"[p.90 - SM] [The change became so complete that Herrera, whom nothing in the world seemed to surprise, was very much surprised during his first visit ...]

And further:

> «*Elle est édifiante, dit la supérieure en la baisant au front*». [She is edifying, said the mother superior, kissing her forehead.]

But the reassurances of mother-superior were not sufficient for Vautrin-Herrera. He intended to achieve, and he did achieve, an enhancement of faith and desire - what a contradiction in a convent! - which should ensure total devotion, besides God, to Lucien:

> "*Le lendemain du jour où vous serrez lavée dans les eaux du baptême, vous ne vous séparerez plus*" [p.96 - SM] [Next morning when you will be purified by the holy water, you two will never be separated again.]

And for the experiment, Lucien himself had to be prepared as a guinea pig. First, the money problem has been eliminated. It was achieved, though not without recurring difficulties, by mysterious means. The literary fame, once so coveted, proved to be neutral anyway, continuing to be a fact based on past achievements now consolidated within the laboratory conditions created by Vautrin, who will now be able to tell Lucien:

«*Je suis l'auteur, tu seras le drame*» [p.131 - SM]. ['I am the author, you will be the drama']

And here we have the moment of great transformation in the novel.

The story unfolds now under a perfect stage control by Vautrin-Herrera-Collin. Lucien II moves in a quite different fashion as a *directed* actor. Of the many possible examples, a central point on the new, more complicated stage, is the *salon* of the *duchesse de Grandlieu*. Here Lucien behaves according to his new role:

"*[Il s'est] habitué à regarder le salon des Grandlieu comme son champ de bataille*" [p.135 - SM] [He got accustomed to consider the salon of the Grandlieus as his battlefield.]

It is the laboratory in which it is not he who is performing the experience. The experience is performed *on him* and therefore he is left, purportedly, on his own to do battle. At this time:

«*Lucien allait à la messe à Saint-Thomas-d'Aquin tous les dimanches, il se donnait pour fervent catholique ... etc.*» [SM p.136] [Every Sunday Lucien went to the mass at St. Thomas of Aquino, pretending to be a fervent catholic ...]

Yet, at the same time

«*Il aimait Esther, et voulait mademoiselle de Grandlieu pour femme!*» [p.137 - SM] [He loved Esther and wanted mademoiselle de Grandlieu for wife!]

We have now Lucien as a "mirror" of himself. It is he who moves from *salon* to *salon*, it is in contact with him that we recognize a world. He doesn't compare to Don Quixote on the road, or Chichikov moving from place to place. It is rather the *Neveu de Rameau* whose close relative he seems to be. Less proletarian, less dependent on the tolerance and charity of others - but for Vautrin-Herrera. He is the factor by which Vautrin pulls the world into his laboratory. In this "laboratory" we meet Nucingen, the shady world of the police, and then, of course Contenson, *cet Épictète des Mouchards*, called *philosophes*. He is the representative of that type encountered in Paris who

> «...*n'est plus un homme, [mais] un spectacle! ce n'est plus un moment de la vie mais une existence, plusieurs existences.*» [... is no more a man, but a show! He is not simply a moment in life, but an 'existence', several 'existences'.]

Nucingen is a new piece on the board on which Vautrin plays his game. He is a banker, but of a different type than Gobseck. The old usurer would never have fit into *this* game. Why? The answer is simple. Because Gobseck himself was the experimenter and his money the catalyst. Instead Nucingen, a much less sophisticated fellow, is himself, to some extent, an object of experiments. We learn that

> «*Dès qu'il s'agit d'un caprice, d'une passion, l'argent n'est plus rien pour les Crésus: il leur est en effet plus difficile d'avoir des caprices que de l'or. [SM p.183] ... Nucingen n'avait aucune fantaisie; il devait donc se jeter dans sa passion pour Esther avec un aveuglement sur lequel comptait Carlos Herrera.*» [p.184 - SM] [As soon as it comes to a caprice or a passion, money doesn't mean anything for a Croesus: for such one it is more difficult to have a fancy than money ... Nucingen had no fantasy; therefore he had to abandon himself to his passion for Esther with that blindness on which Carlos Herrera counted.]

No Gobseck who could claim to possess the world without effort. Here the banker is possessed by Herrera. Apart from other love affairs. He was necessary for Vautrin's plans, which he didn't hesitate to disclose to Esther:

«*Il s'agit ... de tirer Lucien d'embarras. Nous avons soixante mille francs de dettes, et avec ces trois cent mille francs nous nous en tirerons peut-être*» [p.197-SM] The matter is ... to save Lucien from embarrassment. We have a debt of sixty thousand francs, but with his (i.e. Nucingen's) three hundred thousand francs we may find a way out.]

Not that it was a real debt in financial terms. We recall that Lucien needed money for his new way of life which was steered towards marriage with a *mademoiselle* de Grandlieu. Nucingen had the money and Esther had to get it from him. This apart from the complicated plot by which a choice of other shadowy personalities, embroiled with the police, were also tapping the baron's purse. The lovesick Esther's role was thus to drag Nucingen into the play. And she was to be sacrificed: and at some point, after yielding to Nucingen, Esther committed suicide. Her death, however, unlike Coralie's, was most perfectly stage-directed to help us know "everything" about Nucingen, his wife, the *salons*. And the experiment ended when Lucien, now well provided, yet imprisoned as a consequence of the intrigues of Herrera's enemies, committed suicide in jail, just days before he was to be freed as innocent of the crime first attributed to him. This is the story. And in all fairness, it is less exciting than the procedures of the stage director, the manner it was engineered.

The novel would end here, but we know that we have to dispose of Herrera in a way. He will be saved, "honorably". The king of the underworld becomes a champion of justice. This epilogue type of addition to the *Splendeurs et misères* is much more interesting than the central portion of the Esther/Lucien story itself. Yet it is more about the biography of the stage-director than the art of stage directing which brings about the play as acted out - and which was to be stressed in the above notes.

Some Laboratory Tricks

Having recalled the heroes and the unfolding of their stories, let us now complete the earlier methodological considerations.

The Chardin-Vautrin novels offer also an introduction to the manner in which we may read again, for additional pleasure and insight, many other literary works produced by a great variety of authors. This happens to be so because the novels quoted here as exemplary, make very explicit the use of the "experimental" method. First we notice that these stories are about parallel lives. But they are not a fictional variety of the kind of comparative biographies we received from Plutarch. These stories are rather the parallel lives of the same individual placed with studious deliberation in two different circumstances. By the nature of the novel, the "parallel lives" have to succeed each other in time, but they could be read as well as *potential lives* of the same personage. In the here discussed Balzac samples the principle applies to most everybody, main as well as episodic characters, according to an interesting matrix of interacting flows. And their interconnecting network affords us the possibility to quote even minor episodic characters as epitomes of the method. An immediate example is offered by madame Bargeton. In her case the *physically same person* appears as *two moral personalities*, one in the small town and another one in Paris. In each case she is placed in fundamentally different "experimental situations" in which she then, so to say, interacts with Lucien. The main hero himself is then manipulated by two different "masters" into two sets of different circumstances offering thereby the story of two parallel lives ... of the same person. Yet nothing is completely arbitrary. The main personality's subjective motivations are the same in all situations. What was to be revealed is what this very same motivation effects in various states of the world external to the hero. In the case of Lucien Chardon the subjective motive played upon in the novels is his longing for *gloire et fortune*. Whenever this obsession is efficaciously activated by somebody, with intention or just by accident, he will prove to be a rather revealing medium. And such effect can be achieved even by an essentially honest, destitute fellow-poet just as by the ruthless Vautrin-Colin-Herrera. The moments of activation are extremely similar in both cases.

Case I. Daniel D'Arthez: Lucien and Daniel get to know each other in the *Bibliothèque Sainte Geneviève*. Daniel's kind and friendly approach, by which he overwhelms Lucien, are the advices of the experienced *poeta doctus*. [Remember the discussions about the dramatization of the novel? And the expansion on Walter Scott's virtues, as well as his failings due to *les moeurs hypocrites de son pays,* or 'the hypocritical mores of his country'?] Daniel was good-hearted; not an absolutely necessary poetic attribute. He even pawned his watch to buy the firewood he needed to heat up his frozen room when first receiving Lucien. And there, in the now pleasantly warm room, Lucien was served with the advices meant to lead him to the desired destination when:

"Au bout de dix ans de persistance, vous aurez gloire et for-tune."[p.184-IP] [At the end of ten years of perseverance, you will achieve glory and fortune.]

And accepting the advice:

«*Le poète ne discuta pas les conseils de Daniel, il les suivit à la lettre. Ce beau talent déja mûri par la pensée et par une critique solitaire, in-édite, faite pour lui non pour autrui, lui avait poussé la porte des plus magnifiques palais de la fantaisie. Les lèvres du provincial avaient été touchées d'un charbon ardent, et la parole du travailleur parisien trouva dans le cerveau du poète d'Angoulême une terre préparée.*» [p.186 -IP] The poet didn't discuss the advices of Daniel, but followed them literally. This beautiful talent, ripened by the thinking and by an unpublished *critique*, made only for him, has opened the gates of the most magnificent palaces of fantasy. The lips of this provincial character have been touched by glowing charcoal, and the words of this Parisian workman found a well prepared ground in the brain of the poet from Angouleme.]

Notice: to have Lucien act according to the advice and will of his benign adviser he must already have had *le cerveau ... préparée*. One precondition was, of course, the desire of *fortune et gloire;* and also the bitter disappointment suffered by Lucien in Paris, noticed by the good Daniel:

"Vous paraissez chagrin, monsieur?" [You seem to be grieving?]

The very same happened to Lucien when - *Case II* - returning to Angoulême, with all his *illusions perdues* plus suicidal thoughts, he met Vautrin-Herrera who also clearly evaluated his state:

«*Vous me semblez avoir du chagrin.*» [You look like one who has a grievance.]

And Lucien surrendered to the will of a new master. Vautrin invited the sad poet with the same promise of *gloire et fortune* to join him:

«*Ainsi montez. Nous vous trouverons un duché de Courlande à Paris, et, à defaut de duché, nous aurons toujours bien la duchesse.*» [So mount. We will find in Paris a duchy of Courland, and if not a duchy, we could always find a duchesse.]

A compromise solution. But it worked. And so started "Case II" dominated by Vautrin - and the accomplishment of a new type of great novel.

ESSAY NO.5

Of Art and Obsession: Notes on some Modern Short Stories

"Old" and "New" Short Stories

I am referring to the larger class of writings which go by the name of "short story" or, in other languages, *novella, nouvelle,* and *Novelle,* or, in the ancestral, even shorter version as *novellino* and *fablieau.* The earlier variety of storytelling indicated by Boccaccio as *"novelle, o favole, o parabole, o istorie che dire le vogliamo"*, which happily survives in our day along with other worthy and more recently emerged variety of the genre, was a simple linear story, sometimes merry, sometimes sad and quite often didactic, yet seldom loath to propagate moral or even political ideas. The jocose, prankish, indeed bawdy, in the lot was, of course, popular. We know - don't we? - that the vicarious enjoyment of sin in literary representation does not necessarily lead to the reader's damnation; and if the mild sin substitute is offered by skillfully assigning action and suspense and also avoiding explicitness, particularly the kind which deprives the reader of the satisfaction derived from exercising his own fancy, then the author can also be confident of his redemption. At least in the history of literature. Since, as we learn from Boccaccio, no story, however obscene the event may be which it recounts, can displease "when told in decent words". [Or: *"niuna [storia] sí disonesta n'é, che, con onesti vocaboli dicendola, si disdica a alcuno*"]. The genre's immediate particular, shared by its old and new varieties, and which is not independent of shortness, is its poignancy and intensity achieved by concentration. But the older variety's own strength showed itself in the colorful diversity of subjects chosen for their very color and diversity and often offered in artfully sampled garlands which constituted themselves fine works of art. Authors, collectors, or author-re-teller-collectors of popular tales of happier ages in the history of western literature - the paragon being the never aging Boccaccio - have never given themselves to the obsessive recounting of stories with features which would suit only some peculiar paranoia. Though this sets them apart from many of their more recent fellow story-tellers, it is no point in looking for a "scientific" assessment of whether this is indeed the primary distinctive feature of "classical" short stories. The continuing pleasure gained from reading the *fabliaux,* the *novellini,* the *Pentamerone,* the ever lovely *Heptameron* by Marguerite de Navarre, and, above all, the *Decameron* justifies them *ipso facto.* The reader's joy, which offers him a part in the early author's own joy to tell stories (*"Lust zu Fabulieren"* - Goethe), cannot be cast in scientific sentences. Yet I would still take the risk of a sweeping statement: the old *novella* author's uninhibited pleasure in rendering *any* entertaining story seems to have been lost for many of the greatest modern short story tellers as their new mode of recounting emerged to predominance in the late 19th century. The anxious search for specific states of mind, or particular types of "ends" or "solutions", or internal patterns of the *content* (i.e. not only of *the way the story is told*), may have helped us (did it?) to understand more about and penetrate deeper into what is called the "human condition". But the price of learning amounted often to the loss of uninhibited, elementary joy and relaxed serenity. I realize that such a statement, though maybe vaguely suggestive, as I hope, is anything but precise. If after some effort, following the pattern of modern literary scholarship, I would succeed in making myself better understood, "clarity" may come about by sacrificing the picture of much of what I want only *to point at.* So I will try to be cautious and push clarity only as far as clarity goes, calling rather upon examples to illustrate the hazy yet essential rest.

Before coming to my (so it might seem) arbitrarily chosen examples, I would like to propose the interested reader the following experiment. Take your *Decameron* or your *Canterbury Tales* and put it on one side of your desk.

Then, with an eye on it, compose according to your own reader's taste, and without following any professional critic's advice, your own modern story collection, your short story anthology: one or two from Chekhov... one or two from Faulkner or Hemingway... or any other major story teller of the last hundred or hundred and fifty years. Put them on the other side of the desk. And now think about what you may find different and similar between the two collections. There will be many common and as many different things to be noted. So did I when I played this game the results of which I try now to recapitulate. There are, however, good chances that you will notice the following: the older writers covered the whole spectrum of human condition and sometimes, as in the paradigmatic case of Boccaccio, structured them by type and kind of occurrence or general idea; while the newer writers seem to have parceled out between them short segments of that same spectrum. They may be, so to say, deeper, but none of them alone is able to give us a World Picture, not even through the totality of his stories.

So much, for the time being, about the *novellas* as components of a *collection with a wider scope.* Let us now move a step closer to the illustrative sample.

In one particular point short stories are, at least potentially, the closest thing there is to drama, and this by their potential of being poignant. This was true in all ages. But the "new" *novella*, the one which appeared in the late 19th century, is characterized by the maximal and very successful *technical* exploitation of this potential at the cost of freshness and spontaneity. The pleasure of simple stories is thus substituted for enlightenment through dramatic insight - the story teller of the class of Chekhov, whether intentionally or not, addresses his public in a manner reminiscent more of the ancient dramatist rather than the Renaissance fabulator. Maupassant, among the last great masters of the "old" type, still tells us a *good story;* however, Chekhov also achieves the dramatic effect reminiscent of the ancient tragedy writers. (The new "trend" has, of course, forerunners. Think of Balzac's *Chef-d'oeuvre inconnu* or Flaubert's *Un coeur simple.* But these were exceptions even in their *oeuvre.*) Yet, on the technical side, unlike tragedies (or comedies, the "inferior" genre, by Aristotle; the "superior" one if you believe Joyce), the great short story of the "new" kind does not always come to a resolution within the time segment to which the text confines itself. In the case of Chekhov, the "end" of the story suggests the beginning of a long path on which the hero will continue his endless walk into nothingness. And so it is in Gorki's best short stories which in a few instances

- (don't believe Nabokov!) - are a match to Chekhov's. Closer in time to us: Hemingway's heroes are very often made to stop - since the text stops there - at just a step before the End, Death, which they challenge, alternatively, from so many sides. A set of such stories constitute a repetition of experiments in the variety of approaches to the End.

Here, once again, I was about to yield to the temptation of a general formula, this time for: "what is common between drama and the modern short story, and what sets them apart?" This has to be given up. After all, the purpose of art is to lead us beyond what we are ever able to logically and tersely formulate. (Yet - never to forget! - not to substitute itself for what can, and therefore should be, logically and tersely formulated.) But the evocation of examples can help us sense the variety of ways pursued by art to achieve its ineffable purpose. And reading means, ultimately, to engage in the type of exercises translated into the notes from which I propose a random sample. Or random it seems from "outside". In reality they are personal, thus subjective - thus *not* random from "inside". And sifting through the lectures to be discussed may lead to some methodical understanding of what I will later call *storyworthiness*.

This is *a warning concerning the examples chosen*. They are only a few and may carry the bias of personal fancy. The choice, that is. But not necessarily the substance of the discussion. Therefore it may be considered that whenever "Russian", "American" or "German" modern short stories are mentioned, the generalization does not necessary apply beyond the exemplary sample. The characteristics discussed may not stand for the respective national literatures, though the excellence of these literatures may be mirrored in them. All examples chosen stand, however, for that spectrum-slicing mentioned above; for the gloomy human landscape they reflect as well as for particular narration techniques which apply to their dismal subject.

Approaches to Despair: Chekhov

It is fitting to start with the greatest. In the world of Anton Pavlovich the story does seldom end in a denouement, tragic or otherwise, while its thread is hopelessly absorbed in a monstrous, timeless-eternal, sad future. There is a large class of Chekhovian stories (and plays) which, though relating of people seemingly worlds apart from one another, conclude by stranding their often unaware heroes in the same deep mire of un-analyzable hopelessness.

And the fascinated reader returns time and again to the same stories as if trying to do what apparently the author himself attempted: to pursue anew either the same path, or again try a new one to find out whether it leads to the same or, perhaps, some other destination. Yet all (or, anyways, most) of these Chekhovian paths converge to the unarticulated gloom of an end which cannot be deciphered.

There are other ways in life, of course. Pursuing them could lead to a variety of experiences and outcomes. It is the choice among these ways which is the brand of the artist. It is *as if* he would have tried to find other paths and destinations, yet with little success. He repeats his experiences and produces an amazing number of virtuoso variations on the same dismal theme. And indeed, virtuoso variations of a given theme reveal the technical excellence on which we should dwell. To explain this I propose to rehearse some of the memorable reading experiences.

"Vanka" provides a good starting example. It is an unjustly neglected little piece of paradigmatic significance. It is an epitome of the Chekhovian *novella* perfectly articulating the designs of his experiments - repeated and well controlled - with human destiny. Let's recall:

> "Vanka Zhukov, a nine year old boy, who had been apprentice to Alyahin the shoemaker these three months did not go to bed on Christmas eve."

Though his master, mistress and the journeyman went to the midnight Mass he, Vanka, used the occasion to write a letter to the only person close to him. In the village. Not *a* village, this village or that village but THE VILLAGE. Since for him existed only THE CITY, otherwise Moscow, with all its wonders - ("in a shop window I saw a fishing hook for sale, fitted up with a line, for any kind of fish, very fine ones" and "I saw shops where there are all sorts of guns, like the master's at home") - and THE VILLAGE. And he wrote to his "Dear Grandfather, Konstantin Makarich":

> "And I am writing you a letter. I wish you a merry Christmas and everything good from the Lord God. I have neither father nor mother, you alone are left me."

The grandfather in the story was

> "employed as a watchman by the Zhivarovs, he was short, thin but extraordinarily lively and nimble old man about sixty-five whose face was always crinkled with laughter"

and him, this "Dear Grandfather" did Vanka implore:

> "for God's sake have pity on me, take me away from here, take me home to the village, it's more than I can bear. I bow down at your feet and I will pray to God for you forever. Take me away from here or I'll die."

Vanka made the ultimate trial to escape the horrible life of which we receive only a hint. Finishing the letter he wrote the address on the envelope: "To Grandfather in the village", after which "Vanka ran to the nearest letter box and thrust the precious letter into the slit".

Here the story of Chekhov ends - and the endless monochrome future of the "hero" begins. There is a quasi-tragic discrepancy between what the reader knows and what the main character of the story is able to grasp. *We, the readers, know* that letters thus addressed never reach destination. *Vanka doesn't know.* He is trapped, seemingly forever. No "tragic" end of the hero is bringing home to the reader the ineludible decision of the gods. The case is brought down to earth.

"Vanka" is a good and concise example for the study of Chekhov's world and his art of representing it. We can use it as a paragon of the structure of most *novellas* of the great Russian author. Its essential features will be met again in other Chekhov stories. To recall: *the sense of tragic despair is transmitted by the separation between what the hero in the story grasps or is willing to recognize, and what only the reader understands.* Here the suspense, unlike in its "classical" versions, is not built into the story by postulating the ignorance of the reader who will end his reading by achieving "recognition". The reader knows more than what either of the stories' characters, and this makes the tension permanent.

Before continuing let us return to an obsessive reference: the tragic hero of the Greeks is also unaware of his fate; yet neither is the reader or spectator aware of it, unless having prior knowledge of the mythological tale. In the development of a Chekhovian story, however, the reader will realize that the hero misses, ignores or, as in a few cases, because of lack of courage or determination, fails to take into account one particular element of reality, thereby failing his entire life. A case in point is Vanka who found out from

> "the clerk at the butcher's whom he has questioned the day before ... that letters were dropped in letter boxes and from the boxes they were carried all over the world in troikas with ringing bells and drunken drivers".

But the clerk forgot to tell him - and therefore Vanka didn't know while we know - that a letter has to show something called a mailing address. This very "small detail" is probably the source of a tragedy; no illegitimate and insane illusion but a plausible hope is nurtured by the hero, and he will continue to do so long after *our* story, the one we read, ends and until - we clearly, painfully anticipate it - the sad outcome will dawn on him. The Chekhovian heroes' hopes and illusions are never illegitimate in the sense that they were ever impossible and nothing but irrational constructs of a weak person's daydreams. They always carry some, if often only week, seldom sharply pronounced, realistic potential. If noticed by the personage in the story and properly used, it still may offer a chance of accomplishment, though never its guarantee. What is, however, guaranteed is failure when a detail is overlooked, a chance missed, an element ignored or perhaps sacrificed to pointless reveries, revealing thus man's tenuous mastery over his destiny - or at least the author's perception of such.

There are thus three essential features we have to take into consideration when comparing the "classical" and the Chekhovian sense of the tragic. The first is the similarity in the characters' *peripeteia*, that "change from good to bad" emphasized by Aristotle who explains us that it "comes about as the result not of a vice, but of some great error or frailty" (Poetics, XIII 4). But, second, while the "error or frailty" of the classical, "Greek", hero consists in something he may have done that he shouldn't have done, the "error and frailty" of Chekhovian character, coming as if from our own non-heroic environment, consists in *avoiding* to do the right thing. Finally, as already mentioned, it is the manner of conveying the sense of tragic which, in the here studied short stories, speculate on *the difference between the knowledge of the character and that of the spectator/reader*. This is probably a new approach to tragedy. Chekhov developed it further in his plays which, however, do not fit the textbook definition of Tragedy.

The Variety of Chekhovian Despair

The world of Chekhov may be as wide as everybody else's, but in his stories this world narrows down, almost always, to a tiny, remote black point which absorbs everything. To recall some of the better known examples:

> - The case of the doctor who considers a mental patient as being the only person worthy to talk to; then he himself ends up trapped in the mental asylum; one can be "interesting" and "different" only inside the Ward, shut out from the monochrome world of the "sane".

> - The perfectly normal yet disillusioned bourgeois and the distinguished lady (with a pet dog) continuing on a path of recognized hopelessness. No exit here either. And no "tragedy". Here it is the lack of will which leads them to that all absorbing tiny black point.

> - Neither is the hero "falling" in the brilliant story of a "Duel" but ... marrying his adulterous and widowed lady companion, and *then* swallowed by the endless Banality. [Their end is still better than those of most others, but, in the context less convincing.]

> - The merchant (in "The Ravine") who ends up robbed by his daughter in law employing his own tricks and comes to be seeking the heartfelt charity of another, beggar poor, ever despised and neglected, daughter in law. This is a paragon of failure by deliberately ignoring the obvious: what everybody can see, the merchant chooses to overlook.

Of course, it could be easy to dismiss all this as sentimental crap or didactic platitude if every step would not be so perfectly plausibly worked out.

The Virtuoso Perfection.

The minute exploration of human decay is best evidenced when the process is imitated in a description of dramatic tension. I quote as typical and also of masterly perfection the example of the country teacher Marya Vasilyevna - "she had been teaching school for thirteen years" - whom we surprise traveling to town "*In the Cart*" driven by Semyon, to pick up her miserable salary. The road she passes over is just a limited portion of the endless passage through the wasteland of her life. The brighter days she may have enjoyed once, are now absorbed in the fog of an unfathomable past. She was born in a well-to-do Moscow family. But

> "her father died when she was ten years old, and her mother died very soon after. She had a brother, an officer; at first they used to write to each other, then her brother stopped answering her letters. He had lost the habit. Of her former belongings, all that remained was an old photograph of her mother, but the dampness in the school had faded it ..."

Now she was a "schoolmistress", which reduced to plain atomic facts meant that

> "her quarters consist of one little room and a kitchen close by. Every day when school is over she has a headache and after dinner she has heartburn".

Sitting in the wobbling cart she stolidly rehearsed the few clear features of her tiny world's picture, when a streak of brightness flashed through the dismal autumnal landscape only to be swallowed up again by the indefinable Nothing:

> "she was overtaken by a landowner named Hanov in a carriage with four horses, the very man who acted as examiner in her school in previous year". [Hanov, noticeably aging], "was still handsome and attractive to women".

Well, certainly to Marya Vasilyevna, to whom it was a mystery why this wealthy bachelor imposed upon himself this exile:

> "what could his money, his interesting appearance, his refinement get him in this Godforsaken place, with its mud and boredom?"

This strange fellow kept presenting globes to the school. But "who had need of globes here?" The Universe was reduced to a small muddy spot. In such a place globes only illustrate their very irrelevance, and Hanov, though by his own election, was reduced to the level of Semyon "jogging slowly along over an abominable road and suffering the same discomforts".

Hanov drove close by, saluted Marya Vasilyevna with a friendly greeting and joked about the road with Semyon. The reader doesn't know what he was thinking. Yet we learn about what crossed the mind of the young lady. As they drove alongside and while Semyon and Hanov exchanged opinions about the road, she noticed that

> "he is really handsome" [and that] ... you can't understand ... why God gives good looks, friendliness, charming melancholy eyes, to weak, unhappy, useless people - why they are so attractive".

When Hanov turned right, leaving them, the sound of his departing rig kept the sad sweetly soothing thoughts alive for awhile: "She wanted to think of beautiful eyes, of love, of the happiness that would never be". And then a second's bright thought - "His wife?" - vanished in the gloom of her daily concerns. After a short stopover at a roadside tea-house, Semyon decided to drive, unlike Hanov, straight across the shallow, muddy river:

> "'Where are you going?' Marya Vasilyevna asked Semyon. 'Take the road right across the bridge.'
> "'Why, we can go this way just as well, it's not so deep'
> "'Mind you don't drown the horse.'
> "'What?'
> "'Look, Hanov is driving to the bridge, too', said Marya Vasilyevna, seeing the four horse team far away to the right. 'I think it's he.'

"'It's him all right.... What a blockhead he is. Lord have mercy on us! He's driving over there, and what for? It's all of two miles nearer this way.'"

On the other bank, Marya Vasylievna arrived wet and dirty "and she began to cry, she didn't know why".

The story as such, in its broad outline is not yet "Chekhovian". What makes it characteristic is the subtle dynamics of the three main actors, Marya Vasilyevna, Hanov and Semyon. First, not to be forgotten, there is only one perspective, one single vantage point and that one is shared by the author and Marya. We know what she says *and* thinks. Of the others we know only what they say. In the case of Semyon that is little ambiguous: what the simple, boorish and malicious peasant says, leaves little room for interpretation. Hanov, instead, whenever speaking, widens rather than limits the fields of possible interpretations of his personality. Marya tries to find one, but not very hard, and permits her bittersweet reveries to swallow any clear thought about the man who may - just may, only because it's nowhere denied - have had an interest in her. It is *one* of many hypotheses compatible with his behavior. Another one is that he was totally indifferent and engaged only in neutral conversation as a ritualistic exercise in good manners and conventional joviality. We, and Marya, could have found out the truth had she made some attempt to pursue a conversation with Hanov, to take away Semyon's "initiative". She did not. Indeed she did not answer at all to Hanov. It was only Semyon who plainly and rather impertinently "conversed" with the rich landowner while Marya's thoughts prevented her to utter any word. A thin, weak thread of hope: had she (belatedly) used the faint potential of her position as schoolmistress she could have ordered Semyon, with only a very slim chance of success, to change direction following the trail of Hanov causing, who knows, a new encounter and some new beginning... And had she attempted earlier on the road a conversation to start something "social", the result, whatever, may have been revealed only in a "long story", e.g. a novel. But since she did not, the short story conveyed to us comes quickly to its sharply focused sad end - and Marya's "real" life continues in the untold Nothing.

Hopes in the World of Chekhov are always slim, and seldom, if ever, obvious. But their existence cannot be denied; potentially they are always present, and if somebody attempts to activate them they may, by the small probability coefficient with which the real world endows most hopes, come to fulfillment. How slim such hopes are is revealed in many of Chekhov's stories by focusing on the faint thread in the dense web of events and relations which may lead to the contrary of the outcome we get anyway.

Chekhov's hero never runs against a wall. He/she engages in some action with the hope of an outcome which ignorance, if he is brave, or lack of strength, if a wimp, will make him/her, fail but not with big éclat; just trapped in endless hopelessness to which he arrives on a track lined with instances of dramatic suspense worked up by hopes.

Of Russians, Americans and the Dramatic Story Subject.

In the later American short story we meet a different brand of heroes. And a different brand of obsessions than the ones haunting the Russians. It seems, however, that this time the obsession is shared by a nation through its mythology: it is the lone, unyielding fighter. True, he (almost) always overcomes in the movies, but gains only Pyrrhic victories, if any at all, in the "high-brow" short story. In contrast to the hero's dissolution in an un-paced future in the dramatically concentrated Russian (primarily Chekhovian) short story, the American hero, chosen by some of that country's eminent writers, will first brace for a sortie. If these American heroes have some remote relative in the Russian literature it may be Gogol's Akaky Akakievich. His single-minded, persistent pursuit of a redeeming purpose - in "The Overcoat" - sets him apart from his later-to-come compatriots defeated by their dreams, and makes him akin (though still towering above!) many of Hemingway's best penciled characters. And he is defeated: the hero falls victim not to the whim of gods - those glorious times are long bygone - but to everyday meanness, thieves and the indifferent Law. And he dies. But here the kinship ends, since Akaky Akakievich's ghost haunts all those who tormented him in life and, as it behooves a good Russian, be he a good Pravoslavnic Christian or just a godless revolutionary, he also does something to better the world or at least to teach it of the better, by punishing the haughty and unjust Important Person:

> "The encounter had made a deep impression on him [the Important Person]. From that time onwards he would seldom say:

'How dare you! Do you realize who is standing before you?' to his subordinates".

American literature, of course, has its share of successful lone fighters. But it so happens that as the country and its wealth and culture grew, the best, the sharpest drawings in its short story literature became biased towards human failures.

To be precise: bias does not mean exclusive interest. But it often becomes such. And it may be so because success, even if achieved through dramatic battles and great sacrifices, provides fulfillment. Success doesn't call for investigation. It is accepted. Defeat is always contested and the search for its sources is renewed time and again. This is essentially different from Chekhov's own *Comédie humaine,* which is the sad procession of defeats, failures and unavowed capitulations. As American literature progresses, more and more characters join the procession as they emerge from "experiments" performed in a growing number by many authors from Melville to Faulkner or Hemingway. The great short story of both, Russians and Americans, is only too often about the defeated, however, the respective types of the defeated are different. Common is the mode of concentration on single-point targets. The subsequent examples should illustrate this.

I picked a macabre example to stress these particulars. It is from Faulkner's "New Orleans Sketches". Its title is "Sunset". If positioned against the backdrop of Chekhov's "Vanka" the essential differences between the "Russian" and "American" literary approach to failure could be sharply drawn. The story is about a Negro youth and is introduced, as if by a motto, by a news item from "The Clarion-Eagle" about a "Black Desperado Slain". According to the newspaper report he has terrorized a town for two days killing two Whites and a Black man, and then has been shot and killed by the machine gun fire of a National Guard unit. I didn't check whether the newspaper quoted is real or is part of the fiction. This, probably, has been clarified by scholars. Much as I respect their learned endeavor, I do not believe this to be relevant. I take it as stated and discover an instance of how a story may come about. The purported news clipping states that: "No reason has been given for the black's running amuck, though it is believed he was insane. He has not been identified." Perfect! So one can go back to the set of *possible* causes and pre-histories without the constraint of the knowledge about a "true" one, and develop a story relevant to one of them, since every single event or point in a man's life can be either the beginning or the end of an infinity of possible tracks. Not any tracks, but only those which are compatible with its starting point. The choice is made by the story teller. A lot has been written about the motives of such choices - and in many cases, the only thing we can say with reasonable certainty is whether the attributed motive is *compatible* with the fiction; even if confessed by the author himself. "Truth" is irrelevant. Important, however, is not the reason but the fact of the choice made, and in the quoted story it is yet another case of an American loner's tragedy. A young Negro - (that he is *young* is already a choice, because it is not said in the newspaper clipping) - coming to New Orleans from some remote plantation he never left before, "carrying his shotgun and his bundle" and braving the wild city traffic, brutish passers-by, cussing cops etc. succeeds, after some failed attempt, to get on a boat which he thinks to sail to Africa:

"Ah wants to go back home, whar de preacher say us come fum".

"Africa" was for him what the "Village" was for Vanka and the information he got from the preacher was just as true yet just as worthless as what the Muscovite butcher apprentice said about the workings of the postal service. Here the mean white man should be added who takes the youth's four Dollars for a fare to ship him to "Africa". After a river crossing:

"The white cap'n, the mad one, leaned down from the front porch above his head.

"'All right Jack', he roared, 'here you are. Help us put them barrels on the board, and Africa is about a mile across them fields yonder'".

He was deep in "Africa" when after having shot in the dark something he took for a lion, the hunt on him began:

"Whew! Dese Af'ikins shoots niggers jes' like white folks does."

And they killed him too:

"His black, kind, dull, once-cheerful face was turned up to the sky
and the cold, cold stars. Africa or Louisiana: what care they?"

Russian heroes vanish. Americans fall - and then vanish. Or again: they
"win" - and then vanish. Clichés? Yes. But not mine. Life's? The frequency of
the choice by the last hundred or so years' greatest story tellers puts its stamp
on the genre. Whatever the historic, sociological etc. reasons for the choice
of a subject, it, *the subject, determined the structure and cadence* of many, major,
short stories. Faulkner may have protested whenever he or any of his American
friends was compared to Chekhov. Granted, their stories, their fantasy were in
many respects different. Yet it so happens that the greatest concentration of
their talents was likewise directed towards the drama of failure. The Russians
just started sooner. And technically the conveyance of the drama or tragedy
happened with similar means. Once again, the defeat of the main character
originates in his unawareness of a, normally, paltry detail. The simple introduction of such a detail, reveals a whole world. In the case of the young man
killed by the National Guard, the simple knowledge of how far away Africa
was, could have been the source of a different story, a different conflict, may
be a happier end. As if Vanka had known the address of his grandfather. But
it was this simple device by which the quoted authors conveyed the implicit
tragedy of loneliness.

Hemingway and Compatriots

It is easy to list those characters in Hemingway's short stories that are not
of the lost, failed, abandoned and vanishing type. But one will have trouble
finding their exploits as interesting and as exciting when compared to any personage in his gallery of the defeated. In a fine book reviewing the "procession"
of two centuries of American literature, Alfred Kazin writes that "Hemingway's
greatest gift was to identify his own capacity for pain with the destructiveness
at large in our time". If I well understand it, that "destructiveness at large in
our time" means that Hemingway was picking instances of human destruction and destructiveness (i.e. destruction in actual and potential sense) from
whatever is our time "at large", and concentrate on it. It comes up in his work
in a variety of forms but in a singularly sharp, striking form in his short stories.
The story-teller develops a particular method to bring home the moments of

dread one step before a fatal end or, beyond the physical fall, their extension into eternity. To convey metaphorically what I mean, I will borrow a striking instance from a short story of an older contemporary of Hemingway, namely Sherwood Anderson:

> "Once, when I was a tramp, I saw a kid killed by a train. The kid was walking on the rail and showing off before some other kids, by letting them see how close he could let an engine come to him before he got out of the way. And the engine was whistling and a woman, over on the porch of a house nearby, was jumping up and down and screaming, and the kid let the engine get nearer and nearer, wanting to show off, and then he stumbled and fell. God, I'll never forget the look on his face, in just the second before he got hit and killed...."

Many "kids" in Hemingway's short stories are assuming the challenge to let an engine come close to them, though not necessarily to show off before "some other kids". It is either to try themselves or, to experience the thrill of that last minute's danger: an experiment in Manhood - a Hemingwayan obsession. The point which is crucial on a failed life's trajectory marks the moment when the "kid" stumbles and falls. There are some who stumble, fall and are crushed to death by the engine; and there are those who survive physically the trial remaining with the burden of heavy moral and/or physical affliction. To sharpen the focus on such individuals, two parallel techniques have been developed - and this is so even if we may never be able to find out whether Hemingway ever really wanted the development of such techniques. They certainly came about in the process. In the case of fatal ending it is the stress on the last minutes, clustering around the deadly instant, which are focused upon with a sharpness which increases as the story progresses. In the "survival" version, the moment of great challenge is referred to only in back-flashes palely crisscrossing and thereby stressing the dark background of an aimless eternity.

The representation of death, central in Hemingway's story telling, offers an exemplary case for the superiority of the written/read word in comparison to the theatrical representation. Though it is the case of only one instant, the last, in everybody's life, it stands, *pars pro toto*, for the mentioned excellence. It was well understood by John Dryden when he explained that

"... there are many actions which can never be imitated to a just height: dying especially is a thing which none but a Roman gladiator could naturally perform on the stage, when he did not imitate or represent, but do it; and therefore it is better to omit the representation of it.

"The words of a good writer, which describe it lively, will make a deeper impression of belief in us than all the actor can insinuate into us, when he seems to fall dead before us." (*Of Dramatic Poesy*)

Hemingway's short story work continues a series of ideated experiments reproducing in dramatic focus the variety of possible ways of coming close to that moment which makes dread cease. He leads us to converge to that caesural instant, no matter whether marked by physical death or the beginning of endless banality. Aim and method of approach are best revealed in a much celebrated yet not his best (to be sincere: not a very good) story. "The Snows of the Kilimanjaro" is anything but a masterpiece yet one is tempted to call it a "programmatic *novella*". If somebody will take me on, insisting that - perhaps - Hemingway never meant to make it "programmatic", I will yield to the claim. From the reader's point of view, the *intention* of the author bears little relevance to what his output turns out to be; but the *outcome* reads like a program for the structure of many others of his stories. Including many which he wrote before. Chronology is also irrelevant. In "The Snows" the major interest of the Hemingway stories are outlined with an almost theoretical precision. We can read it again and single out a sequence of instances which may serve as guidance to many other stories, whether the characters are social relatives of those in "The Snows" or just boxers, matadors, soldiers, vagabonds, crooks.

The hero, a writer on his death bed, is far away from Paris or the Mississippi. He is right in the middle of Kenya at the feet of the Kilimanjaro:

"Now he would never write the things that he had saved to write until he knew enough to write them well. Well, he would not have to fail at trying to write them either. Maybe you could never write them, and that was why you put them off and delayed the starting. Well, he would never know, now."

These regrets are followed by the remorse for having so often tormented his wife:

> "She was very good to him. He had been cruel and unjust in the afternoon. She was a fine woman, marvelous really. *And just then it occurred to him that he is going to die."*

Awareness of the approaching death. After remembering some of the stories he never came to write, his thoughts return to the ultimate reality:

> "So this was how you died, in whispers that you did not hear. Well, there would be no more quarrelling. He could promise that. *The one experience that he had never had he was not going to spoil now. He probably would. You spoiled everything. But perhaps he wouldn't."*

It is this "one experience he had never had", the experience of Dryden's paradigmatic gladiator, which is now to be conjured. And then, after some more "unwritten" stories:

> "He had just felt death come by again.
> *"'You know the only thing I've never lost is curiosity' he said to her."*

This dreadful curiosity which when fully satisfied becomes meaningless! Because it can be satisfied only when it devours the curious who cannot enjoy the satisfaction of the discovery. But the gradual approach to the cutting point heightened the hope of thereby coming closer and closer to the "idea of death", while still available for its perception. This might have moved Sherwood Anderson's kid who "let the engine get nearer and nearer, wanting more and more to show off". If the kid had been a writer he may have invented other "kids" - e.g. toreros - whom he had sent closer and closer to the End. It, the End, can never be perceived but, may be, approaching it asymptotically (remember your high-school calculus?) one could get the "feel" of it. However close somebody is to that point where a stretch of the time-line is cut, there is still an infinity of points left to explore. (Remember Zeno of Elea?)

The writer in "The Snows of Kilimanjaro" is out for the Experience (of which the reader may get some too) before he is swallowed by the snowy rocks. We get more of it, deeper, chilling and horrifying, in the stories in which this program of "the one experience he had never had" was perfected and applied. It is interesting, to quote a set of major examples, in how many variants the last minutes of a bullfighter are explored. It is some romantic inquiry in yet other aspect of "manhood". This is interesting, of course, worthwhile and, in the given case, good reading. But it becomes good reading only because of the build-up of the last minute thrill. The variety is rich. We shall quote first the typical case reminiscent of that child in front of the "engine". Thus we see the young Paco ("The Capital of the World"), employed as a help in a hotel kitchen in Madrid, mimicking a bullfight in which he is supposed to be the matador. His associate in the adventure is Enrique, the dishwasher, who was meant to play the matador in this "corrida" and admitted it was fear, *miedo*, which kept him from going into the real arena. And while playing "bullfight" in the kitchen he warned his young friend Paco about the dangers of the game. Yet he went along with the game and accepted to be the "bull":

> "Running with head down Enrique came toward him and Paco swung the apron just ahead of the knife blade as it passed close in front of his belly and as it went by it was, to him, the real horn, white-tipped, black, smooth, and, as Enrique passed him and turned to rush again it was the hot, blood-flanked mass of the bull that thudded by, then turned like a cat and came again as he swung the cape slowly. Then the bull turned and came again and, as he watched the onrushing point, he stepped his left foot too far forward and the knife did not pass, but had slipped in as easily as into a wineskin and there was a hot scalding rush above and around the sudden inner rigidity of steel and Enrique shouting. 'Ay! Ay! Let me get it out! Let me get it out!' and Paco slipped forward on the chair, the apron cape still held, Enrique pulling on the chair as the knife turned in him, in him, Paco".

This was the End. Time and again we participate in the experience of the bullfighter's last minutes. He does not always die. Nevertheless he falls as when in "The Undefeated" his *coleta* will be cut off by a caring friend while wounded, under anesthesia on the operating table. Death by charity. Death - which means the end of the only possible *meaningful* life.

As Hemingway came closer to the asymptote the shorter and more charged became the recount. No precedents of the death of Maera, the bull-fighter, are given. Only the Death itself is told - in less than half a page. It is tried out again:

> "...They laid Maera down on a cot and one of the men went out for the doctor. The others stood around. The doctor came running from the corral where he had been sewing up picador horses. He had to stop and wash his hands. There was a great shouting going on in the grandstand overhead. Maera felt everything getting larger and larger and then smaller and smaller. Then everything commenced to run faster and faster as when they speed up a cinematograph film. Then he was dead."

Well, is it really so? Countless times *invented and told,* and when at last experienced - never told again.

> [The *corrida* example provides a good illustration of what I called poignancy of a short recite when compared to the last few pages of the novel *Sangre y Arena* by Blasco Ibáñez. A parallel reading of the rather voluminous novel with the quoted page of Hemingway offers the opportunity for a good comparison of two reading experiences originating in the description of two very similar events.]

What happens to bullfighters can happen to soldiers or boxers. The choice of the subject originates in an eternal research. No new subject in literature, not new in American writing. Think of Melville's captain Ahab. His dramatic fight with the whale could be separated as a short story of an intensity we more frequently encounter later in the American literature. Isn't this story of the same strain as Hemingway's "Old Man and the Sea"?

Of Some Short Stories by Thomas Mann

We certainly understand that most of Chekhov's main characters walk slowly into a cloudy, dismal world of purposelessness. But the impossibility of that world's dissection is relative; only when writer and reader alike, keep the view from the angle of that deceptive hope which leads the uncertain steps of the Chekhovian character, only then is the sight of his future not only dismal but also garbled. After all, the dark world towards which they are heading but of which not much is disclosed in the Chekhovian narrative, has been densely populated by characters of many other writers. Is the Hell of a mental asylum in which Chekhov's Doctor is trapped not like the one in which Gogol's "Madman" has written, much earlier, his diary? Looking from outside and from a certain distance, a bottomless hole looks dim, impenetrable. Scrutinizing it more closely and carefully, frightful images will surface from under the gloom of those aimless "futures". Indeed some, to become heroes of another class of stories, may even have started out, and ended as well, in the middle of this world of shadows; and yet others may have emerged from it, redeemed perhaps, more often, however, as graduates from the Devil's apprenticeship. But as they are damned and, within that world of darkness, having abandoned *ogni speranza* at the gate, they may still become objects of research and emerge with sharp, monstrous contours.

The choice of some of Thomas Mann's short stories to illustrate the point may seem - perhaps it is - arbitrary. Yet their relevance will follow, as I hope, from the discussion itself.

So: how is it in the Nothing and what may come out of it? The story of "Tobias Mindernickel" is paradigmatic for Thomas Mann's search for an answer. The Tobias in the tale is an old, enigmatic man, living in a shoddy tenement, who seldom leaves his miserable flat, and then only for an aimless walk during which he is always exposed to harassment by the proletarian neighborhood's malicious children.

> "One had the impression, however strange this may sound, that he was deprived of that commanding sense of perception which directs every individual's scrutiny of the World of Phenomena: he seemed bewildered by any appearance, and his unsteady eyes were slithering to the soil to avoid people and things alike."

This is the *impression* we may have of him; this is what we see of the man who, himself, looks as if he were to see so very little. We don't know - the writer does not tell us since he probably doesn't know either - how Tobias became as we now see him. So we may list a number of hypotheses which, according to our and the author's knowledge, are compatible with a fellow such as Tobias. First comes to mind a possible affliction by Fate. But then he may just

> "simply not be up to the tasks of Existence, while his suffering appearance of frustration and silliness conveys the painful impression as if Nature had deprived him of the required measure of balance, power and spine which are necessary to live with the head upright."

But while the causes of his affliction, the sources of his behavior remain hidden - the "imitation" of Tobias being not "genetic", so to say - his simple actions reveal his directions: we don't know where he was coming from, yet we discern, slowly, slowly a scaring, fateful character.

One day, while Tobias took once again a walk, a neighborhood boy stumbled, fell, hit his face in the pavement, and his nose started bleeding. The boy was one of those who indulged in the usual harassment of the poor tramp. Tobias jumped to his help, stooped and bent over him, compressed the bleeding wound with his handkerchief, caressing the ten year old with kind words of consolation. Tobias was now superior: he could afford to be kind.

A second "act" in the drama started when Tobias acquired a dog. He named the poor beast Esau, brought it home and taught it the rules of doggish obedience in the usual way, by using food to inculcate the requisite conditional reflexes. Now Tobias was master, exercising his prerogatives with sordid joy. But - do you remember professor Pavlov's dogs? - at some point, when the commands were no more followed by tidbits Esau, desiring to enjoy some relaxed digestion, refused to follow orders, comfortably stretching out his loins on the floor. The desperate master:

> "Esau! ... you ought to come even if you are tired."

This was not Esau's view.

> "Listen, ... obey, or you will find out that it is not wise to irritate me."

The desired reaction did not follow. Thus a raging and desperate Mindernickel went about to cruelly strap the poor creature:

"What, you don't obey? You dare not to obey me?"

No, Esau did not obey while listening to Tobias' tough lecturing given in the same tone as if by "Napoleon in front of a company which has lost the Aquilla in battle". Yet, ultimately, a strange love affair between dog and his master got started. It lasted until one day, when the frisky Esau escaped from the flat, happily playing with the hated street- kids. "On this day Tobias strapped Esau strongly and bitterly." Yet, once again, a great change in their relationship came about when the frolicsome Esau got badly wounded by the big kitchen knife used by Tobias to slice food. Now the Master was again kind, caring and tender. Until Esau felt much better and could dispense with cuddle, actually refusing all caress and jumping happily around. Then the following happened:

> "... with a mad jerk [Tobias] grabbed the animal while a big blank object glared in his hand, and with a single cut, running from the right shoulder deep into the breast, sent the dog to the floor, - it uttered no sound, fell simply on one side, bleeding and shivering."

And then Tobias:

> "My dear animal! How sad is everything. How sad are we both! Do you suffer? Yes, yes, I know you suffer - how pitiable you lay in front of me! Yet I, I am by your side! I comfort you! I will take my best handkerchief..."

It was no use to do so. Tobias disappeared again in the dark. His only hope of escape from darkness and depravity was to rule over something, anything. Yet this proved to be illusory.

We have here an experiment with a soul which, first confounded with the original Chaos, wants to emerge from it and acquire a distinct shape. Specifically it is the trial of a weak Will which wants to constitute itself as World - by proving itself against something deprived or craftily bereft of will. It is also a grotesque, caricature like close-up of the elementary stuff of which dictators of the totalitarian breed are made. Its variety was a permanent preoccupation of the author who wanted, and often succeeded, to go beyond what was ideologically muddled in Schopenhauer's representation of Will. In Thomas

Mann's work we can discover an impressive gallery of individuals whose main effort is directed towards shaping themselves into distinct personalities from the formless Nothing which, indistinct, absorbs them. And some of them reveal possible mechanics of the tyrant's mind which historic, psychological and sociological studies can only suggest. Tobias Mindernickel was an actor on a reduced scale and highly concentrated, therefore a striking drama of the would-be tyrant who, being ill-favored for success by objective circumstances and subjective endowments as well, inevitably fails; yet because of his failure the narration is able to forcefully direct the reader's attention to the minute details of those forces which motivate such individuals.

Mann often repeated the experiment, in novel and *novella* alike, changing some or many of the "parameters" defining the subject and then exposing them to similar tests. Thirty three years later it was Cipolla, the magician - or: *Forzatore, Illusionista* and *prestidigitatore*, as he introduced himself to the public of the Italian sea resort - who was to be "subjected" by the author to an experiment similar to that we witnessed in "Tobias Mindernickel". (And I do not believe that my analogy with a "controlled experiment" is far fetched, as it may first sound.) There are two major changes in the character of Cipolla, compared to Tobias. The *forzatore* has emerged to daylight now for a longer while as a performer, whose art consists in bereaving others of their will, thus making them obey his commands. This is exactly what Tobias tried and where he failed. Further, the *prestidigitatore* was more intellectually sophisticated: he explained and justified the purpose and general relevance of his art. This is dangerous, especially in the case of Thomas Mann who only too often, though mostly in novels, lets his characters talk essays. Lengthy ones! But the story is not spoiled in this case. Cipolla introduces the public (thus the reader), right during the performance, into the frame of his ideas, so that the ideological discourse becomes perfectly absorbed into the narrated action. His show begins by having a young man in the stalls induced to first mock him, Cipolla, for his funny behavior and then to come up to the stage, being this time exposed himself to the mockery of the *illusionista*. Said Cipolla:

> "'I like you *giovanotto*. Would you believe it that I noticed you for quite a while? People like you enjoy my special sympathy: I can use them. Obviously you are quite a guy. You do what you want to do. Or did you ever do something what you didn't want to do?

Something not willed by you? Listen, my friend, it must be comfortable and fun not always to play the tough fellow who has to come up with both, the will and the action. Division of labor has to prevail, after all - *sistema americano, sa*. For example, would you now show your tongue to this select and dignified society? I mean your whole tong, down to its roots.'

"'No', said the lad with hostility. 'I don't want to. It would demonstrate poor manners.'"

Yet, ultimately he obeyed. It was Cipolla's trade to make others enjoy the "comfort" of complying with his will while being "freed" of their own; and the exercise offered also an insight into his motives. When another proud, self-conscious member of the public expressed his intention to resist some of the *forzatore's* attempts to influence him, his subsequent defeat was introduced by the following lecture:

"'Thereby you will make my job more difficult' said the *cavaliere*. 'However, this will not change anything on the outcome. Freedom exists and so does Will; yet the Freedom of Will does not exist, since the Will which targets its own Freedom vanishes in a vacuum.'"

The able juggling with confusing words, which sounded well yet remained beyond logical control, was part of the art of subduing other people's willpower. The ambiguous pseudo-philosophical statements employed by Cipolla with perverse delight in all the various instances of subjugation demonstrated that evening, were also amply lavished upon poor Mario, a young waiter, a *cameriere*, whose humbling was to be the climax of the show. Mario who, like others, made some vague attempt to free himself from the *forzatore's* power, foundered and abjectly obeyed. Cipolla teased Mario about some love affair of his, his feelings for a girl Silvestra - (the information was provided, thanks to the powers of the conjurer, by the *giovanotto* previously humiliated). Then he impersonated, so to say, the desired girl, in a fashion which impressed the poor youth as credible, yet disgusted part of the public.

"'Kiss me' said the hunchback. 'Imagine that you have the permission! I love you. Kiss me right here', and he pointed the tip of his forefinger at his cheek, close to his mouth, while straddling his hand, arm and small finger away. And Mario stooped and kissed him."

Cipolla succeeded in conjuring what Tobias failed to obtain: love by submission. But was this the end of it? A snap of the jugglers lash awoke Mario who, as soon as he realized his humiliation, burst down the scales of the podium amidst the laughter and applause of the crowd.

"Below, while still fast running, he turned around straddling his legs, then raised his hand, and two flat sounding detonations cut through cheer and laughter."

This was, of course, Cipolla's end. Without belittling the political moral of such an end to the story, often stressed in critical literature, it is really of only secondary importance, especially since it can be stated in plain terms without artistic imitation. However, the insight it offers into the mechanics of domination is of considerably more significance, and the mastery of its dramatization warrants its choice as an exemplary *novella*. It is in an important sense a sequel to the Tobias story: a renewal of the experiment, with a twist. In the case of Tobias it was the would-be conjurer who ended the story by unintentionally eliminating the object he tried to dominate in order to secure its love. In the Cipolla case, it was the "object" that with an aroused self-conscience cut the thread of the story after the essentials have been revealed. And in both cases this was the end of a completely analyzed monster. Even the actions which brought about the respective ends had strong common structural features: first, there is an abrupt movement as reaction to whatever happened before - Tobias "... with kind of a mad yank grabbed the animal" and Mario instantly burst down the scales of the stage; second, for Tobias: "a big blank object glared in his hand", while for Mario: "he turned around straddling his legs, then raised his hand"; and finally, Tobias "with a single cut, running from the right shoulder deep into the breast" killed Esau, and Mario with "two flat sounding detonations cut through cheer and laughter" and finished off Cipolla. However, important is not who did physically end, because both, Tobias and Cipolla were by now equally disqualified for what entitles to existence in literature, namely to have a story. A further story, as it was. And neither was able to have one anymore, neither could go beyond the role of a "ruler" into which they stylized themselves.

About Storyworthiness

There are two kinds of individuals, if examined from a literary point of view: those who have a story worthy to be told and those who have no such. Now, we cannot set rules as to who is and who is not fitting the admission requirements into one or the other class. We just realize that many types which we may not have recognized as such prove to be worthy of a story when we encounter them in the tale of a great writer. However, those whom the writers have deemed worthy of a tale may be so in a variety of ways. Nothing surprising about this. Still, I have the feeling that a very large group of modern short story heroes or, just plainly, characters, can be ordered in two major classes. It is first the class of those characters whose (worthy) story tells about their exit from the state of storyworthiness; and then it is the class of those characters whose tale relates about their striving - striving, not necessarily succeeding! - to graduate from story-unworthiness to a state in which they would count for a recounting. Many of Gogol's, Chekhov's and, in more recent times, of Hemingway's heroes, for whom the above selection was relevant, belong to the former category. Less categorically, yet I still believe that many of the major short story characters of Faulkner are sharing their company. In general, Russian and American literature are important suppliers of membership in this class. The second group of characters comprises also those of Thomas Mann, chosen for heir exemplary nature.

Of course, a trial to give oneself a form, to emerge from nothingness into storyworthiness, ought not necessarily end in tragedy or have a perverse outcome. So, the class itself is richer in variety than the discussed examples might suggest. There are more dignified and successful ways of emerging from ignominy or oblivion. But the advanced position which the two classes of heroes have gained in the modern short story is a fact. This still doesn't mean exclusivity. We discussed only paragons of a new way of story telling: the art of micro-precision to describe small spots in the human landscape which are epitomes of the whole. And this method is imperceptibly absorbed in the parallel world of the "old" *novella* which continues to flourish also in our century.

ESSAY NO.6

Rituals of Dignity

Randomly collected marginal notes
from much cherished readings.

Of Myths in Literature

We are inclined to recognize some positive significance in rituals only when they are viewed in association with specific forms of religious observance or, perhaps, some patterns of political practice. This understanding seems to be, by and large, correct though probably not all-inclusive. A distanced yet careful observer of a variety of widely differing religions will be able to identify a very important common characteristic of their rituals, the scope of which reaches far beyond the particular form of these ceremonial exercises. This common feature - documented also by scholarly research - reveals itself in the attempt to make the participant re-live an historic or mythical event with the aim of achieving identification with that occurrence's heroes and/or their purpose. E.g., when Christians participate in the annual ritual of the Easter-Resurrection procession, anywhere in the world, or on the Via Dolorosa itself; when Jews repeat for centuries the Passover rituals miming aspects of the Egyptian captivity and the Exodus - in these and in many other cases, the declared purpose is the intimate association of the faithful with these events through reliving by imitating their unfolding as recorded in the respective scriptures. This, of course, can be easily understood since it is explicitly stated to be so in the relevant religious commendations. And while it may not be always as obvious as in the quoted cases, all religious rituals seem to have a similar purpose, whether achieved or not, whether clearly stated or accessible only to the careful observer peering beyond the screen of observances.

Other rituals, often performed conventionally or without deliberation, are sometimes viewed and, if recognized, appreciated only for their aesthetic character; no less often, particularly in our time, they are rejected by some as superfluous fancy. It is difficult to assess how much of feudalism's elaborate ceremonies of knighthood or, in plainer modern times, the scrupulous practice of five o'clock teas, were rituals of association, and how much of these was added theatrical "superstructure" having no purpose *outside* the play itself. But the presence, at least *in nuce,* of a desire for identification with a person, an object, a state or status is unquestionable in most cases. The performance of an orderly sequence of ceremonial acts as substitutes for a desired, hence not or not yet extant, state; as practice for the achievement of a desired state; as evocation of a past state or purported participation in such - is present in the rituals of religion and patriotism, of love and courting, of statecraft and, indeed, subversion and crime. Rituals are produced at any time when the bond with a desired, yet still not achieved or likely un-achievable state has to be strengthened as well as when they are needed to perpetuate an existing bond. The "state" aspired at can be, of course, a *state of mind.*

To achieve this, the production of rituals remains a permanent, everyday affair of Man, and literature has, and has had, a tremendous contribution to its development. A particular form of literary ritual or, more exactly, *ritual reported and analyzed within the literary work,* has emerged in earlier times, but appeared more frequently in the post-WWII period. It first struck me in the 1960's when a friend gave me to read an earlier (1956) Goncourt-prized novel by Romain Gary, *Les Racines du Ciel,* "The Roots of Heaven". Ever since, I was looking for instances illustrating the "discovered" phenomenon. I found several more examples in fine works which, however, like Gary's novel, can not claim a place in any literature's future classical heritage. Well, there are exceptions, of which some will be discussed. Yet all instances to be discussed illustrate affirmations of a type of literary fancy which will probably develop and endure. The phenomenon also struck me as a sign of our times as well as a *carrier of creative potentials,* as a particular device of truth representation. This requires, of course, a more precise explanation.

At first reading it seems to be easy to comprehend what is *literature as ritual* and *ritual in literature,* what the particulars of the two are and what their differences. Whether we consider such purposely religious or quasi-religious exercises as the programmatic public reading of the Hebrew Scriptures since Ezra and Nehemiah, the solemn public recitations of Homeric poetry by the ancient Greek rhapsodists, or just the versified ceremonious love simulations of troubadours, and indeed the great variety of more relaxed forms of literary communing in latter, more pragmatic centuries, the ritualistic role of an important part of literature appears as obvious. Moreover, it will turn out that much of what is usually judged to be "pure literature" carries with it an important ritualistic element as soon as it becomes the object of purposeful cultivation. As for the *ritual in literature* it is by definition the presentation of rituals of any kind as part of the narration in a literary work, such as a practice of the characters in a novel. This seems to be simple and obvious. Yet it became a not so obvious an aspect of a particular mode of literary representation; it became an instrument of cognition of human types or conflicts, of states of the world etc., by the mediation of the characters' rituals. The specific rituals to be addressed here appear in some stories in recent literature. They impress as the foundation of the hero's definition and a means to reveal human relations difficult to reproduce, comprehend or empathize with otherwise. This should now be illustrated with examples from the above mentioned novel in which I first chanced upon the idea. The first examples should than be followed by a discussion using yet other examples, including one most important classical case offered by Franz Kafka. No comprehensive study is implied. This is rather to be viewed as a heuristic exercise.

Two Parables from *Les Racines du Ciel*

A careful researcher may provide similar examples also from past literatures though the purport of those instances could prove to be limited. There is something peculiar about the cases to be discussed, and this is to be reviewed. First, as said, the examples from Romain Gary's novel.

The novel is about a French political prisoner in a Nazi concentration camp who, after the war, becomes a lone fighter for the survival of ... elephants. He takes on poachers, authorities, ruthless colonists etc. in then French Africa, to protect this endangered species. His decision to engage in this quixotic adventure is traced back to his camp experience. One day, in the camp, he fancied elephants *freely* roaming across the African savannas; he thought of them as symbols of freedom, and the idea gave him strength to resist and survive. Now, to pay his gratitude, he engaged in a fight to save them. In a more roundabout fashion, the whole story could serve as an illustration for our inquiry. Yet more than the novel, some episodes, flashbacks emerging from this former camp inmate's memory, prove to be of paradigmatic significance for a special form of story telling.

First example. There was a fellow among the "politicals" in the camp called Robert. A strong man in every respect: his cheerful conduct was of an effective moral support for all inmates, and his fist commanded respect even among the hardy "common law" neighbors of these forced laborers.

> "One day ... he entered the barrack miming the attitude of a man who offers his arm to a lady. [...] Robert, followed by our surprised gaze, walked through the barrack while continuing to offer his arm to the imaginary lady, and then made the gesture which signified offering her a seat on the bed. In spite of the general apathy, he raised some interest. [...] Now he caressed her [the imaginary lady's] chin, now he kissed her hand ..."

and when one of the fellows scratched some hairy portion of his body, Robert warned him:

> "Watch your behavior... There is a *grande dame* among us."

After some laughter and jokes:

> "Well, I warn you: from now on things will change. You will stop complaining, to begin with. You will make an effort to behave in front of her as if you were men. I say 'as if' because this is what counts. And you will, dam' it, make an effort to be clean and dignified; if not, you will have to reckon with me."

Not much resistance was shown:

"There was some hoarse laughter, but all of us had the confused feeling that in our state, *if we do not accept some convention of dignity to keep us upright, if we do not hang on to a fiction, a myth, all what remains is to submit to anything or even to become collaborators.*"

The moral of the men suddenly improved and everybody did the best to please the lady. After a short while, the Nazi camp commander found out about all this and ordered Robert to surrender the lady so he can transfer her to an army brothel. He was the type of a "sophisticated" Nazi who liked to torment his victims playing their own game while making it clear to Robert that:

"I understand these things Robert ... I was born to understand them. This is my trade, and this is why I got high up in the Party. I understand [these things] ... and I detest them. *That* is why I became a national-socialist. I don't believe in noble conventions, *in the myths of dignity.*"

Robert did not surrender the lady and got a month of solitary confinement.
Second example. One day, while carrying heavy loads, Morel, the main character in the novel, discovered a glowworm, fallen off on its back and fighting in vain to get again on its tiny legs.

"Morel bent his knees, balancing the sack on his shoulders, and with a movement of his index put the bug back on its legs.
"He repeated this twice while on the course. The publisher Revel, who marched in front of him, was the first to comprehend what this was all about. He let his approval be known by a grunt, and instantly jumped to the rescue of the first glowworm which dropped in front of him. Next, [the same was done by] Rotstein, the pianist, who was so slender that one might have said that his body tried to imitate his delicate fingers. From this moment on, all the 'politicals' went about to rescue glow worms, while the 'common laws' went by swearing."

The 'politicals' didn't stop even during the regular twenty minutes granted for rest. Yet soon they were noticed by sergeant Grüber.

> "This one was not an ordinary brute. He was educated and used to be a teacher before the war in Schleswig-Holstein. He instantly recognized the enemy. He sensed a scandalous provocation, a demonstration of faith, *a proclamation of dignity*, inadmissible for people who were reduced to nothing. ... He threw himself in the battle. First he went against the prisoners, seconded by the guards who didn't quite understand what was going on, but were always ready to clobber. ... Sergeant Grüber understood quickly that this was not the thing to be done if the enemy were to be struck where it hurts most. Thus he did something which was very disgusting but also very pathetic in its inability to achieve the desired result: he ran around on the turf, the eyes fixed on the soil, crushing with his boot every bug he could discover."

Analysis by Parable

That things like this happen in captivity is known to us from the memories of many, told, re-told or written. That exactly this happened or not - the story with the fictitious lady or that with the beetles - is not really relevant. What is important is the ability of the story to reveal characters in *and by* their relation to the thus chosen rituals. Particular characters. Any story, any parable, if good, does the same thing. But the stories about *rituals of dignity* are a special kind of revealing conflicts, exposing characters. None of the personae in the above quoted two episodes was actually involved in a *real* event: the lady was a fancy and the glowworms couldn't have any practical consequence in the real world. Yet they revealed aspects of humanity (and inhumanity) difficult, if at all possible, to describe in meaningful scientific propositions. A pure fancy was required for such.

Consider once again the case of Robert: an unarmed, overworked slave facing the "sophisticated" Nazi commander. The commander had chosen to humiliate his man, not by beating or torturing him, but simply by robbing him of his dignity which consisted in ... "nothing", "*une connerie*" as one of the inmates called it, while still going along with it. And the commander was powerless, because in the case of a refuse - a risk which he knowingly took upon himself, the gambler - he could even kill Robert while still remaining humiliated in front of his own soldiers having not gotten "the lady". And Robert?

> "He had a good time, he had a good time thinking the SS men *cannot deprive him, by using force, of this invisible figment of his mind,* that it depended entirely on him to agree to surrender her..."
>
> ".. The commander paled slightly.... he realized that he got into rough waters. His two SS men were only an additional proof of his helplessness. He was at Robert's merci. ... He had no soldiers and no weapons which could expel that fancy from the barrack."

A conflict around a ritual! - of which we learn from a parable. And it is the same in the second example with sergeant Grüber:

> "Because he may have been able to beat to death the detainees and squash all the glowworms, but what he really wanted could not be achieved, it was beyond his range and couldn't be shot."

And even though he squeezed the strength of his slave laborers, they continued the defiance also while resting. Thus Rotstein, the pianist, who was particularly affected, lay on his bed seeming to be completely lost, and yet defying the odds. A fellow inmate approached him:

> "Hey, Rotstein! Rotstein!
>
> "Yes.
>
> "Are you still alive?
>
> "Yes, but don't interrupt me. I give myself a recital.
>
> "What are you playing?
>
> "Johann Sebastian Bach.
>
> "Are you crazy? A *kraut*?!
>
> "Exactly. Just because. To reestablish the equilibrium. One cannot let Germany forever on its back. We have to put it back on its feet.
>
> "We are all on our back, groaned Revel. That's a birth defect.
>
> "Keep your mouth shot. I can't hear what I am playing.

"Large crowd tonight?

"Maybe.

"Pretty ladies?

"Not tonight. Tonight I play for sergeant Grüber"

This is unlikely to have happened in "real" life. But then, this is fiction; the invention of yet another ritual, related in a story stressing aspects of our lives which resist conceptual discourse.

Some Types of Rituals in Literature

These stories illustrate the difference between *myth-making* and *myth-living*. We are accustomed to see literature as either the source or the conveyor of myths. In this case, however, literature conveys not a myth but the story of those who invent it for themselves to live by it, in it. Everybody knows that the story is "not true". Yet everybody discovers by it a piece of a different world. There is no Don Quixote here, who fights injustice, real or perceived, wherever he encounters it. No Béranger [of Eugène Ionesco], the last fighter against the "real" rhinoceroses. The heroes we have so far considered don't fight; they don't exist. They remind and - may we say it? - delight.

They may also fall, and yet they are not tragic. But they have comic varieties as well as sad, yet serene, versions. And they are in the centre of interest of authors who depart from the classical line without playing the experimental games. We can sample a few examples from post-WWII Italian literature. The heroes I casually quote are constructors of myths which they live by the rules of a ritual, engage in actions ritualistic and "sterile" - sorry for the quotes, but, oh, "real" words are lacking - and discover for us a world thereby. Let us pay some attention to the comic yet sad - not *tragicomic*! - variety and pick an example. The author is Giovanni Arpino. (If you want some biographicals, look up in the Who's Who. He may not yet be there. Bad for the Who's Who!) And one of his sweetest stories I so gratefully recall is: "*Randagio é l'eroe*", or, a bit freely translated, "The Vagabond is the Hero". It may also be: "Going astray is heroism". Let's give up and pay attention to just a few instances in the story.

Giuan is a poor, rather awkward fellow who lives in Milan in happy marriage with his *Olona*. He is crazy while she is kind of reasonable. Giuan is an artist. A painter of sorts. He makes a living by copying in various sizes, for the tourist market, Leonardo's *Last Supper* in which, for some reason he always manages to best reproduce Judah and Bartholomew. Why? This may get an explanation in the context and has certainly something to do with his way of relating to a world in which so many disgraceful and outrageous things are going on. Something had to be done:

> "We can't go in and out of this world just so. Not leaving behind any trace, as millions of other poor people. And we are old by now, my old mouse."

And when, at some point, he complained about being old and bored, Olona made it clear that:

> "You may be bored, but not old. Neither are you tired. You need something new. I don't. I am happy. Yet who knows why. But you need to invent for yourself a new reason to stay in this world. I know it."

And he found new things to do, to be able to leave a trace behind, while still keeping himself in this world. Thus night after night he and Olona left their home, on bicycle, to "correct" the ugly stains left on the walls of the city by some most outrageous graffiti. This was a ritualistic guerilla warfare of a painter against shame and disgrace, against the abuse of reason and human feeling. With a can of paint and a paintbrush he stopped at some of the most offensive inscriptions and responded in kind. Some place he read:

> *"La dittatura alle teste di cazzo."*

No matter how embarrassing it is for the translator, it has to be faithfully reproduced if the reader of these notes is to understand the nature of the whole exercise. It would read in English: "The prick heads - give'em dictator-ship!" It was obviously the expression of radical discontent with some who do not "understand" something they "should"; be that the proletariat or the *camicie nere*, the black-shirts. But Giuan understood to change the text into something of a redeeming message. With just a few strokes of his brush it now became:

"**Solo** *La* **mia** *ditta cura le teste di cazzo.*"

Gesú

Thus the "quotation" signed *Jesus* proclaimed that: "Only the touch of my finger will heal [cure] the prick heads." It was "a Jesus who, just like him, cared little about the purity of the vocabulary", as Guido Piovene noted in his introduction to the story. Essential was the purity of the truth, not of the language. And the whole thing was not simple. The original text was written on the wall in a place difficult to reach, and the reader of the story is kept in a long suspense while Giuan and Olona were pondering the odds of the different manners to get to it. (At some point she even compared Giuan with King-Kong.)

One little illustration of a character in a great little story. Giuan had a hundred more ideas, some to frighten, others to elate. But he will end up in an asylum. Was he not more comfortable there? [Remember Chekhov's doctor in "Ward 6"?] He was hopeless. His ritualistic exercises did not save him, but they saved at least his dignity - and his story which reveals the malaise in a "consumer society":

"Fantasy is dead ever since a bowl of soup is no more a problem."

Well, sad as it may seem, fantasy is still alive where the bowl of soup continues to be a problem. It also offers ritualistic substitutes discovered by another Italian writer, Domenico Rea.

"Europe's Calcutta"

Naples. Dying trades, growing misery. The coachman, *un cocchiere,* without authorization:

"The foreigner comes to Naples with the specific purpose to be shown around in a coach. He leaves eagerly his hotel, searches, spies around, doesn't notice anything, and suddenly a taxi emerges, or one of those ruffians who lease cars for the tour of Sorento. And us, we have to live in hiding".

And when a cop shows up he will be fined. Or, money lacking, jailed. One day *in carcere* for four hundred Lire.

"The fine being one thousand, I am assured two and a half days. Sometimes the cop is a brave chap and makes it two thousand. This adds up to five days. But I am married and have six sons. What guts must I have to go to stay comfortably in jail, five days, knowing of those who wait for me like hungry beasts".

Like wolves. *Lupi.*

"Maybe tomorrow I would be able to return home - (in a village, at forty minutes distance in a horse cart). You know why I can't go home every night? Because, as I told you, my six kids are like wolves. You recall the wolves coming down hungry from the mountains during those frosty days? Such are my kids. As soon as they see me appearing under the ark of the tilt they are crying: 'Pop, pop, are you back? Did you bring bread?'"

So he will return only when he will have the bread.

There are thousands, even worse of, in the world of Domenico Rea's "Neapolitan Chronicles", in which the misery of the "blind flesh of the deepest slums" blotted out the last feeble relics of human dignity. Or has it? Rea discovers the pockets of resistance. Sometimes it is myth making - an ancient remedy; some other time it is the small-time social rituals of the poor. Here myth making may not even be the correct term, though the sociologist would apply it to this phenomenon. It has nothing to do with the myth-making poet's inventions: Virgil didn't really believe (or did he?) that Aeneas' erring companions were the ancestors of the Romans. The maker of the myth made it for the consumption of others, not for himself. But the poor *lustrascarpe* or shoeblack of Naples lives a parallel life in his stories which shine-over the sordid reality:

"People are oblivious of the fact that one time, in Naples, the class of bootblacks was so highly respected that one of its representatives had the pleasure to give lessons [in his art] to a King of pure blood and glorious lineage".

To be sure, historic details are irrelevant:

"Whether this King was an Anjou, a Bourbon, or a Savoya - doesn't matter". [What matters is that] "*there was* a king with whom the art of giving luster to the shoes was in high esteem."

But those times were gone. The lack of care for the shine of shoes, and with it the economic decay of the trade once respected by royalty, was a clear indication of general decadence. Though not everywhere!

"I told my son, go to the American consul, fall to his feet, clean his shoes and let yourself be expedited to America, a land great in all respects, and you will see how much a shoeshine is valued there. He is like a merchant there - and what a merchant! With shops as big as a ballroom, with ten, twenty chairs and dozens of employees; and very often a barber and a bootblack pull together - one to wash the head and one to clean the shoes - and make millions."

Things were so bad these days that this aging *lustrascarpe* had to admit that:

"If we do not organize, we will end up like the *cocchieri!*"

It was not quite clear what the union was supposed to stand for, because

"who would want to clean his boots knowing that he has to abide by a tariff instead of just getting away with alms? If we at least would have the King! The King, yes, he would help us".

And, if you have doubts then listen to this:

"the King let his servants and his lackeys do everything: they dressed him and undressed him - because he was the King. But in one thing he wanted his own hands to serve him. One day he sent for master Cicilio Girona, my grandfather, and sending away all those present, told him: dear Cicilio, you got to teach me how to clean shoes *alla napolitana* and I present you with anything you want, a palace or a forest, a ship or a coach with four horses, whatever you please." But nowadays, "those youngsters don't even know that when Garibaldi arrived to Naples the first thing he asked for was a shining-to-mirror of his glorious boots by the hands of a Neapolitan master!"

Never mind that these boots may have been meant for the King. But, as said, history is irrelevant here.

History is irrelevant. When one "invents" a world of Dignity one also has set the stage for the ritual plays mimicking life in the fictitious surroundings. Whether in a Nazi KZ or the slums of Naples, the horror of the present can not only be dreamt away but also - as long as there is still life and some physical strength left - lived away.

So in Anacleto's winery, which he inherited from his forefathers. In the days of his grandfather (just as in the days when "the great and heroic figure of his great-grandfather, who first hissed the branch", the *frasca*, on the distinguished joint's doorpost) the winery was always crowded. Now? On one end a *cocchiere*, this time one who earns more than the one with the six whelps, eating his own fish and ordering half a liter of wine. *Terzigno*, the more expensive one, and not the cheaper *Posillipo*. (The *cocchiere*: "Posillipo? What's that?" *Anacleto*: "*Posillipo* is smooth. It relaxes. It gives you sleep and forgetting". *Cocchiere*: "Yet I want to remember something". - Quite an unusual fellow. One who drinks to remember, not to forget.) On the other end a poor *lustrascarpe*: no ancestry conversant with royalty. Neither too many *quatrini* in his pocket:

"In his pocket two hundred Lire, and he could not decide whether to buy a piece of bread, cheese and one quarter of wine, or to bet it all on wine, the one which put a smile on the face of the stranger. He was, however, both, hungry and thirsty. When the *cocchiere* spread salt on one of those anchovies, peppered it, and slang it into his mouth with the levity of a youth who makes an estival dive in an inviting sea, then the bootblack closed his eyes ..." - It was a fight. But then: "Wine for me too. One quarter", and answering the relevant question: "I also want the Terzingo".

It is impossible to reproduce in a short relation that concentrated, pill-size, masterpiece of Domenico Rea, so rich in insights and dramatic sequences. Here is a preliminary attempt:

- Anacleto is concerned about the poor man overspending; tells him about it.
- A silent, disdainful look by the *lustrascarpe*. No word and
- a stunned Anacleto opens the tap of the Terzigno barrel
- serves the wine and adds - nobody asked him - a thick slice of bread (unfortunately "I am out of cheese", and the other: "later I will clean your shoes");
- the two customers, unknown to one another, in a wine-softened mood, hope for a contact;
- Anacleto pitches in with conversation; and
- when it comes to payment, he charges only 25 lire instead of 50; stressing his generosity with an allusion and
- the "rich" *cocchiere* offers his anchovies to the bootblack who lifts the evening to a joyful high: "I own 175 Lire, we put it on another litter of *Terzigno*."

A new story, indeed, a new reality began.

"Anacleto already bowed under the barrel to refill the bottle. He felt now much better. Outside a heavy rain started, but in the joint a beautiful evening set on".

The outline here given just suggests the story. What can we say about it? That it is a parable of the Victory of the Good? Well, it is. Except that it isn't. It is that something which the story *shows* but plain speech cannot *state*, if not in shallow generalities. The cathartic exercise of the actors *in the story* generates a parallel and different world; it is reality engendered by myths about glorious grandpas which are dignity substitutes for those who in this world would otherwise be bereft of such.

The Ritualized Country: a Story by Kafka.

The examples quoted seem to be randomly chosen. It may be so from the point of view of any systematic researcher. This, however, is an exercise of a reader who chanced upon these stories during many years of informal, i.e. non-deliberately chosen, yet careful reading. And the presentation of the so far quoted examples happened in the order in which this reader (writer of these notes) chanced upon them. The works cited may have their own chronological sequence in the history of literature; but here their order is according to the reader's own timetable. Literature has, of course, its history, i.e. the record of its unfolding in time. But at any moment in time all literary works of the past are simultaneously available to the reader's choice. They have a parallel existence. Well, this is *one* of their forms of existence. So we may consider them according to the type of subject they treat and as if they had been written at the same time. If we study a literary work according to *how the work came about*, then we cannot ignore historic time. However, if we try to understand some particular traces of human behavior, *some*(!) of them, as represented in literary works, then historic time may be ignored. At least to some extent. This is the case with the literary representation of rituals of dignity. Therefore, after the examples meant to *suggest*, hardly to *clarify* the subject, we may get access to major works seldom viewed/read from this viewpoint. Two of such will be discussed. The first is a *novella* by Kafka titled "*Beim Bau der chinesischen Mauer*", or "Building the Chinese wall", the second is a novel, *El Hablador*, by Mario Varga Llosa.

Kafka's is one of the finest short stories ever written and systematically misread in Academia. It discusses the creation of a parallel, ritual world, for a whole nation. Of course, all the above discussed examples were about ritually created parallel worlds by and for individuals. This, however, is about the same for an entire great nation. The Chinese may have offered the example because, well, they have that famous Wall. But no interpretation of *their* history should be associated with these allegorical Chinese wall builders. What is the story about? You may have read it, but the following short rehearsal is meant to stress its relevance in the present context.

The storyteller talks to us in the first person implicitly confessing that he has to "interpret", because the facts are not entirely satisfying when we were to look for an explanation of the enormous and collective building effort of a great nation. Yet, being a very disciplined storyteller, he still refrains from too much "interpretation". We should not forget that the storyteller himself was one of the builders of the Wall. He is therefore a constructor not a "deconstructor". So we, the readers, may follow his example and use the allegory for our own illumination. Since the story may be an allegory of some of our own experiences, desires, dreams or disappointments, wherefore we may likely empathize with the Wall's builders.

Now, most everybody who knows about the non-fictional Chinese Wall thinks that it was built to defend that vast land:

> "The Wall was meant to offer protection for centuries; therefore the unavoidable preconditions for the job were a most careful construction work, the employment of the building wisdom of all known times and nations, and the builders' unremitting awareness of their responsibility."

Please, read again the last part of the quoted text: the Wall may have been built as a defense against invading barbarians but, as it turned out, the effort was founded on "the builders' unremitting awareness of their personal responsibility" [*dauerndes Gefühl der persönlichen Verantwortung der Bauenden*].

How was this personal sense of responsibility to be achieved? The answer is implicit in the description of the work process itself and its planning. To discover it, two most important things have to be noticed while reading again the story.

First, the reader learns that the art of building became a most important educational discipline in China's schools no less than fifty years before anybody was actually directed to go about the gigantic construction work. Thus learning about building, construction became part of the culture. Obviously, minds and souls had to be well prepared before the hands themselves were duly instructed. We also read that the first-person storyteller himself started his training as a child. But could the barbarians not have attacked in the meanwhile? It is nowhere written, but they might have. And why shouldn't they have attacked when the conditions were still favorable? Why not faster? They may have but, so we conjecture, some sort of defense might already have existed. After all China was there and was great also before the Wall.

The other thing to be stressed are those *Teilbauten* or "partial constructions". Pieces of the Wall, short, not yet connected stretches of it, were built at a considerable distance from one another. Could it not have been done by slowly moving the Wall ahead in a continuous line? From a technical point of view it might have been even easier and less costly, but the building program had also a moral aspect. The country was big, its borders very long, and a slow advance along a single line may have driven the many-many builders to despair. Because

> "the hopelessness of such a diligently pursued work which, however, couldn't have been accomplished even during a long life, would have driven the workers to despair, thus making them useless for the work. Therefore the system of partial construction was chosen."

Thus, given the envisioned time-length of the construction work, a sense of achievement was kept alive in the workers by moving them from place to place, to those many *Teilbauten*. It was this *ritual of the changing construction sites* (not a technical necessity) which, by enhancing a feeling of accomplishment, kept their dedication alive. Wherefore

> "they took leave from their homes as ever hopeful children, while their joy to participate again in that popular work could not be defeated."

The *ritual itself* was just as important as the practical purpose of the work. Yet all this required the creation of special people, wherefore the previous, five decades lasting education, was seen to be an absolute prerequisite. It achieved

> "that every well educated person was a mason by profession, infallible in the art of building infrastructures."

Still, nobody really knew the leaders of this enterprise. - The storyteller thinks that given the prevailing confusion, we may only conclude that the "leadership" really intended it to be so. This may seem untoward from a technical point of view, yet it explains *the ritual of wall building*. But do not forget: this explanation in rational terms cannot go very far. And it was well understood by many.

> "In those days many, indeed the best, had a secret principle: try to understand with all your powers the instructions of the Leadership, yet only up to a certain limit. When you reach that limit stop reflecting."

Careful reading will reveal something often overlooked, namely that Kafka believed in the power of the parable which can cast light on things (not "explain" them!) beyond rational discourse. And that also a parable may be further enlightened with yet another parable. And so the parable of the Wall engenders other parables. Let us continue.

We learn that

> "In fact that 'leadership' existed since ever. and so the decision to build the wall. Oh, innocent peoples of the North who thought that they caused this enterprise! Oh, innocent Emperor who thought that he in fact gave the orders! Yet we, the builders of the wall, know it differently and keep silent."

Yet they thought to serve the Emperor. Well, not necessarily the present one. Who knew him anyhow? He was faraway. Somewhere. Because

> "our land is so great that no story can reach its boundaries, and even the Heaven scarcely envelops it - and Peking is only a point, and the imperial palace is just a tiny little point".

> "The Empire is immortal, but any single Emperor falls and collapses."

There is a legend which explains everything. Somehow, this Emperor, unknown to the people, thinks of everybody and tries even to communicate with everyone. He is said to be dying and yet we find out that he is still preparing a message addressed to "*you*", i.e. "the individual and lamentable subject", or "dem Einzelnen, dem jämmerlichen Untertan". Who is this person addressed in the story as the second person by the first-person raconteur? This is not disclosed but we find out that a messenger is "now" on his knees by the side of the dying Emperor's bed who whispers a message into his ears. And then, after "now", we learn about the messenger's adventures while trying to overcome the countless obstacles on the way to "you". In fact he hardly can get through the many rooms and gates of the imperial palace. He tries, and tries, but will never get even through the last gate to enter the capital. His is a hopeless trial to make the message reach "you".

> "Still, you sit at your window and dream about it. Thus appears the Emperor in the hopeless and hopeful imagination of our people."

In fact, as said, the Emperor himself is not known to the people. The present one is confounded with some earlier (eternal?) one. Thus they believe in the presence of one from the remote past "while confounding the present rulers, with the dead ones" [*die gegenwärtigen Herscher aber mischt es unter den Toten*].

Neither do the people care for current political events. An example would offer that odd rebellion in the province neighboring the one of the storyteller. One day a beggar therefrom brought a manifesto to the village. The priest read it aloud, but everybody had a good laugh just after two pages. The peculiar dialect of that province added to the fun. And that was all.

> "So willing we are to obliterate the present."

What kind of a life was this anyhow? Was there also some lack of loyalty towards the Emperor? In fact not, because

> "There exists probably no nation more attached to the Emperor than ours in the South, yet our fidelity is of no benefit to the Emperor."

And this is so because the people lives

"a life which is not subject to any law prevailing these days, but heeds only instructions and warnings which came down to us from ancient times."

The institutional concept of an empire was never clearly spelled out in the minds of this people. But no matter how different may have been the inhabitants of the countless villages and many provinces of China, there was a unifying factor which coincided with their hope for the Messenger. This was the building of the wall, because

"especially while working on the construction of the Wall and thus contacting the human material [involved], a sensible person could travel through the souls of all provinces."

And thereby the weakness of an imperial government in the present day was substituted with a strong sense of human cohesion.

"And this is why I don't want for now to continue investigating this subject."

However, the reader should continue his own investigation by recalling yet another parable. Because parables can be understood (not "explained", "interpreted", "analyzed" etc.) only by other parables.

El hablador

This time it is the story of the individual, lost in the world, who finds himself again, and restores his endangered dignity, by joining the others in a ritual. Does it, or did it really happen? The story about it becomes reality for the reader. Yet it may also recount something that actually happened. So we are told by Mario Vargas Llosa. He speaks about the ancient tribes lost in the jungle of his native Peru, endangered by what some call "civilization". Yet they did not loose each other. At least not some of them such as the *Machiguengas*. Their tribal islands, scattered in the wilderness, kept communicating with each other through perambulating individuals. They wandered through the woodland from one tribal site to the other, and informed people encased there about each other, keeping thus their feats and traditions alive. Who were these men? Even careful observers from outside were at a loss when trying to explain or even name their functioning. Such was the case of Mr. and Mrs. Schneil, anthropologists who first could not decide whether such an individual was a *curandero* (magician or witch doctor) or a *sacerdote*. Finally they agreed that he may be a little of both, yet still something different. Among the *machiguengas* they had a name for them, but how to translate it? Mrs. Schneil made an effort:

> "Some time, you may call him a conversationist. Or better an *hablador* (rhetorician)."

And Mr. Schneil agreed:

> "Yes ... I believe this is a best approximation. *Hablador*, rhetorician."

The *habladors* went from place to place in the sylvan diaspora of the *Machiguengas*, and kept them united with their stories. The *Machiguengas* preserved themselves *by* the *habladors*, the peddlers of stories *about them*. Thus comments the author of our story:

> "This is an obvious proof that telling stories could be something more than a simple pastime. ... [It could be] something primordial, something on which the simple existence of a people depends."

This he said in a conversation with a friend from the university who is in the center of the story. This friend had a rather unusual background in Peru. His father was a Jewish businessman who, while living and running his business in a small backwater town, met and married a native woman of mixed background. She converted to Judaism and they moved to Lima. Their son, the friend of our author, was called Saul whom his father attempted to educate in the Jewish tradition. This could prove to some, and under specific circumstances, a handicap. Not for Saul. He had, however, another handicap: he was ugly. Very ugly; wherefore he was mentioned as the *Mascarita*, the little mask. His double marginality made him interested in the fate of the *Machiguengas* about whom he often conversed with his university colleague who, as mentioned, appears as our first person story teller. But *Mascarita* was deeply and personally involved with their destiny and problems and felt frustrated with his friend's apparently only "academic" interest. Thus, the author reports, that during one of their conversations, Saul Zuratas

> "exclaimed, disappointed, as if this connection would depreciate my curiosity: 'thus it is for its literary aspect that you are interested in the matter. Well, don't make yourself any illusions. It is most likely that it were those gringos who told you the story about the story-tellers. But things are not as they appear to them.'"

Mascarita was impressed by the resistance of the natives; their centuries lasting resistance in spite of all hardships and persecutions.

> "Well, he retorted, a Jew is more prepared than others to defend the right to exist of minority cultures. After all, as my old man says, the problems of the *Boras*, of the *Sharpas*, of the *Piros*, is our problem for now three thousand years."

Would anybody be surprised that Saul became an *hablador*? Hardly. But this is not the issue. It is the *search* by the author, by many authors, and by men, for meaning and dignity, which is illustrated in the stories about heroes with whom all those who are in search of such values, empathize. And if they don't exist, they invent them!

Some may combine to build a wall of defense. Such may, of course be very important also in a direct, practical sense. But the ritual of congregation on the far away building sites, and the communication with those who remained behind, is equally important for *dignified* survival, and not only in a physical sense. And those, equally spread on a large territory, who are deprived of the power to build a defense wall to protect themselves, keep their collective existence continuous by the efforts of those who unite them by stories. All this may be "literature". But the works recounting them offer us a parabolic *mimesis* of human dignity. And sometimes reality itself produces the kind of "parable" illustrated by the examples here collected. Thus in the memoirs of a Jewish woman from Hungary, now a writer living in Canada, we read something reported from the real world, a story which may by classified in the same group as the parables of Romain Gary. In her book *"Journey to Vaja,"* (Vaja being her native town in Hungary), Elaine Kalman Naves mentions the case of a strictly religious Jewish woman, a former servant of her family, who even in Auschwitz made an extra effort to keep pride and dignity alive. While doing daily, and with no rest, the most burdensome slave labor in the camp, she "made a distinction between the Sabbath and weekdays by hauling loads on the holy day on one arm only". She couldn't avoid work on Sabbath, but she stressed the holiness of the day by a gesture which was "but a ritual". Yet thus Blanche saved the dignity of the day on which God rested.

ESSAY NO.7

Aristotle, Kant and Stephen Dedalus: Nacheinander and Nebeneinander (and sometimes Durcheinander)

Statement of the Problem

This essay is about something seldom encountered in literature, namely the *literary imitation of the cognitive process* the purported final result of which constitutes, normally, the substance of the philosopher's systematic, conceptual discourse. We encounter in Joyce's Ulysses several such exercises in *cognition imitation*. One of these is included in the *Proteus* chapter of the novel's first part where two German adverbs, *nacheinander* (one after another) and *nebeneinander* (one by the side of another), are included in the text. Very meaningfully! Only given the bias of many analysts, the German usage was interpreted as a concealed reference to some less recondite literary or "aesthetic" theory. This author has also his biases and tends to understand the mentioned section as an imitation of the thinking process of Stephen Dedalus who endeavors to verify a long process in the history of philosophy by, once again, *imitating* man's experiential recognition of time and space. We may call it an exercise in practical epistemology performed by Stephen Dedalus. Whether *time* or *space* are "categories" as for Aristotle, or, instead, "forms of perception or intuition" (*Anschauungsformen*) as for Kant, is the subject of conceptual argument between philosophers. But is also the object of Stephen's "experiment" to be reviewed in a manner alternative to some interpretations submitted in the expert literature.

This is not the first attempt to establish the contextual meaning of the two German expressions appearing in the third chapter of the first part of Ulysses. Best known is the interpretation proposed by Fritz Senn which, however, is difficult to fit into the train of thoughts of that Stephen Dedalus walking on a sandy beach.[1] It is not very convincing even when we call to the witness stand the well read "artist as a young man", knowing about Lessing's *Laokoon*. It is, of course, nowhere written that readers were not entitled to their own "stream of thoughts". Indeed, much of the pleasure of reading translates into such. Thus, spurred by some simple, spontaneously occurring *associations d'idées*, we may collect the possible, perceived or only purported references to Lessing's *Laokoon* in the works of Joyce and try to understand with their help Stephen and his use of apparently irrelevant German words. This may not be completely unjustified even though we may have to postulate that, in the particular case mentioned, Stephen availed himself of a dictionary of German synonyms to substitute *nacheinander* for Lessing's mostly used *aufeinander* - which is *not completely*(!) synonymous with the former because it does not always refer to a process in time. It is mostly used for "one on top of the other". So why did Stephen do that? But did he really do it? Well, in what follows an alternative explanation will be proposed which is meant not only to cast additional light on the peculiar usage itself but also, and thereby, to complete the reader's intellectual portrait of the artist as a mature person. It is essential, however, to always carefully discriminate between the reader's (or readers') stream of consciousness or stream of thoughts and that of the characters in the novel. Sometimes the two may coincide. But we may attribute our own associations to a character in the story if and only if they are compatible with the logic or drift of his thinking. Mere coincidental indications in the biography of the author are not necessarily explanatory of the hero, his behavior, words and thoughts. Neither should a term which appears in two different texts be viewed as having necessarily the same contextual implication in both.[2]

Two essential qualities are setting apart Stephen Dedalus from all other characters in *Ulysses*, and we will have to keep them in mind when trying to better understand his way of reasoning, illustrated also by the usage of the quoted expressions. Of these qualities, one is better known and more often explicitly addressed in critical literature: Stephen is not simply an "artist" or a poet, but most specifically a *poeta doctus* of a particular brand. He studied in a Jesuit college, a type of school where, in Ireland as elsewhere, the attention paid to Aristotle went far beyond of what Iñigo Loyola might have thought necessary when dropping out from the University of Salamanca because of his lack of proficiency in Thomist philosophizing. The peripatetic connection in Ulysses was, of course, carefully studied and cogently analyzed by Erwin R. Steinberg[3] and others. We also may discover that during his one day Dublin adventure, Stephen Dedalus is in a continuous dialogue with the Stagirite. In recognition of this fact, our attention will concentrate on the poet's philosophical *extension* of what we all understand to be Aristotelian reasoning. Since he very early felt the need of such complement. We just have to remember Stephen "as a young man" treating his dean to the following ideas:

> "For my purpose I can work on at present by the light of one or two ideas of Aristotle and Aquinas. [...]
> "I need them only for my own use and guidance until I have done something for myself by their light. If the lamp smokes or smells I shall try to trim it."

Which he will do in Ulysses with the help of yet another philosopher - but not before fully using a few more ideas of Aristotle. And to comprehend this we, the readers, will have to complete the picture of the *poeta doctus* in a manner which may first seem - yet will turn out *not* to be - arbitrary.

This we will try to achieve by answering the question: where did Stephen find the two German words and to what extent are they relevant for the understanding of his intellectual personality? In most cases the interested critic or reader will try to infer (or rather conjecture) an answer from what has been identified as the *author's* readings. But this is not exactly what we are looking for. We want to find out what the character *in fabula* appears to have read. The question may be asked: can any book read by the character, but not by the author, affect the story? Indeed: is there such a thing as the "readings of a character" with which the author is not familiar? The answer has to start with the simple fact that no matter how "completely" the life of an author has been studied, everything, including his readings, will never be completely discovered. However, we know about the character all that is revealed in the story. Yet in order to fully understand him we have to make the same associations as he does. To make the same associations *he* does, *we* have to have in stock some of the information stored also in *his* mind which, however, may not always be revealed in a clear statement. But we may have a way around this. *We* may have some literary information or knowledge which is *logically(!) compatible* with an incomplete statement of the character in question - whose stock of knowledge we never share completely - and thus conjecture that our hero's frame of mind is affected by it. In our case, this will give us one of the *possible* traits in the portrait of Stephen. Such conjecture may be *plausible* yet not necessarily a substitute for a *true* inference. We know, of course, that true inferences cannot be made without the complete and unambiguous statement of all the premises - which is never the case in a novel. With all this in mind, we will come to the conclusion that the sequence of thoughts in which *nacheinander* and *nebeneinander* crop up is not in debt to chapters XVI-XVII of Lessing's Laokoon, which are completely off the stream of Stephen's thoughts, but - plausibly! - to Kant's *Kritik der reinen Vernunft*. And in a very significant way, as we will see.

The second major characteristic of Stephen Dedalus is revealed by the distinctive quality of his own *streams of thoughts* or *consciousness*. We know, of course, that also Leopold Bloom as several other characters in the novel reveal themselves to the reader through the peculiar variety of their *interior monologues*. However, Stephen, unlike Bloom, is also, and always, aware of the manner in which his continuous contact with the external world translates into a flow of consciousness. We may say that his is a *two level stream of consciousness*. First, there is the straight process from the perception/awareness of the external world to its translation into thought. And then, there is the awareness of this very process and its transformation into a higher level of consciousness. Thus the "second level" process follows and envelops the first one. And Stephen becomes preoccupied with finding out - is this a "third level"? - how all this comes about. Here he calls for the help of Aristotle and when this will prove not to be enough, he will try to complete the explanations of the Greek philosopher. With all this in mind we should attempt yet another reading of the here relevant sections from Ulysses.

An apology to the reader for some inevitable repetitions: we attempt to find out how Stephen *continues*, implicitly, what he explicitly states in the Joyce-reproduced portion of his stream of thoughts. Hence, we have to make clear first *that which is to be continued*. Such calls inevitably for some repetitions.

First: **Mainly the** *Nacheinander*

On a *first level*, Stephen will experience the very same world as others in the novel, yet often the filter of his memories will discriminate among impressions according to whether they connect or not his erudition. This is the way in which his perceptions become consciousness, thoughts. Everybody he meets, as everything he sees, hears or touches - the *same people and things* which might be met, or respectively seen, heard or touched by anybody else - is often associated with the teaching of some philosophical authority. Here comes in the *second (and third) level* of his consciousness: his philosophers are the source of teachings about how this process of perception-to-thought comes about and unfolds, and Stephen engages to test their instruction. We can follow thus the track of his reasoning as it is translated into quasi programmatic references to his principal guide, who is not one of the authorities of the turn of the century often quoted in the critical literature concerning those "streams of thought", but the one he names with Dante: *il mastro di color che sanno*, or "the teacher of [all] those who know". We don't have to "interpret" or conjecture. We are quite explicitly taught how to translate Stephen's experiences into a particular picture of the world by starting from his direct perceptions streaming through his mental screen shaped mainly by Aristotle. Thus we receive one *actual* picture of the many *potential* ones dormant in things, people, or events contacted. Every character in the story may actuate yet another *potential picture* latent in the same thing. Stephen reveals one of the many, but his particular role is also to reveal the mechanics of the process. Let's try to follow one of his exercises - with some inevitable repetitions.

Stephen, sitting one night in the *Biblothèque Sainte Geneviève*, where he was "sheltered from the sin of Paris", remembers teaching class in Dublin. It was about Milton's elegy in which the poet remembers a friend, Lycidas, who died while the boat in which he was crossing over to Ireland hit a rock and sunk. It was studied by the boys, while the teacher's mind was reflecting the verses as well as the faces and every movement of the students. We read first the Milton lines:

> "Weep no more, woeful shepherd, weep no more
> "For Lycidas, your sorrow, is not dead,
> "Sunk though he be beneath the watery floor...

Stephen, of course, knows the continuation of the verse to be quoted later. And if we want to know what *he* thinks, *we* will have to rally our own memory and recall a little bit more than initially quoted:

"So Lycidas sunk low, but mounted high
"Through the dear might of him that walked the waves."

Already after the first quoted fragment we learn about the thoughts which the poem occasions in the mind of our poet-teacher:

"It must be a movement then, an actuality of the possible as possible. Aristotle's phrase formed itself within the gabbled verses ..." [p.21]

The idea of "movement" - this time of Lycidas' *body* - is the actuality of the possible, but also carrying other, new, potentials. This is not all that clear. Therefore it is useful, before returning to the "*movement*" and following the indication of the above quotation, to first recall the teaching of the Stagirite about the Soul which is said to be:

"... first actuality of a natural body potentially possessing life." [*De Anima - On the Soul*, II, 1, 412a, 25][4]

We do not expect here any precise translation from the philosopher to the poet. And it may be that Milton has not considered explicitly the connection which cropped up in the mind of Stephen. But, then, it could just as well have been part of his thinking. Yet, in the case of Stephen these thoughts are part of his personality as we find out from his continuing reflections. If we read in *De Anima* that "matter is potentiality, form actuality" [II, 1, 412^a, 10] and further that the "soul is the actuality of the body" [II, 1, 412^a, 23], its form definition that is, then we comprehend Stephen's thoughts, and their consecution, as well. Or we may try, anyway. Namely if, as a *major premise*, we identify form with the actuality of "all that is", and take "soul as actuality of the body" for a *minor*, then we understand that:

"The soul is in a manner all that is: the form is the form of forms." [p.21]

231

We have bended a little the rules to obtain this syllogism but then, Stephen doesn't have to pass an undergraduate exam in Logic. He only has to testify for his thoughts. In this respect most interesting is the fact that he measures any of his ensuing contacts with his surroundings on the propositions of *De Anima*, and later, in one particular instance, on Kant's *Kritik der Reinen Vernunft*, or Critic of Pure Reason. Kant? Yes, quite distinctly, though the philosopher is not named. It may not be important - (what is important?) - but it could certainly be interesting to read, reread, the first three chapters of Ulysses as a literary illustration of Aristotle's treaties on the soul and some sections in his Metaphysics. Thereby we will also discover the methodological program of the entire novel: seeing, recording and shaping thoughts, and Stephen's manner of completing his teacher. With Kant's "intrusion", among others. Here is the well known example to be repeated and further examined. Walking on the beach, Stephen meditates:

> "Ineluctable modality of the visible: at least that if no more, thought through my eyes. Signature of things I am here to read, seaspawn , seawrack, the nearing tide, the rusty boot. *Snotgreen, bluesilver, rust: coloured signs. Limits of the diaphane.*" [p.31]

If it sounds familiar, it is not only because of Jakob Böhme's "*signatura rerum*", but mainly because you sometime read also this:

> "The visible, then, is colour, i.e. that which overlies what is in itself visible; by 'in itself' we mean not that the object is by its definition visible but that it has in itself the cause of visibility. Every colour can produce movement in that which is actually transparent, and it is its very nature to do so." [*On the Soul* II, 7, 418^a, 30]

This is not modern science, but it is no medieval mysticism either. The "diaphanous", the transparent, carries the color which, however, depends on the *body* which carries it as a potential:

> "Limits of the diaphane. But *he* [Aristotle] adds: bodies. Then he was aware of them bodies before of them coloured. How? By knocking his sconce against them sure." [p.42]

"Knocking his sconce against them" will be the movement to which we will have to return.[5] The philosopher's approach is to be repeated: he sees and touches. He offers a generalization of what will appear in the novel as particular experiences of individuals. But does he go far enough? What remains when we abstract from the visible? Aristotle, naturally, introduces the audible. But is this enough? Try an answer to this. Here is a trial in praxis:

> "Stephen closed his eyes to hear his boots crackling wrack and shells. You are walking through howsomever. I am, a stride at a time. *A very short space of time through very short times of space. Five, six: the Nacheinander.* Exactly: and that is the ineluctable modality of the audible." [p.42]

What has the *nacheinander* to do with the "ineluctable modality of the audible"? Just wait and see. All that we are told about happens during **time**: *nacheinander,*[one after another] and in **space**: *nebeneinander* [side by side]. Time and space are framing any movement. Yet only the *movement* is mentioned by the Stagirite, stressing that whatever is "audible" is so by movement; no sound without movement:

> "[because] that which produces the sound is blow. So if there is only one condition [body] present, there can be no sound; for the striker and the thing struck are two different things [such as the 'boots crushing' and the 'crackling wrack']; so that what produces the sound sounds against something else. And no blow occurs without movement." [*On the Soul*, II, 8, 419^b, 9-13]

Aristotle does not elaborate on movement's conditions. He does not mention that even *a very short space of time through very short times of space* refers to the mental frame of movement. For him time and space are just another couple of categories, some of lesser status, and not the frame of all perceptions. In the *Categories*, he takes them for granted as a simple matter of fact:

> "The rest, that is, time, place and state, are so clear that I need say no more than I said at the very beginning - that a state is intended by terms such as being 'shod', 'armed', and the like,

whereas place is intended by phrases like 'in the Lyceum' and so forth." [IX, 11b, 10-15][6]

Yet the assumption of such frame, independent and above categories, is necessary, and what follows now in Stephen's mind amounts to a Kantian intrusion in the Aristotelian discourse. As the boots moved on the sand and produced the sounds of "crushing crackling wrack", they moved not only *nacheinander* but *nebeneinander* as well:

"My two feet in his boots are at the end of his legs *nebeneinander*." [p.43]

Thus the *nacheinander* and the *nebeneinander* frame "the ineluctable modality of the audible"; they are not contrasted, as suggested in all references to Lessing pertaining to opposing forms of representation, but strictly connected as the time/space frame of any re-cognition.[7] It is as if Stephen had read - or developed by himself - the following ideas:

"*Denn das Zugleichsein oder Aufeinanderfolgen würde selbst nicht in die Wahrnehmung kommen, wenn die Vorstellung der Zeit nicht a priori zum Grunde lege. Nur unter deren Voraussetzung kann man sich vorstellen, das einiges zu einer und derselben Zeit (zugleich) oder in verschiedenen Zeiten (nacheinander) sei. [...] Verschiedene Zeiten sind nicht zugleich, sondern nacheinander ...* [Kant: Kritik der reinen Vernunft*, B 46-47][8] "For neither simultaneity nor succession would come to be perceived, were the representation [or intuition] of time not being given *a priori*. Only under this assumption can we perceive things as existing at the same time (*zugleich*-simultaneously) or at different times (*nacheinander*). [...] Different times are not simultaneous, but in succession [*nacheinander*] .."

These *Anschaungsformen*, or "forms of intuition" seem to be associated by Stephen - a philosophically lettered young man - as a complement to the Aristotelian theory of perception because

"... *damit gewisse Empfindungen auf etwas ausser mich bezogen werden* .... *imgleichen damit ich sie als ausser- und nebeneinander, mithin nicht bloss verschieden, sondern als in verschiedenen Orten vorstellen könne, dazu muss die Vorstellung des Raumes schon zum Grunde liegen.*"[*Kritik der reinen Vernunft*, B 38]

"... in order to have certain perceptions [sensations] associated with something outside me, ... and also [in order] to be able to perceive them separately and side-by-side [*nebeneinander*], that is not just different [between them] but also [situated] in different locations, we must already have the representation of space as a given."

By observation Stephen tries to reconstitute the theory with as many funny asides such as quoted above:

"My two feet in his boots are at the end of his legs, *nebeneinander*." [p.42]

Repeat the philosopher's lesson in an everyday walk: the peripatetic philosopher's in a peripatetic manner, and then go a stride further. A program for Stephen; a program for Joyce. To read "the signature of all things" as being *nebeneinander* are necessarily perceived *nacheinander*. And to follow how their *potential* as rough matter becomes *actual* thought, form.

Did Stephen read Kant? Well, for once, his usage of the two German terms is not simply coincidental. It has a perfect *Kantian* contextual justification; it is the time/space framework which follows as a next step in the reasoning about movement, which on its turn explains the sound made by the "boots crushing crackling wrack". (No Lessingian contrasting of poetry's *aufeinander* with the objects simultaneity, i.e. *nebeneinander*, as in painting.) And though Stephen may have never read Kant's *Kritik*, he could have had access to some of the countless popular presentations in German of the critical philosophy in which Kantian terminology was always faithfully employed. This vocabulary was stock-in-trade of such literature.

Remains the *Nebeneinander*

We stopped above at the "ineluctable modality of the audible". We remember that

> "Stephen closed his eyes to hear his boots crush crackling wrack and shells".[p.42]

i.e. to have his boots impinge upon the wrack and shells to produce *sound* which comes about only by *movement*. But farther in the paragraph he becomes scared:

> "Open your eyes. No. Jesus! If I fell over the cliff that beetles o'er his base, fell through the *nebeneinander* ineluctably." [p.43]

Now what should this mean? The fact that Hamlet (I, V, 70-71) was also warned against falling over the "cliff that beetles o'er his base" does not yet provide an explanation, but just another instance illustrating the meaning of the *nebeneinander*.[9] We may rather have to try an explanation fitting the earlier suggested philosophical context: a young peripatetic philosopher, also a poet, tries to confront and test the lines dispensed by his *mastro* at the Lyceum, in a controlled, practical, experience. First, he associates the concepts of *De Anima* with what he sees. Then, the solid things are perceived by the senses, as if "knocking his sconce against them", as the master did. Yet, third, any such act is *movement* leading further to *the audible*. So the audible is conditioned by movement, being "impossible without a movement from place to place"; or, may be, caused by movement. The Stagirite may [just may] imply that here *post hoc*, that is *nacheinander*, is also *propter hoc*. But then, does movement exist in the first place? We know that, among others, the Eleats have questioned it - [remember Zeno's *aporias*?] - and Aristotle was not happy with them. Furthermore, any philosophical view denying the principle of contradiction, such as the impossibility of a *tertium* to the movement/non-movement alternative, was unacceptable. Can movement/non-movement be true simultaneously? Can it be indifferent whether we move or not? The practical behavior of humans disproves it:

"Otherwise, why does a man walk to Megara and not stay home, when he thinks he ought to make the journey? Why does he not walk early one morning into a well or ravine, if he comes to it, instead of clearly guarding against doing so, thus showing that he does not think that it is equally good and not good to fall in?" [Metaphysics, IV, ch.4. 1008^b 14-17][10]

Thus every wayfarer should learn from Aristotle that if the principle of contradiction holds, and they disregard it when choosing their actions, they could easily fall "through the *nebeneinander* ineluctably", which is any "well or ravine" or some "cliff that beetles o'er his base".

Other Uses of the Terms

Painting represents things in their coincidence, *nebeneinander*, while poetry in their succession, *aufeinander* - such goes the argument of Lessing. Yet we have to be more specific as the German poet indeed is. There are two kinds of successions in poetry: that of the text and that of the reader. If the text contains a simple description of an assemblage of things, these will still be *nebeneinander*, except that the reader has to take cognizance of them *aufeinander*, i.e. during the time framed process of reading. [In a painting the same things can be seen *nebeneinander*, simultaneously - if you are not very picky in matters physical optics.] Lessing does not seem to particularly favor plain descriptions; they may not be poetical. Therefore he thinks that a good description can be given gradually by telling a tale in which the things in question are involved and recognized as their various aspects emerge in time, in succession, i.e. *aufeinaderfolgend* [not necessarily heaped *aufeinander*.] But all this is a far cry from the physical perception-experience of Stephen where the terms discussed have a different contextual justification. They refer to experiencing the external world and not an artistic work imitating it.

The *Nebeneinander* and *Nacheinander* have been properly employed, and often, also in classical philosophical scholarship in the days of Stephen Dedalus (and James Joyce) and Leopold Bloom. The example to be quoted will be relevant to such literature but also suggests the essential difference from the interesting usage of Lessing.

Just consider that Stephen, intensely interested in classical philosophy, Aristotle in particular, reviews the relevant literature of his own time [as his author did in Trieste?] and chances upon the *Griechische Denker* of Theodor Gomperz. In chapter 9 of the sixth book, he will find the author discussing the fact that the two greatest philosophers of the Greeks, Plato and Aristotle, have neglected the "norms [we would call them "laws"] of the natural process" (*"Normen des Naturgeschehens"*), commending at the same time some of the pre-Socratics as not being guilty of such negligence. Still Gomperz finds an excuse for the two great men: they seem to reflect an essential characteristic of the history of ancient science, and of all science, as a matter of fact, namely that

> *"... die Wissenschaften, deren Gegenstand das Nebeneinander der Dinge ist, ungleich früher zu einem hohen Grad der Vollkommenheit gediehen als die Disziplinen, die das Nacheinander der Vorgänge, vor allem mittels des physikalischen Versuches ergründen."*
> "... those sciences which have the side-by-side appearance of things [*das Nebeneinander der Dinge*] as their object, have advanced earlier to a higher degree of perfection, then those disciplines which investigate *the succession of processes* [das Nacheinander der Vorgänge], mainly by means of physical experiments."[11]

Thus Stephen could find here, in the context of the Greek philosophy so familiar to him, the terms which, though common in general German usage, were employed earlier when Kant was defining the framework of world perception.

All the above mentioned connections are *possible*, not necessary. Yet they fit into the context of Stephen's silent deliberations in *Proteus*. They offer one possible consistent completion of his thinking, in logical *nacheinander*, avoiding any *durcheinander*, [or upside down] of references to who else used such and such terms. So, by placing the thoughts of the hero in the context of his potential readings, we achieve one *actual* intellectual portrait of the artist as a mature poet, from among several *potential* ones. Since, in their tumultuous stream, not all formless potentials are given to become actual form.

NOTES

1. Fritz Senn: *Aesthetic Theories*. Note in James Joyce Quarterly, vol.2, No.2, Winter, 1965.

2. The fact that Joyce or his character may have had doubts about the relevance of Lessing's "aesthetic theory" would not, in itself, disprove the claims of Fritz Senn. In this connection and in consideration of the philosophical implications of the present discussion, we would like to remind the reader that the term "aesthetics" or "aesthetic theory" has at least two different employments, both known to Joyce and Stephen but, somehow, often escaping the attention of the litterateur. This is most important to realize regarding the German philosophical context of the fragment discussed. When we read in a learned study that "Stephen's whole theory of aesthetic forms ... is German to the core, deriving from the tradition that includes Lessing, August and Friedrich Schlegel, Kant, Schelling, and Hegel etc. etc.", then we should not forget that in the particular case of Kant there is the "transcendental aesthetics" which is a branch of philosophy concerned with the way in which the perception of the external world by our senses is transformed into thought by the human mind. And this has a lot to do with the Stephen of the *Proteus*, as to be shown. (The quotation is from "The Aesthetic Theory and the Critical Writings" by Robert Scholes and Marlena G. Corcoran in *A Companion to Joyce Studies*, Z. Bowen and J.F. Carens editors, Greenwood Press, Westport Connecticut, 1984.) - It seems that

the "Lessing connection" has taken a strong hold on the minds of many Joyce commentators. An example would be an article which discusses a book by Wyndham Lewis criticizing Joyce's time/space approach. It is "Time and Space (with the emphasis on the conjunction): Joyce's Response to Lewis" by George Otte, in the *JJQ*, vol.22, Nr.3, 1985. We read there about a relevant section in Proteus: "In the episode's introductory overture - [to be sure: not in any concluding *overture*! - T.S.] - we find Aristotle alluded to [as in 'Bald he was and a millionaire, *mastro di color che sanno*'], Lessing implicated [most obviously by the terms *nacheinander* and *nebeneinander*] ..." "Implicated" by whom? Because the quoted terms do not, certainly not "most obviously", implicate Lessing. There is another implication. Please follow the argument in the text.

3. Erwin R. Steinberg: *The Stream of Consciousness and Beyond in Ulysses*, University of Pittsburgh Press, 1973. Contextually interesting is also: *Cognitive Process in Writing*, Lee W Gregg and Erwin R. Steinberg editors, L. Erlbaum Associates, Hillsdale N.J., 1980.

4. All quotations from Aristotle's *On the Soul* are according to the translation of W.S. Hett in the Heinemann-Harvard 1957 edition.

5. The reader who may have encountered in some critical writings, as this writer did, observations claiming that in Proteus the contradiction between Platonic "essence" and the world of perception may be investigated, should recall once again that "he [Aristotle] adds: bodies". It is "them bodies" one is aware of before "them coloured". Because, you see, nobody "knocks his sconce" against preexisting Platonic essences. So, please, remember: for Aristotle, and Stephen Dedalus, the *phenomenon* originates in *things*. N.B. This was a piece of the stream of consciousness of the author of this essay.

6. According to the translation by Harold P. Cooke in the 1983 printing of *The Categories* in the Heinemann-Harvard edition.

7. Recall again and again the allusion to the experience of the *joint existence of time and space*: "I am a stride at a time. A very short space of time through very short times of space."

8. All German quotations from Kant are according to the 1956 Felix Meiner, Hamburg, edition.

9. Shakespeare just supplied a good phrase. Doesn't he ever so often? But there is nothing "Shakespearean" here to concern us.

10. According to the translation by Hugh Tredennick in the 1961 printing of *The Metaphysics* in the Heinemann-Harvard edition.

11. Theodor Gomperz: *Griechische Denker,* [most recent edition in] Eichorn Verlag, Frankfurt 1996, vol. III, p.65-66.

ESSAY NO. 8

The Game of Cracked Looking Glasses Played in Episodes of Joyce's Ulysses

For Stephen Dedalus:

> "Drawing back and pointing, Stephen said with bitterness: 'It is a symbol of Irish art. The cracked lookingglass of a servant.'"

For Leopold Bloom:

> «... les hommes méconnus se vengent de l'humilité de leur position par la hauteur de leur coup d'oeil.»
> [.. disregarded people avenge the humbleness of their status by the haughtiness of their eye's glance."] (Balzac)

A Little Theory

I only hope that old fashioned schoolmasterly pedantry will not be reproached to him who tries to assess how Joyce measures up to the poetical standards outlined by Aristotle. Such reproach, whether justified or debatable in the case of other poets, is out of place when the work under scrutiny is part of a long, almost continuous struggle and argument with Aristotle's Poetics and several other writings of the Stagirite. It is the reader's neglect of Aristotle which often limits access to some of the finest pieces of modern writing; and this is, sometimes, the case with even the most conscientious readers of Joyce's Ulysses as well. Most obvious is, of course, the frequent recurrence of references to, and discussion of, Aristotelian principles in philosophical excursi embedded in the narrative. At first reading, this seems to be hardly in strict abidance by the principle according to which in an imitated action "the structural union of the parts" would be impaired by "unnecessary" episodes or essayistic asides: "For a thing whose presence or absence makes no visible difference is not an organic part of a whole" [Poetics, VIII, 4]. Thus we may be tempted to belatedly question, among others, the usefulness of the library discussions in part II chapter 6 of Ulysses. Yet, thinking it over carefully, we should change our mind. If we were to segregate those discussions from the novel, we might gain, perhaps, fragments for essays or scholarly lectures, but at the same time we would certainly damage the novel itself by depriving the portrait of Stephen Dedalus, as a maturing artist, of some essential traits, indispensable to understand his actions. A hero of tragedy or comedy introduces himself by *speech*, which explains often his actions. And an orthodox peripatetic would ultimately remain entangled in his own confusion concerning the difference between rhetoric and plot-construction. The lover speaks of love; the warrior of war; the *Malade imaginaire* lectures about his imagined sickness, Falstaff about highway robbery, Richard III about his own and general wickedness; and Stephen Dedalus, most naturally, about poetry and poetics as he learned it from Aristotle and repeated it with Aquinas during his college days, when he acquired the subtle art of putting through an argument - and to "unsheathe [his] dagger definitions" (II.6.) - from the soldiers of Saint Ignatius. (Twice, during that day of his life which is reported by Joyce, did Stephen, in the heat of a discussion, invoke the help of the founder of the Order of Jesus: "Ignatius Loyola, make haste to help me!" Though, in all fairness, the reader may be confused about what help should be rendered and by which Loyola. Was it that Iñigo Loyola, the dropout from the University of Salamanca, ruled by insight and revelations, whose lack of proficiency in Thomist philosophizing would have disqualified him as an adviser in Aristotelian wisdom? Or was it the one upon whom the doctors of the University of Paris bestowed, rather reluctantly, the title of *magister artium*? Well, probably the latter, as suggested by many explicit and implicit references in the novel.)

Yet how does Ulysses live up to other peripatetic requirements? If we substitute "Comedy" for "Tragedy", the latter being inferior to the former according to Joyce, then Ulysses fulfils both the basic structural requirements for epic poetry *and* for theater. It most definitely is long, as obligate for the former, yet it satisfies in an amazing and fascinating way what was thought to be mandatory only on the stage, were the play is supposed "as far as possible, to confine itself to a single revolution of the sun, or but slightly to exceed this limit; whereas the epic action has no limit in time" [Poetics V.4]. Indeed, Ulysses starts at breakfast time, but the next breakfast is only talked about; when you finish the book - ("during a single revolution of the sun"?) - the next breakfast still *will* be served. And yet, several worlds have revealed themselves in so short a time.

And what about the excess of episodes? Are they not of the kind which unnecessarily burden the plot? Not to speak of the complete or unfinished stories, some of them small masterpieces in their own right. If we were to pluck one or the other off the main story, the plot may not really fall apart, and perhaps we may get a better "disciplined" literary work. However, neither does the underlying, supposedly austere work of art disappear in the garb of "inessentials". There is no need to resent these episodes and no need to abandon them. They are, sometimes, expressions of that urge of the poet which Goethe called *"Lust zu Fabulieren"*, i.e. the joy of telling stories, and which offers pleasure to the reader as well. And in the Ulysses they are a lot more; because it is the first great novel in which the unity of plot comes about, without a main concatenating action, as a mosaic of episodes. A preliminary warning against a possible misreading of this apparently bold statement: the novel is not simply viewed as a *frame for episodes*. It exists as a dense web of such to reflect the peculiar epistemology of the author and his characters. Epistemology? Yes. This should follow from the arguments developed in sequence and the exemplary cases quoted from the work. Since every section, episode, or argument quoted, is meant as illustration of Joyce's method and general concept, as once said: "Parts constitute a whole as far as they have a common end" [Paris Notebook, 25 March, 1903]. No summary of the novel will be given, only approaches for an assumed *second reading* will be put forward.

Perception, Reflection, Story

This risky definition of "Ulysses" as the first major novel in which the unity of the plot comes about by the assemblage of a mosaic of episodes, needs to be defended in a more elaborate fashion; especially against many of the widely held opinions on what is to be viewed as original, i.e. as a "first" in it. Trying to extract from the many writings on the subject a (statistically) consensual characterization of what constitutes the excellence of Joyce's novel, we will obtain the hypostasis of two aspects, most frequently cited as essential. The first refers to the content of the story as connected to its purported Homeric paragon; the second addresses the technique of narration, specifically the use of the characters' *stream of thoughts* or *consciousness* as its main medium.

As for the first widely quoted aspect, I would take upon myself the risk of claiming that we could quietly neglect it along with some of the scholarship cast in parallels between Homer's epopee and Joyce's novel which, though obvious in their very broad outlines, have no more than casual significance for "Ulysses". To see the point in this remark, test yourself: shut out from your memory everything you ever read in Homer and see whether Joyce's Ulysses is still meaningful to you. And should you have trouble reading Joyce's story, it is not because you neglected Homer and the celebrated scholarly associations. It is rather the *technical novelties* employed by Joyce in telling the tale of the wanderings of Stephen Dedalus and Leopold Bloom which have to be given special attention to help the reader overcome his difficulties. Also the philosophical references which crop up in the mind of Stephen are an indispensable element of the plot's construction. The experienced World "streams" through the conscience of the characters. But each and every Conscience is a passive one, given at the moment when the story starts - and when the "streaming" sets on.

There is, of course, a lot more to the "stream of thoughts" issue. It is not to be forgotten that this device is not for the first time used in story-telling; and though it *provides for the first time the main building blocks of an entire novel* it is the peculiar mode of combination of these blocks which makes for the excellence of this particular plot and that celebrated "first" in literary history. (For those who can read German I would warmly recommend the *Leutnat Gustl* of Arthur Schnitzler. The "stream of thoughts" of the *Leutnant* is a masterpiece of the genre. And you may also find a translation.)

When a personage in "Ulysses" steps on the stage, so to say, he doesn't act. He watches others acting, and what he sees - always by peering in his "cracked looking glass" reflecting those others - and comments upon silently within his mind, is what we read. Before Joyce and as far back as Homer, a story's *personae* participated in an action, intrigue, scheme, within the plot; and we found out about their adventures while "watching" *them*. Now we also find out about character "A" by using character "B" as a mirror reflecting him; and we learn about the actions of B by looking in the "mirrors" of A, C... etc. We also experience the world and the drama of those who walk about or cross the Dublin stage through the recordings, on the pages of the book, of their streams of conscience.

The Game of Mirrors

To explain this I will reach back to the Socratian metaphor of a moving mirror as paragon of the futility of "imitation", i.e. art. By changing the value of this metaphor, from negative, as it was advanced by Socrates, into a positive heuristic allegory, we may gain the correct approach towards the novel. Let us try it.

Any story, naturally, implies the separation of the storyteller from his characters and their action. Not very much is changed in this respect when the tale is recounted in the first person: what we read or hear is always from the fixed or moving vantage point of *one* story teller. When he moves, the vantage point changes. *His* vantage point; and the reader beholds what the author purportedly sees. It is essentially that what we can see in *one* mirror. Yet the separation between the writer and the viewed "object" i.e. characters and their actions *and* thoughts, was not always perfect. Indeed, fine writing has always aimed at overcoming this limitation of perspective by all kinds of attempts to "imitate" the view from "inside" the story, i.e. from the perspective of some of the implicated characters. Their direct speech or their "interior monologues" were a manner frequently adopted to reveal a perspective other than that of the storyteller yet, of course, "imitated" by him. The "stream of consciousness" representation is a step ahead in that it "imitates" primarily those thoughts which the characters would not communicate in direct speech. It means that the writer's mirror returns now not only the view of things or persons and their movement but also the reflections of another mirror. If we look into the writer's mirror, another mirror's reflections, purportedly inaccessible at first, will become visible.

A novel usually offers a plot of interacting personages. Joyce's "Ulysses" instead reproduces the crisscrossing of their streams of consciousness. If consciousness is reflection or mirroring of the external world as sifted through the *a priori* given memory filter of each character, then their blend of thoughts can be viewed as a complicated system of mirroring.

A mirror may choose and change angles, can move around things, record and - start reasoning. One mirror. But then there are several mirrors which may choose and change angles, move around things, often the same, record and - reflect each other. You look in one of them and see what the others reflect and what may not be visible for the direct sight. A complicated game of reflections sets on and the artist discovers their geometric order.

Thus two men of widely differing backgrounds, walk out one morning into the streets of Dublin, move from place to place and, until they meet to face and reflect each other, they reflect the world roundabout; and the "world", other men and women in the same city, reflect them. But they not only see each other, they also spy (or remember having seen and spied) on each other. (Want another metaphor? Think of a periscope.) They peep in each others backyard but reveal *directly* very little of their own.

Take Leopold Bloom, for example. The best naturalist novelist, possibly some elder contemporary of Joyce, had he decided to tell Bloom's story, would first have given some physical description of him, then told us about his family and/or general background, which information would have been properly mixed with the writer's own philosophy; then a small set of events lived by Bloom during the day would have been built up with descriptions and conversations leading to dramatic tensions and one sort or another of denouement. And it could have been a masterpiece. If the short story genre had been selected ("within one revolution of the sun") then, among others, we could have seen Bloom walking on the seashore, engaging a conversation with some pretty girl - who is crippled. Had Dr. Freud already spread his teaching, a number of other avenues could have been developed. Either a love story with the lame girl - had our writer been Stefan Zweig. Or one could have added Bloom's frustration for not being able to gratify his wife's, Molly's, desires, and satisfy her artistic interests as well. In the meanwhile we may also have been told the parallel story of

Molly engaged in forbidden love with her impresario; possibly all phases of it for the reader's enlightenment.

Yet in all these stories an author would have given his view of Bloom, from his, the author's angle. Bloom would also have had views, which he may have expressed according to the wishes of his inventor; should the latter not have chosen telling us first about them "on his own", so we should know why a man with such and such views is expected to act in one instead of another way. Or, again, why a man to whom such and such things happened is expected to hold one instead of another view. But we will always have to build up our view of the man and his world by having to follow the moving mirror carried by the author himself. How to see what is not reflected in the mirror? By placing another mirror, facing the sight invisible to us, and then reflecting it in the first mirror. We could multiply the mirrors facing one another from different angles and we would get something which can be a physical metaphor to Joyce's novel.

There is a catch to the mirror metaphor: each and every one of the numerous mirrors is the construction of the same author. So, in order to have such a literary construction succeed, the writer must have seen the world from as many points of view with equally sharp eyes. Thus, to have this peculiar art-form successfully cultivated, talent is not sufficient, neither *own* experience, however rich and varied. A very special sort of empathy with the experiences of *others* is required to convey us their record: you have to be several mirrors simultaneously which reflect one another. Balzac knew many; he saw through poor père Goriot, *he* was amazed by Vautrin, *he* dissected with his sharp lancet the motifs of Tascheron, *he* sympathized with Lucien Charon, *he* laughed at and dreaded Nucingen and *he* told us all *he*, Balzac, knew about them and so many others. And only seldom, very seldom, did we find out how they were thinking of one another - (Vautrin and especially Gobseck are the major exceptions, the latter being a path breaking instance) - but in a way always recordable by the outside observer. Joyce *knew* many and *was*, amazingly, many. He didn't know only Stephen Dedalus. But he knew quite well something most unlikely: a *Kaiserlicher und Königlicher* Jew, indeed, to be more precise, a *Magyar Kiralyi Zsidó* (i.e. a Royal Hungarian Jew); he seems to have known him from *inside*. Not from *outside* as Bloom was seen by Stephen Dedalus. But Stephen has never seen the World, i.e. Dublin, through the eyes of Bloom, or of anybody else for that matter, but Joyce obviously tried and often succeeded.

The gallery of individuals whose eyes Joyce has "borrowed" is incredible, and we will have to stop later on some aspects of their "technique of seeing". We should first dwell on a significant instance of the Joycean "world construction" to explain and justify the change of accents in this reading.

The Facing Mirrors - I.

The examples chosen for this discussion, as will be seen, are not arbitrary, but the order of their discussion may be, though not according to this reader's/writer's own "stream of consciousness" (some moments of which may be inserted in square brackets within quotations). Let us start with Leopold Bloom.

Bloom's complete police file type definition which is given only in the third part, is good to be recalled (since we go through the book, now, for the second time - don't we?):

> "Bloom, only born male transubstantial heir of Rudolf Viràg (subsequently Rudolf Bloom) of Szombathely [translates: Sabbath-town, but the city really exists -T.S.], Vienna, Budapest, Milan, London and Dublin [the wandering Jew - eh?] and of Ellen Higgins [Ruth or Jezebel?], second daughter of Julius Higgins (born Károly) and Fanny Higgins (born Hogarty)" [p.558]

And further we find out that Bloom was baptized no less than three times:

> "by the reverend Mr. Gilmer Johnston M.A., alone in the protestant church of Saint Nicholas Without, Coombe; by James O'Connor, Philip Gilligan and James Fitzpatrick, together under a pump in the village of Swords; and by the reverend Charles Malone C.C., in the church of the three patrons, Rathgar". [p.558]

Thus Leopold Bloom was most of his life a Christian of various denominations. Recounting earlier, but still in the third part, that he was insulted and molested by an individual for his jewishness, Bloom explains to Stephen:

"..I, without deviating from plain facts in the least, told him his God, I mean Christ, was a Jew too, and his family, like me, though in reality I'm not" [p.525]

So we shouldn't doubt: no deviations from plain facts occurred! Except that it will not be easy to find out what the plain facts were. We have to place a mind-recorder inside Bloom's skull and follow him on his daily adventure, learning from the recordings about his encounters and subsequent thought associations.

After performing his morning routine, Bloom leaves home for shopping, and after a short stopover at the Post Office! - remember the fancifully sentimental epistolary exchange of "Henry Flower" with a named Martha Clifford? - he enters the church of All Hollows through "the open backdoor"! Where else? Why? To pray? For the time being he assesses, "mirrors", facts which produce several revealing thought reactions *not likely to be expressed in direct speech:*

Fact: a poster calling "save China's millions" noticed by Bloom;

Reflection: "Wonder how they explain it to the heathen Chinee. Prefer an ounce of opium". [Yes sir, obviously only in the West is religion - according to Karl Marx's dictum - "the opium for the people". In China it may be that opium is the Christianity of the "heathen Chinee".] [p.65]

And then, entering the church and watching the service:

Fact: "the priest bent down to put *it* into her mouth, murmuring all the time. Latin."

Reflection cum **comments**: "The next one. Shut your open mouth. What? *Corpus*. Body. Corpse. Good idea the Latin". [p.66]

Fact: "He stood aside watching their blind masks pass down the aisle, one by one, and seek their places". [*He* stood aside. It was "*their* blind masks" which passed down the aisle.]

Reaction: "Something like those mazzoth... Look at them. Now I bet it makes them happy. Lollipop. It does". [p.66]

Quite obviously the associations are similar to those which old man Rudolf Virág (Rezsö), as we will know him, would also have made. Mazzoth! Yet still: it is not *the* mazzoth but *"those mazzoth"* which "makes *them* feel happy". And it is *they* who

> "then feel like one family party. Same in theatre, all in the same swim. They do. I'm sure of that. Not so lonely. In our [read: their] confraternity." [p.66]

Bloom knows, of course, about the Church. Here is an adopted outsider's cool assessment of facts:

> "Wonderful organization, certainly, goes like a clockwork. Everyone wants to. Then I will tell you all. Penance. Punish me, please" [p.68]

But he does not participate:

> "Then all settle down on their knees again and he sat back quietly in his bench".

They knelt in front of *their* Savior (*"your* God") but *he sat back* and watched what was going on within their isle. He was outside but with an eager interest in the islanders. In all their variety: when he continues his walk he will arrive to a point where he will recall:

> "Huguenot churchyard near there. Visit some day." [p.68]

Bloom comes from an isle; a tiny one in an archipelago of many isles. And so does Stephen. The view on and from these isles changes with the beholder. Their *views* plus their *memories* define what they are. This time let's see Stephen Dedalus remembering having peered over to the reserve where Bloom was supposedly coming from. When Mr. Deasy, the headmaster of the school where Stephen is a teacher, treats him with an anti-Semitic tirade, images of the past suddenly loom up: Stephen remembered as he saw *them* doing something what the like Mr. Deasy might (and often do) call *their* true way of worshiping. It was not in a Synagogue. Yet it still is symmetrically suggestive of Bloom's visit to All Hollows:

> "On the steps of the Paris Stock Exchange the goldskinned men quoting prices on their gemmed fingers. Gabbles of geese. They swarmed loud, uncouth about the *temple*[!], their heads thick-plotting under maladroit silk hats. Not theirs: these clothes, this speech, these gestures. Their full slow eyes belied the words, the gestures eager and unoffending, but knew the rancours massed about them and knew their zeal was vain. Vain patience to heap and hoard. Time surely would scatter all. A hoard heaped by the roadside: plundered and passing on. Their eyes knew the years of wandering and, patient, knew the dishonors of their flesh." [p.28]

Stephen sees. *Them*. From without. Everybody sees everybody else, naturally, from without and tries to re-compose the "within" from what the surface betrays. As far as this is possible. What is missing from the picture is added by musing over the impression. Stephen does it just as Bloom. Also in the class room. A page from the algebra book of a not very bright yet kind student engenders the following "stream" of ideas in Stephen:

> "Across the page the symbols moved in grave morrice, in the mummery of their letters, wearing quaint caps of squares and cubes. Give hands, traverse, bow to partner: so: imps of fancy of the Moors. Gone too from the world, Averroes and Moses Maimonides, dark men in mien movement, *flashing in their mocking mirrors the obscure soul of the world,* a darkness shining in brightness which brightness could not comprehend." [p.23]

Never mind that those "symbols [moving] in a grave morrice" are the invention of a Frenchman of the late sixteenth century, it is the "dark men in mien movement", the two of them, who are remembered. Why? Mostly because of their "mocking mirrors" in which they are "flashing ... the obscure soul of the world". Mirrors again. Mocking mirrors. A little bit like Bloom's on whom the mirror metaphor is so often, and quite explicitly, applied by Joyce. Bloom: a mirror whose surface is cut and polished by the memories it bears. Thus when, at some point, he rehearses his childhood memories:

> "... Leopold as he sits there, ruminating, chewing the cud of reminiscences, that stayed agent of publicity and holder of a modest substance in the funds. He is young Leopold, as in a retrospective arrangement, *a mirror within a mirror (hey presto!) he beholdeth himself.* [...] *But, hey presto, the mirror is breathed on and the young knighterrant recedes, shrivels, to a tiny speck within the mist.*" [p.337]

Yet, there is little doubt, that the *little speck* never disappears. It will remain structural part of the sieve through which the impressions stream when becoming consciousness.

The Facing Mirrors - II.

In the third part, after Stephen and Bloom will meet, the infinite sequence of the reciprocally reflective pictures of two facing mirrors, is outlined in one of those question/answer type of catechistic characterizations, which reads:

> "Did either openly allude to their racial difference?
> "Neither.
> "What, reduced to their simplest reciprocal form, were Bloom's thoughts about Stephen's thoughts about Bloom and Bloom's thoughts about Stephen's thoughts about Bloom's thoughts about Stephen?
> "He thought that he thought that he was a Jew whereas he knew that he knew that he was not." [p.557-558]

(Notice that there is no enquiry starting at *Stephen's thoughts about Bloom's thoughts about Stephen*. There is a break in the pattern of questioning/answering, in this chapter! It may be that such preoccupation with the interlocutor's thoughts is characteristic only of those who "knew the rancors massed about them" and whose "eyes knew the years of wandering". But this is dangerous thinking: it is "interpretation". Let's continue reading again, that is more carefully, what is *in* the text.)

Straight reading of this reduction of thoughts "to their simplest reciprocal form" is a bit confusing. So let us try to spell it out in easily tractable symbols of the algebraic kind. Student Sargent may have had trouble with it, but we are better, though probably less kind. Let S stand for "Stephen" and B for "Bloom". A thought of either of them is:

$$S(T), \text{ i.e. "Stephen thinks that T", and}$$
$$B(T), \text{ i.e. "Bloom thinks that T"}$$

where we may substitute for T the particular symbol of a specific thought or class of thoughts. For example:

$B(S)$ is "Bloom's thoughts about Stephen"; $S(Jb)$ is "Stephen thinks that Bloom is a Jew".

Now, "Bloom's thoughts about Stephen's thoughts about Bloom" writes:

$B(S(B))$

And "Bloom's thoughts about Stephen's thoughts about Bloom's thoughts about Stephen" writes:

$B(S(B(S)))$

But this may, of course, go on and on, such that in the potentially endless series, just as the endlessly repetitive pictures in two facing mirrors:

$B(S(B(S(B(.....$

We have to apply a cut at some point - if we want to have a story. And, in fact, B and S also stop at a point: they cannot avoid the limitations of the human mind. The best chess players couldn't.

Important is to recall that we may cut only somewhere on the right of the series, as we did so far, never the first item on the left. For example we may transform

B(S(B(S(B(....

into

B(S(B)) or B(S(B(S)))

but not into

S(B(S(B(....

by abandoning the first "B("; because that would be tantamount with "the other mirror", of the two very subjective ones, being put at the beginning of the thoughts. So we have only the representation of Bloom's viewing of Stephen. Thus:

"He [B] *thought* that he [S] *thought* that he [B] was a jew", i.e.: B(S(Jb))

being confronted (by substituting "*thought*" with "*knowledge*") with

"He [B] *knew* that he [S] *knew* that he [B] was not", i.e.: B(S(B(-Jb)))

shows that Bloom recognizes the contradiction in his and Stephen's presumed picture about himself, as reflected in what he "thought" in opposition to what he "knew" (and knew that S knew that....etc.). But the contradiction between (Jb) and (Jb), the negation of (Jb), is what Bloom's story is all about.

This instance is also paradigmatic for the novel's approach: the characters "see" and spy on *themselves* in the "mirror" offered by somebody else's personality. But a real mirror on the wall offers itself also to Bloom as an instrument of self-reflection, contemplation. It reflects the objects around itself, various matrimonial gifts, and Bloom sees them in it. Then:

"What composite asymmetrical image in the mirror then attracted his attention?
"The image of a solitary (ipsorelative) mutable (aliorelative) man.

"What final visual impression was communicated to him by the mirror?

"The optical reflection of several inverted volumes improperly arranged and not in the order of their common letters with scintillating titles on the two bookshelves opposite." [581]

The library: what our heroes read is part of their personality; the books are used to characterize them. And the mirror, once again, is not simply a metaphor but an instrument of discovery.

All these are not plain, clear mirrors, but biased ones, like the broken one friend Mulligan held out to Stephen in the first chapter:

"Look at yourself, he said, you dreadful bard." [p.6]
"Drawing back and pointing, Stephen said with bitterness:
"It is a symbol of Irish art. *The cracked lookingglass of a servant.*" [p.6]

It is the pictures reflected by such cracked looking-glasses which are collected in Ulysses, and it remains for the reader to figure out the rules of that peculiar optical geometry with the help of which the "true", underlying, matters of fact can be reconstructed. A few more exemplary exercises may clarify this point.

Bloom's Thoughts and his Cracked Looking Glass

Ulysses is a dense web of interlaced threads. None is, or only few are superfluous. Yet the whole cannot be comprehended without specifically identifying each. Still, pursuing each line separately means missing out on the connective webs. Pursuing simultaneously all is, at first, impossible. Repetitive reading is the way of not only identifying new threads but also detecting connections between those already discovered. And gaining new insights. Let's follow again some of the old, often discussed, threads and try to find out about more connections.

Bloom's obsession with his origin has frequently been commented upon. The highly perfected "inside picture" which Joyce has given of a person so utterly remote from his, Joyce's, background, has yet never been properly appreciated, nor the *technical devices specific for the character* which he employed, adequately analyzed. The Bloom-Joyce discussion in expert literature centers often around personal matters and gossip: literary gossip supplemented by some small talk material collected during scholarly trips to Trieste, Zurich, Paris, etc. Whom was Bloom fashioned after? Was it Ettore (better: Aron Hector) Schmitz - Italo Svevo? Or was it the father of that Amalia Popper, secretly (secretly?) loved by "Giacomo" Joyce? Because, according to Richard Ellmann, *signor* Leopoldo Popper "may have furnished the first name of Bloom". (He may, in fact, have been the source of more than the name. We read in James Joyce's "Giacomo Joyce": "Her father and his son in a carriage. They have owls eyes and owls' wisdom. Owlish wisdom stares from their eyes brooding upon the lore of their *Summa contra Gentiles* ... Ay, they love their country when they are quite sure which country it is".) But then, if you open a Budapest address directory from 1908, as I did, you will find quite a few Jews called Leopold, i.e. Lipót, as well as Rudolf/Rezsö. It was fashionable in the Hapsburg Empire, that after the 1867 "*Ausgleich*", many a Hungarian Jew honored the ruling house by borrowing the first names of some of its members. So why does it have to be signor Popper? And if so: why is it important? And if we want to conjecture about the name, can't we find anything in the book itself? Item: Bloom went to a used book dealer to find some reading for his wife Molly:

> "He laid both books aside and glanced at the third: Tales of the Ghetto by Leopold von Sacher Masoch. - That I had, he said, pushing it by." [p.193]

He had it, the book of this Leopold (a gentile for a change) whose name is at the origin of the term "masochism", not least because of the quoted tales which Bloom "has had". But is it essential of what pieces is Bloom composed of? Remember Balzac:

> «*La littérature se sert du procédé qu'emploit la peinture, qui, pour faire une belle figure, prend les mains de tel modèle, les pieds de tel autre, la poitrine de celui-ci, les épaules de celui-là. L'affaire du peintre est de donner la vie à ces membres choisis et de la rendre probable*» (*Cabinet des antiques*). [Or, a little freely translated: "Literature uses the same procedures as the painter who, to make a nice figure, uses the hands

of one model, the legs of another one, the chest of this one and the shoulders of that one. The job of the painter is to lend life to these selected parts of the body, and make them verisimilar".]

It is irrelevant where the composing elements of Bloom are coming from; and irrelevant - though not uninteresting - the history or the plain gossip, which is used to trace their origin. Important is what the composition has yielded, and what this result is relevant to:

A man walks about the city and sees things, people, actions. As he sees them he records the simple facts in his mind. The simple elementary facts, however, are the same for everybody. But then not everybody makes the same choice of the facts to be noticed, let alone the same mental associations with the present experience. The difference of angle is determined by a past some have and some others have not experienced, and by the selection memory makes from its inventory to associate remembered past with observed present.

An example, relevant for Bloom-construction, from part II. chapter 4. Returning from Patrick Dignam's funeral and arriving to the window of the newspaper printing shop, Bloom "stayed in his walk to watch a typesetter neatly distributing type" for the news about that very same event. Follows: *Bloom assesses facts*, translates them in "*Protokolsätze*" (though he couldn't have read yet Wittgenstein to know that this is how they are called), and adds his own considerations:

> "Reads it backwards first. Quickly he does it. Must require some practice that. mangiD. kcirtaP."

So far this is what everybody could have seen and most everybody could have said. But then comes *Bloom, the brooder:*

> "Poor papa, with his Hagadah book, reading backwards with his finger to me. Pessach. Next year in Jerusalem" -

and a lot more of the same kind follows before returning, without interruption, to the first impression of the printer's job which will close the circle:

"How quickly he does the job. Practice makes perfect. Seems to see through his fingers." [p.101]

Bloom seems to screen everything through the memories he holds of his ancestors. His experiences make countless times a full circle, from fact back to fact, yet passing through either the memory of dad Rudolf, or the Jews or, in a not so roundabout fashion, "Jerusalem".

Item: Bloom left his home in the morning, first just for a short while to buy his essential daily victuals, and when reaching the pork butcher's shop

"he halted before Dlugacz's - [what a perfect K.u.K. butcher name! - though some erudite claims that he was a Jewish pupil of Joyce at the Trieste Berlitz school - T.S.] - window, staring at the hanks of sausages, polonies, black and white." [p.48]

Entering the shop he "took up a page from the pile of cut sheets". He picked the page because a peculiar advertisement struck his eyes. Of course, it was printed there and hardly could anybody have read anything else. Yet, not anybody could have had the same interest as Bloom in the conspicuous announcement (discussed in all the articles around the "Zion motive") about "The model farm at Kinereth on the lakeshore of Tiberias". When he left Dlugacz's with the kidney and in the possession of the wrapping paper, "he walked back along Dorset street, reading gravely" the report of the planters' association called Agoudath Netaim - and not "*Agendath* Netaim" as it is misspelled, faithful to the original, in all subsequent editions. [Why the "Agen" lapsus? May be that recurring "*agenbit of inwit*"? Ask your favorite shrink. These fellows always have an explanation for things like this.]

And the planters' association - by the way, founded in 1905, well after this 16th of June 1904 - keeps returning, in the most unlikely associations. One single exquisite example: Bloom is out to shop for a present for his adulterous wife. Passing the windows of "Brown Thomas, silk mercers" he is struck by a good idea: pincushions! Why? "I'm a long time threatening to buy one. Stick them all over the place. Needles in window curtains". Contemplating the silk mercers' merchandise supply, Bloom produces yet another stream of *Protokolsätze* - everybody else could have made similar ones - followed by associations not everybody was liable to make and which may have been normal only among people living about the *Seitenstaetter Gasse* in Vienna, the *Rumbach utca* or thereabouts in Budapest, or passing by the via *Donizzetti* in Trieste, yet most unlikely among most inhabitants of Dublin. Remember this:

> "Gleaming silk petticoats on slim brass rails, rays of flat silk stockings.

> "High voices. Sunwarm silk. Jingling harnesses. [You see, of course, the caravan approaching. Don't you?] All for a woman [some Middle Eastern Molly], home, houses, silk webs, silver, rich fruits, spicy from Jaffa. Agendath Netaim. Wealth of the world." [p.138]

There is no experience, or almost, which Bloom makes in Dublin without these associations. Yet the experiences themselves and their literary representation are ordered within a peculiar frame systematically neglected by almost all the scholarly writers on the subject. *It is the urge to display one's own peculiar or biased scholarship which leads to the critic's secondary associations, who often forgets about the very glue which keeps the story together, and which is:*

The "General Thirst" as Axis for the Story

Associations may be predetermined. But so may be our choice of things we want to see. When our eyes meet things of only casual interest, we easily slip into unlikely or, at any rate, unexpected associations with what compulsorily preoccupies us. When under no external compulsion and when relaxing critical control over our erring thoughts, we do not necessarily notice anything or everything within the physical range of our eyes, but will unwittingly choose to notice what we subconsciously and compulsively *wish* to see. And we introduce in the web of our physical picture a thread spun of remembrances selected by our urges. Leopold Bloom and Stephen Dedalus walk through the same city, often meet the same people, witness many of the same events, yet they don't pick the same angle to get to the same component for a picture of their respective Worlds. The author, the poet, slips alternatively in *their* respective skins, pursues *their* "Odissey", records *their* images and translates them into the novel which he submits to the reading public. The reader reads the book, which means walking out into another World, subjects it to his own scrutiny, makes his own associations and sees in it images of his own will. Many features are discovered by everybody. But some go unnoticed, for the same reason for which the heroes of the novel make so often different associations and reveal different elements of the same world of simple facts.

A striking example is the motive of drinking, drunks and drunkenness. Noticed, of course, but never as an essential feature of the novel, never as what it is indeed, namely a fundamental characteristic of Bloom's Dublin picture as reflected in his own "cracked looking-glass", and seldom considering fine little technicalities by which Joyce conveys this picture of a biased picture. The careful reader will also discover this motive as the substance which glues together the web of episodes - a little bit like the river in Huckleberry Finn. How? Let's follow once again Bloom's trail.

Bloom leaves his home to go buying that pork kidney at Dlugacz's, but before arriving:

> "He approached Larry O'Rourke's. From the cellar grating floated up the flabby gush of porter." [p.47]

And then follows a "flabby gush" of thoughts about the "General thirst", the culmination of which is the following:

> "Good puzzle would be to cross Dublin without passing a pub. Save it they can't". [p.48]

And another good puzzle for the reader: *read Ulysses from cover to cover skipping "only" every episode on drinking, drunks and drunkenness and see whether it still keeps together.* It would be an Aristotelian test of the unity of the plot. Says the Stagirite: "For a thing whose presence or absence makes no visible difference is not an organic part of the whole" (Poetics, VIII,4). Take the booze out of Ulysses and the essential components of two world pictures, Bloom's and Stephen's as well, will be lost and *the narrative itself will fall apart.* Let me submit the outline of a proof.

The picture and the facts are the same - the associations different. Right in the first chapter, friend Mulligan, smelling the money Stephen is expected to receive that day as wages of his teacher's job, says:

" - Seriously Dedalus. I'm stony. Hurry out to your school kip and bring us back some money. Today the bards must drink and junket. Ireland expects that every man this day will do his duty." [p.13]

The "men of Ireland", those in the novel at least, will not fail to do their duty. What is to come is foreshadowed by Stephen's "stream of consciousness" while walking on the seashore, "along Sandymount strand", after having received his humble wages:

"*Ineluctable modality of the visible*: at least that if no more, *thought through my eyes. Signature of all things I am here to read*, seaspawn and seaward, the nearing tide and the rusty boat." [p.31]

And see he does: sad recollections in the desolate landscape. They deluge the beach. And then a signal of what is to come:

"Unwholesome sandflats waited to suck his treading soles, breathing upward sewage breath. He coasted them, walking warily. *A porterbottle stood up, stogged to its waist, in the cakey sand dough. A sentinel: isle of dreadful thirst.*" [p.34]

Stephen's *Weltbild* will come forth later in accomplished drunkenness. In the meanwhile, Bloom goes on his way. Leaving Dlugacz, he considers the ad of Agoudath Netaim:

"A barren land bare waste. Volcanic lake, the dead sea: no fish, weedless, sunk deep in earth. No wind would lift those waves, grey metal, poisonous foggy waters. Brimstone they called it raining down: the cities of the plain: Sodom, Gomorrah, Edom. All dead names. A dead sea in a dead land, grey and old. Old now. It bore the oldest, the first race. ***A bent hag crossed from Cassidy's clutching a noggin bottle by the neck***. The oldest people. Wandered far away

over all the earth, captivity, multiplying, dying, being born everywhere. It lay there now. Now it could bare no more. Dead: an old
woman's: the grey sunken cunt of the world. - Desolation." [p.50]

Two desolations. One framing the other, one entwined with the other.
The "barren land" which bore the "oldest race" and "the oldest people" frame
the Dublin hag with the bottle. And Bloom noticed the "noggin bottle" at
about the same time when Stephen chances upon the porter bottle "in the
cakey sand dough", that "sentinel" of the "isle of the dreadful thirst". This is in
the first chapter of part two, Bloom's part. In the twelfth and last chapter of this
part, late in the evening,

> "on a step a gnome totting among a rubbishtip crouches to shoul-
> der a sack of rags and bones. *A crone standing by with a smoking
> oil lamp rams the last bottle in the maw of his sack.*" [p.351]

Is this *crone* the same as the *hag* who walked in the morning through the
desolate landscape of "dead land, grey and old" while "clutching a noggin bottle by the neck", closing her day in the slummy nighttown where the picture is
completed with "a drunken navvy"?
And Bloom continues his wandering and - we are again at it - arrives at the
church of All Hollows. First was the host, the Corpus. And further:

> "The priest was rinsing out the chalice: then he tossed off the dregs
> smartly. Wine. Makes it more aristocratic than for example if he
> drank what they are used to Guinness's porter or some temperance
> beverage Wheatley's Dublin hop bitters or Cantrell and Cochrane's
> ginger ale (aromatic). Doesn't give them any of it: shew wine: only
> the other. Cold comfort. Pious fraud but quite right: otherwise
> they'd have one old booser worse than another coming along,
> cadging for a drink. Quite right. Perfectly right that is." [p.67]

Admiration for the "wonderful organization" which "goes like a clock-
work" and a pragmatic approval of the "pious fraud" by the thrice baptized
Leopold Bloom in the sarcastic language of the son of Virág Rezsö. The
haughty look of the humiliated. Remember Balzac?

« ... *les hommes méconnus se vengent de l'humilité de leur position par
la hauteur de leur coup d'oeil.*»

And Bloom - he wouldn't be otherwise Bloom, would he? - never ignores
the business aspect of drunkenness. It is sticking to the booze like Agoudath
Netaim to everything else. Read again the economic considerations he makes
when inventing the puzzle, never to be solved, about the pub-free crossing of
Dublin at the entrance of Larry O'Rourke's:

> "Where do they get the money? Coming up redheaded curates
> from the country Leitrim, rinsing empties and old man in the cel-
> lar. Then, lo and behold, they blossom out as Adam Findlaters or
> Dan Tallons ....
> Off the drunks perhaps. Put down three and carry five. What is
> that? A bob here and there, dribs and drabs. On the wholesale
> orders perhaps. Doing a double shuffle with the town travelers.
> Square it with the boss and we'll split the job, see?" [p.48]

Some more beer economics follows and is taken up again before entering
the church in an unlikely association with his fancy love-letter exchange with
an unknown woman:

> "Lord Iveagh once cashed a seven-figure cheque for a million in
> the Bank of Ireland. *Shows you the money to be made out of por-
> ter.* Still the other brother lord Ardilaun has to change his shirt
> four times a day, they say. Skin breeds lice or vermin. A million
> pounds, wait a moment. *Twopence a pint fourpence a quart, eight-
> pence a gallon of porter, no, one and fourpence a gallon of porter. One
> and four into twenty: fifteen about. Yes, exactly. Fifteen millions of
> barrels of porter.*

> "What am I saying barrels? Gallons. About a million barrels all
> the same.
> "An incoming train clanked heavily about his head, coach after
> coach. Barrels bumped in his head: dull porter slopped and
> churned inside" [p.65]

Bloom enters the church and subsequently follows his way to Patrick Dignam's funeral, attends it, goes to the Freeman's Journal and the Evening Telegraph, then meets "A somber Y.M.C.A. young man" who gives him a throwaway heralding the coming Elijah, his eyes meet the misery of Stephen's sisters, Simon Dedalus' daughters, whose wife had fifteen children by "their theology". Then the brooding Bloom takes on the priests:

> "Increase and multiply. Did you ever hear such an idea? Eat you out of house and home. No families themselves to feed. Living on the fat of the land. Their butteries and larders. I'd like to see them do the black fast of Yom Kippur." [p.124-125]

Sic!! Did we arrive? Not yet. Just a few more lines:

> "As he set foot on O'Connell bridge a puffball of smoke plumed up from the parapet. Brewery barge with export stout. England. Sea air sours it, I heard. Be interesting some day get a pass through Hancock to see the brewery." [p.125]

And then the final picture:

> "Regular world itself. Vats of porter, wonderful. Rats get in too. Drink themselves bloated as big as a collie floating. Dead drunk on the porter. Drink till they puke like Christians. Imagine drinking that! Rats: vats. Well, of course if we knew all the things." [p.125]

Yet Bloom is also from this very same Earth, and he is hungry. *And* thirsty! After skipping one dirty pub he settles for another. No problem to find another one when you skip one, and he doesn't seem to be up to solve the puzzle he himself invented. After ordering a cheese sandwich:

> "Like a few olives too if they had them. Italian I prefer. *Good glass of burgundy; take away that. Lubricate.*" [p.141]

Company he enjoys is that of Nosey Flynn who already is working on his grog when Bloom goes about his burgundy:

"His midriff yearned then upward, sank within him, yearned more longly, longingly.

"Wine.

"He smellskipped the cordial juice and, bidding his throat strongly to speed it, set his wineglass delicately down." [p.141-142]

Discusses with Nosey chancy horses and Molly's recital engagements, yet comes back to the great pain he is just about to drown into the mellowness of burgundy:

"Wine soaked and softened rolled pith of bread mustard a moment mawkish cheese. Nice wine it is. Taste it better because I'm not thirsty. Bath of course does that. [Does it really? In the tower Mulligan said of Stephen: "The unclean bard makes a point of washing once a month" - T.S.] Just a bite or two. Then about six o'clock I can." [p.143]

Well, he may, but in vain:

"Six. Six. Time will be gone then. She..."

Yes, she, Molly will have accomplished the crime of adultery with her impresario. Bloom knows it, suffers in his quiet way without doing anything about it. *His* consolation, *their* consolation:

"Mild fire of wine kindled his veins. I wanted that badly. Felt so off colour. His eyes unhungrily saw shelves of tins, sardines, gaudy lobsters' claws." [p.143]

The distraction offered by the sight of food is a good start for long considerations about nutrition. But how long can he stay off his obsessions? Not very long and his food thoughts converge with iron necessity:

"Orangegroves for instance. Need artificial irrigation. Bleibtreustrasse»." [p.143]

Remember *Bleibtreustrasse*, Berlin? Head office of Agoudath Netaim. The long, smart and witty considerations about food, its social implications, not forgetting its sexual effects preoccupying the betrayed husband - ("Fizz and Red bank oysters. Effect on sexual. Aphrodis"; or: "Caviare. Do the grand".) - along with sexual reminiscences, come to an end and Bloom goes on his way. "When the sound of his boots has ceased" owner Davy Byrne and Nosey Flynn comment on the strange character whom they suspect, admiringly by the way, to be something of a free-mason:

> "Ancient free and accepted order... They give him a leg up...They stick to you when you are down... By God they did right to keep the women out of it." [p.145]

This is what you see in Nosey's cracked looking glass and more: the drinking subject. We read:

> "God Almighty couldn't make him drunk, Nosey Flynn said. Slips off when the fun gets too hot. Didn't you see him look at his watch? Ah you weren't there. If you ask him to have a drink, first he outs with the watch to see what he ought to imbibe. Declare to God he does" [p.146]

But Bloom walking towards Dawson street is happy for having imbibed something:

> "Feel better. Burgundy. Good pick me up. Who distilled first? Some chap in the blues." [p.147]

Well, well, the haughtiness is gone, yielded to a friendly tolerance for the "chap in the blues" who invented distillation. (Surprise! Noah is not mentioned nor the paragon of earthly happiness in the Bible: every man under his vine and fig tree - possibly to be achieved through Agoudath Netaim. Bloom could have fiddled ahead through the fig leaf to ... Well, not quite. The impresario was already on his way.)

All the above references, as the quotations illustrating them, were meant to suggest the main links of the dense lattice framing the mosaic which makes the story and the description of its main characters. The concluding (and conclusive) summary of this description will then be given in that catechistic penult chapter:

For Bloom:

> "What in water did Bloom, waterlover, drawer of water, watercarrier, returning to the range, admire?

> "Its universality: its democratic constancy to its nature in seeking its own level: its vastness in the ocean of Mercator's projection;" [p.549]

For Stephen (after Bloom's suggestion that he may wash himself):

> "What reason did Stephen give for declining Bloom's offer?
> "That he was hydrophobe, hating partial contact by immersion or total by submersion in cold water (his last bath having taken place in the month of October of the preceding year), dislike the aqueous substances of glass and crystal, *distrusting aquacities of thought and language.*

> "What impeded Bloom from giving Stephen counsels of hygiene and prophylactic..?
> "The incompatibility of aquacity with the erratic originality of genius." [p.550]

So did Stephen see it. On Bloom's side of the street it showed differently. It was not the "erratic originality of the genius" which had to be kept drunk to stay live. In the nighttown hallucination, the ghostly appearance of old man Virág, in terms of a paraphrase of Salomon Mosenthal's "Deborah", addressing his son warns him:

> "One night they bring you home drunk as dog, after spend your good money" [p.358]

This was not to happen. It rather happened that *"Leopoldleben"* brought to his place the drunk Stephen of whose own "good money" not much was left.

Gerty or Mirroring the Tragic

The Odyssey continues: Museum and Library are almost the only places in this book in which there is no drinking. Yet there is a lot of drinking going on in Barney Kirnan's joint where a "patriot" named "the citizen" subjects Bloom to anti-Semitic abuse. The citizen and his drunkenness return in the next chapter as a motive. The sublime Gerty MacDowell, sitting on the beach, playing her (cracked!) mirror game with the unknown Leopold Bloom, has her own streams of consciousness marred by the terrible thought of drunkenness. The gentle story of desire is flashed through with the ugly story of her father's - he turns out to be the "citizen" - addiction to "that vile decoction which has ruined so many hearts and homes." [p.290]

Gerty MacDowell:

> "...she was sincerity itself, one of the bravest and truest hearts ever made, not one of your twofaced things, too sweet to be wholesome." [p.290]

She was sitting on the beach:

> "And then there came out upon the air the sound of voices and the pealing anthem of the organ. It was the men's temperance retreat conducted by the missioner, the reverend John Hughes S.J." [p.290]

And then the bitter arrest of attention:

> "How sad to poor Gerty's ears! Had her father only avoided the clutches of the demon drink, by taking the pledge or those powders the drink habit cured in Pearson's Weekly, she might now be rolling in a carriage, second to none." [p.290]

Nobody in this book is given to quietly enjoy chewing his or her favorite dream or melancholy fancy without the motive of drunkenness flashing through their mirror and tightly associating with their thinking. It should remain for the student of the writer's motivations to figure out why Joyce gave in the hands of many of his major characters a mirror turned towards drunkenness, while distributing them in space in such a manner as to return to the reader their thus arrived at specular insight. For us, the readers, it remains only to simply assess this fact. And as far as the targets chosen by the author are concerned, we have only to remember the "young artist's" considerations about Aristotle's failure to define terror and pity as emotions begotten by tragedy.

Stephen tried earlier (in the "Portrait") his own definitions: "*Pity* is the feeling which arrests the mind in the presence of whatsoever is grave and constant in human suffering and unites it with *the human sufferer.*" *Terror* is likewise an *arresting* feeling which, however, unites with the "*secret cause*" *of suffering.* They are static in the sense that they do not prompt the subject to motion. Thus they are opposed to *desire* and *loathing* which do engender motion in the sense that "desire urges to possess, *to go to* something; loathing urges to abandon, *to go from* something." But: "The tragic emotion, in fact, is a face looking two ways, towards terror and towards pity."

We may now distinguish, on our own, between the reader's and the hero's perception of the tragic. The purpose of tragic poetry, as explained by Aristotle, is to cause pity and terror in the spectator or reader who, by the mediation of the plot and the evolving action, experiences the undoing of a hero; but this does not mean that the heroes in the plot, however tragic their situation may be, also and necessarily sense it as such. In the quoted case, Gerty witnesses the un-heroic downfall of *her* hero, her father, by "that vile decoction" and is "*arrested*" by a deep feeling of compassion. This *we* understand as a tragedy, though we may "see" it through her eyes. Bloom, instead, is loathing the victims and "*goes away*" from them without compassion; at least before meeting and "rescuing" Stephen! Is the non-heroic downfall a legitimate source of tragic emotion? It probably depends on your definition of heroic and tragic or, otherwise, on whom you are more familiar with: Gerty or the citizen. For Gerty the "citizen" is a tragic hero. To the reader, Gerty's "grave and constant suffering" causes the "arrest" we call pity and "unites" us with Gerty.

[Excursus. The motive of drunkenness flashes again and again through Ulysses, yet it punctuated also, with the same hidden meaning, the "Portrait". So it was during Stephen's lecturing about the *aesthetic stasis:*

"They lit their cigarettes and turned to the right. After a pause Stephen began:

"- Aristotle has not defined pity and terror. I have. I say...
"Lynch halted and said bluntly:
"- Stop! I won't listen! I am sick. I was out last night on a yellow
drunk with Horan and Goggins.
"Stephen went on:..."

The incident is there, yet Stephen could not be stopped until he reached
the main conclusion to justify his own *Ars Poetica:*

> "...To speak of these things and to try to understand their nature,
> and having understood it, to try to slowly and humbly and con-
> stantly *to express, to press out* again, from the gross earth or what
> it brings forth, from sound and shape and colour which are the
> prison gates of our soul, the image of the beauty we have come to
> understand - that is art."

And this is how Gerty Macdowell was to be shaped.]

Gertrude MacDowell and Leopold Bloom were examining each other,
longingly - and this is the most important subsidiary reciprocal mirroring
game in the novel. The "consciousness" of each of them is streaming out in
appropriately contrasting language. Gerty's language, the only one she commands to transcend the banality of the quotidian, is the verbiage of cheap romantic novels; yet, unlike these products of lowbrow literature, her thoughts
testify of genuine suffering. She "exchanged glances" with Leopold and

> "under the brim of her new hat she ventured a look at him and *the
> face that met her gaze* there in the twilight, wan and strangely drawn,
> seemed to her the saddest she had ever seen". [p.292]

And further:

> "*Yes, it was her he was looking at and there was meaning in his look.*
> His eyes burned into her as though they would search her through
> and through, read her very soul." [p.293]

Now the pastiche of sweetish housewife's literature brings us back once again to the fundamental image composition:

She saw that he saw ... but not much more. Just a simple addition of the Bloom-picture as returned from a corner of a loathed and feared world:

> "She could see at once by his dark eyes and his pale intellectual face that he was a foreigner... He was in deep mourning, she could see that, and the story of a haunting sorrow was written on his face." [p.293]

And yet further:

> "His dark eyes fixed themselves on her again, drinking in her every contour, literally worshiping at her shrine. If ever there was undisguised admiration in a man's passionate gaze it was there plain to be seen on that man's face. It is for you, Gertrude MacDowell, and you know it." [p.296]

Was it? Bloom, after a good while and many a thought streaming away, realized that Gerty was limping:

> "She [as she saw herself] walked with a certain dignity, characteristic of her but with care because - because Gerty MacDowell was..." [p.301]

And Bloom fell back into his cynical outlook:

> "Hot little devil all the same. Wouldn't mind. ... That squinty one is delicate." [p.301]

Follows some strange, morbid gratitude after vicarious gratification.

> "Did me good all the same. ... Still it was a kind of language between us" [p.305]

Quite a scenario for makers of dirty movies. And they didn't miss the opportunity. It seems to be all what they got out of the novel, just as the censors who once prohibited its distribution in the United States.

By the laws of this novel, streams of thought, which first have a parallel thrust, will bend, meet and become a dialogue. Partly! Because the dialogue will continue to be punctuated with thoughts in bracket which the characters don't communicate to each other. Only to us, the readers. The place of the dialogues is then the Nighttown. The place description and the recounting of various meetings imagined, dreamt, invented etc., reads like the pastiche of a, may be German, expressionist tale - and is not the strongest part of the novel. (Alfred Döblin had done it better.) Still, it occasions those meetings which help the story ahead. Or, more precisely, it provides location for the rendezvous of the hitherto parallel streams to complete the picture of characters through their direct confrontation. So it does for Gerty and Bloom, but not very successfully in this particular case. So we read:

> "GERTY: With all my worldly goods I thee and thou. (*She murmurs*) You did that. I hate you.
> "BLOOM: I? When? You're dreaming. I never saw you.
> [...]
> "GERTY :(*To Bloom*) When you saw all the secrets of my bottom drawer. (*She paws his sleeve, slobbering*) Dirty married man! I love you for doing that to me. (*She slides away crookedly ...*) [p.361]

And sometimes also the story seems to slide away crookedly - unless we are aware that we have to follow the game of cracked looking glasses. Which for now, we stop here.

ESSAY NO.9

Whereof We May Say Parables: Between Broch's "Unknown Magnitude" and Musil's "Törless"

"It seemed a limbo of painless patient consciousness through which souls of mathematicians might wander, projecting long slender fabrics from plane to plane of ever rarer and paler twilight, radiating swift eddies to the last verges of a universe ever vaster, farther and more impalpable". [James Joyce: A Portrait of the Artist as a Young Man].

"'Wissen sie', sagte Kapperbrunn, 'die Mathematik ist so eine Art Verzweiflungstat des menschlichen Geistes ... an und für sich braucht man sie ja wirklich nicht, aber sie ist so eine Art Insel der Anständigkeit, und deshalb mag ich sie gern.'" ["'You know', said Kapperbrunn, 'mathematics is kind of an act of despair of the human spirit.... After all we do not really need it, but it is sort of an island of decency, and this is why I rather like it" [(Hermann Broch, Die unbekannte Grösse, 1933)]

Between Statement and Parable

"Whereof one cannot speak, thereof one must be silent" - with this advice concludes Wittgenstein his Tractatus Logico-Philosophicus. And when the Motto to his treatise, quote from the poet Kürnberger, is accepted as a justification of this rule, then the honest lover of wisdom will yield to the empire of a stern, laconic discipline, since

"... alles, was man weiss, nicht bloss raushen und brausen gehört hat, lässt sich in drei Worten sagen." ("...everything we know, which is not simply the rustle and bluster we hear, can be expressed in three words").

Science, the claimant of knowledge, does not always abide by such rule, yet its history follows the path leading from the colorful loquacity of alchemists to the terse economy of the mathematical idiom employed in modern physics. We have learned to state more with a minimum of words which scientists assign either to the "things" they observe, or to the results deduced from these observations, abiding by the iron rules of mathematics. Well, as far as possible. Yet, the larger the domain of things whereof we can speak, the longer the frontier which surrounds it, and while it expands, it increases our awareness of the immensity beyond it, along with all the questions one cannot ask and all the anxieties "whereof one cannot speak." And I already sinned against the rule by pretending to state what cannot be stated: when talking about the "domain" of the speakable and its "frontiers", I used a language which carries a precise meaning only in relation to things intuited in space. Yet I slipped away from, well, the *domain* under scientific command following the rule I hereby propose: "Whereof one cannot speak meaningfully - as 'meaningful' is defined by the philosophical kindred of Wittgenstein [of the Tractatus!] - one may speak in parables and metaphors". This is what art does; and it *is* what it *does*. How could we distinguish in literature between plain nonsense and the enlightening parable, that periscope which helps us peer beyond the high walls surrounding that whereof we may speak? I don't think the answer is so difficult to be found. The parable doesn't state, assert, contend or propose; instead it *conjures experiences* by the metaphor of a story, verisimilar or not, or it offers an image which *suggests without stating.*

Can we live without that "beyond-the-speakable"? How can we answer this question? Unless by parable, hardly by anything else. Is that whereof one can speak fulfilling? (And, by the way, what is "fulfilling"? - if not filling full, to the rim, a pot, a bottle, etc.). The most frequent negative answer to such a question has different roots. For some it is justification for meaningless talk, marketed as philosophy. ("Science cannot explain human nature". Probably. Mostly because nobody has yet told "science" what is meant by these two words "human nature". And beware of those who volunteer to "explain" it "without" and "against" science!) For others it is simply the result of a disappointing trial to expand the domain of those things whereof one can speak. Many of the latter walked the rocky road of science; they know about the austere pleasure of advancing on it and the pain of disappointed trials. They also know that for those who took upon themselves the heavy yoke of precise speech censored by the rigor of mathematics, there is no smooth road paved with soft words. Their knowledge of the limits of meaning prevents them from unloading their grief in that type of shallow verbiage which so often is peddled as "philosophy". Therefore they also shun the Parable. They have learned the difficult art of translating an idea on something whereof one *may* speak, into meaningful speech. However, they don't know how to master the speech, how to forge it into a parable when they want to point beyond the limits of that whereof the mathematical and logical Censor authorizes limited freedom of speech. But, because of their awareness of incomplete expression and their reluctance to soak their anxieties, hopes, desires and passions - *they* also have such - in the narcotic of prohibited talk, their bewilderment may be deeper than the confusion of those who booze up on meaningless speech. *Beyond that whereof one can speak there is an "unknown magnitude" which they cannot find by solving the rationally underspecified equation system of their experience.*

The two novels, indicated in the title of this set of notes, were chosen to illustrate the problem as above adumbrated. The justification of the choice follows from the discussion itself. Still, the knowledgeable reader of these notes may be surprised by the counter-chronological sequence of the discussion: first the Broch novel, and only then the better, better known, and more widely appreciated small novel of Musil. It is not possible, indeed not even necessary, to justify this choice *a priori*, since the justification should follow from the subsequent discourse. However, the friendly reader is invited to forget about the historic sequence of their publication; think of the two books as if published simultaneously. And one more thing. The Broch novel is a much simpler exercise, which concentrates more specifically on the problem of the limit between that whereof we may speak and that which can only be pointed at - by a parable. It can offer itself as an introduction helping the reader to discover in Musil's novel this particular issue enshrouded in a much more complex plot. Thereby the reader will not commit the frequent error of just simply not noticing its presence, as many of the so very learned critics do.

Broch's Parable

"The Unknown Magnitude", *"Die Unbekannte Grösse"* by Hermann Broch [I use my own translation of the title], published in 1933, is the story of a young mathematician, of whom we learn to be in an endless quarrel with his limited language, in a feverish, incessant quest to absorb every experience within the meaningfully expressible and, so he hopes, mathematically testable. It is not Broch's best novel, but it is a particularly significant one. It is not simply the story of a scientist. Such would, in itself, not be new in literature. The new and exemplary about it consists in the fact that the scientist *in fabula* meets the author on the common frontier of their respective domains: the line where scientific expression stops and the parable begins. That the scientist in the story and the poet are both aware of the limits of human expression may also be due to the fact that this poet, Broch, walked himself for awhile the roads of science. Broch, as Robert Musil, his compatriot and older contemporary, are among the few masters of literature whose hostility to nonsense talking originates in their experience with science, as its students and, at some time, its practitioners. Therefore they have a good understanding of both the scientist's own "human" problems and the poet's risk of being inebriated by shallow verbiage. Such awareness can be encountered, though seldom, also in the works of other writers, who gave the issue something we may call a "parabolic treatment". A case in point would be Hermann Hesse, whose parable of the *"Glasperlenspiel"* develops the fantasy of a world in which a chosen and respected minority of initiated, cultivate, in arcane rituals, the acquired stock of what is presumed to be secure and lasting knowledge. It is meant to stress the contrast to this our "age of the feuilleton" as it was characterized by Theodor Herzl, himself a feuilletonist despising the abuses of his trade, characterized by the rule of thin talk. But Hesse's is a humanist's parable, while Broch's (and Musil's) is, so to say, an insider's relation. It tells, of course, about the limits of scientific and generally meaningful speech when it tries to come to grips with problems "human"; but it also reveals the limits of literature in handling similar problems when the writer, scientifically trained, educated in respect for rigor and precision, has an unforgiving mathematical Censor nestled in the back of his mind. Writers like Broch and Musil could not afford

themselves that type of writing ("philosophical novel") in which the main exercise consists in making the heroes talk "whereof one cannot speak". So they tried
parables about it, little understood in their time by those who practiced - wrote
or read - literature outside the spell of the Vienna School of linguistically obsessed positivist philosophers. (As for the latter, we know that they read very little literature, and quite a few of them had an atrocious literary taste, Wittgenstein
included.) I admit, the proposed reading exercise of the two mentioned novels
carries the bias of these introductory considerations. But, then, is this bias any
worse than all the others?

"The Unknown Magnitude"

A short review of the story is required, also and mainly because all the
deprecatory writings about this novel ignore the particularities of its language
which introduces the reader into the main problem: the discovery of the frontier between the scientific idiom and the language of the poet. Hereby I would
also like to caution the friendly reader of these notes that what he may have
read as Broch's own disappointment with this novel should not be taken as a
precise, unbiased, *strictly literary* judgment. I rather propose to follow the advice found in a recently published book on "mathematical traces" in literature
in which it is said about Broch's own disillusioned judgment:

> "*Ob dieses Urteil gerechtfertigt ist, kann allenfalls im Anschluss an eine
> Analyse des Romans entschieden werden*" "Whether this judgment is
> or is not justified, can be decided only following an analysis of the
> novel".] - [Knut Radbruch: *Mathematische Spuren in der Literatur,*
> *Darmstadt,* 1997.]

This brief review will thus purpose the rehearsal of some of the specifics
in the characters' speech.

Richard Hieck was one of five siblings, three boys, two girls, of a lower
middle-class Austrian/German family. The father, now dead, used to be a
small office clerk, a "*Beamter*", who once worked in an unspecified "office"
("*das Amt*"), doing an unrecorded job. Nothing in his cheerful, still young
widow's home, not even a photograph, reminded of this man of strange habits,
taciturn yet kind, uncaring about his family and surroundings, hiding in the

darkness of his own thoughts, which, if rarely expressed, then in metaphors or parables. A man who didn't speak whereof one should not!

On a beautiful summer Sunday afternoon the mother proposed an outing with the children. Other fathers may have followed the advice. This one refused the proposal, with a kind, friendly laughter, saying: "The World burns within us, not outside of us" (p.16). Does anybody know what this "means"? This time he didn't take his family along for a walk, but one evening - he was "a man of the night", a "*Nachtmensch*" - he took the oldest son, Richard, by his hand, walked with him out in the country and there, unexpectedly, went about plucking flowers in the dark night under the cloud-covered moon ("*verdeckte Mondnacht*"). One would have expected him to bring the flowers home, to offer them to mother; that would have been "logical". Yet he dumped them from the bridge into the river while issuing another one of his enigmatic, obscure declarations: "Stars in the water". Nothing was clear about this man, nothing clear-cut, nothing unequivocal.

> "And it was to some extent a rejection of his influence and of the paternal character, that made Richard cling so doggedly to school and study: in the school and its regularity he found at least part of that [desired] unambiguous state of which he was deprived as a child. And for the same reason he soon acquired an attachment to things clear and mathematical, an inclination which, during mathematics classes, was to take the shape in a hope that one day he himself will teach the class these beatifying unequivocal things" (p.18).

Richard - as student and then as professional mathematician - went about making his dream come true in the usual manner of those who search for *happiness* (or just *serenity*?) *in clarity*. He labored to bring as much experience as possible under the hood of a precise statement, in his case a rigorous theory, thoroughly tested by exposing it to the stern control of mathematics. His father knew very little unambiguously and struggled all his life with his experiences trying to command or exorcize them by an occasional metaphoric saying or act. Richard, instead, tried to bring within the command of rigorous speech all experience and didn't make allowance for things "whereof one cannot speak". The latter were only in pre-scientific limbo; progress meant bringing them within the fold of science. There is a simple question we are not told that he might have asked: what causes such an urge in man, what makes him desire such clarity? Since the *desire* itself can hardly be expressed without ambiguity, in a manner Descartes would call *clairement et distinctement.*

His sister Susanne was a different reflection of the father. She didn't care about learning and understanding. She had faith in God and the Savior, and prepared to join a convent, transforming her little room into a chapel, with saints' images covering the walls. Richard envied and loved his sister. But while slowly yet successfully advancing on the academic ladder and becoming assistant professor at the University, Richard felt that "the purpose of the sister was considerably more honest and straightforward" (p.29) than his. In fact he knew *what* his science was capable of; however, it was not clear to him *why:*

> "He wanted to achieve something with the help of mathematics, something which was outside mathematics in the same way as Christ was outside the Church which served him. Yet he never got beyond targets inside mathematics. What was his aim?"

He couldn't find an answer. Susanne had an aim: "marrying Christ". But what was his? He experienced by now "the burning joy of cognition" yet realized that "cheerful it is not". Science could provide joy, never serenity.

While Richard respected Susanne's own way leading out of the same dark ambiguities bequeathed by their father, he displayed an occasionally hostile aloofness to the approach of his intelligent, brilliant yet utterly sarcastic (cynical?) senior colleague at the University. Dr. Kapperbrunn was mathematical assistant to Professor Weitprecht, physicist, and chief of Richard as well. To Kapperbrunn, who liked hiking in the woods, climbing mountains, skiing, and didn't despise pretty girls either, mathematics was a different matter:

> "You know...mathematics is kind of an act of despair of the human spirit.... After all we do not really need it, but it is sort of an island of decency, and this is why I rather like it" (p.14).

This is not unheard-of in literature though only seldom so honestly and clearly stated as, so long ago, by Stendhal:

«*Mon enthousiasme pour les mathématiques avait peut-être eu pour base principale mon horreur pour l'hypocrisie..*» ["My enthusiasm for mathematics was probably based on my abhorrence of hypocrisy".] [*La vie de Henri Brulard*, ch. 34]

Stendhal writes amply about his struggle with sciences, but he never managed (did he ever try?) to take on the problem with the instruments provided by fictional literature. Broch, and as we will further see, Musil did exactly this. Yet, the ghost of Stendhal will creep into these stories several times. But, of course, we ought to know-to-see that such a ghost exists. Now, in this story Kapperbrunn made a step ahead of Stendhal's approach to mathematics: for him this science was a self-protecting ritual of honesty in a world of unchecked lies, a ritual practiced like a sport for the sake of one's moral health, but with no major purpose outside it. (Kapperbrunn also haughtily despised any "dirty" applications of his science, such as in physics - of which he made a living. The "island of decency" as a brothel? I am afraid he would have willingly and sarcastically admitted it.)

The major difference between Dr. Kapperbrunn and Richard Hieck consisted in the former's realization that there is something which will eternally remain beyond that whereof we may speak, while the second stubbornly persisted in his dogmatic conviction of everything to be mentally comprehensible and translatable into rational discourse.

But things were to change when a new experience brought real life home to Richard. While continuing to work for his physicist chief and give mathematical lectures, his, now Dr. Hieck's, academic duties were complemented, for monetary reasons, with some very literal moonlighting at the astronomical observatory - quite a departure from those earlier days when "the father's love for the nocturnal sky...kept him away from astronomy as from a forbidden land" (p.25). The lectures were mostly about symbolic logic and set-theoretical subjects.

"His position became respectable; he was counted among the prominent. His paper was published in Crelle's Journal [the famous mathematical periodical – T.S.], a significant event, by any rates, in the small world of the Institute" (p.70).

And then, the ailing professor Weitprecht, leaving in very bad shape for a health resort, invited him to put in order his enormous pile of notes, which were likely meant to be his scientific legacy. The good Dr. Kapperbrunn, helpful as always, volunteered not only with advice but with his connections:

> "Don't worry....we will round up a negro".
> "What?"
> "Well, a negro, or should you like it more, a pretty *negresse*; after all you will not do this all by yourself...some of the girls will consider it as an honor, only we are not supposed to tell Weitprecht about this" (p.70).

After a short and pragmatic review of the possible candidates, Kapperbrunn decided for a young mathematical lady - not exactly the type he himself would have invited to a ski party.

How a Mathematician Falls in Love

Richard never had many illusions and hopes in matters of love. His looks and awkwardness gave him reason enough to be skeptic. But then, there were things about love far beyond his simple understanding. One night, walking home from the observatory, he stopped at a little garden restaurant, took a table, ordered a beer and while sipping it, examined with interest the couples of lovers enjoying a good time at the neighboring tables:

> "He compared his bulky and awkward body with that of the young lads who emerged from the dark with their lasses in crosswise embrace, and it seemed to him impossible that a woman should ever be able to put her arm around his clumsy body. Such was not to be expected, no matter how famous a mathematician he may become one day. Yet these thoughts ... were interrupted when a man, twice as big and heavy as he, appeared with a tender, swarthy girl and took a table not far from his: at first he decided that this man has obtained for himself the tender girl either with money or by sheer force. Yet he had soon to realize that the girl was hopelessly in love with the

giant fellow, and this realization, which should have given him some consolation, rather increased his bewilderment..." (p.44).

Not for long. On that very same evening, returning for a walk to the observatory garden, he experienced a new feeling

"as the night penetrated him and filled his lungs, awakening in them a little angel ... the cowered and offended angel of the child".

The simple, straightforward, inexpressible and a little vulgar took hold of him:

"In the forest the wind rippled from time to time through the pine trees. Richard had beer in his belly, the stars above his head, while an angel in his bosom spread his wings" (p.45).

This may have been just an ironic and slightly vulgar paraphrase by Broch of Immanuel Kant's dictum about "the star spangled sky above me and the moral principle inside me", when he recorded that "Richard had beer in his belly and the stars above his head"; but both states, the philosophical recognition and the plain physical fact may sometimes generate the same results, namely the permission for the "little cowered and offended angel" inside everybody to "spread his wings".

Not long after this "discovery" came the "*negresse*" proposed by Kapperbrunn

"in the person of Ilse Nydhalm, student in physics in the sixth semester ... with brown hair, pale skin, grey eyes, average height and slim, ... slightly myopic and twinkling" (p.79).

When Richard gave her the necessary instructions to sort and organize Professor Weitprecht's papers,

"Ilse Nydhalm, softly frowning her eyebrows, listened with growing concentration, until she finally put on her spectacles and started making stenographic notes. And after he finished, she said shyly and slowly: 'Yes, so it is, thus it is, for sure'" (p.80).

Richard lectured. Ever more often, more intensively, purportedly to explain scientific matters to Ilse. So he believed at the beginning when:

> "every clarification of a scientific situation was also always an elucidation of his own aims, and the fact that he could achieve and express such clarity was as a liberation from everything he left behind, it was the beginning of a sigh of relief and of the promise of Light..." (p.81).

Yet it was only the beginning of a liberating sigh and the Light was still only promised, because the mathematical Censor claimed abidance by his rules of discipline. Richard realized that he went beyond the verbal necessities of this most laconic of all sciences. He slipped into the sweet yet hazy field of rhetoric! Periphrastically employing Wittgenstein's dictum, I would say that Dr. Richard Hieck, mathematician, has discovered something one cannot meaningfully *speak* about, yet he broke the rules: he *talked* about it. And his scientist's conscience tormented him, not only because he talked past of what can be spoken, but because he did so by abusing the purity of science:

> "... that he had to talk about [all] this in front of a girl, that *the liberating and beatifying illumination came about only through speech,* was a betrayal not only of Mathematics, but also of the essence of his life".

Betrayal to the talkers! Not so long ago it was his hostility towards Kapperbrunn which was nurtured by the "hatred replete amazement" [*hassüberfüllte Verwunderung*] in face of

> "that man's profligate ability to connect words into half-ordered speech without a clue about the *essential* on which all the rest depends, [and which is] *the only thing worthy of expression*" (p.39).

Long was the way Richard Hieck left behind.

> "It was a complicated and completely un-transparent act of treason he had perpetrated, and which led him along a tortuous path back

to the Sinful and obscurely Anarchic! Oh inaudible and lonesome sound of the Universe! *But every unprejudiced observer could have noticed that since awhile Richard Hieck was increasingly granting attention to his looks*" (p.81-82).

The Speech of a Mathematician

Richard Hieck became aware of his sin. But he was never completely innocent. He always peeped beyond the walls surrounding the speakable, and for what he "saw", metaphors volunteered to build the parable. Yet the metaphors which liberated his speechless mood were those peculiar to the scientist. Were they any worse than those used by the rest of us? If we will try to remember a little of our high school math and physics it will be "clear" that Richard's suggestions were not accidental at all. He was all along pinning metaphors, verbose little devils, to his thinking. And we could reproduce his entire curriculum with the help of his metaphors. Hieck, of course, was a mathematician and mathematics was for him "something very exciting, yet one couldn't say about it anything, since one couldn't know why it was exciting" (p.14). But one could use it to say all kinds of non-mathematical things, or better: to suggest them. This fact was seldom considered by thinkers of times past ... and was never really exploited in literary creation before the end of the 19th century.

The literary significance of the mathematical metaphor was once outlined, namely in 1766, by Georg Christoph Lichtenberg in a witty and caustic essay, noticed only by few: "*Von dem Nutzen, den die Mathematik einem Belesprit bringen kann*", or "About the profit which mathematics may offer to a *bel esprit*", and then quickly forgotten. If somebody would like to do in our times a study in the same vein he could peruse the "Unknown magnitude" as a first major store of examples (of the type to abound somewhat later in the "Man without qualities" of Musil), perfectly fused in the narrative. These are interesting not only because the writer, telling the story of a mathematician, must out of necessity employ the language his hero is expected to use, but also, and more importantly, because the metaphors supplied by the quantitative sciences are generally enriching the expressive potential of literature. In fact, this device has been used, though seldom, since ancient times. Lichtenberg gives us an early, just slightly limping example for the metaphoric employment of *negative magnitudes*, showing that they are

> "used in Psalm 62, and it says so much with such boldness, that twenty hexameters, with all their roundabout precision wouldn't suffice to express it".

And he is probably right when he refers to verse 10, Psalm 62:

> "Men of low degree are vanity, and men of high degree are a lie. *If they be laid in the balances they are together lighter than vanity.*"

which translated in *algebrese* means that lie has a negative sign. (I couldn't find anything else in Psalm 62 which may lend itself as a mathematical parable.) Yet, no matter how far back in time we go to collect examples like this, we will realize that they constitute only a repeated accident.

Not so the book we examine. This modest novel of Broch has a multitude of examples illustrating *a three-level use of the mathematical (and related scientific) metaphors organically absorbed in the story.* First, there are the accidental cases, those which may occur to everyone. When, for example, Richard is associating the cutting out of a timber beam from a trunk, with a problem of maximum in classical calculus; and, if you delve a little in your memory to pick out something of what remained there from your high school calculus, then you will understand what he means. This is one example of the easy ones. Then, second, there are the metaphors of a man who simply has no other source for images but the preoccupation of his life. These will penetrate Richard's mind as his resistance against them declines with the progress of his love affair. Yet there is a third, most important, source of mathematical metaphors which refer to a special class of experiences "whereof we may not speak", experiences which only higher scientific knowledge can engender. Let me insist on the last two groups as they are used in the unfolding of the narrative.

Christmas was approaching. Part of the fatherless family, the mother, Richard, Susanne and Otto, the artistic printer's apprentice ("I learn now copper engraving....We don't really need it in the shop, but it is part of the trade"), gathered for the holiday, while Emilie was somewhere in Berlin and Rudolf, who knows?, may be in South America. Has the spirit of Christmas overcome only the religious Susanne? Not quite, a mathematician also yields to the solemnity of a holiday, and finds the right expression:

"And without any real connection Richard realized that Christmas descended as a white lull, with an instant removal of all noise, and, ... a friendly introverted madness of the world. *A point of instability on a stable curve*" (p.30).

He realized perfectly well how imprecise this mathematical metaphor was, that it was only a substitute for something he was not supposed to talk about:

"[only] the Devil may find his way out of this" (*"Der Teufel mochte sich da auskennen"*) (p.30).

A metaphor only for the initiated which, one would expect, would have irritated anybody unfamiliar with the idiom, but in fact it was an atom of those of which his "treason" was slowly to be built up.

As it was at Christmas so it was on New Year's eve. Otto proposed wine to the assembled family. This was first opposed by Susanne and Richard - ("I am against any kind of alcohol" - quite a strange explanation for those who knew him) - but they yielded to Otto's insistence who reproached their lack of holiday spirit (*"Ihr habt keine Spur von Feierlichkeit"*). When, however, the artist returned with a jugful of wine he was received by big brother with a physics exam question: "Why is the pitcher overlaid in the summer but not in the winter?" The attempted vengeance of the scientist failed; Otto didn't pay much attention to it and when the time of coffee arrived there was a tilt toward the "third-level" metaphors:

"*Richard suddenly thought about the theory of groups.* And this abstract theoretical construction became instantly the fringe of a faraway, unspeakable life. He let the rest of his wine flow into his stomach and had under the jacket a fat and pleasant feeling" (p.37).

Double betrayal: his main love affair, group theory, used as a metaphor for fuzzy perceptions, mixed with alcohol, made him even more confused! [And I cannot help remembering and mentioning Leopold Bloom, in Joyce's *Ulysses*, with his haughty views on drinking, originating in his "aquacity", when himself accepting the consolation of a good glass of burgundy: "His midriff yearned then upward, sank within him, yearned more longly, longingly - wine". Well, under jacket or the midriff, the "pleasant feeling" of yearning "longly, longingly" is certainly beyond that speech, meaningful to the scientist].

The faraway unspeakable life claimed its right to verbal, metaphoric expression also from somebody else:

> "It was nothing astrological and mystical, and should the awesome hypothesis about the expanding and then again contracting universe come close to being a metaphor for human breathing, it was still more than a superficial comparison when Ilse Nydhalm came to perceive with every breath of hers, as a new and great expression of her entire being, the indissoluble unity between *what is thought and what is experienced, what is thinkable and what is liveable [zwischen Gedachtem und Erlebtem, zwischen Denkbarem und Erlebbarem]*" (*p.96*).

An amassment of words about that whereof one should not speak. And if you think that these "words" are borrowed from science! You have as a first "given" Einstein's daring theory of the expanding universe expounded, in his time, in the dry, compelling language of mathematical physics. And then, you experience the awe it inspires. Yet who can experience such awe? Obviously only those who have the utterly rational education leading to grasp the theory: science expands the domain of the frightful; whereby I don't mean "the bomb", but science's formidable ability to expand the frontiers beyond which lurks the ever expanding unknowable, the dread we cannot speak about. But apart from this, the awesome discovery offers itself as a metaphor *only* to him who is familiar with its expressible side, helping to insight and recognition, that type of "recognition" which

> "hovered like a multiple echo under the vault of existence, and the words which carried it, the voice which carried the words, floated

on the reverberating sound waves of the spheres and yet in [that recognition] itself".

Thus Ilse and her maker, Broch, arriving at the end of science's wits adopt the dark language of the poet, when interrupting one of Richard's exercises in scientific rhetoric:

> "'It is in fact frightening that a man has discovered and thought all this'.
>
> "Yet above the awesomeness of this thought hovered, even more frightfully, the *second meaning of the World*, hardly to be understood, hardly to be expressed either in mathematical forms or in a word, and still lifted above all dread; a strange coolness and free movement of the brain, an exciting transposition into a *second order reality*, which did not correspond to anything anymore and yet carried in itself the evidence of the perfect truth" (p.97).

This is hardly anything the philosopher (of the positivist persuasion) would call a meaningful statement. It is not, of course. In a philosophical exercise, developed on its own, as an expression of insight, it would possibly leave us exactly where we have been before reading it. But within the novelistic parable it is an indicative illustration of the attempt of our heroes, and often of us, to try to erode with word-floods the foundations of those walls surrounding the limited province of that which can be meaningfully expressed. It is not the frivolous talkie-talkie type of poetry, the pretext for those who avoid to know, who think that indulgence in verbosity is good enough an excuse for not being able to extract a square root. Rather it is the expression of a controlled and dignified resignation of those who tried knowledge and, in spite of the poetic intermezzos, cannot fool themselves with words. Because they realized, as Richard Hieck did during that very same session, that:

> "The essential is not expressible. The ultimate truth like the deepest sin [are] the limits of the Word. He looked towards the nocturnal plain, avoiding to meet the eyes of Ilse.
>
> "Love.

"Instantly he remembered the word; it horrified him, but he was unable to associate anything with it" (p.98).

Because, you see, when you are a scientist you expect from yourself to use only words with which you can associate something, maybe even to reduce them all, as Bertrand Russell once proposed, to "object language". One wonders what "love" would mean in such a language. Something of this kind preoccupied Richard who now "was confusedly reminded of human copulations, and recalled even more dimly that he himself had been part of such", all this, while "the nocturnal sky shined like a wet swimming suit". Yet, all this was not quite what the remembered word was meant to convey. When he continued his "treacherous" rhetoric

"he said something what he so far never formulated, indeed never even thought of: 'he who succeeded to achieve so much insight as to encompass the whole Process, is immortal... I mean subjectively immortal'. And immediately afterwards he was ashamed" (p.98-99).

But Ilse was on the right track when, noticing a shooting star, she said:

"'I wished something for myself...' and as he waited in silence she added awkwardly: '...that you may achieve this immortality.'"

The limits of the Word? It is rather the ability of the Word to convey "the second meaning of the World", to picture "a second order reality".

Ilse Nydhalm had it easier because she didn't let herself be tormented by her own internal Censor. She even allowed herself the indulgence of a wish, to profit from the sight of a shooting star. Richard got nervous, indeed angry when a metaphor, even a scientific one, slipped through his tight control system. It was so when another student, preparing her dissertation under his supervision took her leave for vacation. Erna Magnus was first meant by Kapperbrunn to be that "pretty negresse", but then he realized that the rich girl with too many worldly interests wouldn't provide the dedication needed to order Professor Weitprecht's scientific-literary heritage. Richard inquired about her going "to the mountains" for a vacation and thought that "the mountains, to which Erna Magnus may go, were doubtless bigger, more copious and mundane than those in which Kapperbrunn spent now his time. And that between the life which roared incomprehensibly through those mountain brooks and the abstract life of the Institute, Erna Magnus established a peculiar connection, a very peculiar connection indeed, which reached as far as the room of Susanne".

The girl, whom he once wanted to show around the Observatory, mockingly remarked, in lieu of a farewell, that "I have tormented you enough… You have it easier with Ilse Nydhalm, isn't it?" And now it was Richard's turn to find a graceful way out, by both answering and neutralizing the joking insinuation of this very feminine Erna Magnus, a lady "so incomprehensible to have anything to do with electron charges", whose presence, however, enhanced somehow the femininity of all the other girl students, including Ilse:

> "'Miss Nydhalm's work is completely different from yours'.
> "'I would think so'. Laughing gently and warmly, Erna Magnus took a loving couple under her protection. She was a real woman. Yet, instantly, her laughter remained suspended in space and *Richard came to think of a chemical or physical catalyst, the presence of which is absolutely necessary for the effecting of certain reactions, but which itself remains outside that reaction*".

It was a strange realization that the presence of a woman, of the kind hardly to be reached ever, should act as a catalyst in the budding love affair between Richard and Ilse. But was it this? What kind of a silly indulgence is this comparison?

> "The metaphor about the catalyst doesn't state anything [*besagt nichts*], it was not a theory; his urge for theory construction has not been satisfied. He took gloomily the file with the research results of Erna Magnus: 'Well, to see you in the fall'" (p.105-106).

The word "Love": how strange and inadequate it was. The experience of love required more searching for expression. Richard realized "that he owed something to Ilse Nydhalm, and that he owed also to Love something that could not be substituted by mathematical conversations". And yet when he tried to transcend them it was still mathematics to provide the only language in which he was able to find the quieting metaphor: he saw

> "love, or whatever it was to be in its place, as *a curve swinging to-wards infinity, eternally converging to it,* [the "world" he hoped for himself and Ilse – T.S.], yet never reaching it" (p.116).

(Apropos: Among the examples proposed by Lichtenberg we read that "what is called an asymptote in higher geometry is apt to describe many things in Nature, succinctly and yet with a precision rarely offered by any [other] paraphrase".) And he could understand everybody else's tranquility and adequacy only in such a translation. Thus, in the chapel-like room of Susanne "the pictures [of saints on the walls] suggested to him the symbolics of an impenetrable algebra" (p.118). As he got more and more accustomed to using these little metaphor-devils, he also arrived at the full realization that they offer, if not the means, at least a comforting surrogate for "*das Wort befreiend aus der Ruchlosigkeit des Unzulänglichen*" or "the Word liberating from the profligacy of Inadequacy", as an ever inadequate translation would render the adjective-turned-noun "*das Unzulängliche*", which in German is often fraught with some philosophical second meaning. This quote is reminiscent of the last verses of Goethe's Faust in which the *chorus mysticus* characterizes the place of Faust's ultimate salvation:

> "*Das Unzulängliche,*
> "Hier wird's Ereigniss;
> "Das Unbeschreibliche
> "*Hier ists getan;*"

i.e. what was unfulfilled, inadequate in the world of our senses [*das Unzulängliche*], becomes here an accomplished occurrence; what escaped description (the "Word") affirms itself in action or in material facts. The inadequate and inexpressible cannot be mastered ultimately through speech, controlled by logic:

"The grasping of the incalculable by means of the calculable, this is what it is all about, and when it fails then all what remains is the sharp dividing line between the two" (p.129),

and only the metaphor or parable can venture beyond it. May I add this?

Tragedy led the story to a rather poor conclusion. Otto, the artistic printer took his life because he suspected (without foundation) that his comely, young mother had an affair with his best friend. This might have offered stuff for a good story in the vein of another Vienna fad of the time, namely psychoanalysis. But it was not to be. It is not clear what exactly this episode, the best developed of all, with unquestionable literary merits, was meant to become. In the novel it served only as a powerless excuse for a basically happy-in-sorrow family reunion (the elegant Emilie was back from Berlin) of which Ilse Nydhalm was part ("Pretty your little bride" said warmly a homely Emilie). And all this was then patched over with some remarks about Rudolf's acceptance of the fact that "the solitary cognition of love, the moral law, [is] valid without proof" (p.141).

By proclamation, of course (confusedly remembering Kant's "moral law", probably), and not by fully developing the drama of recognition, leaving us an unequally composed yet highly relevant novelistic torso.

Between Hieck and Törless

The dictum of Wittgenstein quoted at the beginning of this essay is the 7th point, and the last, of his Tractatus. All the six previous points have numerous numbered corollaries and scholia. Thus point 1. is elaborated in paragraphs 1.1 to 1.21; point 2. - from 2.01 to 2.225 - and so on. The seventh point is the quoted phrase and nothing more, since nothing can follow after it. The rules for the speakable have been discussed in the previous six sections and he did not consider - not in the Tractatus - that whereof one may tell parables, that is the use of words beyond that whereof one may speak.

The somewhat awkwardly told story of Richard Hieck is a parable meant to teach us of a difference we cannot properly speak about: the difference between *the Word as metaphor for the unknown and the Word abused as substitute for knowledge*. For him the Word is no substitute for what can and should be known as it so often becomes within some literary-artistic fashion. But Hieck discovered the metaphoric use of speech, however awkwardly and painfully. Reading his story we may become aware of the fact that as the understanding of the world in the language of science becomes more and more demanding, we become, more than in the past, exposed to the seduction of those who supply cheap and sweet rhetoric surrogates. It is some sort of ordered production of verbal substitutes for precise knowledge by which demagoguery of all brow heights, from the lowest even to the highest, preys upon people's minds. It was the fear of being soaked down the mire of empty talk which made Richard seek refuge in the precision of the mathematical idiom. His father, whose strange ways he wanted to avoid, didn't really sin against proposition number 7. Not in a major way. He did not speak a lot about what tormented his thoughts, because he couldn't find meaningful words, or meaning to the words. The occasional metaphoric utterances underscored rather than denied his shunning of shallow talk. But Richard didn't yet learn about this other use of the word. He arrived to it on the road which in his case led through mathematical studies.

Broch's novel was first published in the fateful year 1933. He understood it, as a manuscript at the Yale University Library testifies, as a search for an answer to the following question:

> "in what way can a man dedicated to science ... coming from his own specialized field, arrive at the solution of that *Erkenntnisrest* [or 'that rest beyond cognition', manifested in the great questions of death, love, the fellow human - T.S.]? Does such a road exist?"

Important is not Broch's attempt to answer in this truncated note but rather how the question is answered by the novel itself in which it seems to appear as the mystical *Erlebniss* [or life experience] *beyond knowledge,* yet not as *substitute for knowledge.* True, our awareness of what is "beyond" and what is "instead of" is not always very strongly differentiated. Yet it is the "beyond" which Rudolf Hieck was led to experience. He never thought of trading the *knowledge* achieved for some *insight* never to be gained. Therefore the reader will also learn only about one aspect of the tension between science and human experience. Another aspect should be focused upon for the reader of Robert Musil's "Young Törless".

This masterpiece of short novel writing has been published in 1906, twenty-seven years before the "Unknown magnitude". Better known, widely read, discussed and commented upon it would seem to be a fully exhausted subject. It is not. One important aspect of it emerges when we re-read it in a trial of gaining additional insight into the problematic complexity of Richard Hieck's story. All this seems to be a very strange recommendation by the standards of many critics. Yet I propose a trial.

There are many threads of which young Törless' life is plaited; one is marking the path of liberation from the mind of mystical demagoguery to rigorous thinking. It is also the narrow, accidental path which leads from oppression to liberation, from human degradation to human dignity. For Törless the path led through mathematical "revelations". And for us, the readers, it reveals the other side of the tension between the urge to speak and that whereof we may not speak. This is the reason why the (re-)reading will invite us to comparisons with the "Unknown magnitude".

Young Törless

The superiority of Musil's novel consists in its high dramatic tension which reveals, through action and direct speech, the complexity of a major human conflict concentrated in the microcosm of an aristocratic junior college somewhere in the Austria of the late XIX and early XX century. To direct our attention to what is most important to me, often treated as an episode of lesser and misunderstood significance, we shall briefly call the role of the story's main personae. Apart from the hero, the son of *Hofrat* Törless, a rather shy and pensive, intelligent and philosophical youth, we have:

Beineberg: son of a commissioned cavalry officer who hated books and intellectual controversies in general, but had a propensity towards a special kind of readings.

> "These had to be books ... which were like a symbol of a sacred Order and a guarantee of transcendental revelations. Such he found only in the books of Indian philosophy, which didn't seem to him to be simply books, but revelations, realities - cryptic works like the books of medieval alchemists and sorcerers" (p.19).

Beineberg inherited from his father "the habit to read in books in which no word was supposed to be moved from its place" if the cryptic meaning was to be preserved.

Reiting: an "admirer of Napoleon", manipulator of people, attracting yet frequently changing followers. He "knew no greater pleasure than pitting people against one another, subdue one with the help of the other, or revel in extorted favors and adulations"(p.40) which could barely hide the victim's repressed hatred of his tormentor.

Both Beineberg and Reiting, individually and in association, lived secret lives in the seclusion of a forgotten roof chamber of the old Institute building contriving plots to gain power over others. The younger Törless participated in all this up to a certain point and they tolerated him for two major reasons. First because they needed some sort of recognition from an outsider and second, because he was of a particular use for them:

> "The mind of Törless was the nimblest. Once set on a particular track, he was exceedingly fertile in ideating the most subtle combinations. Nobody else could predict with greater precision the variety of possible effects to be expected from the behavior of a person in a specific situation. Yet he failed, lost interest and could not muster the required energy whenever he was to make a decision on his own risk, based on the conclusion that one of the available psychological possibilities was the certain outcome to be expected and acted upon" (p.41).

To analyze and predict the behavior of others: he was good at and thus useful to Beineberg and Reiting. To use and abuse others directly: he either had scruples or was too weak.

Bassini: the weakling in the story, the typical victim and the main experimental object to test and reveal the characters of the other three. His pecuniary means were not up to his spending habits and consequently he was permanently in debt. Also to Reiting, who used this as a method of extortion and subjection. And this is the source of the main intrigue.

To pay off his debts to Reiting, Bassini breaks into the lockers of other students. Reiting finds out his secret and, threatening to deliver him to his colleagues and the school authorities, achieves to subject Bassini to humiliating (and sadistic) trials in power and domination. These were to serve as practice in domination for a would-be "Napoleon" and to offer also Beineberg a subject for his occult investigations. Törless also becomes involved, and the "experiments" take place through several weeks in a room in the loft of the school.

The ensuing story is a thorough introduction in the mechanics of human degradation and the book was also - rightly - celebrated as a prophetic foretelling of the emergence of the Nazi Man. It tells about Bassini becoming the guinea pig for the education of would-be "supermen"; and about Törless breaking away from the gang. We will dwell only upon one aspect of the awakening of Törless which is about the fine line separating knowledge and parable.

The Mathematical Puzzle of Törless

The shy "Törless was afraid of them. But he was afraid only as one fears a giant known to be blind and stupid..." (p.49). This knowledge kept him throughout the exercises of Bassini-tormenting at some distance from the other two. Then, "during mathematics classes, an idea suddenly occurred to Törless". It was an idea about some philosophical problem in mathematics, seldom to preoccupy the average student: an idea far away from the demeaning and dirty nocturnal exercises, yet bound to disrupt the course of the horrible routine.

Every one of us learned at school that the square of any negative number is a positive number: negative multiplied by negative yields positive. This is adopted as an axiom in some renditions of the principles of algebra and is an undisputed rule in computation. It doesn't follow from observing reality; it is not an *a posteriori synthetic statement,* to use the terminology of the philosopher. Yet it works in practice: all computations which are at the foundation of those marvelous and frightful creations of technology which we use and abuse, work perfectly well in spite of something so strange for the laymen that the product of negatives be positive. It becomes even more puzzling when we want to extract the square root of a negative number. Now square roots of positive numbers may be positive or negative, but negative numbers do not occur to have square roots, because no square of any number can be negative. Right? Wrong. Negative numbers have "imaginary numbers" as roots: if you square an "imaginary" number you get a negative number. But imaginary numbers are, of course, *imagined* rather than "real". Yet imagined though they are, they

also "work" in the world of real, tangible things. Törless, who was not yet beyond the level of his turn-of-the-century high school math, wondered:

> "Is it not like a bridge of which [only] the pillars on two ends are in
> place and which we may yet cross as safely as if it would be entirely
> built? For me such computations have something dizzying.... *The
> weird thing about it is the power which lies in such calculations and
> holds us tight so that we land safely again*" (p.74).

We have here a new rendition of the same mystery which puzzled already
the young and studious Stendhal:

> «*Suivant moi l'hypocrisie était impossible dans les mathématiques ...
> Que devins-je quand je m'aperçus que personne ne pouvait m'expli-
> quer comment il se faisait que: moins par moins donne plus (- x - =
> +)?*» ["According to me hypocrisy was impossible in mathemat-
> ics ... What happened then to me when I realized that nobody
> could explain me how it was possible that minus times minus
> gives plus (- x - = +)?"]

Since his teachers weren't smart enough to explain him the mystery:

> «*On faisait bien pis que ne pas m'expliquer cette difficulté (qui sans
> doute est explicable car elle conduit à la vérité), on me l'expliquait
> par des raisons évidemment peu claires pour ceux qui me les présen-
> taient. Monsieur Chabert pressé par moi s'embarrassait, répétait sa
> leçon, celle précisément contre laquelle je faisait des objections, et
> finissait par avoir l'air de me dire: 'Mais c'est l'usage, tout le monde
> admet cette explication. Euler et Lagrange, qui apparamment va-
> laient autant que vous, l'ont bien admise.*» ["They did worse than
> just not explaining to me this difficulty (which is beyond doubt
> explainable since it leads to truth); they gave me some explana-
> tions which were rather confused, if you consider who gave them.
> *Monsieur* Chabert [the math teacher - T.S.] being prodded by me,
> got embarrassed and repeated his lesson, the one namely against
> which I made objections, and ended up by having the nerve to

tell me: 'But this is the usage, everybody accepts this explanation. Euler and Lagrange, who apparently are worth as much as yourself, have admitted it."]

Yet Stendhal, as Törless, understood that "the weird thing" must make sense *car elle conduit à la vérité*, that truth which consists in the power to "hold us tight so that we land safely" from that "unfinished" bridge. [And some philosophers would claim that it is not "as if" we would cross safely a not yet finished bridge, but rather that bridges, real ones, can be safely thrown only when such logical problems have been given a logical, however counterintuitive, solution. Thus, in the minutes taken by students during "Wittgenstein's lectures on the Foundations of Mathematics" in Cambridge, 1933, we read: "It was suggested last time that the danger with a contradiction in logic or mathematics is in the application. Turing suggested that a bridge might collapse" (p.211). And whenever it does not collapse, even though its engineers abide by the *rule of signs*, well, then there is no contradiction ...].

Now, the problem of imaginary numbers doesn't bear any relevance to matters of human morality, or so it seems. Still it was to trigger a major moral conflict. At the beginning it was just an intellectual puzzle for Törless. Then in search for an answer, he visited first the math teacher. The answers of the teacher were totally unsatisfactory; they didn't go beyond the suggestion that longer and more persistent study of and preoccupations with mathematics will lead the student to a better understanding. This was the usual teacher's cop-out plus references to the philosophy of Kant which allegedly said the last word about some innate urges of ours under which we may comfortably order the puzzling rules of mathematics. Earlier also Törless accepted - such was the convention in better society - that Kant was the last word in philosophy, so you have not to bother with philosophy anymore. Now, exactly this has changed. Since it was no more clear whether Kant had the answers or was used only as a cop-out pretext, Törless decided to further investigate.

In his search he also addressed Beineberg, thinking that his colleague's interest for the metaphysical could be enlisted for a fruitful discussion and common preoccupation. Instead, Beineberg acted like some lesser degree substitute Mephisto who tries to use Faust's doubts and hesitations to make him assume the fateful pledge; he quoted several other puzzles or "contradictions" of mathematics, some of those which already in the time of the story have been quite elegantly solved by set-theorists and geometricians (generating, as solutions go, other puzzles), and added:

"I think, if people would be too conscientious, Mathematics wouldn't exist at all" (p.73).

Mark the difference to Kapperbrunn for whom mathematics was an "island of decency" in a world of foul rhetoric! For Beineberg, the problems of Törless were not here to be solved by rigorous logical labor but a hindrance on the short-cut offered by the insights of what he fancied to be "Indian philosophy". For a man who trained himself in the ruthless exercise of power

"all those laces...of which we are told by the professors, are so thin that we may not yet touch them, they are dead - frozen".

"They are dead". "Alive" is something else: "liberation" from all rules of consistency of which mathematics is the paradigm.

Only shortly before the math discussion Beinberg explained to Törless:

"Now you can see what this is all about. The urge to let Bassini get away is of a low, external origin. [...] For me it is a prejudice I have to get rid of as of everything else which distracts me from my interest.

"Precisely the fact that I feel it difficult to torment Bassini - I mean to humiliate him, oppress him, depart him from me - is good. It requires a sacrifice. It will have a cleansing effect. I owe myself to learn on him every day, that the plain human existence doesn't mean anything - it is simply an apish exterior resemblance" (p.60).

And human existence did really not mean anything to him as we already could have found out earlier:

"As far as Bassini is concerned, I think he would be no big loss, whether we turn him in or beat him, or whether we torture him half dead for the pure pleasure of it. *'Cause I cannot imagine that such a man should really mean something in the marvelous mechanism of the world"* (p.56).

There is no *necessary* connection between loathing logical labor and any form of mysticism of your choice, be that of the subtle variety of some oriental seer or of the gross, vulgar, beastly brand professed by Beineberg. If he would have known anything about the origins of algebra, the science of which important parts came down from India traveling with an Arabic name, or of number theory, under which some of Törless' problems are subsumed, then he may have learned that metaphysical contemplation and rigorous dedication to "all these laces" could be fruitfully paired and live along with those moral "prejudices of a low and external origin". But the purpose of a literary work, or any work of art, is not to demonstrate necessary connections. Wherever such are assessed or inferred they will be absorbed in the body of science. Yet, the epic (and dramatic) work comes about by confronting the vast mesh of possible yet not necessary connections, and then by un-plaiting some of the trajectories they contain as a potential.

Mathematics and Mutating Insights

When Doktor Richard Hieck, in an accidental instance, experienced the unspeakable emotion named "love", he was also forced to recognize for the first time (in other words: he gave up resisting the recognition), that logical rigor and semantic hygiene do not always apply. Thus insight beyond knowledge sprang of an emotion.

When Törless was struck by Beineberg's insistence to shove away as "irrelevant" everything to which logic does apply, in order to expand the dominion of that inarticulate darkness in which the pseudo-oriental mystic felt homely, he also arrived at a recognition: the muddled verbiage in which Beineberg washed out problems to be dealt with in plain logical terms, is the same poisoned spring of which the beastliness of the nocturnal experiments swills.

Hieck gained happiness in discovering serene landscapes in the world of emotions *beyond* knowledge. Törless discovered the dreadful consequences in a world of dark emotions meant to *substitute* knowledge.

Chancing upon a subtle and difficult problem of learning, Törless tried out a variety of approaches as suggested by his immediate human environment, specifically the math teacher and Beineberg. The disappointment with both in matters mathematical, enlightened him about the humanity of each, or better the lack thereof. Beineberg's answer in terms of easy yet ill-temper fraught rhetoric engendered a mutation in Törless' insight:

Törless (after an infatuated lecturing by Beineberg):"Neither may your assertions be so sure, after all".

Beineberg: "How can you say this! They are the only sure thing. But why shall I bicker with you about this?! You will come to see, dear Törless; I would even bet that one day you will show a goddamn interest for what implications this may have. For example, when we will arrive with Bassini as I...."

T.: "Leave this please.... I would right now avoid mixing these things together".

B.: "Oh, why?"

T.: "Just so. I simply don't want it. It is disagreeable to me. Bassini and this [the mathematical-philosophical issue discussed] are two different things for me; and I don't cook two dishes in the same pot" (p.83).

What for Beinberg were two things of one and the same kind, things to be subordinated to the same purportedly mystical insight allowing for the dehumanizing experiments, appeared to be two "dishes" different in kind for Törless. They were not supposed to be cooked in the same pot. This realization did not come about by necessary reasoning! It came about by a sequence of experiences; not by a chain of deductions.

First, it was the participation in the nightly *séances* during which he himself contributed an occasional "idea" to the search for the bottom, if any, of human baseness, while basking a little in his own meanness as well. Then, a cold intellectual problem, the question of imaginary numbers, surfaced. The confrontation with this problem revealed to Törless the miracle of practical, tangible, this-worldly relevance of those purely mental constructions which constitute the edifice of mathematics. It lead to the recognition of the fact that some outgrowths of the human mind are applicable with success, according to their peculiar grammar, to the world of our senses, while others, such as the "insights" of some unnamed oriental mystics, are pure guesswork. This has drawn a clear divide across the so far inarticulate muddle of his ideas, beliefs, concepts, learning games and perversely acquired insights. Finally, this recognition lead to the end of any further participation in those "experiments" in the loft. Of these only a vague, unexpressed and then fading homosexual interest in Bassini survived. When, subsequently, a desperate Bassini offered himself naked, begging for protection against Reitling and Beineberg, Törless, refusing the offer, interrogated Bassini once again about his odd, shameful and painful encounters with them. It was only for a short instance when in the old perverse way of "learning" he answered to Bassini's complaint that "you torment me...":

> "Yes, I torment you. But this is not my purpose. I want to know only one thing: what is called forth in you when I cause my questions to penetrate you like a dagger?" (p.104).

Yet this was no more one of those "experimental" questions he occasionally contributed to the exercises of Reitling and Beineberg. It happened just so, in the heat of an interrogation about the most recent goings-on in the roof chamber, and right after it he explained to Bassini:

> "I do not want to torment you. I want only to force you to tell the whole truth. Maybe in your own interest" (p.99)

- since he was already prepared to bring all this to a conclusion in one way or another.

It was, as we saw, a sequence of intimate experiences which lead Hieck to the discovery of the trans-logical. The components of this sequence had no necessary connection with one another as steps of a mathematical or logical consecution may have. The rejection of the anti-logical by Törless was the end of a sequence of similar nature. It is particularly interesting to follow his reaction after the fruitless meeting with the math teacher. Instead of being disappointed with science, he became disappointed with some of its practitioners who answered, as the math teacher, in the confused language of the "outsider". Thus it was up to him to look for an answer and he started with a dramatic and categorical move:

> "It was to be a marvelously enjoyable afternoon. Törless pulled all his poetic exercises from the locker where he kept them stored. He settled with his papers by the fireplace, and abided, unseen behind the screen, all by himself. He turned the pages of one booklet after another, tore them slowly to very small shreds and committed them to the flames, one by one, every time savoring the subtle emotion of parting."

It was the poetical exercises he had to get rid of in a ritual of liberation before a new dawn:

> "... Tomorrow I will carefully review everything and I will surely gain clarity" (p.79).

Yet this was not to happen right the next day, but when the moment came to disclose everything to the school authorities he already gained clarity:

> "Törless felt that the moment arrived when he will speak clearly, distinctly, confident in victory about what was in him first so unclear and tormenting, and then so lifeless and deprived of strength" (p.136).

Well, well; he should speak "clearly, distinctly", "*klar und deutlich*". Descartes crept in again as in Broch's novel. Yet none of our two authors volunteered to give us a definition for that "*claire et distincte*", a definition still owed to us even by the founder of analytical geometry. And it was as with all major recognitions. Musil explains:

> "... A great recognition [*Erkenntnis*] comes about only to a half within the halo of the brain. The other half emerges from the darkest depth of our innermost, and it is essentially an affective state on

the tip of which Thought sits like a blossom. Törless needed only an emotional shock to bring this urge to the fore".

It was this urge to recognize the distinction between things which ought not to be "cooked in the same pot", when he was talking to the investigation commission of the Institute's teachers:

> "'Maybe I was mistaken with the irrational numbers: if I think of them in some sense along mathematical lines then they seem to be quite natural; when I view them in their own peculiarity, they appear to be impossible. Yet this is where I might be mistaken, since I know very little about them. But I wasn't wrong about Bassini... *No I wasn't wrong when I spoke about a second, hidden, unnoticed life of things*! [Just remember Hieck's "second order existence"! – T.S.] I don't mean it literally - not that the things are alive or that Bassini has two faces – but *in me was a second one which looked at things not with the eyes of reason*. Just as I feel when an idea comes to life in me, so I do also feel that something else is alive in me when I look at things while my thoughts are at rest. There is something dark inside me which I found incommensurable with my thoughts, a life that cannot be expressed in words and yet it is my life...'

> "'... Now, it is over. I know now that I was mistaken after all. I know: the Things are the Things and will always be like that; and I will always view them in one or the other way. Sometimes with the eyes of Reason, sometimes with those other ones...and I will never again try to check one against the other'.

> "He fell silent. He thought it most natural to leave and nobody prevented him from doing so" (p.137-8).

His speech was not clear yet, but Törless had learned to keep the irrational in its own "pot" and neither to mix it in the other "pot", nor put it in its stead.

Long ago I read these two novels as stories in their own right. Broch's I experienced as a minor love story (and as a love story, minor it is indeed!) of people whom we are seldom inclined to think of as lovers. Musil's I recognized as one of the stories about the emergence of the human material which performed the horrors of our century - which it is, in a major and powerful way, as often recognized. Later, however, I reread them with philosophical awareness and discovered an essential common element: both are parables of the seventh (and my apocryphal eighth) proposition in Wittgenstein's "Tractatus". The authors' intentions are irrelevant; they may not care for any particular philosopher but they grew up as writers in the same philosophical environment and had to confront the same problems. Neither finished here with their discovery - Broch continued the road of parabolic exploration of the world beyond that whereof one may speak and arrived, through "The Sleepwalkers" [*"Die Schlafwandler"*], at the poetic masterpiece of "The Death of Virgil" [*Der Tod des Virgil*]. Musil transformed the Törless, escaped from the stuffy atmosphere of the Institute, into one Ulrich, "The Man Without Qualities" [*Der Mann ohne Eigenschaften*], mathematician by background but not trade, who struggles for the expansion of the field of rationally controllable and for keeping the irrational in its pot - without talking it out of this world in the shallow parlance of popular science bigots.

And the reader's discovering turnabout was also liberation from the "psychoanalytic" abuse which is only too often offered as critical analysis of these books.

> [P.S. Törless is, of course, a great boon for the literary psycho-analyst. At one time I thought to present each and everyone of them whom I encountered during my reading adventures with a photocopy of Musil's essay: *Der bedrohte Ödipus* ["The Endangered Oedipus"]. But then I realized that this would be, apart from costly, also a redundant exercise; just as Musil's essay was. Because he, purportedly, targeted litterateurs implied to have the following two characteristics: (1) they are followers of some teacher to be found along the spectrum extending from Freud to Jung; (2) they are endowed with a good sense of humor. But this is a contradiction.]

ESSAY NO.10

The Novel of a Mathematician

- About the "Man Without Qualities" by Robert Musil-

Er ist hochmütig mathematisch, aber kommt auch nicht weiter. Traum eines Logikers... [v.5, p.1952]

[He is superciliously mathematical, yet he doesn't get any farther either. Dream of a logician ...]

Yet another introduction! And the reader of this essay is certainly justified when asking: why? First remember: the author of *"Der Mann ohne Eigenschaften"*, or "The Man without Qualities", Robert Musil himself, felt also quite uneasy about several aspects of his novel, and struggled with the idea of an "explanatory" preface during the entire duration of the writing - which didn't end with the completion of the work. The reasons of his concern will be addressed, explicitly and implicitly, in the subsequent discussions. Not here, in this purported "introduction" to the essay, which is itself, as said, an "introduction". One of the many. Here, a simple justification will be offered for this "again". Because, you see, anybody would be entitled to ask: "is it not simpler and easier to just read the novel without an introduction (other than that proposed by the author himself, with ideas scattered in countless notes, articles, diary pages, etc.)?" It would be, if the conscientious reader had not been already overwhelmed with introductions, interpretations, "readings", or that peculiarly German exercise [which often inspires French caricatural variations] called *Deutung* - a term which, if translated, would lose its particular flavor and deprive you of a pleasant, relaxing smile. Some of these - and they justify the subsequent notes - have successfully distracted the reader of the novel from what is actually *in* it. They bask with voluptuous nostalgia in the story, perceived ("interpreted", "read", etc.) as yet another representation of a world which - unfortunately, oh! - was soon to crumble under the illusion-plated cover of moderate happiness and innocent *Gutmütigkeit*. Reading some (please: *some!*) of these papers, one has the impression that the authors themselves are among the marginal characters of the Musil novel, just barely mentioned or only suspected to camp somewhere in the same Vienna, say in the smoke cloud of the *Cafe Central* or, perhaps, *Griensteindel*. (God, how happy they would be to be really there! Never mind that ill-heated, ill-smelling *möbliertes Zimmer im vierzehnten Bezirk* which naturally goes with it). In reality they are much farther in time and space, but chew all the same, and with great delight, stories about that great performance at the *Oper*, the going adventure of Alma Mahler, or the last literary antiques of Karl Kraus. But it is they who also supply the more scholarly information about what otherwise the reader on the North-American continent may get only from Walter Cronkite's zoological television shows complete with the *Fledermaus* and *Lipizaner* horses. Anything against it? Absolutely nothing!! Except that it would be useful if the reader were to change, slightly, the angle of the lens through which he reads the book and discover *in* the book something of which the critics who polished his lens don't seem to know a lot. And this little variation will lead to the understanding of the difference between what Musil had to offer and what most of the countless other writers of the same historical-geographical definition have supplied.

No ample discussion should enlighten us. Not in this short (short?) introduction to the subsequent introduction. Rather a suggestion is to be made by quoting an example which is a perfect epitome of the confusion in which otherwise worthy scholars of literature address this particular subject. The instance to be reviewed is part of *the translation of a quotation* from an early and revealing article by Robert Musil about "The Mathematical Man" - *Der matematische Mensch*, first published in 1913 without signature. Why to review a translation? Well, because translations do often reveal misunderstandings. There is an Italian saying: *traduttore traditore*. The translator is a traitor.

It certainly often happened that a translator/interpreter deliberately mislead his employer. But even the most honest and dedicated translator may unwittingly become a traitor. To himself. Because as long as he does not have to translate, we may not find out about what he doesn't know. However, as soon as he translates, we have an easy time finding out about what is missing from his store of knowledge, particularly about his lack of information pertaining to the subject matter of the translated text.

The fragment discussed is from a book on *"Robert Musil and the Crisis of European Culture 1880-1942"* (University of California Press) signed David S. Luft. First I will quote the relevant section in Musil's article in the German original; then the translation of David S. Luft; and finally my own translation. (And if you have a friend whose German is better than yours, ask him/her to help you choose the correct translation or to improve on the existing ones.) In all three fragments the phrase to be discussed is either in bold (in the German text) or in italics (in the two translations).

Here is the fragment in the German original:

> *"Wir plärren für das Gefühl gegen den Intellekt und vergessen dass Gefühl ohne diesen - abgesehen von Ausnahmefällen - eine Sache so dick wie ein Mops ist. Wir haben damit unsere Dichtkunst schon so weit ruiniert,* **dass man nach je zwei hintereinander gelesenen deutschen Romanen ein Integral auflösen muss, um abzumagern.***"*

Now the Luft translation:

> "We beat the drums for feeling against intellect and forgot that without it - aside from a few exceptional cases - feeling is a thing as dense as a blockhead. In this way we have ruined our imaginative literature so badly *that every time one reads two German novels in a row, one must pause a moment to vomit.*" [op.cit. pag.112]

And this is the translation proposed by me:

> "We blubber our defense of *Feeling* against the *Intellect* while forgetting that feeling without intellect - apart from a few exceptions - is something as thick as a pug. We arrived thereby to ruin our

literature to such a degree *that after two German novels read one after another, one has to solve an integral to loose some weight."*

Now *vomiting* - of which there is no mention in the original! - and *solving an integral,* after having read two German novels of the turn of the century, have something in common. They both have a cleansing impact, only on completely different organs. By vomiting (a physician friend told me) one may cleanse one's stomach and ease one's mood. But solving an integral after those two feeling fraught novels which fattened the soul and restricted blood irrigation of the brain, is an operation of *intellectual cleanliness.* Musil, by naming that exercise in calculus (or mathematical analysis), meant exactly that sort of *intellectual hygiene* of which the "pure" litterateurs and "artistic minds" deprive themselves. And they not only deprive themselves of the benefits of rigorous mental gymnastics performed *more geometrico,* but also open the ways for all kind of abusive interpretations. The quoted translator betrayed in this fragment the poor standards of understanding for many aspects of Musil's writings, breeding those misreadings which prevail in the now flourishing Musil-industry, a sub-sector of the even more prosperous *fin de siècle Vienna* industry. You certainly cannot understand the complete message of Musil characters, such as the earlier Törless, and now that Ulrich "without qualities", when you refuse to make the effort required to comprehend the language they employ. Because "integral solving" is built into the novel; it is *in it.* But could be sensed only when you are aware of the simple *existence* of such before starting to read the novel. And for those who already enjoyed reading this fine book, the subsequent, well, "introduction" should offer a few clues about how to discover in it delightful, yet neglected, aspects. This may be thus a little "how to" exercise for a second reading.

One could quote without end from the critical literature instances testifying for the total incomprehension by the traditional litterateur of important aspects of Musil's discourse. To make all this useless (and to observe traditional humanistic politeness), the best solution, of course, is a measure of familiarization with that culture which is the "other" in relation to the one constituting the frame of your own preoccupations. If you adopt this as the postulate of your approach to the puzzling variety of human creation, then you will achieve what Goethe's Faust only aspired at:

"Dass ich nicht mehr mit sauerm Schweis
Zu sagen brauche, was ich nicht weiss"
[That I never again with sweat soaked brow
Should have to say what I don't know.]

I. The Programm of the Novel

(1.1) From Törless to Ulrich

Remember this momentous instance from Musil's first novel:

"It was to be a marvelously enjoyable afternoon. Törless pulled all his poetic exercises from the locker where he kept them stored, settled with his papers by the fireplace, and abided all by himself, unseen behind the screen. He took one notebook after another, turned the pages, tore them slowly to very small shreds and committed them to the flames, one by one, every time savoring the subtle emotion of parting." [v.6.p.79]

He now wanted to get rid of the verbose sham he used to call poetry, and he did so with a specific purpose:

"Tomorrow I will carefully review everything and I will surely gain clarity."

Törless freed himself from the underworld of his mystical-brutal college companions and celebrated the liberation with the ritual annihilation of things which reminded him of this nightmarish period of his time at the Institute.

About Törless' future, the novel offers only vague hints. There are many possible futures open for an individual thus defined, and the poet is free to make a choice according to his interest, experience and knowledge. He may also, either develop the ensuing life story of the same hero or, abandoning continuity, just pick out characteristic dramatic moments of his formation, graft them upon somebody else's life, see what potentials, if any, they activate in the new subject, and then develop them into an independent story. In the process of Törless' enlightenment, *the extension of the path which first lead from a problem in the foundations of mathematics to the discovery of the connection between crime and verbal mystification,* offered a subject worthy of exploration by "parametric" variation of circumstances. By a slight mutation, one could create an individual already enlightened about the foundations of mathematics, who also considers this science, beyond its purported immediate utility, as the paradigm of responsible, disciplined thinking. Then one might pursue his behavior and record his experiences in a society marching to its doom, through and by what will prove to be Crime, a crime covered-up with a thick cloud of ideology-charged verbiage, by the artful employment of muddled talk to convey imprecise thinking.

This is what Robert Musil attempted to undertake when ideating Ulrich, the hero of his long, unfinished - indeed unfinishable, as we will see - novel: "The Man without Qualities". [I would like to apologize for the above "Musil attempted" to whoever may read these notes. This is quite against what I should say if I were to strictly follow my own principle: *the intentions of the author are irrelevant,* because we have no sure way to know them. But it so happens that what we actually got in the novel is *as if* he had pursued the line of reasoning suggested above. But we should not guess; we should rather identify and emphasize aspects often neglected by conventional criticism, yet extant in the text. Except that *all words in the text ought to be understood.* Plain German is not enough for that.]

(1.2) Mathematical Precision and Semantic Cleanliness.

Mathematics and physicism, as philosophical *attitude* married to language criticism was, of course, a remarkable though still marginal feature of Vienna's turn of the century *Kultur*; and Ulrich was its obvious product. The influence of Mach, on whom Musil has written his doctoral thesis, but also that of the later emerging Wittgenstein, whom he quotes in "The Man" almost verbatim, without bothering to ever mention his name, as well as that of the "Vienna Circle", which flourished between the two world wars, is obvious in the thinking of Ulrich. The scientific sophistication of Musil places his own theoretical and Ulrich's "applied" language criticism, as activated in the novel, several stories above that of Vienna litterateurs such as Karl Kraus. Yet Musil shares with intellectual rebels of this environment the insight into the connection between a disgraceful, often criminal reality and the rhetoric screen meant to hide it. As the architect Adolf Loos claimed to have uncovered the connection between useless, un-functional, pompous decoration, burdening utilitarian architecture (and "applied art" in general) and the actual or potential criminality of the builder, so the novel-dialogues in which Ulrich engages will reveal a connection between pseudo-poetic word-setting as well as political rhetoric, and society's criminal cowardice manifested in its avoidance of grievous problems by enveloping them in a cloud of such verbiage.

The translation of his worldly experience into rigorous intellectual expression will be a programmatically expressed purpose of Ulrich's; at least in the *first book* of the two. This can be achieved only by fighting verbal mystification in politics, psychology or poetry. What was to become Ulrich's view on all this can be succinctly characterized by a quotation from one of those numerous, insightful and witty Musilian posthumous fragments, the one "On Princes and Street-names" (1925):

> "It seems thus that it was premature to view language as the element of difference between man and beast, since progress appears to point in the opposite direction. In fact the primeval man was convinced that one who knows the name has also the power over the thing or person [it designates]; he took language at its face value and used it with precaution. Nowadays no one fears that something can happen to him who uses language thoughtlessly and negligently." (v.7,p.791-92.)

We understand, of course, what is meant by this not very happily formulated statement which is, nevertheless, representative not only for the book's philosophy, but also for Musil's difficulties in putting through its message. Those whom he criticizes actually *do* behave like the "primeval man", because they believe that giving names to things will make them their master. *Thereby*(!), i.e. by "using language thoughtlessly and negligently" and taking it "at its face value". That this is what was really meant, will be amply developed in the novel - with as many essayistic explanatory twists.

Ulrich is an exception in his time. He knows, we are suggested, how words ought to be used. Therefore he wages a small scale guerilla warfare against the monster of semantic pollution; not with the purpose of liberating mankind of its pernicious delusions, but to protect first himself by making it his habit to reduce the Expressible to precise wording, while also continuously expanding the field of what we may meaningfully talk about. But what about the rest, that which is beyond meaningful verbal expression? The poet's own way of transcending this frontier is by suggesting the sights beyond it through the behavior of his fictional characters and the plot of their actions. Musil does this too, and in a masterly fashion. But not always. In the novel he often yields to the lure of the "beyond" and tries to approach it riding on the crest of sometimes (not always!) very fine essayistic asides. These offer readings worthy on their own of your studious attention. In most cases. But are not valid substitutes for a good story which hence has never been finished. More will be said on this in subsequent sections of this discussion.

Of the many things which characterized that year 1913, when the story begins, one was the forceful advancement of what the philosophically unsophisticated would be inclined to call the "domain of precision": science and technology. It became commonplace that while people increased their command, in knowledge and use, over their physical environment, (for good or evil - would read the skeptical addition of our environmentally concerned contemporary), the more obvious became their inability to get even with problems of humanity, leaving them to the confused and shallow "expertise" of those who claimed dominion over some undefined and indefinable, nebulous empires of "spirit" and "soul", *Geist und Seele*. The still young Ulrich, when working in an engineering bureau, was deeply puzzled by his brave and able colleagues, who were a perfect reflection of this contradiction:

> "They proved to be men closely attached to their drawing boards, who loved their profession in which they displayed an admirable competence; but they would have perceived a proposal to apply the boldness of their [scientific and technical] thinking on themselves, instead of their machines, as tantamount to transforming a hammer into a murder weapon".(p.38)

The boldness of scientific thinking wasn't yet to be applied to man's problems, still Ulrich searched for the way which leads towards solutions for as many of them as possible. Well, not so simply formulated! He was not deprived of "feelings", something usually opposed to "knowledge" by the self styled knights of "spirit" and "soul". Still, as he was to put it in a conversation with one of the main female characters of the story:

> "I have more feelings inside myself than you would think. But I want to protect them against all those discourses which are but idle words". (p.31)

This was not to be meant a simple academic exercise, or simply a "professional" search for philosophical adequacy by a character who, if viewed as a reflection of his author, was trained in the Austro-empiricist, more precisely: *empiriocriticist* school of the great physicist Ernst Mach, and has just arrived - with a measure of uncertainty - to the threshold of the logical positivists. Beyond this was a trial "to apply the boldness of their thinking" on himself and the permanently scrutinized society with which he developed a very peculiar intellectual commerce constituting the subject of the novel. Did he succeed?

There is no unambiguous answer to this question because there is no end to the trial. Not because the novel hasn't been finished, so that we have to contend with putting together ourselves, probably according to our own taste, some sort of an end from countless, often contradictory, posthumous fragments. But also because there is never an end to the trial to expand the domain of the meaningfully expressible; and because laying bare those who cannot stop talking about what we ought to be silent, is a continuous process.

(1.3) The Stage

The environment, as we recall, is pre-WWI Vienna, mainly a section of its high, very politically and *Kultur*-minded, society. The hero, Ulrich, is to function as an experimental reactive in this environment, a factor meant to provoke revealing responses. But it is not just another novel, however good, about the "crisis" of Austria, or Europe for that matter, before the great conflagration. That celebrated crisis is now only of historic interest and the Musil novel is only a secondary document of the period. Its timeless significance consists in the method as to be discussed, and which is new and distinctive in the art of novel-construction. The historic context was, of course, inevitable. Musil lived that history which, however, was mainly the supplier of experimental subjects for an enquiry which went well beyond the frame of yet another "*Kulturroman*". What exactly does this mean? Here are a few remarks, just for starters: the novel is an experiment in which the *limits of knowledge* in matters human are tested through the adventures of the characters, *the frontiers of the expressible explored*, and connections between modes of expression on the one hand and social behavior and human action on the other, exhibited. That above mentioned high society offers the matter on which the experiment is to be performed. If the novel contains also interesting elements for an understanding of the historic time of that experimental matter, this is implicit and secondary, however interesting. [Does anybody seriously believe that Balzac or Stendhal are important only because they testify about the "crisis" of France during the *Restauration* or the July monarchy? Who, other than a historian, gives nowadays a rotten eggshell for Charles X or Louis-Philippe and the "crisis" of their regimes?]

So it is 1913 and the stage is Vienna. A committee is convened to organize the celebration of the anniversary of the Emperor's 70-th year of reign. It is meant to compete with a similar action initiated in the neighboring "upstart" empire of the "Prussians", the victors of Königgrätz, who will have to be defeated this time on a ground on which the Habsburg elite thought itself to be stronger. It is the field of "*Kultur*" and "*Geist*" in which the "Parallel Action" is expected to reap Victory. And the Committee has to dream-up something which should make the festivities "a celebration of cultural superiority" over the "barbarians" in Berlin. The Committee, an assembly of distinguished personalities, didn't yet arrive to some concrete practical proposal in the unfinished manuscript of the novel; instead, its activity, the vain busying of its members, revealed the connection between semantic fuzziness and the collapse of the Hapsburg Empire. It showed the impossibility of semantic beguiling of the Inevitable which was already on the march before the Parallel Action could even have been launched.

This is, very broadly speaking, the spindle around which action, characters and ideas are clustered in the first book (two parts) of the intended novel in two books (four parts). Then slowly, slowly, the man with positivist philosophical background is discovering the metaphysical. And thus the main thread of the story gets lost, and characters, principal and episodical, will overwhelm the story each with their own "novel". The disintegration begins already in the second part (first book), but the fragments beyond it wouldn't have made it to a coherent fourth part anyway. The composing elements of the novel, instead of tending towards a skillfully crafted convergence, acquire an un-checkable power, fall off the construction scaffold and continue to progress on their own trajectory, at their own speed. Is this a failure? Not at all. It is just simply a novel which engenders other novels; it is an unfinished, probably impossible to finish, cycle. And I will try to propose a reading exercise in which the fairly rounded first two parts should be viewed as a starting point for the reading of several subsequent individual novels. This cannot be achieved by straightforward reading; and Musil knew it only too well when he dissertated so often and in so much detail about

(1.4) The Need for a Preface.

To be sure, action and narration are heavily fraught with the author's long, occasionally *agaçant*, yet more often insightful and witty essayistic excursi. But can we dump the ballast and still retain a clear novelistic work of art? - as we probably would be able in the case of Proust. If we were to scratch off some of the gratuitously sprinkled critical and essayistic stains on "*À la recherche du temps perdu*", the century's finest epic work would still, in unharmed elegance, cast its sadly revealing brilliance. In the case of Musil, however, we will have to live with the philosophizing plus. Not only because it can be enjoyable reading on its own, though when stripped off the main body of the work we may be inclined to read part of it as a collection of, however inspiring, literary café aphorisms. But also because it introduces us in a new type of novel. It is no more the exercise, so deeply despised by Socrates, to carry a mirror around in the world and capture a variety of images and actions. It seems that the "optical" approach to story telling has achieved the most it could in the 19-th century novel by alternating focus and vantage point of mirrors and lenses. Here a new type of story-telling comes about, which requires - because it is new, unfamiliar! - some, so to say, reading instructions to be considered by the unaccustomed reader. This is at least the opinion of Musil and we do justice to him and a service to us, as readers, when we review the arguments he adduces in favor of this massive blend of an unfinished novel(s) with unfinished philosophical ingredients. Musil himself was irritated by this fact, possibly to be interpreted as inconsistency, and reacted sometimes with an offensive sometimes with a defensive explanation. In some (posthumous) "General considerations"

(1930-42) to the never ending novel, Musil wrestles (once again) with the idea of a preface meant to offer the reader an adequate explanation of what he was doing. When overwhelmed by the difficulty of coping with the great mass of his riotously outpouring ideas, never obeying any rules of form, he frequently applies a peculiar logical fallacy which I may call *argumentum contra lectorem*. Its trail is worth to be followed:

> "The stories written these days are all very beautiful, significant, profound and useful, temperamental or insightful. But they [the stories] have no introductions. Therefore I decided to write this story in such a manner that it should need an introduction in spite of its length". (v.5, p.1935)

Further he writes:

> "The readers are accustomed to ask [the writer] that he tell them about life and not about reflections of life in the minds of people. This, however, is justified only in so far as these reflections are a poor, conventional reprint of life. I try to offer them [the] Original, [and thus] they will have to suspend their prejudices". (v.5, p.1937)

Now, suppose that the reader suspends indeed his prejudices. But does the author himself feel liberated from their burden? It doesn't seem so, and we surprise Musil, the priest of rigorous thinking and meaningful expression, talking-away his own sins:

> "It seems that a lot is superfluous in the first volume and is included there only for its own sake."

This is fact; but here is the excuse:

> "According to my opinion, narrated episodes may be superfluous and put there for their own sake. Not so ideas".

This is of course a declaration which explains *why the book is as it is* and not *why it ought to be so*. Then we read about the essayistic additions:

"The reflections about the combination of ideas and sentiments contained in this volume afford me to explain [the essayistic surplus] in the following way: *the main impact of a novel should be on our feelings*. Ideas have no right to be there *for their own sake*. At this time - [obviously when ideas are not there for their own sake] - they cannot be expounded as a philosopher would do it, i.e. they have to be 'parts' of a structure [*Gestalt*]. This is particularly difficult. And when this book will succeed [sic!] it will be Structure [*es wird Gestalt sein*], and the objections [claiming] that it resembles a treatise etc. will become meaningless. The richness of ideas is part of the richness of feelings" [whatever this means, anyway - T.S.]. (v.5,p.1941-42)

The book, even though unfinished, succeeded for many good reasons yet none of those claimed in the above quotations, which are nothing but hazy wishful thinking expressed in a concentration of undefined terms - exactly the thing Ulrich was fighting against! And his loathing of confusion is a little like Don Quixote's hatred of injustice. But this is an intellectual adventure story and thus still calls for an explanation.

Upon human actions lays a thick stratum of speech, which often hides motives and mechanics. Acts and actions are talked away by complicated structures of verbiage which the positivist philosopher would call "meaningless". Yet there is a hidden meaning to them. While things and relations can be talked about, revealed and explained in meaningful speech, there are also specific systems of verbal expression which are meant to hide the real thing. Searching for methods of translation between speech meant to talk-away and the things it wants to hide, is probably a perfectly legitimate field of scientific and scholarly endeavor. But it, in itself, however ably performed by the philological virtuoso, will not provide us with however little experiential insight into people who talk around their world, who express false joys to cover their fear, who pin comforting terminology on things they don't understand, pretending to have thereby gained understanding, who flood in verbiage dim feelings which don't yield to words etc.etc. Such insight we may get, if at all, by the representation of their actions as connected to their talk.

Such experience comes about by a new form of *mimesis*. If Musil wanted to defend his work against the "readers ... accustomed to ask that one tell them about life and not about reflections of life in the mind of literature and people"

he may have answered them: "Life" is also the people whose preoccupation is life's reflection (or distortion) in minds. They live their life as an exercise in reflecting Life. Their *acting* means *reflecting*. They don't carry the mirror in Socrates' parable. They *are* the mirror. And if they are philosophers they are a "philosophical mirror". And if they are critical they are a "critical mirror". And critical mirrors are choosy; they go after a particular *bête noire*. Now, why are these thought to offer less legitimate novel subjects than anybody else? Ulrich was a man of a particular background and his reflecting surface had one particular cut and polish. From this followed also a special approach to society and its members whom he saw through their language play meant to beguile the inevitable, and analyzed it in essay-like excursi. Characteristically this came to us "From an empire which collapsed because of a language error", as the title of a chapter reads.

(1.5) A "Mathematical Man"

In the vanity fair of verbiage in Vienna's high society, Ulrich has the function of the testing acid. It is *as if* he would always ask to whomever he speaks: "would you kindly be more precise?", or: "if we accept your premises let's see what the consequences are" etc. etc. We may say "as if", because Ulrich seldom actually does it in an explicit manner, though he quite often would come close to such formulations. Therefore everybody fears him, yet everybody likes him too. He is charmingly social (ladies appreciate that) and very intelligent (a nuisance to gentlemen who, nevertheless, court his sympathy). And he is everybody's bad conscience.

Ulrich was a thinker, something of an "applied" thinker, however strange this term may sound, who tried to apply the boldness of scientific thinking on everything in life, exorcising the imprecision with which our speech is fraught, the muddle in our speech which prevents us from solving our problems by avoiding their clear definition, and ultimately gives free way to major historic crimes.

Who was this Ulrich? He was the son of a very rich, retired, yet still upwards influential lawyer, quite unhappy with his son who "accomplished" only things which were "valuable and useless", but whom he generously subsidized nevertheless. So Ulrich could afford the elegant life of the elegant imperial capital in his elegant little *palazzetto* which in its elegant structure had something of the sweet rottenness in which the story unfolds:

> "Exactly speaking, its supporting arches were from the seventeenth century, the park and the upper story sported the dignity of the eighteenth century, the façade was rebuilt and a little spoiled in the nineteenth century, so that the whole offered a blurred picture akin to superimposed photographic images, yet it so happened that nobody walking by would fail to stop uttering an 'Ah!'"(p.12).

Well, it was perhaps something of an epitome of that odd composite which was the Habsburg Empire, and just as comfortable as the dual monarchy was for those who were endowed with the requisite means and furnished with the appropriate privileges. And equally un-reformable! Ulrich tried hard, studied journals of architecture and interior decoration, probed his own wits and technical knowledge - and gave up, accepting the place without further concern for aesthetic rigor and enjoyed its lush comfort. That very lush comfort he was to deny himself in matters intellectual! No question, he needed that kind of luxury for the type of activities in which he engaged after the first two phases of his life. These two phases are to be shortly recalled.

The *first phase*: military education, service as military officer (cavalry) and finally the inevitable affair with a bourgeois lady, a banker's wife.

> "The financier had an interview with the minister of war, whom he knew personally; subsequently Ulrich had an exchange of views with his colonel, during which he has been offered a clear explanation of the difference between an archduke and a simple officer"(p.36).

So Ulrich decided to become a professional engineer. This was the *second phase* of his early life when "he but changed horses, by moving from cavalry to technology; only the new horse had limbs of steel and ran ten times faster"(p.36).

And after he became an engineer and took up the habit of measuring things by the scale of technological achievements, he suddenly realized how terribly backward Man was whenever called upon to handle his own problems, the ones we call "human".

"The world is simply ludicrous when observed from a technical point of view; impractical in all inter-human relationships; uneconomical and inexact in its methods; and someone accustomed to solve problems using a slide ruler will simply find that *half of all the statements made by men are not worth being taken seriously*"(p.37).

It so happens, however, that an engineer, so intimately familiar with the slide ruler, and whose "statements ... *are* ... worth being taken seriously" whenever referring to his machines, is getting

"diluted in his particularity instead of ending up in the Freedom and wide plains of the world of thought".

In fact, poor him, he relates to the rigorous way of thinking on which his art rests, as the machines he builds to the scientific principles they incorporate; since

"*no machine is capable to apply to itself the infinitesimal equations on which it is based*"(p.38-39).

All this is true of technology but not of mathematics. Mathematics is applicable to everything, including human thinking which brought it forth. This is the major reason why Ulrich decided to become a mathematician, thus opening the *third phase* of his life, the most important one, corroborating the roundabout implicit definitions of the first two books which are said to be finished. More or less.

The reasons of the new choice, though, were not all the way intellectual, yet they explain much of the novel. We learn thus that

"[Ulrich's] love for mathematics was caused by those individuals who couldn't stand it. He was less scientifically than humanly in love with this science". (p.40)

If you now start reading the novel for the second time, keep this quotation in mind! (Also when you want an answer for what prompted me to set on paper these notes.)

Who were those people who couldn't stand mathematics and whom, so it happened, Ulrich disliked? Obviously the shallow word-mongers of "soul" and "spirit". They were those

> "who predicted the decline of European culture because no faith, love, simplicity or goodness was to be found anymore in Man"

and of whom one could say with assurance that

> "during their youth and school years they were all bad mathematicians".

(At least one of those who are likely implied in this passage was in fact a high school mathematics teacher. Oswald Spengler's "Decline of the West", contains a mass of startling nonsense about mathematics and logic, brilliantly criticized by Musil in an article on "Spirit and Experience. Observations for the benefit of those who escaped the 'Decline of the West'" - 1921, even if granting some vague sympathy for the murky decline philosophy. This ambiguous, and not very clear interpretation, was then understood to be a declaration of sympathy for Spengler - which it was not really - by some who should have known better. It could be that they were among those who "during their youth and school years ... were all bad mathematicians".) The Musilian implication is that, because they were bad mathematicians, they abhorred precision and everything based on rigorous thinking. Therefore they also blamed on it everything bad, and bad was everything beyond their grasp.

> "Thus later it was sure thing for them that mathematics, the mother of natural sciences and grandmother of technology, is also the

matriarch of the spirit which ultimately emanated toxic gases and launched fighter planes" (p.40).

Ulrich rejected this tenuous line of reasoning. For him, if the same spirit which spearheaded all the technological achievements of the time (the horrible bloodbaths included) were to be applied to matters human, the results would be no less wonderful yet less dangerous:

> "only people don't know it; they have no idea how one *could* think; if one could teach them anew how to think, they would also live differently".

Mathematics was viewed primarily as an instrument of intellectual education; thus not only as an instrument for the applied technologist. The latter's mathematical needs were anyways far bellow the immense apparatus constituting this science.

Considering that Ulrich became thus a "mathematical man", one is inclined to think that the essay on "The Mathematical Man" published by Musil in 1913 could have been used in its entirety in lieu of that much considered preface to the novel. (I would certainly recommend to any future publisher and editor of "The Man Without Qualities" to use the mentioned article as such, leaving his own comments for the end of the edition. I cannot, of course, find out wether any of those future publishers were or not "during their youth and school years ... all bad mathematicians". Which is not unlikely.) The purpose of the essay was to present mathematics as the mould in which intellectual attitudes are to be cast, and the mathematician

> "an analogy ... for the man of intellect of the future". (v.8,p.1007)

The purpose of mathematics is to serve as a universal drill for the mind:

> "It is foolish to affirm that all this is only about Knowledge, since the *purpose* has now become [the process of] thinking".

I don't know how far Musil's mathematical reading went, but this essay reminds me of a letter written by Carl Gustav Jacobi to Adrien Marie LeGendre in which the "purity" of mathematics is exalted:

"Il est vrai que Monsieur Fourier avait l'opinion que le but principal des mathematiques etait l'utilité publique et l'explication des phenomene naturels; mais un philosophe comme lui aurait du savoir que le but unique de la science c'est l'honneur de l'esprit humain et que sous ce titre une question de nombre vaut autant q'une question du systeme du monde" [It is true that Monsieur Fourier believed that the main purpose of mathematics was its public utility and the explanation of natural phenomena; but a philosopher like him should have known that the only purpose of science is the honor of the human spirit and therefore a question regarding numbers is as important as a question about a World System]. [Quoted in: Felix Klein, *Vorlesungen zur Geschichte der Mathematik im 19. Jahrhundert*, vol 1, p.114, Springer Verlag 1927]

Mathematics is thus viewed as a new form of "high culture", to use the expression by which Felix Klein stressed its significance. But how can a science, purposing only the cultivation of itself, become formative of an attitude? Here is *Musil's* answer:

"With its claims of depth, boldness and novelty [mathematics] limits itself, for the time being, to the exclusively rational and scientific. But this mode of understanding infiltrates everything around it and as soon as it reaches our feeling it will become spirit". (v.8, p.1007-8)

Well, we "feel" were the argument goes, but we would not *say* it any smarter. It is hitting the limits of the expressible. The closest thing to it may be what Dr.Kapperbrunn said in the "Unknown Magnitude" of Hermann Broch, an author whom Musil didn't particularly favor:

"... mathematics is kind of an act of despair of the human spirit ... After all we don't really need it, but it is sort of an island of decency, and this is why I rather like it".

Ulrich's story was meant to be the parable of "the man of intellect of the future", who went about to search for the "island of decency". He had no choice, as soon as he decided to become a mathematician, even though he may have had some doubts as well:

"I had never the intention to be all my life a mathematician." [p.47]

Easy said. Unlike with most other trades, mathematics cannot be given up. Once you got infested with the stuff it will remain entrenched in some corner of your mind and "soul". No escape, poetic or otherwise. You will always have to *essay-out* of it without ever succeeding.

(1.6) The "Utopia of Exactitude"

As Ulrich saw it, the possibility of knowledge with and by precision was obstructed by the fact that man's greatest intellectual achievements, mathematics being their paragon, have never been permitted to enter the field of moral sciences in which shallow verbosity still prevailed.

> "One could classify human activities according to the number of words they require; the more words are needed, the worse the character of that activity" (p.245).

Ulrich's aim was essentially a negative one: *not to* introduce words where there is no positive knowledge; *not to* make words pretend knowledge where there is none; *not to* exhibit verbal-pretence as knowledge. In fact, it can be said that,

> "all knowledge which led our species from the caveman's animal skin covering to the airplane, including all the relevant proofs, would fill no more than a reference library".

This may sound a bit exaggerated if you consider that the book on the "utopia of exactitude" has itself sixteen hundred densely printed pages, and is not finished. Yet the essential of its program is clearly stated within a remarkably insightful essayistic segment:

> "It would thus approximately mean that we should remain silent where we have nothing to say". [p.246]

And all this sounds as if quoting almost verbatim the seventh and concluding paragraph of Wittgenstein's *Tractatus*. [Some insightful critics tried to establish a connection between the second book of the novel and the second part of Wittgenstein's philosophical life, when he seemed to have glided away from the principles developed in the *Tractatus*. This seems to be correct. Yet one could just as well relate the first book with the first period of Wittgenstein's philosophical development.] Yet Musil doesn't remain silent, witness the sixteen hundred pages of the novel. And he is probably justified because much of what he has to convey is unfamiliar to most readers. Consequently some practice and drill is in order. And that is to be done slowly. Only when advancing in his reading up to about the middle of the first book (second part) will the reader get an approximate answer to the question he was asking himself earlier while reading the first 50-60 pages. The question is: how shall mathematics "pervade" life, other than through sciences, and how is it to spread its message of a still meaningful verbal austerity as implicitly and explicitly claimed by the author or his main character. For a long time the reader seems to be at a loss; especially when he knows, as it is so often stated in the book, that mathematics is pure form: it doesn't carry meaning. The patient reader will than slowly, slowly, get familiar with the idea that it is something we may call "mathematical mentality" which generated the series of experiments on which this novel is the lab report. When arriving to chapter 61 the reader will also get a good account of the experimental technique involved. Let us discuss it shortly.

Perhaps the best way of understanding Musil's "Utopia of exactitude" would be to rehearse some elementary knowledge we may have about how scientists perform their experiments. The simplest fact about an experiment is that the scientist probes not "Nature", as commonly and carelessly thought, but a separated and artificially reconstructed partial perception of it. Then, some factors or "variables" or natural elements of the studied process are eliminated or "stabilized". What is to be seen is how this piece of counterfeit "Nature" reacts to excitations artificially induced by the scientist. It is expected that as a result, a scientist's hypothesis will either be confirmed or rejected by the result of such experiment. Whichever be the case, new knowledge is gained which then can be used in two ways. Either as a plausible explanation for real-world natural processes which are, in some way, analogous to the artificial one; or to reproduce, on a standard basis, with some practical purpose, the simulated process. We are used to call this latter type of application a technical invention.

We can think of several problems in mathematics where the approach is similar to that of the experimental scientist. Let me state a simple example which should be accessible to every high school graduate, including the class team's goal tender. Think of a system of two equations (linear, of course) which, however, happen to have three unknowns. It is clear that something like this cannot be solved straightforward. We were told that in order to solve a system of equations we can go about right away to find the unknowns whenever their number is equal to that of the equations. (Never mind that this is by no means sufficient, because necessary it is nevertheless.) But here we have more unknowns than equations. In such cases, we were taught, that the system is "underdetermined" and that consequently we have an infinity of solutions compatible with it. Too bad: it looks a little bit like Nature, where "everything" is possible. Yet, we were also taught a trick to apply on these equations, a trick which comes close to what a scientist does in the laboratory. If we pick one of these unknowns and assign it an arbitrary value, it becomes "known", and thus we have to solve the two equations for only the two remaining unknowns, which is easier. At first sight. We may further see what happens when we alternate the values which make the one chosen unknown to become successively "known" under different values, and then solve every time the system for the other two. We do thus the job of an experimenter: varying one factor we see how the other two "react".

Can we do this in life? Musil proposes an answer in the affirmative and goes about to "demonstrate" it on Ulrich. How is this possible? The answer is that for the time being we have to contend with an utopia.

> "It is a process similar to that when a researcher observes the modification of one element within a complex phenomenon and draws his conclusions; the Utopia consists in the experiment in which we observe the possible modifications of certain elements along with the effects which they may engender in that complex phenomenon which we call life". (p.246)

The element to be chosen and purposely introduced, so to say, in the World, in order to observe its effects is - *Exactness*. Thus: how does the "World" behave when we force upon, or introduce into it "Exactness"? The problem is: how to introduce it? If this were simple, Musil wouldn't have had to write so much about it. Here we chance again upon the paradox so often recurring in the book. On the one hand, if we would apply the requirement of meaningful precision to whatever Musil has to say on the subject, we wouldn't get very far. We would get stuck in the mire of confusion against which Musil fought a lifelong battle by pouring an excess of brilliantly blended essayistic prose upon an assemblage of remarkable stories. They eventually became a great, yet incomplete novel. Still, Musil didn't always respect in "The Man Without Qualities" the limit between what can be meaningfully stated and what only the parable can bring home. A scientific experiment could be mapped, without metaphysics, into a mathematical model, but *"living exactly" means either being exact or suggesting it by a parable.* Otherwise one should be silent about it. Musil talks, sometimes, to much about it. Yet at the same time he produces also parts of the liberating parable.

(1.7) Parables of "Exact Life"

It comes out from the story and it doesn't always square with the essayistic overflow, as the latter isn't always in agreement with itself. First, *Exactness* will become an attitude of Ulrich who checks on every statement and every opinion. For him being exact is thus

> "a habit of thinking and attitude in life [*Denkgewohnheit und Lebenshaltung*] ... [which ought] to impact, as an exemplary force, on everything it comes in contact with" (p.246).

We will by no means be vaguer when saying that his purpose is to watch for logical adequacy and semantic cleanliness, thus getting behind the ideological smoke curtain or making it simply dissipate. The philosopher behind his desk may also try this. But in the case of Ulrich we have a man who applies the philosopher's technique in all his encounters; or at least this is what he tries to do. Ulrich is thus that peculiar excitant in the social experiment which has an uncommon character attribute: the virtue of exactness. Thereby he provokes particular reactions in the other elements of the experiment, which are exposed, against their will, to the attitude called "exactness" and consequently reveal, during the experiment, all those unpleasant secrets sheltered behind muddled talk which we will encounter in the story. So we will find out *how a particular section of the world reacts when an individual obsessed with exactness is thrown in its middle.*

An old parable from the history of sciences shall help understand Ulrich's functioning in the novel. Far fetched as it may seem, the daemons of Maxwell will be the terms of comparison. These were two little devils "thrown in" by the physicist, so small as to be able to direct equally minuscule molecules of gas in directions opposite to those which the laws of physics would have assigned them. The physicist who invented the parable also taught us why any attempt to imitate such daemons must necessarily fail. But the parable itself enlightened us, with the help of those daemons, about important laws of molecular mechanics.

Ulrich is a little bit like these mischievous and intelligent little monsters of Maxwell. He is, of course, endowed with reason and conscience, as well as the will to experiment, and thus will either expose or change the "laws" under which "Nature" operates. The difference is that the "molecules" he faces, unlike those of Maxwell, are themselves endowed with reason. So they may possibly decide what "laws" to choose from. (If you are familiar with Maxwell's story, you may force a little bit its outcome in the following way: the gas molecules are themselves endowed with reason and they themselves, not the daemons, decide to play a farce on the "laws of Nature" by choosing when to exit, and when not, the pipe mouth which separates the fast ones from the slow ones among them. But, of course, as a physicist friend told me: "this is totally absurd".) The upper-class Austrian "molecules" could use their own reason to either gain insight or to fool themselves. To their doom and mankind's disaster they have chosen the latter.

II. The Man Without Qualities - and Some of His Friends

(2.1) His Definition

There are several, partly competing, partly complementary statements about Ulrich, of which we could, with some attention, devise a definition of what is a "man without qualities". Because, mind you, we have to work a little on it. Though Ulrich, a bachelor of 32, is a mathematician, and his author has written a doctoral thesis on the philosophy of a great physicist, an exercise in which he relapses very often while writing the novel, we should not expect from him geometric rigor. In most novels the "definition" of the hero is implicit in the narration. It should be the same in this novel, and to some extent it is. Still, this time we ought to be helped along with some explanations; specifically because the hero happens to be a mathematician, member of a class of *rara avis* in the woods of literature, who consequently reveals traits of character, attitudes, thoughts, indeed passions and whims unfamiliar to most readers.

First, on a much simpler note, the qualities here talked about are not to be picked from the whole set of possible general predicates by which we usually define the character of a person. They are perhaps a subset from which a specific education and upbringing may choose the traits to be grafted upon an elementary personality. In fact Ulrich was richly endowed with many of these:

> "He noticed in himself, with remarkable sharpness, all the aptitudes and qualities esteemed by the society of his time, with the exception of the ability to earn money - something he didn't need; but an opportunity for their application [of his many qualities] eluded him" (p.47).

And because he couldn't find a suitable occasion to apply these qualities and capabilities, or rather hesitated to submerge in the exclusivity of one only application, he did not acquire those capital-initialed *Qualities* which social convention recognizes in men and women of achievement. So

> "Ulrich decided to take a one year leave from life in order to find an appropriate application for his talents" (p.47).

Which is just another way of saying that he went out in the world to seek intellectual adventure or, if we want to paraphrase James Joyce's Stephen Dedalus: to seek [intellectual] misfortune. In the meanwhile he remained an indistinct concentration of potential "qualities" which did not fuse yet into an accomplished personality: "A man without qualities is made up of qualities without a man" to affirm them, we are told.

He met people reflecting the dying splendor of imperial Vienna. Every encounter of Ulrich was a new piece in a puzzle which it is not easy to complete. It is easy, of course, to notice that the final chapter of a history is being acted out. However, this in itself is not enough. Countless other novels tell about the same. And if we see only as much in it, or if our reader's bias picks out only that, then Musil's "Man without Qualities" is just another of the better ones - of which some others are excellent. Yet the particular merit of this book originates in the fact that it tells us about *the same history being experienced by a fellow whose intellectual formation was different from that of most other contemporary writers' or their heroes'.* This makes him to be the carrier of unusual potentials. Some of these were discussed in a previous section referring to the "program of a novel". There it was mentioned that by a slight mutation in its vantage point, the author's (and, implicitly, the reader's) mirror will reveal interesting new human potentials, showing also the width of the new, thus discovered, spectrum. The much stressed *exactness* may now be employed in a variety of fashions. First, in that positive, ever-testing, critical manner: frequently exchanging membership in the set of the "controlled" and that of "free" variables. This may be wholesome; it could be a source of cognition/ understanding and, who knows, improvement of human mores and behavior. But then there is another aspect to it, not to be neglected, when such attitude is sported by a character of whom we learn that

> "he is not responsive to other people, and has seldom tried to put himself in their place, except when attempting to know them so as to be able to also use them for his own goals." (p.151)

Such attitude could reveal another aspect of *exact living* which is dangerously lurking behind the screen of what we may call radical rationality:

> "Comparing the world with a laboratory reawakened in him an old idea about life as it ought to be if it were to please him. It was the idea of the world as an immense workshop, in which the best ways of being a human being (*Mensch zu sein*) are tested, and new ways for it discovered. That the whole big laboratory functioned without a plan, and that managers and theoreticians were lacking as well, is another question. One could, of course say that he himself would have liked to be sort of a prince and master of the Spiritual life. But then, who does not?" [p.152]

This is yet another implicit potential of a man with *the quality of amorality* as defined in the novel, endeavoring to design Man according to standards of laboratory perfection. It was probably never really thought by Musil, but the *planned man* is a facet of what we call today totalitarianism, using an expression borrowed from Mussolini. The concept, never mind the term, has spooked around since ever, from Socrates, to the Nazi man-breeders, to Stalin or Pol Pot. Remember the "engineers of the soul"? They were not really breeding, just "educating" in the name of one who "would have liked to be sort of a prince and master of Spiritual life". It seems, though I am not very sure, that we slipped a little too far from the novel. Yet, if the author can afford himself irresponsible asides, never fully considered for their consequences, then readers should also be forgiven for their associations. Therefore, also to rehabilitate the author, let us rather try to dig out what is actually contained in such statements viewed as a procedure to represent human problems. Because Ulrich has not embarked on that amoral trail, one of the many possible, which may follow from the above quotation of a casual aside. Such may no more be Törless emancipated from his lurid ways. It would rather be some Beineberg or Reiting who learned, after all, mathematics ...

Let's now return to the main track. As said, we have a number of parallel lines running through the book each of which could claim a major novelistic existence. Therefore, to sort them better out, it seems appropriate first establish a short and deliberately incomplete list of the *dramatis personae*. The particular purpose of such a presentation is to review their most intimate qualities, the ones which set them apart in the "line of literature". Let us then examine

(2.2) Some of the Women,

specifically those least independent yet most intimately connected with the personality of Ulrich. Those women namely which have little to do with the main action, the "parallel" one, but will help reveal some of the qualities of the man who may have chosen to ignore having such. [The most important female personages will be given special attention in subsequent sections of these notes, when pursuing the main thread of the story.]

There is no denial that Ulrich liked women and they, charmingly responsive, favored him as well. Yet he was never able to abandon himself completely, be it either to carnal love or to the joy and serenity sought, and often found by other men, in the company or in association with a woman. No matter which bracket in the conventional classification of love affairs his connections with ladies were to be appropriately subsumed, these *"mondaine"* adventures were always polluted by the sharp, nasty and indeed caviling sight of the critical *raisonneur* in him. Specifically *a critical raisonneur with the training of a mathematician, aware of the amorality of science.* And I have to repeat it: *amorality of science,* which does not necessarily require the *amorality of the scientist* as the *Geist und Seele* people of all times would be inclined to make you believe. The reader has sometimes the feeling that the women, some of them anyway, were cast in for some epistemological experiment: "let's see how these girls, with their primitive, unsophisticated approach, *perceive* the world, and how they reflect in speech whatever they understand of it". And then: how the spectrum of *their* reflection is analyzed by Ulrich's own prism. [It reads as an arbitrary hypothesis. That it is anything but arbitrary will be seen in connection with "The letters of Susanne".]

The first woman to appear, and then quickly disappear from the novel [did she really disappear?] is acting as the epitome of a society which is to constitute the object of philosophical scrutiny. It happened thus:

An elegant lady and an equally distinguished looking gentleman were walking along a busy street of Vienna, when they noticed, at some distance ahead, an agitated crowd gathered at a place where a heavy auto-truck stood paralyzed with one front wheel on the curb of the sidewalk. The crowd formed a circle around a man laying on the pavement, blood-covered yet alive. The poor fellow was hit by the truck while carelessly trying to cross the street, and now, compassionate bystanders were busy helping him with comforting words while waiting for the ambulance. When the elegant couple came closer and saw the man outstretched on the ground

> "the lady had an unpleasant sensation under the heart, in the stomach pit, which she thought entitled to qualify as compassion" (p.11).

It was a "vague and paralyzing" sensation in a very literal sense: she was as if locked in that sensation without being able to free herself from its grips. Her compassion was the source of an unspecifiable urge. But because the urge was unspecifiable, it heavily burdened the conscience. It had to be gotten out from there to ease that "vague and paralyzing sensation". Unexpectedly the gentleman came to her rescue:

"These heavy trucks, as they are used nowadays, have a much too long breaking distance".

What a perfect relief! Do you get the point?

"The lady felt thereby relieved, and thanked with a kind look. Sometime in the past she heard this expression, yet had never an idea what a breaking distance actually was, and didn't really want to know it; *it was sufficient that the horrible incident could be ordered under some heading, thus becoming a technical problem which was no more of her concern*" (p.11).

Careful reading of this first chapter is advised against the possibly misleading paradoxical suggestion of its title claiming that "in a significant way, nothing emerges from it". In fact it enounces the *Leitmotiv of the novel*. The dominant theme of the entire work is quite obviously stated in the above quoted episode. It is about the part assigned to words whenever something is to be covered up: the elegant lady was liberated of that unpleasant and paralyzing stress between the heart and the pit of the stomach, by relegating it to the field of some technical expertise. Further, it turned out that all this was possible by simply discovering that there is a word, a term, which guarantees that stomach-upsetting sensations have been safely classified away. Without the necessity of enquiring what is behind that word! Because, you see, this is now the business of the experts.

The full significance of this episode is by no means obvious. Still, if the author, who otherwise does not display much preference for music, has chosen to introduce some sort of a leading theme, he will have to prove it to be such in the next chapters. The proof of the *Leitmotiv* is in the reading.

The subsequent female personae who step into the story reveal examples of the variety of human perception and reaction to the world. Thus, two subsequent mistresses of Ulrich are two antipodes of elementary world perception. The first is Leontine, a 25 years old *chanteuse* in a medium-sleazy variety theatre, a beauty by the fashion standards of yesteryear, sentimental but also revealing herself as utterly voracious when dining in Ulrich's little palace.

"Ulrich decided to call her Leona, and her possession appeared to him as desirable as a lion's skin prepared by the furrier (p.22)".

Quite nasty, all considered. But then again, the lady "practiced occasionally prostitution". At least this is the name of the activity performed for a living by somebody "who doesn't sell her entire person for cash", limiting the deal to some services of the body. This trade and the lack of social and intellectual sophistication made her not only a plain and straightforward person, but yet another pragmatic professional. Provided, of course, we pluck off the social value-label stuck upon the name of her trade. Because

"when one knows, for nine years now, ever since she was sixteen, the meanness of the daily wages paid in the vilest musical joints, while one has the head stuffed with the prices of garments and lingerie, when one faces every day the deductions, the avarice and the abuses of the owners, the bonus for the food and beverages of pepped-up patrons, the room bills in neighboring hotels, the haggling and settlements in a businesslike fashion, then, all that what a layman enjoys as extravagance, turns out to be a profession, subject to logic, pragmatism and status regulations" (p.23)".

We have here a clear and value-free statement. The question is: what is the role of Leona in the whole story? At first reading it seems as one of those superfluous episodes which, by Aristotle's teaching, if cast away, wouldn't harm the plot. Unless, of course, there is an arcane connection which makes the episode necessary. And this hidden requirement may very well be the contrast Leona offers to the character of the other mistress of Ulrich.

This new mistress was something of a split personality. A lady of the good society, the wife of a judge (who "abused her" in the first year of their marriage), who loved Ulrich and was tormented by her sin-burdened conscience. Ulrich called her Bonadea, because he met her first, unexpectedly appearing as a redeeming *Dea ex machina*, when he was wounded and fallen after having been mugged on the street. [Mind you: in pre-WWI Vienna! Not South Bronx, today.] Then he promptly started with her a love affair. Bonadea sinned, and suffered because of her sin which was akin to "living a double life as some burgess who, respectable at daylight, was a train robber in a secret resort of his conscience; and this quiet, impressing woman was oppressed by self-contempt as soon as nobody was holding her in his arms" (p.42).

And when she was overcome by "remorse between two moments of weakness" one had to go along with her urges of respectability:

"One had to be true and good, compassionate in all disasters, and to love the Imperial Family, respect everything respectable and behave with the tact required by the side of a sickbed" (p.43).

Question: who is Bonadea and why do we need her? On her own she may do a good showing in some minor story of Arthur Schnitzler. Or perhaps Stefan Zweig, who might have taken her very seriously. Or again she could have been fixed-up to be exhibited as another excellent piece in Musil's gallery of women. Though, probably, she may never have become such a perfect little masterpiece as any of his "Three women". In the context of this novel-rhapsody Bonadea is another epitome of a desperate search for ideated verbal and ideological incense smoke meant to overwhelm and exorcise the sinful reality. She wanted some unspecified "grand purpose" for her crime. But she couldn't find it.

"Bonadea was missing The Great Idea to be associated with the great excitement which overcame her every time she came near her lover" (p.266).

These were those occasions when she strongly felt an urge "to express some idea" yet could find no help in Ulrich whose own ideas, she found, "were lacking dignity". Indeed not only dignity was absent from Ulrich's frequent bedside perorations, but they were also keeping intact and sharpening the contours of that cruel picture of reality she so badly wanted to escape. Bonadea suffered

"because of his unfriendly, exaggerated and peculiar manner of treating her with *thoughts instead of feelings*" (p.265).

This was the suffering Ulrich inflicted on so many others who were in search of a "great idea" and a "great purpose".

Not to everybody though. Here is the youth friend Clarisse, who married another friend, Walter, the musician, painter, litterateur etc. etc. - a failure with countless qualities. Walter, who submerged aimlessly in the Viennese obsession with *Kultur,* was exactly the opposite of Ulrich - and Clarisse was in the middle between the two. She was intelligent, undecided, rejected the *Kultur*-cloud of "*Geist und Seele*", yet she was lacking the notions and method to overcome the mess. Hence she offered an image on the basis of which a lady commentator thought qualified to dismiss her as "hysteric". Yet the easiest way to characterize her would be by comparing the ways in which she related to, respectively, Ulrich and Walter.

To Ulrich:

> "She had no favorable opinion of mathematics, and she never held him for as talented as Walter. He was intelligent, he was logical, he was knowledgeable in many fields; but is this more than barbarism? In the past he played a definitely better tennis than Walter and she remembered his ruthless hits and her strong impression that this fellow will achieve what he wants, something she never felt in connection with Walter's painting, music and ideas" (p.53-54).

To Walter: she told Ulrich about a dream of hers in which

> "a creeping creature wanted to overwhelm her while she was sleeping; it was soft-bellied, tender and gruesome; and this big frog meant the music of Walter"(p.49).

This corroborated what Ulrich already knew about her, namely

> "that whenever Walter played Wagner, with bad conscience, and as if practicing a juvenile vice, she denied herself to him for weeks."

Walter associated his Wagner cult with his support for German nationalist extremism. Once when he prepared to go out and participate in one of their demonstrations, a disapproving Clarisse asked:

"'What do they get out of it when they are yelling?'" [Walter:]
"What does one get out of life these days anyways! When they are
on the street they constitute a procession: one feels the body of the
other! At least they don't think and don't write: something may
emerge out of all this.'" [p.605]

It did, as we all know, a couple of decades later.

Yet Wagner or no Wagner, Clarisse, who permitted herself many unconven-
tional gestures, was often quite rude with Walter, whom she frustrated in his
desire to become a father. (She would have liked a child from Ulrich.) A characteristic example is offered in one of those drafts which comes up in the editor's
assembly as chapter 96 of the second book, where she, while just about to take a
bath, rather coarsely repulses Walter's nuptial advances thus presenting an image
difficult to render in translation without losing the entire point:

"*Clarisse sah heftig und schön aus.*" Or: "Clarisse looked impetuous
and pretty". [p.1430]

while a beatuful chapter started outlining her mental problems.

[Some critics are compensated with these episodes for not getting to
understand everything to be read in the novel. But some others may
also be disappointed. E.g. the critic of the *Corriere della Sera* (3 Nov.
1996) who commenting on a recent Italian translation discusses on
a whole bedspread size page almost only the trials and tribulations of
Clarisse. Expanding on the first Walter-Clarisse-Ulrich encounter, in
which the "chemistry" between the last two seems to have much excited him, he had to sadly complete part of his analysis in frustration
because *una delle scene più erotiche della letteratura moderna si conclude
senza coito* (or 'one of the most erotic scenes in modern literature ends
without coitus'). But then, had he read more carefully the rest of the
work he could have been richly, even if not explicitly, compensated.]

But, given her choices, the lot of Clarisse was not easy. Wagner was spook-
ing around even in her family. In a letter to Ulrich (in the second book) she
complains about her brother, a psychiatrist:

"Whenever you introduce him to somebody he would say: 'But I am neither nor musical'. Because given that his name is Siegmund he wouldn't like to be seen either as a Jew or as being musical. *He was begotten in Wagner-drunkenness*". [Italics in the original - p.713]

Now the Clarisse-Walter-Ulrich trio often acted out small philosophical dramas which we, apart from enjoying and appreciating for their own merit, could also view as a guide to the concept of the greater drama in the novel. On the one end we had Walter who felt best in the lukewarm security of the "emptiness of his music". On the other end was Ulrich who preached austere precision against the "obscene emptiness" with which human problems were approached. During one of their triangular colloquies he argued as follows (*à propos* a leading personage involved in the Parallel Action):

"The scientific man is in our days a totally unavoidable fixture; one cannot wish *not* to know! And [yet] never before was the abyss dividing the experience of an expert and that of a layman as deep as in our days. Everybody can notice this on the performance of a masseur or a pianist; one wouldn't send a horse in the racetrack without special preparation. Only in matters of being human does everybody feel the calling to make decisions." (p.215).

And while Ulrich continued his harangue:

"Clarisse gave signs of tending to agree. Walter instead smiled like a fakir..."

From thence Clarisse crops up, mostly in posthumous writings, in various situations - *some to be discussed in subsequent sections of these notes* - proving to be a remarkable stuff for a novel. One interesting exercise would be to collect these fragments and unite them with the help of our guesses. Nice, no doubt, but off the track of the main novel. She will end up as some sort of yet another recreational philosopher and in a mental institution. There are a quite few such in the novel and she is among the most interesting ones.

Recalling now the quoted characteristics of the three ladies so far mentioned, a short stop is advisable in order to make an attempt to figure out their role in the web of the novel in which neither of them will be assigned any significant role within the action proper, the *"parallel"* one that is. Indeed, by all the efforts of Musil to involve them in some way or other, they remain essentially on the sidelines. This applies to episodic figures, such as Leona and Bonadea, and to the major character Clarisse as well. Are they, perhaps, introductions, sketches, of the whole approach? Could any other choice of persons have served equally well to fill the empty spaces on the canvas of this big composition? Obviously any such choice had to be made from the totality of individuals with whom an Ulrich type was most likely to meet. This condition is fulfilled; the choice is indeed verisimilar. Yet, why are these elaborately detailed extras all women? Walter, the husband of Clarisse, is one of only two or three major male characters in the book who are not involved with the main story of the "parallel action". At the same time, with one and only one exception, all women with any noticeable part in the book are *not* involved with the main frame story. (Bonadea craves to get involved, but she will remain outside throughout.) We don't know why. And we shall not probe the *intentions* of the author. I may occasionally slip into such obnoxious exercise, but it is essentially *un-literary*. We, the readers, could get some clue about their role from a couple of feuilleton type exercises published by Musil in 1925 as

(2.3) The Letters of Susanne

I like to stick to my principle according to which a novel has to stand on its own. So why to discuss "The letters of Susanne"? Because *this* novel, with all its grandeur, can be viewed as a sandbox, or rather a *Baukasten*, containing innumerable elements of which one or more nicely rounded, action oriented *complete* novels could be built. Some of these elements were forgotten outside the box, or sold separately. Great writers must also do something for a living. Now this Susanne was worth a part along Leona or Bonadea, because she is so much more interesting, as revealed by her two letters. About the motivation to write Susanne's letters we find out from yet another letter, this time written by Musil to a publisher, that

> "the exterritorial status of the woman in this world of men offers a convenient vantage point from which one may talk about everything in the same tone. [...] I send you here the first of Susanne's

letters. This time it is still a feuilleton type of product, but the sequel could be more serious without losing its facility or, perhaps, to be made to alternate between chatter and earnest irony, if so it pleases. I have sufficient material since I could cast all my essayistic work and part of my novel (sic!) in this form." [v.9, p.1754-1755]

It is indeed the "exterritoriality" of the woman which warrants the roles of most of them in the novel: the woman proves itself as "convenient vantage point" [*behaglicher Standpunkt*] for the man without qualities. But Susanne was omitted. And this is a pity, because her two letters, particularly the first, are formidable, up to some of the best pages in the novel. She has something which sets her apart from all of Ulrich's women. She is not simply the testing acid always available when required to analyze men and their world, but also, and at the same time, the observer who records the results of the experiment. Susanne is a feminine Ulrich, to some extent, and this may have made Musil to keep her out. Nevertheless she is worth a few additional words because she provides some evidence for that "convenient vantage point" of all the women in the novel.

In the first, the best, of her two letters, Susanne reports to a friend, a lady, about her meeting in a train compartment with a one-eyed gentleman. It is a most remarkable piece of the "stream of consciousness" type of literature in only four master-pages, relating the silent exchange of glances and glimpses between the two. But while this short masterpiece deserves a special attention in a more general literary context, it is the second letter in which Susanne becomes a feminine Ulrich. From her "convenient vantage point", guaranteed by her feminine "exterritoriality", she examines the world of men and spells out its contradictions. When spelling out the inconsistency of her husband's actions with his principles, she speaks with an almost Ulrich-like sarcasm:

> "Once I possessed a friend [*ich habe einmal einen Freunden besessen*] who was a physicist. ... He told me that each and every one of those so curiously tattooed symbols, which he called mathematics, would permit him to write a very terse formula which enables him, at any time and without any effort, to deduce all those particular cases, which he would never be able to consider in their totality. ... But what are general propositions worth when they only keep you from

addressing either of the special cases? Yet all statements of which my hubby infers his 'general responsibility [principle]' are of this second kind. [...] They [the men] build up the world of only general principles and will have to permit lots of exceptions in order to keep the whole thing together. Thus hubby requires that the State do more for the Christian idea; yet he never goes to church and all his business associates are Jews. He finds it nice that we live in a modern democratic age, but for nothing in the world would he agree that [in this democratic age] there should be no Highnesses, princes, counts, eminences and the like; etc." [v.7 p.638-639]

We recognize the rudiments of an Ulrich reflected by a woman of the kind not developed in the novel. Because, it so, happens that while the women in the novel do the required job from their "particular vantage point" by acting, or reflecting in action, they will never arrive to actually formulate complicated opinions like Susanne. They are subject to the same inconsistencies as the men Susanne was talking about, but only some of them will have occasional glimpses of the truth as Susanne or Ulrich have.

(2.4) The Sins of Bonadea and Those of the Empire

So we return to the original task of trying to identify the role of these female characters in the context of the novel. We may consider them now also as a "how to" exercise. As an example, the "sins" of Bonadea should introduce the reader into that complicated mesh of problems of the old Habsburg Empire which turn out to be of "linguistic" nature. Thus Bonadea, without philosophizing, will help us understand the contradictions of the kind Susanne tried to point out between the thinking and the actions of her "hubby" and which are wearing away the structures of the Empire. An instance is offered by a discussion between Bonadea and Ulrich about the sexual criminal Moosbrugger. The reader shall return to chapter 31 for the details of this conversation which ends as follows:

"'Thus', said Ulrich, 'you are always on the side of the victim and against the deed ... Yet if you were to direct your judgments consistently against the deed itself ... how would you, Bonadea, justify your adulterous acts!'" [p. 120]

This type of contradictions is studied by casually observing the behavior of the women. But the story does not stop here because the cases are only introductory examples for a much greater problem which could be most conveniently called *the Empire's linguistic fragility*. It sounds like a joke but it is not. It is rather the true background of the novel's action and, well, its implicit philosophical message.

III. The Empire's Linguistic Fragility - Matters of Definition - Once Again

Beside the philosophical definition of the main character's intellectual personality, implicit also in his choice of friends, the description of the stage on which his story unfolds requires some additional specification and this in a very unorthodox fashion. It shall start with a real life based anecdote, historically confirmed and re-told in the novel. It is the story of a crooked, jobless shoemaker from Berlin. Never mind that he was a Prussian, because the tale of the *Schuster* can be quoted as a perfect epitome of the "linguistic crisis" of the Austro-Hungarian empire in those days when the *Man without qualities* was the honorary secretary of the Parallel Action. It so happened that the shoemaker, dressed in a captain's uniform bought from a peddler of second hand cloths, stopped an army patrol on the streets of Köpenick, a Berlin suburb, ordered the soldiers to occupy the town hall and, claiming to execute "orders from the highest quarters", seized the municipal treasury, while arresting the mayor and sending him, under escort, of course, to the police headquarters in Berlin. The thief was later (not during the well protected operation!) arrested, the newspapers, particularly the liberal ones, celebrated, stories and plays (Karl Zuckmeyer) were written about him, movies were produced (an excellent one, as late as the 1960s, with Heinz Rühmann as the "captain") and, as it was rumored, even His Imperial Majesty deigned to a hearty laugh when the case was reported to him. No soldier was reprimanded! The duty of a good Prussian soldier was to obey the orders of his superiors without asking questions. The fellows were up to everybody's legitimate expectation when following the orders of the "captain of Köpenick". Iron discipline was the foundation of the Kaiser's Germany! But there was a problem: *without* this iron discipline the town-hall in Köpenick wouldn't have been robbed. Not that from then on banks and safes could be comfortably burglarized with the help of military patrols. Still, the funny occurrence, which made the "captain" an instant hero, at least as far as the liberals were concerned, came to illustrate the many contradictions within apparently solid social arrangements, covered-up with catchwords such as "discipline".

The mention of this case in Musil's novel is connected to another "linguistically" dubious affair, this time in Austria, were

"all the time things happened for which no one could find fast enough the proper name." [p.448]

The case referred to was the extremely distressing action by the employees of the Imperial and Royal Telegraphic Company, who suddenly decided to strictly and scrupulously apply the countless service regulations on which the activities of this particular branch of the communications industry was supposed to rest.

"It has thus been revealed, that strict abidance by the law could lead much faster to a total work stoppage than the most unruly anarchy." [p.448]

All this was called "passive resistance", and in the English of today we call it less ambiguously "work to rule". But was it "passive resistance"? Resistance to what? Certainly not to the law. Since the employees were strictly abiding by it. So you better don't call it "passive resistance", because it is not that. But then again it meant sabotage of the communication system. And it did so very successfully. So, here we have another small news item disturbingly reminding that words, which seemed to precisely designate well established things, are in fact not only unable to do so, but are actually obscuring the real state of affairs. We call "discipline" - the armed protection of an act of robbery; and we call "passive resistance" against the established order - strict abidance by its laws. The examples quoted may have only an anecdotic character if taken out of context. But within the novel they are an exercise meant to mediate the understanding of a much more complicated language confusion, that of the Empire, the language mess which offers the real background of this story.

The Habsburg empire, or as much as remained of it after Solferino and Königgrätz, is perceived by the reader, in Musil's ironic yet nostalgic characterization, as a grid of confusions which nobody in the story could un-mesh intellectually, and hence translate into clear and distinct terms. Everybody in the story hides his or her confused feelings and undigested perceptions behind a fuzzy verbal screen, in the hope to be thus relieved of the responsibility to face the difficult reality. It is the case of many: of the elegant lady, confronted with a horrible street accident, who first thought it to be her duty to pretend that her feeling of disgust is but "compassion", only to get rid of it all by hiding behind the incomprehensible technical term "breaking distance"; of Bonadea, who was all the time indulging in words she thought to be "ideas"; the daughter of a Jewish banker, Gerda Fischel, who made strenuous efforts to talk away the explicit and little ambiguous terms of hatred, as "symbols" of something she could hardly specify; of Diotima, the *grande dame* of the novel and her distinguished company basking in the verbiage of the Parallel Action - and many others. And the same applied to the odd ethnic mosaic which was the Austro- Hungarian Empire, the "linguistic" troubles of which are worth more than simply being quoted for their caricatural nature. Let's address them, borrowing a bit from Musil's analytical performance, starting with the terminology purportedly mapping the complex reality of the dual monarchy:

> "Thus it was, for example, imperial-royal [*kaiserlich-königlich*] and it was imperial-*and*-royal [*kaiserlich und königlich*]; the corresponding acronyms, k.k. and k.u.k., being assigned to every thing or person" [p.33]

and expanded by Musil into the name of Kakania for the entire complex Habsburg realm. Kakania was not simply an ironic colloquial convenience, but a genial terminological solution for characterizing a problem which in reality could never find a solution. Only a novel could "solve" it. And this was the problem:

> "The inhabitants of this imperial and royal imperial-royal monarchy had to face a difficult task; they were supposed to consider

themselves imperial and royal Austro-Hungarian patriots, but at the same time also royal Hungarian and imperial Austrian [patriots]." [p.450]

The latter part of the obligation didn't put much strain on Hungarians. Their case was rather straightforward, "since Hungarians were first and foremost Hungarians" to themselves. In their case name and ethnicity were in perfect agreement; name of the people and the country were also largely coinciding. But while the Hungarians were "first and last Hungarians", the Austrians were in trouble because "there wasn't indeed a proper name for them". [p.451]. Now, this may sound a little strange to our contemporary who knows that the overwhelming majority of the inhabitants of the present day tiny Republic of Austria are calling themselves, seldom in a doubt, Austrians. But then there was no Republic of Austria but a huge, heterogeneous compound which called itself "the Kingdoms and Lands represented in the Imperial Council [*Reichsrath*]" which included such funny places as "the very Shakespearean kingdoms of Lodomeria and Illyria". What could an inhabitant of this Empire answer when asked about his nation or strain?

"He naturally couldn't answer: I am one from one of the Kingdoms and Lands represented in the Imperial Council, which don't exist".

It would have sounded much too silly,

"and if only for this he preferred to say: I am a Pole, a Czech, a Slovene ["Illyrian"], a Croat, a Serbian, a Slovak, a Ruthene [Ukrainian], or a Wallah [Romanian]; and this was that so called nationalism." [p.451]

Thus a particular bureaucratese language was developed, purporting to offer one single umbrella which was to be spread above the many heads of this unruly Babylonian hydra. Yet the monster always managed, somehow, to show its ugly, numerous, and fearfully vindictive heads, at the edges of, or by simply cutting holes into, the umbrella's flimsy linguistic web.

"Names" (as in logic) or "nouns" (as in grammar), are supposed to be associated with classes of objects having some common set of characteristics. When we say "apple", "star", "math teacher", or "the class of all individuals called Romuald", most of us know what the words designate. But when we decide to give arbitrarily chosen names to classes of grown-up humans, members of our species within which we all share the prejudice about our rationality, then things are not always simple as with the Romualds and math teachers. In the case of apples and stars we have a clear separation between him that classifies and the classified objects; it doesn't really matter whether the fruit on the tree or the Great Bear agree. In the case of human classes, such comfortable separation is not possible. If *A* insists classifying *B* as a patriot of the Kingdoms and Lands represented in the Imperial Council, or anything else for that matter, while *B* rejects the definition as well as the context, then the outcome will be the one very clearly defined by Musil:

> "Ever since Creation it never happened that a living being should have died of a language deficiency. Yet we have to stress that this is exactly what happened to the Austrian and Hungarian, Austro-Hungarian dual monarchy, namely that it died of *unpronounceability [Unaussprechlichkeit]*" [p.451]

But were not the German speaking people of narrower Austria *the* Austrians? Well, if the Empire had meant only them by that name - it would have fallen apart even without a lost world war. So, what if they had stressed the *differentia specifica*, insisting on the adjective-complemented name: "German-Austrian" [*Deutsch Österreicher*]? The fact is that after Kakania fell apart, this term gained a genuine, however undesired meaning, but in the days of the Parallel Action, putting too much emphasis on it was tantamount to subversion. What was "German" after all? It was exactly that "barbarian" Empire which the Parallel Action intended to defeat with "cultural superiority". Between insisting on German identity and claiming union with that other Empire, naturally under the supremacy of its *parvenu* emperor, there was a thin, very thin, barely visible line. Crossing it would have been equivalent to rebellion. So, while "Austrians" such as Poles or Slovenes, Italians or Czechs, never had doubts about their identity, the German Kakanians were unable to find their own. Moreover, many tried to find it outside their country. Thus we read in a (posthumous) strange digression that

"almost every German [Austrian] had a natural feeling of community with the Germans in the *Reich*, and that it was only the inertia
of historical processes which separated them for the time being."
[p.1494]

In spite of this, monarchic loyalty prevented them from admitting that
they haven't gotten any "Austrian" identity. To make good for what was missing they employed the ersatz of funny terminology.

But what has all this to do with a novel? Would it not better fit into a study
on the social and political function of language? It may, but then we would
be missing out on an important account to be dwelt upon in what follows.
Humans live their lives acting, feeling and then speaking. In the case of Musil's
characters a lot of real action is substituted by speech. Their speech is interesting not for the ideas they convey; these are not always meant to be valuable
or even extant. However, the progression of a character's speech discloses the
living or experiencing of the world also by persons who seldom act meaningfully; it can be dramatic on its own, or even tragic. A succession of international
catastrophes, such as two world wars, were germinated in the words of every
character in the novel who, in some way, were to face the "German-Austrian"
identity crisis. They faced a problem, "resolved" it with a word; encountered
a new problem, this time originating in the conflict between the previously
chosen word and some aspect of reality it wasn't able to cover - and invented
another terminological trap. This went on until such characters ended up as
caricatures or, as in one case, dead.

On the caricatural side we have, most importantly, count Leinsdorf, who
ideated the Parallel Action. Long after we learn about this and the count's
function as the Action's *spiritus rector*, we are assured that

"It was not without interest for a foreigner to find out how a sea-
soned and highly placed Kakanian, such as Graf Leinsdorf, came to
terms with these difficulties." [p.451]

Namely the ones which caused ultimately the lethal "inexpressibility" of
the Empire. This was an operation in two stages:

Stage 1. Of the Austro-Hungarian complex he tacitly separated one element with a clearly homogenous structure and doubtful loyalty to the empire:

"[of Hungary] he never spoke, just as one doesn't speak of a son who makes himself independent against the will of his parents".

Still there were also others who would have liked to act like that son, and hence in stage 2, he arrived to designate these, e.g. Poles, Slovenes, etc., as "Austrian tribes" or "nationalities". That had something to do with his background in international law which supplied him with the idea that a Nation, i.e. not a *nationality*, is something on its own territory. Now, if all these "tribes" or "nationalities", all of them, together, were to make a "Nation", then the best thing is to have them gathered under the roof of the same statehood.

And part of this enterprise was the Parallel Action, the nature of which we would have trouble to understand without permanently keeping in mind Kakania's anomalous structure reflected in its "language games". [Excursus: Isn't it typical that the philosopher Wittgenstein, who made of *language games* such a big issue, was himself an Austrian?] - So now we may return to the more intimate aspects of the great undertaking.

IV. The Linguistic Fragility of Moosbrugger

And then there is Moosbrugger, the sexual offender. What a delight for "psychological" literary criticism! The poor, homeless, maniac tramp, a carpenter of sorts, alternating resident of prisons and lunatic asylums, was on trial for having murdered a prostitute. All this happened parallel to the Parallel Action. Parallels don't meet, of course, but they can be connected by crossway bridges or fastened together with a strap. After all, much of the novel is like a bundle of parallel fasces, each of them a story on its own, straight rods with undefined ends. Such one is Moosbrugger's. But once again, the attention granted him goes beyond the interest which novelists have always demonstrated for criminals of all varieties. He is interesting for Musil and Ulrich - and the reader as well! - as yet another facet, or rather a caricatural epitome, of the Empire's linguistic fragility. Or, put it in a more general context: as a pathological illustration of man's failure in his eternal struggle for verbal expression, for the command of the World by the Word. If it pleases the reader, he may interpret Moosbrugger as yet another metaphor for the verbal cloud-covering of crimes, whether these crimes are against the law or within the law or, indeed, in strict abidance by the Law. But it is wiser to forget the metaphor and follow the brilliantly described case story on the linguistic inadequacy of some human beings studied on the particular case of a criminal. After all we may view a literary-novelistic work, once again, as an organized, well controlled experiment, the purpose of which is to reveal aspects of real life or at least, as experiments go, some truncated facet of that very "real life". In this case the reactive used in the experiment happens to be a lunatic. But remember: it may not always be the *intention* of the author (as it very likely was that of Musil) to develop an experiment, but in good novels it *works out as such.*

So Moosbrugger is just another exploration of the empire of "inexactness". The advantage of the Empire itself consists in the fact that nobody can defeat its language games *when using the same kind of weapon or defense,* i.e. the shield of muddled talk. Hence it will be defeated in a world war where the argument poured forth from the barrel of the gun. But the killer was defeated by those who were countering his murderous knife with an incomprehensible talk, that of the clauses in the Law, often as powerful as guns. Moosbrugger, though not very bright, understood as much that words have some sort of power. If you know how, when and against whom to brandish them, you may gain your case. The stranger they sound the more powerful they may be. So he collected words:

> "Such words he learned in bedlams and prisons; fragments of French and Latin, which he then fitted into his diatribes in the most inappropriate places, ever since he figured out that it is the command of these languages which lent the rulers the right to 'find' against him. For the same reason he used a choice German when speaking during the trial proceedings. Thus he said that 'such must be the foundation of my brutality' or 'I thought of her in an even more horrifying manner than I normally do in the case of such women.'"

He was also aware of the importance of giving a political color to his deeds proclaiming himself a "theoretical anarchist"

> "who could easily and any time let himself be saved by the social-democrats, were [he] willing to accept any favor from these Jewish exploiters of the working and ignorant people." [p.72]

And no doubt:

> "He shared the feeling of simpletons that one has to cut out the tongue of those who are educated. [p.235] [...] He envied all people who learned in their youth the facility of verbal expression. His own words stuck like gum to his palate whenever he most urgently needed them, and it took sometimes a good while till he managed to wrench a syllable and to be able to continue." [p.238]

He even perceived his inability as a virtue. Once his random outpourings of inappropriately chosen and pretentious words were diagnosed by some police shrink as "hallucinations". Based on this, Moosbrugger figured that the faculty of "hallucinating" sets him apart, in a distinguishing way, from everybody else. Thus hallucinating was his field of excellence.

This Moosbrugger fellow may indeed be significant for the "story", but he himself has not a long one. His characterization, the most important and most brilliant aspect of his presence in the book, is widely dispersed. Sometime several hundred pages divide two chapters involving this peculiar bum. Just another torso which we read - we haven't been given a choice - as if we were contemplating the *ébauches* of a great painter. But a painting can be finished without ending the story which it illustrates. It may represent a moment in a mythological tale, the final revelation conveyed by a miracle, a scene, one single scene, of a great battle, or just an anecdotic snapshot from life, and nobody will deny the two-dimensional space-locked work the attribute of completeness if it satisfies certain simple technical conditions. We know, however, these conditions normally don't apply to a work in narrative literature. Normally. But this is not quite a "normal" work. Here master portraits are coming about by severally retouched snap-shots. And the portrait reflects also the viewer. How does the viewer/reader compare to Moosbrugger? Here is a sample:

> "The poor ability in establishing connections between things, the cruelty of his thinking which maneuvers with agreeable terms, without concern for the strain of life and suffering, and which makes any decision so difficult: this is what the soul of the general public and that of Moosbrugger have in common." [p.532]

Thus the fool turns out to be an incomplete and mixed-up composite of the analytically identified elements of our own self. So it seems to be suggested. [And I just hear a good friend of mine mentioning a "surrealistic composition".]

And what is his end? We don't really know. It is also irrelevant, because it anyway remains outside the "parallel" and any other "action". From posthumous fragments we find out the bizarre detail that Ulrich was to help him be freed from his captivity. This may have something to do with what we read at some point in the ever more confusedly ending story:

> "The victims of Moosbrugger were abstract, threatened people, as all those thousands who were exposed to the dangers of factories, trains or automobiles." [p.1463]

This is from a section of the vast confused posthumous bunch. Moosbrugger crops up also in a number of other little fragments, some of them providing enjoyable reading on their own. Thus, for some reason, Ulrich, Clarisse and the Parallel Action's general Stumm von Bordwehr, will visit the asylum where the murderer was interned. But, oh!, in the last minute the odd assembly will be prevented from seeing Moosbrugger, because the doctor in charge of him was unexpectedly required at an emergency. So why the whole chapter? - if it is one. We will certainly never find out. If anything, it offered an occasion for a conversation between general Stumm and Ulrich about military matters presaging the First World War. This conversation is as if coming from the notebook of a mediocre writer but not as a digression in the "novel of the century". Then there is yet another occasion, when poor Clarisse, obsessed with the sexual offender, finds him in the asylum engaged in a card game with two doctors and the priest. Though better than the first arbitrarily enclosed episode, it hardly manages to include Moosbrugger in the novel's web, while he still remains an excellent *étude*. [Nothing changed later when Clarisse, and a little chamber maid of the Parallel Action's first lady manage to shelter him. Do we really have to concentrate also on this?]

The portrait is done, yet the *historia*, which by Leon Battista Alberti has to underlie any picture, is sadly incomplete. Still we are lead to sense, by yet another example, that inadequacy which characterizes our word-blanketed world. We have just an *ébauche*, doubtless a masterly one, of the dangers of the inability to articulate anything but by the abusive employment of words. Outside the book of Musil, and outside the loony bin, Moosbrugger was not alone. There was a variety of Moosbruggers all over the place. The more articulate ones, those who were able to more impressively verbalize the discharge of their purulent guts for the benefit of yet other word-addicts, fared much better and did not even have to use themselves a murder weapon, thus being innocent.

V. Diotima

(5.1) A Lady well Protected from Algebra

She was Ulrich's cousin. He didn't know her until his father, in stern epistolary counselling, convinced him to seek her company and protection. For good reason. Hermine Tuzzi by her real name, the wife of the diplomat Hans Tuzzi, was the Grande Dame of the "Parallel Action". Not only was her salon the regular meeting place of famous people, actual and prospective members of the fuzzily defined committee of a fuzzily defined action, but she also had the double function of an organizer as well as conveyer of that feminine touch thought to be absolutely indispensable in any "intellectual endeavour" - as the parallel action was viewed by its initiator, count Leinsdorf. First of all, as it was stated in the title of chapter 24, hers was "the office of bringing about unity between famous guests and the Soul" (p.98). She was to prepare that

> "Inquiry pertaining to the writing of a statement of intent and the assessment of the desires of participating circles of the public concerning the seventieth jubilee of His Majesty's reign." [p.296]

And most importantly, she took upon herself to preside over that

> "Committee concerned with the writing of a declaration of intent concerning the seventieth jubilee of His Majesty's reign." [p.296]

Because, as one could read in count Leinsdorf's invitation, a committee of this kind was absolutely necessary, given that "a powerful demonstration emerging from the rank and file of the people could not be left to chance." [p.296]

Obviously not. And here was the opportunity for Ulrich's involvement as some kind of a secretary, and, as it will turn out, intimate adviser (and substitute Mephisto; of the Goethean brand, that "*Geist der stets verneint*", (that is: "the spirit which always denies") to Mrs. Tuzzi.

When Ulrich met his cousin, she called herself Ermelinda, instead of Hermine, as recorded in her birth certificate. Though her choice was arbitrary

"she, nevertheless, acquired some day the right to this beautiful name by a flash of intuition [*intuitive Eingebung*], when it [the name] requested entrance to her spiritual ears as a superior Truth" [p.92].

The chosen name was to be obliterated by the one Ulrich has given her. When inquiring about the distinguished lady, his, mostly loathed, acquaintances characterized her as:

-".. a spiritual grace beyond all description".
-".. our most beautiful and intelligent woman".
-".. an ideal woman". [p.92]

Rather unsatisfactory answers by the standard of our mathematical hero whose inclination towards philosophical pragmatism has affirmed itself in a question which required an answer to reveal the "thing" by its "function":

"And who is, after all, her lover?"

Since the surprised interlocutor was unable to produce an answer, Ulrich came to the following conclusion:

"Thus, a spiritual beauty, a second Diotima".

Diotima: a name of great consequence. First in the history of wisdom-loving. Was it not the woman from Mantinea who conveyed to none other than

Socrates the correct understanding of how the Olympians communicate with mortals through the daemon *Eros*? Since a god he was not, if we believe her.

Diotima: a name of great consequence also in the German literature where we have a significant precedent when a Frankfurt banker's wife, Suzette Gontard, was sublimated into a Diotima by her great admirer, the Hellenizing poet Friedrich Hölderlin.

And this new Diotima? She was also destined to be of great consequence. We should remember the accident in chapter 1, when the question came up about who were those distinguished lady and gentleman at the accident sight. We read that

> "they belonged to a privileged social group, wore elegant clothing, were of dignified demeanour, and had on their underwear the initials of their name displayed in the same decorous manner in which they addressed each other; and in exactly the same fashion, that is not turned outward, but on the fine lingerie of their conscience, it was engraved who they were, and that they most appropriately belonged in this capital city and royal residence." [p. 10]

The implication is obvious: though she was not Mrs.Tuzzi, she could as well have been her. Same feelings, same attitudes, thoughts. And a language ridden by fuzziness: when a clear concept is missing the word "soul" can always step in as a substitute. But: *what is soul*? Here is Musil's answer:

> *".. it is something which goes into hiding when it hears about algebraic series"* (p.103).

This is indeed what the novel is all about: a society which goes into hiding "when it hears about algebraic series" or anything which requires the clear and distinct discourse of which the mentioned mathematical example was the epitome. This society is, naturally, lead by those who "during their youth and school years ... were all bad mathematicians" (p.40), wherefore "they couldn't stand it". So they also went into hiding to protect their souls. Some were more aggressive. But not Diotima. She was a charming, feminine variety of the species, and therefore she is not treated so harshly in the novel. We are gentlemen, aren't we? But then:

"What she called soul was probably nothing but a small capital of ability to love, which she already owned at the time of her marriage; yet councillor Tuzzi did not offer the appropriate investment opportunity" (p.104).

Part of that capital was now invested in a vague cause, the "Parallel Action", and in a vague "spiritual relationship" with the rich and influential German businessman Dr. Paul Arnheim.

And whatever may have been solid substance in it, was subject to semantic disintegration:

"She choose carefully her words, fastened with threads of black and yellow [the imperial colours], and burned on her lips the soft-perfumed expressions of the higher bureaucracy" (p.268)

when presiding over her "Committee". This was in keeping with what was designated as her "office", namely of "bringing celebrity guests into unity with the Soul".

She was decidedly beautiful, "indeed ... a hydra of beauty", as Ulrich thought, and this fact had a clear impact on his decision:

"He [first] intended to let the great patriotic action wait for him in vain, but it [the Action] seemed to have taken shape in the person of Diotima and was prepared to swallow him" (p.95).

No dirty intentions! Instead, right from the beginning, Ulrich acted as the Great Logical Inquisitor. When outlining the Parallel Action, Diotima declared:

"We must and will realize a very great idea. The opportunity is given and we shall not miss it",

Ulrich naively asked:

"Do you think of something specific?"

This clearly foreshadowed Ulrich's future behaviour: questioning about the substance of the words used by people in his new surroundings and revealing, when he so perceived, their shallowness. So it was in this opening skirmish when Diotima turned out to be unable to quote anything specific. How could she?

> "Nobody who speaks of the Greatest and the most Important thing in the world means that such really exists." (p.94).

The only possible thing could be an ordering of aims according to degree of preference and thus some precisely defined purpose may end up on the top of the list. But somebody who had ventured into this line of reasoning should probably have been unable to see beyond "those soul-bereft times dominated by logic and psychology". Ulrich was one of them. He was being deprived of the required time-transcending farsightedness. Diotima, instead was endowed with it, only she wasn't able to precisely describe the things sighted yonder. What did she see? Nothing precise and clear. But then this was not her role and purpose. We were suggested that it was symbolic for all her outlook and insight when one day

> "the beautiful woman proclaimed to her followers the need to enjoy the bright sunshine of the year 1914[!] which downed several weeks ago." [p.563-4]

The pleasurable occasion was to be relevant for the subsequent developments.

(5.2) Diotima:an Unfinished Novel

The gallery of characters, those very numerous characters of Musil, call for artistic organization to become a novel. It so happens that the only organizational principle of their coming together in a novel is the meeting, under a variety of not necessarily connected circumstances, with Ulrich, inside or outside the "Parallel Action". However, what strikes the reader again and again is the potential to autonomy of a great number of characters in this Austrian *comédie humaine*. One has the oft recurring feeling that Musil had originally intended to write as many novels as he has main characters - one for Diotima, e.g.; but then, in an urge of unification, he pasted them together with an over-dose of essayistic mortar. Yet we can identify their strong contours and their links in the complicated mechanics of the whole. In this sense, one of the novels absorbed in *the* Novel turns around Diotima. She emerges in the process as a more complex female personality than sensed by Ulrich in the beginning. In earlier stages of their acquaintance,

> "Ulrich occasionally felt with great intensity that Diotima was very beautiful" [p.246]

and he fell into plain romantic dreaminess. But then he awoke and saw in her

> "the spirit of an ambitious commoner seeking the company of noble ideas". [p.277]

Then followed the "sexist" Ulrich:

> "How pleasant could she be ... were she uncultured, negligent and good-natured as a big-framed [*grossgestalteter*] female body always is when not infatuated with extraordinary ideas".

Yet beautiful women often surprise prejudice. So did Diotima, a real "hydra of beauty", with as many appearances of her beauty as men she met and had to face. The hydra revealed two different heads to two very dissimilar men: Arnheim and Ulrich.

(5.3) Dr.Paul Arnheim

He was a leading German industrialist, a Jew by birth, organized by Diotima to participate, as a prominent personality, in the great Action. In spite of his "Prussian" background! Or, perhaps, because of it. As we learn early in the story:

> "... one could say that the Great Idea of Diotima consisted of nothing else but that Arnheim, the Prussian, must take over the

leadership of the great Austrian action, even though it [the Action] was meant to have its resentful edge directed against Prussian-Germany." [p.110]

We may find this either too smart or too silly, but it has something to do with the linguistic inability to handle fuzzy sentiments which are not properly articulated into meaningful expression. So we are explained in chapter 27 where it is said that:

"great, compelling [*ergreifende*] ideas consist of a body, which is solid yet fallible as the human body, and a Soul, which carries its [the idea's] significance, but which is not solid, and which evaporates as soon as you would try to grasp it with cold words." [p.110]

Now, so we are suggested, Arnheim was the "body", the solid stuff, the vehicle of the idea. The reader is of course entitled to think that our author simply did not have a clear idea justifying the presence of Arnheim in this novel with its countless casual encounters. Instead of simply proclaiming the association of that fellow with the Action to be a whim of Diotima, we are served the above quoted tenuous explanation which so strongly tastes of that very proto-Kakanian language constantly criticized, yet only too often, and too bravely, used by the author himself. Ironically! - we are suggested. Why not granting a "hydra of beauty" the right to have whims? The dozens of "essayistic", not novelistic, pages about Arnheim could in fact be simply reduced to the following:

"He [Ulrich] couldn't stand Arnheim ... He found this connection between spirit, business, highlife and well-read haughtiness most insufferable." [p.176]

And the following complement would make for a perfect definition of this character, as far as Musil/Ulrich is concerned:

"This union between the Soul and coal prices was something of a fraud which served the purpose of a divide between what Arnheim did in full conscience and the dim thoughts he expressed in speech and writing. [p.281]

Now Arnheim, though just another example of ideological fuzziness, was nevertheless one who attempted to rationalize his irrationality claiming that truly great things

"do not follow from the strictures and laws of logic but are responses to the riotous urges of the spirit. Logic can be viewed, at best, as having the efficiency of a police force." [p.403]

He also had his secrets. Arnheim loved Heine "in a hidden fashion", often quoting him, thus betraying, may be, some arcane inclinations he did not publicly reveal. All the same, as Ulrich met him, our fine mathematician plunged himself into the confusion of his environment. And the author a little bit too. Do we get now an interesting intrigue, a conflict, a dramatic development? We could, if the Arnheim-Diotima and Ulrich-Diotima connection would not always be drowned in philosophical outpourings which the author is not able to discipline. The fragments we get to read are extremely interesting in themselves containing a promise never to be fulfilled. But something is always missing from the representation of the debating characters. Or, we may also say, that their definition is just given in a *new* manner. Whatever "explanation" you may adopt, test it by comparing the work with other major novelistic accomplishments of modern literature to see what is new, what is different or what is missing. Thus a comparison with Proust could prove to be useful. Of course, it is different, since it is another work. But one important difference is to be revealed. In Proust, apart from talk, also the actions, vices, virtues etc., of the characters are sharply represented in a very direct fashion. Proust's novel is more "behaviouristic", even though the "intellectual" aspect of the characters' behaviour is also properly (sometimes over-) accentuated. No doubt *Törless* was better on this account. It was the perfect small novel. Not the slightest fault in it. Instead, in *The Man* the characters mainly confront their ideas. If we would like to characterize them it would be rather by the degree of fuzziness in their ideas.

If we were to choose from the essay fragments which the characters hurl at each other, the best philosophical representation of Arnheim could be gotten from the following:

"'The sciences?' asked Arnheim further; 'Culture? What remains is the art. Indeed, it is art which is to reflect the unity of existence and its inner order. Yet we know the picture which it offers today. General confusion; extremes without connection. Stendhal, Balzac and Flaubert have already given us, earlier, the epos of the mechanized society and its emotional life. The monstrous existence of the lower creatures has been revealed by Dostoevsky, Strindberg and Freud. And so, nothing remained for us to be done in these days of our lives." [p.197]

Of the many platitudes uttered during such conversations, this one was a little bit less muddled. For the rest, the type of historic pessimism promoted by the German industrialist was exactly what was required to have him offered as the ideal antagonist for Ulrich who, so we are suggested, tried to apply scientific-logical rigour to everything he came in contact with, while living his life "as an essay". When directed by the author to challenge each other, face-to-face or by the mediation of a tale, Arnheim and Ulrich reveal their contradictory attitudes concerning the bearing of scientific thinking on moral matters, or on the matters of everyday life, by clubbing each other with essay fragments - in all politeness. It is useful for the reader to recall two parallel running conversations in the same distinguished company which illustrate this opposition of characters and leads also to the critical point of the entire novel. The first is between Arnheim and General Stumm about the art of playing billiards. Says the great industrialist:

" I never play billiard ... but I know as much that one can hit the ball high or low, right or left; that one can strike the second ball directly or just graze it; that one can drive the ball 'hard' or 'soft'; or to choose between more or less 'skewed' directions; and I am sure there are many more such combinations possible. ... [indeed] an infinity. If I were to express all this theoretically then, apart from mathematics and the mechanics of rigid bodies, I would have to consider also the theory of elasticity; I would have to know the coefficients characterizing the materials used, as well as the effect of temperature; I would have to employ the most subtle methods for the estimation of the coordination and degrees of my motor impulses; my estimate of the distance would have to match that of a vernier calliper; my combinatorial ability would have to be up to that of a slide ruler; not to speak of the estimation errors, the variance index and the fact that the coincidence of the two balls, which is the purpose to be achieved, is itself not univocal, but [is the member of] a set of values clustered around an average value itself dependent on a considerable number of additional circumstances."

Not bad for a fellow who despises science! Yet he also adds:

"You can see ... that I would be supposed to have all kinds of qualities which I don't possess, and to do things which I am unable to do. [...] And yet I approach the billiard board with a cigarette in my mouth, humming a melody, with the hat on my head, not giving much of a thought to the whole situation, then I push the ball and hit target! My dear General, the same happens in life in countless occasions! You are not only an Austrian but also a soldier, so you will understand: politics, honour, war, art, and all the decisive events in life take place beyond the confines of reason." [p.570]

This was probably meant to be a complete intellectual characterization of Arnheim. Now this is a novel; consequently we are not supposed to expect the author to go into detail analyzing and exposing the fallacious use of the cogently expounded allegory of the billiard player - a lovely little piece - to justify the subsequent propositions about the "confines of reason". If Arnheim were to be confronted by somebody in a direct fashion we *may* (!) get an interesting philosophical debate which, however, being a strict philosophical discussion, will not reveal much about the other personality. So Ulrich is not directly confronting Arnheim on the matter. Instead, we will learn about the *here* relevant aspect of his frame of mind from a parallel dialogue, this one with Diotima. However, one additional remark is to be addressed before coming to this ambiguous point; because I started writing these notes to clean the path of a friendly reader from the nonsense scattered around by countless commentators.

One of these is the association of Arnheim with the real-world Walther Rathenau. Well, once again: a novel is a novel is a novel. Even if the author had the intension to make references to somebody in real life, as he probably did, it is irrelevant. The story has to stand on its own. And as far as Arnheim is concerned, no matter how many "wrong" ideas he dispenses - and he was probably manufactured to do such, or so it seems - this opponent of Ulrich hardly provides the most interesting story within the grander framework. He isn't getting any better when toward the end of the novel, in a posthumous fragment, he becomes one of the "new" lovers of Leona. But, if Arnheim were indeed one to have been compared to Rathenau then he might have become a rather tragic and very revealing character. The roots of such a tragic story are, indeed, hidden in the most unlikely fashion in another posthumous chapter. It is when Ulrich, after the death of his father, visiting his sister Agathe, meets in her house, once again, General Stumm von Bordwehr, the militarist-totalitarian. Thus reads (a fragment of) the general's lecture:

> "... people don't need complicated intellects, because they want to trust and have faith. Considering all this, we arrive to the conclusion that when it comes to achieve the order which everybody desires, it doesn't matter whether we can rationally justify it. There are forms of order which have no rational justification, such as in the army where the higher-up is always right, at least as long as there is a higher ranking person at hand. How disturbed I was as a young man perceiving in all this a profanation of the world of ideas! And what do I see now? Nowadays this is called the principle of the Leader [*Prinzip des Führers*]." [p.1237]

The general, of course, foreshadows the *Führerprinzip* of the Nazis and, when asked by Ulrich about the sources of his ideas, he answered as follows:

> "They all ask now for a strong leadership! [...] They already ask for a two-level philosophy and ethic, one for the leaders and another one for those who are led." [p.1237]

A reference to Nietzsche was also made. Yet Ulrich rejoined with an ironic statement purporting to imitate Diotima, and which was also meant to be the final conclusion drawn from the general's peroration:

> "All decisive things occur by bypassing reason, and the grandeur of life roots in the Irrational!" [p.1237]

This is then the point where Stumm and Arnheim meet. The same Arnheim who once treated Stumm von Bordwehr to the allegory of the billiard play and who even earlier expressed ideas dangerously converging to those implied in the *Führerprinzip*. Here is an example:

> "The civilization problem is to be solved only by the heart. By the emergence of a new personality. By the internal image and pure will. Reason has not accomplished more than diminishing a great past to debilitating liberalism." [p.198]

Rathenau and the real-world generals may have met on similar grounds. Only the peace champion of Rapallo missed out on some details he could have discovered with more analytical reasoning and relying less on conditional reflexes. Yet he was never to use the lesson offered to him. It was, as we all know, deadly.

(5.4) The Shadows of Arnheim and Diotima

This particular discussion of one of the major literary works of our century has something in common with all other discussions of Musil's book[s]: it is biased. However, it shares its bias with only few others. Except that it does not suggest that what is neglected in the discussion should be neglected also by the reader. The clearly stated bias is meant to re-establish some balance. Therefore it could grant only a very small room to some most charming, readable, artistically - from the point of view of *plot construction* - remarkable elements of this great rhapsody. If these are mentioned it is in order to point out their connection to the bias, which is not necessarily very strong. The fine little string of episodes to be mentioned *en passant* is about Arnheim's very sensual African groom Soliman, and Diotima's little Jewish maid.

> "We remember that the glowing little maid of Diotima chased from her parental home because of a false step, and landed in that golden shine of virtue which was her mistress ..." [p.1470]

was defeated by her recurring fits of weakness yielding to the amorous entreaties of Soliman. Well, sin was haunting her throughout the novel in which she was never properly fit in. But then there was a thin, yet firm cord, loosely tying most everything in the book:

> "[Rachel] felt love for Diotima. And infinite respect for Arnheim, as well as profound disgust for those wallowing and swallowing individuals whom a good police force would classify as subversive; *- yet she had no words for all this.*" [p.339]

So not even the little maid was able to free herself from the roots of conflict of her age: the inadequacy of language in facing that so complex reality. Had Musil liberated her from even thinking of it, we may have had a nice little, slightly kinky, quite delightful but *no-consequence* story. Even without that odd involvement of Rachel with Moosbrugger's liberation.

(5.5) The Mathematician Slips

Ulrich's ritualistic urge to test everything for its exactness, required itself to be tested. The claims for a possible "exact living" were in most cases justified by exposing the consequences of inexact living. However, it turned out that there was somewhere a line between the two, a line which Ulrich inadvertently crossed. We may say that the story reveals a contradiction in Ulrich's intellectual personality which is a reflection of a yet deeper contradiction in the state of things real. One aspect of these is revealed in a chat with Diotima in the same place where, in some other corner, Arnheim and General Stumm were conversing about billiards. It was *à propos* the recurring questions of Diotima about how "a woman" - she avoided to name herself - is to behave "correctly" when faced with the choice between duty and preference. The mathematician did the same as his opponent on the previous page did: he resorted to something of a scientific allegory, though oddly enough, less ably than Arnheim. Answering Diotima's question Ulrich said:

> "Have you ever seen a dog? [...] You merely think so! You always saw something what appeared to you to be, more or less, a dog. It did not have all the doggish characteristics, while at the same time it had something personal which is not to be found in any other dog. How can we ever do in life the 'right' thing? We are able

to do only things which are never the right ones, and always only more or less something that is right." [A strange consequence of having to restrain oneself to a platonic relationship is to end up a Platonist. And all this by using positivist parables! - as the one to follow. – T.S.] "And has ever a tile fallen from the roof according to the laws of physics? Never! Not even in a laboratory do things behave as they should. They deviate in all directions [from the "laws of physics" – T.S.], and it is just a fanciful construction of our mind when we explain all this as a random deviation of the execution [of the experiment] from a mean to which we ascribe some real value."[p.572]

Scientific correctness is obviously not the purpose here. Though, with small amendments, the above statements can be considered as - tolerably, and very generally! - correct, they are hardly offering a pertinent allegory. Allegories can be taken from science or Chinese mythology, but in order to carry meaning in a literary work they have to relevantly *point at* something in the narrative process. Because, you see, there are certain clearly definable characteristics which make something to belong to "the class of dogs" and not of zebras or unicorns. So the general definition gives the frame for the purported variance, and there is no "incorrect dog" outside the frame. But then, we have here yet another semantically abusive employment of science which not even a mathematician would avoid when aiming at the heart of a lady. The sections subsequent to this quotation provide additional proof for that.

(5.6) Diotima and Ulrich

Of course, we do not expect any character in a novel to have "correct" opinions. The problem is that these philosophical opinions are expounded in so much detail that one would be tempted to take them on in a discussion. Yet this should not happen here, and attention will be paid to them only as indicators of a character. So we pursue the relation between Ulrich and his cousin to see how logically correct thinking is to be employed, in other words how "exact living" passes the test in this odd context. It is interesting that it was to be demonstrated by none other than Diotima when once again confronting her cousin. It happened thus:

Diotima was at the zenith of her platonic affair with Arnheim. One day the distinguished personalities of the Parallel Action, among them Diotima, the German industrialist and Ulrich, visited the imperial library to do a bit of research on their own concerning some past folk jubilees. When they left the library for a leisurely walk, "to enjoy the bright sunshine of the year 1914", Diotima and Ulrich disengaged themselves from the rest. This provided the occasion for an exchange between the two cousins about love, in which the lady talked only about abstract third persons while the mathematician didn't hesitate using names. Diotima, whose secret love (for Arnheim) could hardly be hidden anymore, asked the cynical cousin:

> "- 'When a woman has to choose between her duty and her passion, on what could she rely if not on her own character?
> "- 'You have to choose! - replied Ulrich
> "- 'You permit yourself too much; I didn't speak about myself' whispered the cousin'" (p.566)

But then she asked again:

> "Do you conceive it possible that the thing we call our soul should be able to step out of the shadow which normally conceals it?"

The nasty reaction of Ulrich is hardly relevant, but what Diotima said in sequel was of revelatory significance:

> "When I said 'stepping out from the shadow' I meant to abandon the equivocal, that shimmering concealment, in which we perceive at times all that is unusual. It is spread like a net which torments us because it neither holds us tight nor lets us free. Don't you think there were times when all this was different? A person's self asserted itself more forcefully; some people followed a luminous path; in one word they followed, as they said in early times, a holy course, and miracles became reality, because they were always an ever present *other* reality!" [p.566]

This may not have been all that *clear and distinct*, but it struck like a thunderbolt. A new head of the hydra of beauty showed itself to Ulrich:

"Did we thus arrive to the point where this giant hen talks like me?"

The giant hen was about to produce more embarrassing ideas during this long and revealing dialogue crisscrossing the frontiers of exact living. Here is a sample. Talking about the sentimental link between Arnheim and Diotima, Ulrich afforded himself a serious aberration from his usual speech manners:

"'You and Arnheim are two delicate people; you love poetry; I am absolutely convinced that you are sometimes touched by a gentle breeze of some kind, without knowing what it is. And you want now to apply all the thoroughness of which you are capable to discover the source of it all?!'
"'Don't you always profess that one has to be exact and thorough?' replied Diotima." [p.568]

Of course, this is the point where exactness hits the limit. It does not apply anymore. No wonder that "Ulrich was a little startled". He went about to produce once again one of his long essayistic lectures, but at the end of the line she pressed again:

"-'What shall thus a woman do who, in real life, is in a situation like the one we were discussing?'
"-'To concede.' replied Ulrich
"-'To whom?'
"-'To whatever comes! Your husband, your lover, your resignation, their blend.'"(p.573)

Well, this is not much said for "exact living" and "exact feeling" when love gets into the picture. But the exchange clearly stressed Diotima's fear to choose. As for Ulrich's subsequent proposal of a romance, it was nothing but a substitute for the missing answer:

"Let's try to love each other, as we were but characters of a poet who meet on the pages of a book. However, we should keep out the truss of fat which makes Reality so roundish" [p.573] [Or "as thick as pug"? - as we read about German novels in the "Mathematical Man". It seems that Ulrich explored other ways for slimming than just the solving of integrals.]

And after yet another long essayistic outpouring of her cousin, the "giant hen" made it quite clear that the tirade does not make much sense, saying:

"You spoke fast, soft and long ... Yet you said not a word about what you actually wanted to say. Do you know what you declared here? That we ought to abolish reality! I have to confess that I could never forget this statement ever since I heard it from you for the first time during one of our excursions. And I don't exactly know why. However, you never said how we are supposed to achieve this." [p.575]

Here we have now the hydra of beauty and giant hen in the process of graduating to a positivist and exposing a fallacious turn of the doctrine of exact living.

(5.7) Where Exact Living Becomes Irrelevant

Ulrich finds out about it for the first time in connection with Diotima. *Love* is the testing ground. - It is, of course, all right to play the logical censor as long as one is pacing carefully when crossing into the domain of things which can only be pointed at but never meaningfully spoken about. And love is part of this province. There are good attempts in the novel to represent it, but in the present case the reader remains with the feeling that Diotima could have deserved better.

The quoted conversation indicates the borderline from where Ulrich is to leap into the irrational. In this connection it should be emphasised, once again, that the exploration of this borderline remains the strongest point of *The Man Without Qualities*. He, *The Man*, is some sort of a border guard or customs officer on this frontier. A little corrupt - not always! - but nevertheless alert and watchful. Most examples quoted refer to the manner in which this unique character in the entire novel literature is exerting his functions. The remaining examples should reveal his reflective presence from additional angles, particularly in relation to his association with Gerda Fischel, and to his own sister.

VI. Leo and Gerda Fischel, as well as Hans Sepp

(6.1) The *Direktor* and His Family

It was early in the twentieth century. In Vienna. Hence you could not miss Leo Fischel, neither his daughter Gerda. Not to speak of her lover Hans Sepp.

Leo Fischel was a personality defined by three components often associated since ancient times. He was: (1) a Jew; (2) a banker; and (3) a recreational philosopher. But all in a small way. Though a Jew, he was a "freethinker" who believed in something called "progress"; and when this first component of his personality appeared to be offensive to some, he thought that mankind's advances will soon make their purported resentments an obsolete oddity. But until that happened he never got very high up in the Bank's hierarchy, though his modest yet important position very likely "generated business" - which might have acted in the direction of that much yearned for progress. As for philosophizing, well, he did it, so we read, "ten minutes a day". In reality much more, since the first two above listed components of his personality determined a situation in which he couldn't afford to free himself from the peculiar habit of asking unpleasant questions. Though Leo, unlike Ulrich, never acquired his nasty questioning habits from immersion in the definitional rigour of math classes, he was nevertheless close to the stuff in many of its varieties. Because, precise, clear and distinct specifications were just as important to a banker as they were to a mathematician. The terms of a contract have to be clear and free from metaphysical intrusions! Therefore Fischel was, perhaps, the only character in the novel, beside Ulrich, who still retained a measure of Socratian nastiness. After receiving the circular letter of count Leinsdorf, the *spiritus rector* of the Parallel Action, inviting him to participation, Leo found the occasion to emulate Ulrich in something of a philosophical discussion of the type which, in the novel, appeared to have been within the turf of the man without qualities. Meeting one day Ulrich, Fischel made it clear that he understands perfectly well what progress is, what Austria is supposed to mean, and probably also what the "love for the fatherland" signifies. Yet, he said, he was unable to make any sense of expressions such as "*true* progress", "*true* Austria" and "*true* love for the fatherland". But Ulrich, who of necessity was familiar also with the philosophical work of one of the founding fathers of calculus, produced a prompt answer by twisting a little an important contribution of that great man. For if Leibniz could establish the *law of sufficient reason* (or *sufficient foundation* as the verbatim translation would read) as being explanatory for what we call "reality", Ulrich was able to propose the LIR for everything that has *no* foundation. LIR? Yes, the *law of insufficient reason* or *foundation*. It may not have satisfied Fischel because he still believed in progress as well as in Austria, as so many others of his strain, proving thereby to be indeed unaware of every aspect of the relevant "true" variety.

Fischel closed the conversation with a flattering remark:

> "I said to Gerda the other day that you could have made a remarkable diplomat. I hope you will soon pay us a visit again." [p.135]

Because, so Leo might have thought, Gerda could demonstrate some *true love for the fatherland* when involved in the Parallel Action, of which our hero was already some sort of a secretary.

Then we have Leo's wife, Klementine, who came from a family belonging to the upper ranks of the Imperial civil service. She married Leo, in spite of item (1) above, because she was *enlightened*. And item (2) was not to be despised either seeing that social position and money were not always keeping company to each other in the higher Kakanian bureaucracy. But then

> "The poor had to live to see the spirit of nationalism emerging everywhere in Europe and along with it a wave of attacks on Jews..." [p.204]

affecting her husband and her marriage as well. Most significantly, however, because Gerda, her and Leo's daughter, fell in love with none other than Hans Sepp, a young warrior of the "blood and soil" ideology. How was that possible? It just so happened in a company of students "who may not have been racial anti-Semites" (I wonder) but

"who were against the 'Jewish mentality', by which they meant capitalism, socialism, science, reason, the power and assertiveness of
parents, calculation, psychology and scepticism. Their main buzz-
word was 'symbol'.." [p.313]

This was the ideological rubbish which eludes criticism because it hides
behind "symbols". Symbols cannot be discussed

".. first, because symbols cannot be translated into sober words, second, because Arians are not supposed to be sober, wherefore they
succeeded in the last century only in producing allusions by symbols, and third, because there are centuries which produce only seldom that moment of Grace, so alien to the alienated Man." [p.313]

More or less like Beineberg and Reiting, the colleagues of Törless. But a
conflict between Gerda and them was not to erupt because

"Gerda, who was a smart girl, felt secretly quite suspicious about
these exaggerated opinions, but she was also suspicious of her suspicion which she thought to be a legacy of paternal rationality".
[p.313]

Here we have an excellent subject for a novel on its own. But then, *The
Man without Qualities* is a composite of torsos of excellent subjects for any
number of novels, yet it, *The Man*, never made it to a complete novel. This
Fischel story is, however, interesting on its own. Particularly for a nasty cavil-
ler. Its careful *re*construction ("re-" not "de-", please!) would show us why the
author had to labour so much on his self-imposed Sisyphean literary rock-roll-
ing. It also shows us that when the purported and much praised mathematical
and semantic rigour is inappropriately - i.e. *not* rigorously - employed, a horror
of fallacies may swamp not only the story but the often so delightful essayistic
plus as well. The point deserves some attention. We certainly owe praise to the
musilian respect of the borderline between the positive and the metaphysical,
between what we may speak about and what we may only point at; for Musil
understood that only the literary representation of action, as well as the parable and the metaphor (also the mathematical metaphor!) could provide the

passport for crossing that frontier. But when such "passport" is used for smuggling across the border the author's own perplexity and conceptual confusion then we, the readers, may be in trouble if we ignore the nature of that junk. We ought to know that not every smuggle ware is of better quality than what you may normally get at the corner grocer, even though it might fascinate by the mystery surrounding it.

(6.2) The Frontiers of Unreason

The excellence of this novel consists in the manner in which it guides the reader to discover the borderline between reason and unreason. The "guide" is in fact the mathematical hero who has acquired during his education the ability to ascertain the location and trajectory of this line, while being also endowed with the innate inclination to expose himself to its challenges. Such adventurous trials are often generated by conversations between the characters of the novel. A relevant example should be subsequently quoted.

One night there was company at the Fischels, Ulrich and Sepp also attending. Discussion was about "progress". Ulrich, as usual, developed a theory which, nevertheless, was redundant in the context. Instead, the unsophisticated Fischel managed to clearly define what was behind the muddled verbiage of the young blood and soil warriors:

> "The young gentlemen despise the precision of numbers."
> ["*Zahlengenauigkeut verachten die jungen Herrschaften.*"] [p.483]

And here is the furious answer of Hans Sepp:

> "Yet, by your way of thinking, a wish list [to define progress] will always be summed-up on the bottom-line of your ledger" ["*Aber für ihre Denkweise bleibt das Wunschzettel trotzdem immer nur eine Summe oder eine Bilanz.*"] [p.485]

Of course, let us not forget, that as soon as we depart, rationally, from such words as "progress", since more than words they are not, a *Wunschzettel*, a wish list, is to be provided to avoid any form of ambiguity. But this will then be "positivism".

Later Ulrich proves the same kind of confusion when he, instead of speaking in terms of a *Wunschzettel*, tries to philosophize about "progress" producing an appalling sham of what seems to claim to be taken as a mathematical metaphor. This happened while he remained alone with Gerda. We are presently supplied with some reference to the young lady's academic education in which she was supposed to acquire - no word about *when* and *how* - some notions of mathematical statistics which explain how a collection of observation values yield some average result which then may be viewed as a "law". Subsequently we are explained how this applies to "progress":

> "Then, from a number of observations, we make a number cluster; we devise sections according to magnitude, and see which values [from the cluster] can be placed within their respective range; then we construct distribution series; further we will find out whether the frequency of the [investigated] occurrences is or is not systematically growing or declining; thereby we will find out whether we obtained a stationary series or a distribution function; subsequently we calculate the measures of deviations from a certain value, such as the median, the mode, the mean and the variance etc. and then we examine, with the help of all these notions, the given occurrence." [p.487]

This lecture in elementary mathematical statistics is meant to justify Ulrich's unwillingness to establish a *Wunschzettel* of his own as a measure of *progress*. Follow several pages of considerations related to the philosophy of science as it emerged after the discovery of the kinetic theory of gases, a parade item in popular renditions of certain principles in statistical physics. These considerations, which are purported to be part of a conversation with Gerda, are uncharacteristically confused, uncharacteristic for Musil that is, ending up in the following non-sense analogy:

> "Let's assume that in the moral domain things happen as in the kinetic theory of gases: everything floats around in a random fashion, everything behaves arbitrarily, but when we come to calculate this apparently confused process then it turns out that it leads to whatever it leads! There are momentous coincidences! Let's assume that

a certain amount of ideas are presently floating randomly about; this ["amount"?] will give a most probable mean value; then, this mean value, will shift very slowly and automatically, and this will be that so called progress or historic state; the most important thing, however, is that all this does not depend at all on the personal, particular, movement of each of us. We may think left or right, lofty or paltry, new or old, unfathomable or imperious: it is indifferent for the average value. And it is the only thing God and the world cares for, not us!" [p.490]

Now there is nowhere written that a character in a novel cannot talk nonsense, even when, as it happens quite often, he has very smart things to say. But this piece of nonsensical philosophizing can be most properly tagged with the title of a never openly avowed but widely shared doctrine, a very fuzzy one indeed, a doctrine I venture to call "historic fatalism". This is the refuge of those who, pretending wisdom, abstain from a political stand and thus grant the green light to the like Hans Sepp (or Reiting and Beineberg) whom they so spitefully purport to counter. This time we got the "thesis" in a totally out of place physico-mathematical gibberish. There is no place here to discuss the issue itself. We discuss *a novel*. (Though: attention deconstructors! It would be a delight to work out the theme "underlying" this and related sections, postulating the following hypothesis: Musil wrote these chapters in a time when he was alternating his bedtime reading, night after night, between a treatise of statistical physics and Leibniz's *Theodizee* or *Monadologie*. He was so deeply impressed by the latter that he didn't even notice how the law of sufficient reason, or "foundation", was subtly creeping into the story *via* statistical mechanics - creating a chaotic movement where nobody in his right mind will ever find an "average value".)

It is quite clear that Musil did not take the subject on with the means of a novelist, as he so successfully has done in the case of Törless. The triangular conflict Fischel-Gerda-Sepp, *only witnessed* by Ulrich, is not fully elaborated with the means of the novelist, but rather permeated with essayistic additions, which in this case proved to be of very poor merit. This opinion could be countered by saying that, notwithstanding Ulrich's rather meagre performance in this context, the rest of the triangular story (or quadrangular, if Klementine is included) has not been finished, we having only posthumous fragments of it.

We could see, of course, whether we can put together a plausible story-web from the fragments. This will be avoided here for quite a few reasons. Yet these fragments are interesting on their own, because some are very good reading, never mind how flimsy their connection with the main action. But then, is not the hero, Ulrich in this case, unifying them?

There may be, of course an excuse for all this: Ulrich's interest in Gerda which causes him to talk no matter what only to counter Sepp. So, to some extent, Ulrich appears as a rival of Sepp. This rivalry was most active when the two, in the presence of Gerda, crossed rhetoric swords, "in the jargon of the border zone between super- and un-reason" [*Über- und Unvernunft*] as signalled in the title of the relevant Chapter 113 of the first book. Samples of these discussions testify for what was already clear, namely that Hans was but an illustrative instance of that

> "...soul of a monstrous multiform irrational movement which spooks through our time like a night bird lost in daylight" [p.553]

and which was said to compare in a negative fashion with organized religion and its systematic theological doctrine. True. Except that we do not have here either a comparison of the several relevant *Wunschzettel*. There is certainly a borderline between what can be sorted out in a rational discussion and what is to be suggested by literary/parabolic representation. The first is done very poorly; the second is simply not there. Had the difference been revealed, we would have a conflict-development sparked by a situation in which Ulrich, Sepp, Gerda etc. had exposed themselves by there behaviour, even if their thoughts and discussions had to help along the narration. But we have no "situation", no active conflict, only blah-blah "in the jargon of the border zone between super- and under-reason". And a justification by love, where "anything goes". So it seems that Musil was totally unsuccessful to entwine the conflict of the two languages, so magnificently epitomized in Törless, with the novel of the "parallel action".

Nor were the Fischels, plagued by their own family imbroglio, properly mated with "the great patriotic action". Let us recall their story. *Herr Director*, loathed by his Arian (still enlightened but now doubt-ridden) wife for not going "ahead", decided to do just that. He engaged in dangerous business adventures, and become a "greedy speculator" [*ein erpichter Spekulant*].

First he seemed to gain and, to enhance his status, he even got himself a mistress: Leona. Not without the help of Ulrich. But then he lost everything, Klementine's jewels *compris*. Yet, a new move, and this time he won. A lot, and became *Generaldirektor* of a company, and even got himself a new tailor. In the meanwhile he passed Leona to Arnheim. However, Gerda left home and, as we would call it today, "moved in" with Sepp, or so it seemed at first. The various manoeuvres to recover her - including a Fischel/Diotima meeting - offer the reader fine episodic exercises in character descriptions by a master novelist, without properly fusing them into a "story". Yet the characters continued to philosophize as revealed at an occasion when, once again, the *Generaldirektor* met Ulrich, shortly after the father of the mathematician passed away:

"You inherited?" asked Fischel.
"'Well' said Ulrich, 'quite enough'"
"'I know, we all have our troubles.'"

And then he said exactly what Hans Sepp would have expected him to say:

"Only what can be expressed in numbers is reliable. Believe me, the world would be a much more reasonable place were we to leave it to the mercy of the play of supply and demand, instead of endowing it with battle ships, bayonets, diplomats ignorant in matters economic, or so called national ideals." [p.1451]

With slight corrections one could agree. Yet we still miss out on the whole dramatic transformation of Fischel from a back-room bank executive to the general manager of a big company. A whole history is hidden behind it which can not be represented in the terms of statistical thermodynamics. Whatever the statistical outcome of the whole process, in which Fischel is only a "molecule", it is the individual trajectory of such a molecule which literature *imitates*; physics cares only for the whole mass.

Human life means the movement of each "molecule" in the social context but not by the laws of statistics. And whenever the author has invented the story, the medium of its recounting, the Word, belongs to Maxwell's demons. Indeed, also to each "molecule" separately when confronted with the demons. Also, perhaps, to each "electron" within the human "soul". Since we may tell their story but never determine, simultaneously, their position and velocity. (Now *I* am using such a metaphor; only this time, I hope, correctly.)

(6.3) Hans Sepp

Fischel's trials are strangely entwined with those of Hans Sepp, who will become a tragic reflection of yet another "linguistic" inadequacy. The right-wing radical student is a most ably represented character, though one has an uneasy feeling about him. He is, of course, not a Beineberg or a Reiting. Or more exactly he *is* one like them but in completely different circumstances. Sepp is not in the situation to dominate anybody; no Bassini type is subject to him. In fact he is in opposition to those who dominate, but not because they dominate. It is domineering Kakania which obstructs the fulfilment of his great-German ideal, wherefore he hates the dual monarchy proving himself "politically unreliable" when conscripted by its military. He dreams of an all-German commonwealth with strong and great leaders, Napoleon being their paragon. Yet when he gets for the first time under the dominion of something of a "strong leader", such as a corporal, he comes to realize that

"my innermost is nothing but the lining of a military coat." [p.1498]

It is so because he is not the master, being also placed in a rather humiliating subordinate situation:

"The corporal who tormented him was a milksop of a peasant boy, and Hans looked astonished in his young furious face which did not only express rage ... but [also] all the malevolence of which a man was capable whenever permitted to show it". [p.1494]

To recall once again the first novel of Musil - one can hardly escape the idea that we read the tormented *essay* of a continuation - in the new situation, Reiting or Beineberg was to become a Bassini ending up in suicide. This transformation was at the same time one of the finest epic pieces, fragments rather, of the whole hefty book, reminding the quality of the *Törless* novel at every step of its unfolding. Thus, before throwing himself under the wheels of a train, Sepp "[first] broke his pencil and tore his notebook into small pieces. Then he descended the slope, and after seating himself in the grass by the edge of the gravel track, he scattered the tatters of his spiritual life in front of a passing train. The train strew them all over the place. No trace remained of his pencil, and the bright paper butterflies stamped by the wheels, were spread on the embankment." [p.1516]

Something similar was done by Törless when stepping out from the dark world of his beastly colleagues into the light of reason. Sepp, instead, cut short his life built of word-adorned symbols which crashed at the first contact with their hard, real-world complements. We know - don't we? - that a person living in such a world could endure reality only when having somebody to look up to, somebody able to stylize himself as a "leader", different from the "milksop of a peasant boy". Beyond this the Sepp type would also need to gratify himself by mastery over others. For this it was too early yet, because Herr Fischel just became the *Generaldirektor* of a company.

[Just another *excursus*, sinning against my principle of not looking for connections with real life characters. How come that all those astute critics never properly used the opportunity to construct a parallel between Hans Sepp's thoughts, ways *and* suicide, and those of the suicidal right wing writer Rudolf Müller? The latter, who shot himself at a young age, definitely enjoyed the literary appreciation of Musil, though not his pretences as an ideologist. A research in the subject could yield, perhaps, a good seminar paper. Useful reading is Musil's obituary article in v.VIII, p.1131.]

VII. Slipping Into the Irrational

(7.1) Agathe Between two Mathematical Men

A "second book" of the vast, unfinished, novel could have yet again stood on its own. Indeed it does, as far as it goes, the unifying hero showing himself from a very different side, suggested in the "first book" only in casual digressions. This other part, much of it posthumous, has little to do with the Parallel Action, though several of its characters will turn up again, often cloaked in some artificial pretext. It starts with Ulrich meeting a so far forgotten sister, Agathe, when he arrives in his native city to his father's funeral. Their encounter was characterized by a critic - was he a French one? - as the most beautiful onset of an incestuous relationship in modern literature. I hope Thomas Mann didn't come about to read this remark. The old man might have had a very bad day. As for my humble self, I have to confess that I am totally unable to make dependable distinctions between the qualities of various incestuous relationships. The only thing I could say with relative certainty is that a new, may be interesting novel's giant torso lays before us, though without many of the literary merits of the previous "book", while being burdened with a profusion of redundancies. Here are now a few additional notes of this reader's idiosyncratic perception of the matters.

The comparison with *Törless* imposes itself once again. Keep him always in mind. Also as a gauge of literary quality! We recall how the young man discovered reason while struggling with the consequences of unreason, and decided what Ulrich came also to know: not everything is of the domain of the rational, and keep the "two jars" separated! However, the Man without qualities got into trouble. At some point he tried to cross the border - and this is what the story around Agathe has revealed.

We recall the story starting when Ulrich received the telegram in which his father informed him about his *own* death: *"I notify you about my passing away"*. Remember? Not *impending* passing away! - but the one which actually happened. This would be no problem for most readers who would easily guess that the telegram was sent by somebody according to the last wish of the deceased. And so it actually happened. But while this "practical" aspect of the occurrence was of no consequence, it is likely to generate different thoughts in different minds. For our mathematician it seems to have been just another case of those paradoxes with which various mathematical disciplines and chapters of logic have to reckon. Think of it: a dead man behaves as if he were living, and sends a telegram. Does he belong to "the class of all dead men"? But he was living! Well, then he belongs to the class of all living men. Yes, but this contradicts the implicit self-definition in the telegram which excludes him from this class. So, how to decide? It certainly appeared that

"the present attempted to dominate the future which it never hoped to reach" [p.672].

This, illogical as it may sound, was quite logical, though according to a devil-ridden logic, that is *verteufelt logisch*, while at the same time

"the eerie reek of an angrily decaying volition"

hovered over it. And Ulrich met his sister under these circumstances while carrying such ideas in his head.

Agathe was the wife of professor Hagauer whom she intended to leave because she had no feelings for him. The two siblings discussed him at length. These exchanges were an attempt by Musil/Ulrich to solve two problems, a philosophical and a literary one. Philosophically Hagauer had much in common with Ulrich, or rather *The Mathematical Man* of that early essay. This had to be revealed, as well as the contrasting characteristics, if we were to find out about the motives of that "most beautiful incestuous relationship in modern literature". Now a novel has to be a novel. This is possible only when the characters *act* as well as talk. Platonic dialogues are not novels. But then what do you do when, by the purported logic of the plot, you have to involve a fellow whose actions proper are not really interesting, while you are still compelled to account for him? Because he exists, and he exists because he fits also the essayistic intrusions into the novel, apart from being a cumbersome husband. Here is then the literary problem: what to do with him? Make him utter yet another one of those endless perorations, of which some are interesting, but not always novelistic? This time a new trick was found. Agathe mockingly imitates her husband, rehearsing one of his professorial lucubrations she claims not to understand, reproducing it only to monkey her spouse and poke fun of the fussy prof. So you have yet another philosophical insertion of which you are supposed to think that it is mockingly said as a description of a person by another person. Here is a sample:

"And intellectual breeding means imposing on the mind the discipline which enables man to work himself rationally through longer chains of [given] thoughts, while permanently questioning his own intruding ideas. In other words, this means that he is able to put himself through faultless syllogisms, sorites and chains of consecution, based on induction or starting from symbols, and to test the thus gained assertion as long as all the ideas are accommodated with one another". [p.703]

Agathe pretended not to know what she was talking about and that she was only quoting from memory. But her brother, amused as he was by his brother-in-law's purportedly bombastic scholarship, agreed with him nonetheless:

> "Do you know that in all this what you claim to have quoted, Hagauer is quite correct? It is only funny." [p.704]

No surprise that Ulrich agreed, since he started out even in this new phase of his adventure as a scientist. As a scientist? Yes. Right in the house of mourning with its "eerie reek of an angrily decaying volition". He awoke the morning after his arrival and

> "took his scientific work from the suitcase and went over to the study of his father" [p.686]

and shortly thereafter his

> "eyes stopped right at the beginning on the section presenting the physical equations of water with which he was stuck for quite a while."

And now read this and be surprised:

> "He recalled dimly that he thought on Clarisse while constructing an example on the three states of water, to exhibit on them a new mathematical possibility; yet Clarisse then sidetracked his attention." [687]

There are people, particularly when they happen to be called Marcel Proust, who are able to recall several volumes worth of stories when stumbling once on the kerb of some pavement. Now just think that somebody in the Proust family would have gotten the idea to send young Marcel to science classes where they had stuffed him with a lot of *mathématiques*. Than his associations would have been of the same kind as those of Musil/Ulrich. This did not happen, as we all know. But it seems the mechanics of memory re-living is common to Ulrich and Marcel. Because

> "there certainly exists a kind of remembrance [*ein Erinnern*] which recalls not the word, but the atmosphere in which it was spoken, and thus, in an instant, [the word] 'Carbon ...' flashed through Ulrich's mind, and out of the blue sky, he got the impression that he could make progress were he to know, right now, all the states in which carbon appeared; but he could not remember, and instead he thought 'Humans appear in two [varieties]. As man and as woman.'" [p.687]

So we are at it. We know, of course, that "man and woman He created them". But how much more do we know? Well, we can discover that "carbon" and tasty little madeleines are not so different from one another.

A lot follows about the young Ulrich's memories - we are now in the memory department - particularly about Agathe. *We* could have gotten to it on a shorter way. But *Ulrich* has no shorter ways, and it turned out that "it made him pleasure to remember" [689]. A fit of humanity! Followed by wanderings on the winding and dangerous path of brother-sister love. A real gold mine for those who couldn't find their way with the previous Ulrich. But the epic construction is wanting. Yet the author had obviously a lot to say; not so much a story to tell but to philosophize about love and *feelings*. Now the characters could be put to tell this. But then they would talk a lot more seminar stuff - ever more often undergraduate - than they already did. And the author would again be accused of *not* writing a novel. And quite rightly. Therefore a solution had to be found. It was found. That is, the *Diary* of Ulrich was found by Agathe. This is the legitimate part of "the story". She reads it. Just as Agathe imitated her husband so the diary imitates Ulrich. And now you also can read the diary. If you have patience. Perhaps in installments, as I did. But then, I enjoy searching for the solution of integrals or, perhaps, of some nice little problems in algebra. Therefore I also know how to shed some pounds between two lecture installments while still relaxing. What about you?

Yet there is good, solid material here, explaining the transition of Ulrich and the qualms of an undecided scientist, as one he was. A short catena of quotations shall only adumbrate the series of thoughts, plaited with feelings, which illustrate Ulrich's own "rake's progress". The brother confesses to his sister:

> "When I became a mathematician ... I wished myself scientific success and focused all my efforts to achieve this goal ... And, indeed, my first works contained ideas which were new at the time. Yet they either remained unnoticed or encountered opposition, even though I was generally well received in every other respect. Thus we may also call it Destiny that I soon lost my patience to continue to engage all my strength in driving this wedge." [p.721]

Being asked by Agathe what he means by "wedge":

> "Because this is what the thing I first wanted to do actually was: I wanted to drive it as a wedge, but then lost my patience. ... And it is now clear to me that, had I had more luck or shown more perseverance, I would have been entitled to see myself [...] the leader of a new trend." [p.721]
>
> "'You could make up for it' said again Agathe. ..."
>
> "No, I don't want that! It is surprising yet true that I might not have changed anything on the way things went or even the development of science. Maybe I was about ten years ahead of my time; but people came to the same results at a somewhat slower pace and on different paths ... while it is doubtful whether such a change in my life would have been sufficient to give me a new boost for jumping beyond the target. [...*ob eine solch Veränderung meines Lebens genügt haben möchte, mich selbst inzwischen mit neuem Vorsprung über das Ziel hinauszureissen.*] Here you have thus a piece of what one calls personal destiny which, however, depends on something conspicuously un-personal". [721]

No question that "personal destiny" may depend on many external factors. But Ulrich, earlier so precise and rigorous, has now trouble finding words which should protect him from bombastic orations. His "slip from exactness" will give us a clue about the turn represented by the Second Book, that never to be finished second book. The first revelation is coming from the exchange between the two siblings introducing the above chain of quotations. Quoting in reversed order is justified by the implicit logic of the argument, purportedly a philosophical one, about *destiny*. Agathe initiated the discussion which Ulrich seemed to have first tried to avoid, claiming that

I am not one of those people who like to use this word." [p.720]

But then he will argue that

"in the better informed times to come, the word 'destiny' will possibly be given a statistical content'" [p.720]

I just would love to find out what a less informed person of our (or Ulrich's) uninformed age could (have) read in this. Because a somewhat more informed reader, even if not way ahead of his time, would quickly realize the nonsense. Neither now, nor in the future could statistics state anything about the destiny of an individual. Statistics is about populations, whether of people or gas molecules. The human individual's destiny is the matter of something we call drama or novel.

(7.2) Agathe Learns about the Calculus of Probabilities

Ulrich's frequently recurring dabbling in mathematical statistics and the theory of probability, shows that "exact living" is approaching its limits as the story advances. Once our mathematician claimed that he has a lot more feeling than the adepts of *Geist und Seele*. This claim is reiterated in various forms also in the second book, except that Ulrich now attempts to cover up his limited ability to come to grips with matters human, with a lot of non-sense talk about probability. And the worst is that this happens not only when the discussion is about "love" or that unspecified something called "feeling", where conceptual discourse is anyways seldom relevant, but also in simple matters of human history which, though difficult to fully explain, can nevertheless be addressed in a more rational fashion. It is a pattern which becomes more and more irritating as the story advances. We notice that Ulrich treats every female personality in the novel with some of this stuff. Thus, as we recall, Gerda Fischel was entertained with a limping analogy between the kinetic theory of gases and the way in which the various ideas "floating around" in any historic period converge to some "average" [p.490]. Of course, you may think about this, most charitably, as a metaphor. But it is a very bad one. After all, what is an "average idea"? Then there is the "dog" definition and the inability of achieving in life, history, society etc., anything but statistical averages, as explained later to Diotima [p.572]. And finally Agathe is also exposed to such a lecturing. Chapter 47, Book II, is an epitome of the quagmire which is now sucking down the narration. The title, *Wandel unter Menschen,* is of course challenging to the translator who, at first reading, may be inclined to translate it with "Changing among people" or "Wandering among people", which is non-sense because it is about how Ulrich and Agathe avoided people, to quietly and happily exchange their ideas and communicate their sentiments in recondite verbal rituals. And also to offer Ulrich the opportunity to unload yet another torrent of probabilistic non-sense on his beloved sister. This is a pity because the chapter contains lovely impressionistic descriptions of the town in which they were "wandering" in a sort of incognito, as well as fine conversational elements between the two which are worth more than the pseudo-mathematical balderdash. It also states cogently that:

> "whoever thinks cautiously, will simply say that the world has not been created to conform to human concepts. [...] However, as sure as it is that the world has not been created to match human needs, so certain it is that human concepts are created to correspond to the world, this being their purpose." [p.1097]

And to respond to this purpose we learn that

> "the recollection of the computation of averages, as understood by probability calculus, slipped into these ideas [the ones dispensed by Ulrich].[p.1098] [...] Involuntarily Ulrich transferred the concept of probability more and more on matters intellectual and historical. He did the same when he transferred the mechanical concept of [statistical] average [or mean] into the field of the ethical. [p.1099].

We then are told that the realization of each of the ideas floating around is equally probable.

> "But this assumption [i.e. the assumption of the equiprobability of events] is the fundamental concept from which the calculus of probability draws its substance; that it also characterizes the development of the world, permits the inference, that things would not happen any differently were we to leave everything to be decided by chance." [p.1099]

But are ideas indeed cropping up with equiprobability? Don't expect an answer. - It would be interesting to collect all the "probabilistic" fragments in the book and subject them to a critical analysis. Not because they are terribly wise, but because they circulate around. After all the duty of philosophy is to correct our notions or, at least, to keep them constantly under critical scrutiny. Yet this is a different job from the one of literary analysis, pursued in this essay.

Here the question is not so much whether Ulrich talks wisdom or nonsense. A character in a novel has the right to do either. What is interesting here is that we, the readers, can find out that mathematicians have their own ways of being silly and *thereby* reveal things we may not be aware of. It is all right to censor thoughts and their expression in the name of precision by applying the logical rules which connect definitions, postulates and theorems. Yet such rules apply only to that "whereof we may speak". The rest is the province of parable and metaphor. And when the metaphor becomes technically much to elaborate, then we are entitled to enquire about its structure. As a result, the metaphor will be lost while its verbally expressible content could turn out to be fallacious. Ulrich was very likely aware of such and stopped, midway, his perorations:

> "... he did not want to add anything further, abandoning the apparently inspired venture without getting beyond the introduction. - He had the feeling to have touched something of major importance in a clumsy and fussy manner. [p.1099]

Good idea for Ulrich. Tolerable excuse for Musil.

This novel ran into trouble because the author tried to fuse two (at least two) completely different novels into one. Few Musil aficionados (I almost said *fans*) will like me for this statement. Still, the second book was not meant to be dismissed thereby, except that the first one contains an eminent new element; therefore it has a great pioneering merit. Just as one can live life "as if writing an essay", so one can write a novel, or - as I do - read a book. So we find that the true character of a novel-essay as *The Man without Qualities* is not given by the abundance of essayistic elements it incorporates, or just loosely includes. It consist in *essaying*, i.e. trying out, testing, *within a story, and against the background of real-life situations, an individual who represents a completely new type in literature requiring a new language and technique of representation.* Not that scientists have not yet appeared in stories, good and not so brilliant ones. But because Ulrich is a mathematician the situation is essentially different. Being a mathematician does not simply mean to practice a particular scientific profession. It means to have a particular frame of mind. [Some non-mathematicians may acquire it by contagion.] And a mind in such a state is Ulrich's filter through which all kinds of human experiences are sifted. And when the "world" is strained through such a sieve we get an innovative blend of its countless aspects. Therefore we ought to have an idea about the filter's structure and composition to recognize the blend, the suspensions in it and the dreg left behind. And *therefore* the first book of *The Man without Qualities*, a masterpiece of a new type of novel, requires a more careful consideration of the mentioned filter. This is the main reason of my concentration on the first book's expository qualities. Quite apart of the fact that I decline any competence in matters of incestuous love on which the second book concentrates. I felt a lot more comfortable with the adulterous parts of the first book.

(7.3) A New Literary Genre?

We have to face something which looks like a contradiction, and it should be solved. *The Man Without Qualities* is most definitely one of the most readable *books* written by a novelist in our century. But how about it as a *novel*? Its shortcomings are often excused by the fact that the author had no time to finish the huge work. Now, there is no question that this is an unfinished novel. But could it be finished? It started as a good coherent novel, yet an enormous amount of additions piled up in the process of writing it - sketches of types and situations, short story torsos, comments, some very insightful, some others not really so, also an abundance of uncontrolled, often silly, verbal ballast - without a perspective of incorporation into a consistent whole. Still: it is exactly this profusion of additions which offers the most fascinating reading. Some of the best character portrays and situation descriptions anywhere in modern German literature are to be found in the book. So what is the problem? Absolutely none with the work proper! Be aware of its technical shortcomings and read it with pleasure. Turn its pages as if they were the file of drawings of a great master. Since this is what it is. But the problem is rather with the acclaiming reception by the professional literary critics which may impair the reader's way to the work. First we are said that this is a new type of novel. This wouldn't be so bad yet, if the critics would only know that which is essentially new in it is the story of a character which is totally unknown to them. This novel is the one and only major instance in world literature in which a scientific mind is tested in his reactions to a world where unscientific things happen every day. And most importantly: it is *not* about that "two culture" business invented for the benefit of those who are too slothful to inform themselves about more than Vienna literary café gossip.

ESSAY NO.11

"Le temps retrouvé" and the limits of the Word

- or scratching off the price tag from Proust's novel cycle

«*Une oeuvre où il y a des théories est comme un objet sur lequel on a laissé la marque des prix*». ["A literary work which includes theories is like merchandise on which the price label has been forgotten."]

Proust's Ars Poetica

This novel which concludes Proust's great cycle includes also his very peculiar "*Ars poetica*". Part of it is quite obvious: it is formulated in the numerous essayistic *excursi* wadded between episodes purporting to invite their exposition. Yet much of it comes through in the narration itself which is meant to be (so it appears to a reader like me) an exemplary tale about the genesis of a great literary work. "*Le temps retrouvé*" is a book on literary creation, yet not only because of the assortment of barely disguised normative statements or critical stocktaking enveloped by the flow of the narrative. It is rather the *narrative simulation - mimesis - of the preliminaries of actual creation*, from doubt and despair, through instants of illumination, to the moment of determination, *translated into the process of creation*. Though it fulfils in part the role of the great essay-confessions about a poet's work and method, it is a novel, not an essay; the first major novel in which the recounted adventure is that of a writer's story construction. It is the *mimesis* of the *genesis* of the process of literary *mimesis*. Even the discussion of the choice of techniques of representation is largely part of the story; its evolution is recognized by, and recognizable in the account of the poet's experiences. It is not simply and not only the novel of a poet's trials and tribulations; these "will be" narrated in the "previous" six novels - or "have been" narrated in the "following" six novels - of the complete cycle of seven novels. It may not sound very convincing at first, yet it is, as told, Proust's own *ars poetica*; in narrative form. Unlike Horace's, which was epistolary poetry. A rare and fine insight in the process of the emergence of a work of art, quite apart from whether the appended, often cumbersome, theoretical considerations, those "price tags", really resist critical scrutiny in every single instance. It is the tale of a man, poet by will and talent, who wants to re-create *his* (little known to *us*, the readers) world, in words conveying the most intimate part of his experience without falling into the verbose doodle of his symbolist contemporaries and friends. It was *a trial to find the words*, so limited in their own conventional meaning, to translate the most private, and for the poet most valuable, because unique, part of his experience.

Two major claims are made in the novel in frequently alternating explicit statements as well as implicit suggestions. The first is about the irrelevance of the methods of the late 19th century French novel, aiming the edge of the argument against naturalists, the Goncourts being mentioned explicitly. The second is about the creative power of introspective re-living of a past experience, instanced in memory by an accidental occurrence. Whether and how these major claims are justified by the work as it stands today before the reader, should be reviewed in what follows by examining the degree of correspondence between the author's (more exactly: the first person hero's) declared intention and the final result. This is to be done by reading anew important sections of the work along the lines to be subsequently proposed. The proposed reading exercise should be *a reader's case study on the ability of language to translate intimate experience* while still protecting the work's beauty against inappropriate critical intrusions.

Outline of the Proposed Reading Exercise

So it is the last volume of the cycle which instead of concluding the story commences it anew. Re-reading every earlier volume with "*The temps retrouvé*" open at the relevant passage, is the trick to get out most of these aesthetic and moral experiences which Proust professes to convey. It may also show why the novel cycle is incompletely read when read only once. To avoid any misunderstanding: every good book is worth reading more than once, if you so wish. Still, most other good books are "completely read" when once, carefully, read. Instead, "*À la recherche du temps perdu*" is simply not completely read if read only once. And not only because you forget at the end what was at the beginning of the long-long story. The reasons of this claim should follow from the forthcoming discussion. For the mathematically minded, a metaphor is at hand: reading Proust's cycle is like walking along a Moebius band.

The peculiar relationship between the components of the novel cycle should be shortly outlined as follows. We will be acquainted with the experiences of a young man called Marcel, a member of France's high society. The time of the story covers the period from the late 18 hundreds to the First World War. All this time, though spent in idleness, is nevertheless crowded with illuminating experiences but void of any real achievements; thus the *Time* of this young man seems to have been lost. But he is determined to reclaim it, *to find again the time lost* with the multitude of passively received impressions which fill it, and capture it forever *in a story of this very search to recover it*. Yet the poet's determination is challenged by recurring doubts about his ability to repossess, by the employment of plain words, the unique, intimate and therefore most precious part of his experiences. The last, the ninth volume of the cycle, "*Le temps retrouvé*", tells us how the poet succeeds to finally overcome his doubts, and arrives to the point of perfecting the story we have read in the previous volumes. And we may now start to read them again in full knowledge of the ways in which their construction and composition came about. Thus, by empathically repeating the poetic exercise of the storyteller, we may conjure those most intimate experiences which he meant to recover and save, including *the experience of writing it*. When searching for works on poetic mastery we will find countless examples of "how to" or "how they" writings, from Aristotle and Horace to our most proficient professors. But this is the only major case of *a full mimetic reconstitution of the poetic process*.

The time of "*Le temps retrouvé*" is the First World War. From the point of view of the "time recovery" process the elements of its subject can be arranged, in broad outline, in three major groups:

(I) The doubts of the poet concerning his ability to express anything intimate, unique, "true", beyond superficial experiences. The reading of the "Goncourt diary" feeds these doubts.

(II) The struggle to defeat the doubts, which means to settle accounts with their indirect originator, namely the Goncourt-approach to literature, by picturing the salon of Mme. Verdurin according to the methods of the naturalists (the "Goncourt pastiche"). It aims at demonstrating the inability of the naturalist method to transmit more than the surface impressions of the world.

(III) Overcoming the doubts; this represents 2/3 of the last novel in the cycle. The poet returns to Paris from his second country retreat (the first one was occupied by the Germans in 1915), and is lead by simple accident to discover the ways of transcending some(!) of the limits of naturalistic representation, while at the same time offering us a masterly last-hour picture of the social environment in which he grew older and then start writing. [The forthcoming discussion will also implicitly justify the rejection of the title of a widely read English translation: "Remembering Times Past". It is not about remembering; it is rather concerned with recovering - this is what the *recherche* is all about - and transforming the recovered past into a work of art, thus capturing that particular past forever.]

A Poet's Doubts

The reading of the "unpublished Goncourt diary" confirms earlier doubts:

«*Et quand avant d'éteindre ma bougie je lus le passage que je transcris plus bas, mon absence de dispositions pour les lettres, pressentie jadis du côté de Guermantes ... me parut de quelque chose de moins regrettable, comme si la littérature ne révélait pas de vérité profonde; et en même temps il me semblait triste que la littérature ne fût pas ce que j'avais cru.»* [p.72] ["And when, before putting out the candle, I read the passage which I transcribe in what follows, my lack of literary disposition, of which I had a presentiment long ago by the side of the Guermantes ... seemed to me less regrettable. It was as if literature were not revealing profound truths; and at the same time I felt it to be sad that literature was not what I thought it to be".]

The section following the above quoted lines is about the contradiction between the beauty of beautiful things, and their description, particularly in contemporary French literature, mainly of the naturalist variety, and, last not least, in the purported Goncourt diary read by a sick, bedridden, Marcel.

Still it was not over: "I closed the diary of the Goncourts" and also

«Je résolus de laisser provisoirement de côté les objections qu'avaient pu faire naître en moi contre la littérature les pages de Goncourt lues la veille de mon départ de Tansonville.» [p.83] ["decided to put aside, temporarily, the objections against literature which were suggested to me by the pages of Goncourt read on the eve of my departure [for a medical checkup in Paris] from Tansonville."]

So the abdication was not final. Maybe literature was still "what I thought it to be". If anything, the Goncourt reading prompted a methodic self-examination. It was about ascertaining those safe, stable elements in the "self" of the poet which can survive the doubts planted in his mind by the disappointing, shallow text of the naturalist gurus. Marcel thus set out to examine his "inability to see and hear, which the quoted diary has so painfully revealed" (p.83). The "inability" seems not to have been complete; the first-phase results of the test were not really discouraging.

For seeing:

*«Il y avait en moi un personnage qui savait, plus ou moins bien, **regarder**, mais c'était un personnage intermittent, ne reprenant vie que quand se manifestait quelque essence générale, commune à plusieurs choses, qui faisait sa nourriture et sa joie.»* [p.83] ["There was inside me a character who knew more or less how to **look** at things; yet this character had no continuous existence and revived intermittently only when some substance shared by many things revealed itself, and which was its sustenance and bliss. «]

For hearing:

*«Alors le personnage regardait et **écoutait** mais à une certaine profondeur seulement, de sorte que l'observation n'en profitait pas. Comme un géomètre qui dépouillant les choses de leurs qualités sensibles ne voit que leur substratum linéaire, ce que racontaient les gens m'échappait, car ce qui m'intéressait, c'était non ce qu'ils voulaient dire mais la manière dont ils le disaient, en tant qu'elle était révélatrice de leur caractère ou de leurs ridicules».*(p.83) ["Then this character looked and **listened** but only to a certain depth so that the observation was of no consequence. Like a geometrician who baring things of their perceivable qualities sees only their underlying linear structure, whatever people said escaped my attention because I was not interested in what they wanted to say but the manner in which they said it, as far as this revealed their character or ridicule."]

[A propos: this is probably also what an investigation like the one you just read is all about. The interest is not so much in *ce qu'il voulait dire mais la manière dont il le disait.*]

All in all:

«le charme apparent, copiable, des êtres m'échappait.» ["the obvious, reproducible charm of [all] beings escaped my attention."]

It reads like the logico-philosophical analysis or description of the concept-creating process, though, so far, without any clear distinction of a philosophical stand. First it would satisfy everybody: the average nominalist as well as the realist. The first, even if he were of the neo-positivist persuasion, would agree that "knowing" and "seeing" is the start of picking out the "general essence common to a variety of things". While the philosophical realist, who claims objective existence (i.e. reality) only for the hidden essence spread in countless deceptive manifestations of the sensed world, could also be made happy. However, if the philosophical stand is not yet clear - (such clarity we are to expect from philosophy professors, who often deceive us, but not novel heroes) - the delimitations in respect to the Goncourts are quite obvious: "I" [Marcel] am able to discover common traits, essentials behind observable things, unlike "You" [naturalists] to whom the world to be described is that of the immediately perceivable. This is why literature, as practiced by "You", not being able to break through the limits of the perceivable, is so disappointing to "Me". But is that all what it is to it? Indeed if "*le charme apparant, copiable des êtres m'échappait*" (p.83), does it really mean that there is nothing to my way of seeing or listening? From these doubts new certainties will emerge, slowly, and first only in theory:

> «*J'avais beau dîner en ville, je ne voyais pas les convives, parce que quand je croyais les regarder, je les radiographiais.*» (p.84). ["Even when I happened to dine in town, I never really saw my fellow diners because, while I believed to observe them, I radiographed them."]

But is there no merit to radiography?

> «*Il en résultait qu'en réunissant toutes les remarques que j'avais pu faire dans un dîner sur les convives, le dessin des lignes tracées par moi figurait un ensemble de lois psychologiques où l'intérêt propre qu'avait eu dans ses discours le convive ne tenait presque aucune place. Mais cela enlevait-il tout mérite à mes portraits puisque je ne les donnais pas pour tels?*». (p.84) ["And when I finally made a summary of all that I was able to record during a dinner party about my table mates, the resulting draft turned out to be but a set of psychological laws which were almost totally disregarding the interest which my table companion had in the conversation proper. But did all this deprive my portraits of any merit just because I didn't offer them as such?"]

It may not be without merit. But is there in such an approach no risk of some sociological or psychological generalization which would justify an essay or a study but deprive literature, art, of its essential *raison d'être*? The next passage is meant to assure us of the contrary:

> «*Si l'un dans le domaine de la peinture met en évidence certaines vérités relatives au volume, à la lumière, au mouvement, cela fait-il qu'il soit nécessairement inférieur à tel portrait ne lui ressemblant aucunement de la même personne, dans lequel mille détails qui sont omis dans le premier seront minutieusement relatés, deuxième portrait d'où l'on pourra conclure que le modèle était ravissant tandis qu'on l'eût cru laid dans le premier, ce qui peut avoir une importance documentaire et même historique, mais n'est pas nécessairement une vérité d'art.*» (p.84) ["Is a painted portrait which reveals certain truths about volume, light or movement, necessarily inferior to another very different portrait of the same person which painstakingly reproduces those thousand details omitted in the first? Viewing the second portrait we may conclude that the model was enchanting, while from the first one we may have thought it to be ugly. But all this could have only documentary or even historic significance without being, necessarily, a truth of art."]

It may very well be that it is the first kind of portraying which best reveals the "essence" picked out from the "object" by the artist-"subject"; but if it is so then this is hardly the method of the earlier mentioned geometrician peeling off the accidental disorder from things thus reducing them to plain, abstract, logically tractable forms. The geometrician's truths are equally accessible to everybody; also to the slave of Menon whom Socrates leads into "discovering" something which resembles to what we call the theorem of Pythagoras. But the "first" portrait painter discovers something we can get into only by empathy and not logical reasoning, since it is not really a generalization of a "*vérité d'art*", but just another revelation of sensorially accessible particulars. The "essence" of a person is the "essence" of *that* person, nothing general, either as Platonic reality or in any other sense, as geometry would be. This essence is that which is most particular of that person. If, of course, it is anything more than just blabla. So what do we do with such disquisitions in a novel? For once, do not take them seriously as considerations of the author himself. Read them as the hero's thoughts. Novel characters are entitled to any balderdash. In this case it testifies about the motifs of an angry writer disappointed with the inherited methods of the trade, but a bit confused when it comes to be specific. Never forget: this novel (and novel cycle) *imitates* the motifs and the process by which literary *imitation* comes about. And the quality of the final imitation stands on its own; also because it reproduces plausibly the connection between *nonsensical motifs and meaningful results.*

The confused doubts engender vengeance against those who caused them. The purported Goncourt pages contain a description of a reception at the Verdurins. And these pages are supposed to testify about the shallowness of such literature. Here are a few examples of the "naturalistic" descriptive art.

Madame Verdurin places her literary guest at the table:

«*La maîtresse de la maison qui va me placer à côté d'elle me dit aimablement avoir fleuri sa table rien qu'avec des chrysanthèmes japonais mais des chrysanthèmes disposés en des vases qui seraient de rarissime chefs-d'oeuvres, l'un entre autres, fait d'un bronze sur lequel des pétales en cuivre rougeâtre sembleraient être la vivante effeuillaison de la fleur.*» (p.74) ["The lady of the house, while placing me next to her, explained to me congenially that she made her dinner table blossom only with Japanese chrysanthemums, and this by placing them in vases which were most rare masterpieces. One of these, a bronze vessel, was covered with reddish copper petals seeming to have been dropped by the living flowers."]

A sample of the dishes at the table:

«*... des assiettes des Yung-Tsching à la couleur capucine de leurs rebords, au bleuâtre, à l'effeuillé turgide de leur iris d'eau, à la traversée, vraiment décoratoire, par l'aurore d'un vol de martins-pêcheurs et de grues, aurore ayant tout à fait ces tons matutinaux qu'entre-regard quotidiennement, boulevard Montmorency, mon réveil, - des assiettes de Saxe plus mièvres dans le gracieux de leur faire, à l'endormement, à l'anémie de leurs roses tournées au violet, au déchiquetage lie-de-vin d'une tulipe, au rococo d'un oeillet ou d'un myosotis, ...*» (p.75) ["...

plates of the Young-Cheng dynasty era, capuchin-brown colored on the border, slipping into blueish, with bulging petals of water lilies, and the truly ornamental flight of kingfishers and cranes crossing the morning sky of the same hue of dawn which is caught every morning by my awaking eyes on the *boulevard Montmorency* - plates of Saxony ever so graciously crafted, with sleepy, anemic roses turned purple, tulips with wine-dreg colored indentures, rococo forget-me-nots ..."]

and so on and on with "*assiettes de Sèvres*" and the silverware on which the taste of Madame Dubarry was perfectly recognizable, all dignified in addition by the profusely described fine food served in them. It would be difficult to say whether we have to praise the Goncourts or naturalists in general, for the method they developed and which Proust employs so much better than most of them or, rather, to praise Proust himself for what he might have meant to be a caricature, and which turned out to be a masterly composition. Because it is a remarkable *technical achievement* which may be comparable only to the best of Flaubert. Indeed, never forget to read *À la rechèrche* without recalling the experience of *L'éducation sentimentale*. In the case of the above quoted example a parallel to a dinner party *chez les Arnoux* will prove once again that the description of simple material facts must not deprive the reader - if the author happens to be Flaubert or Proust - of the intimate of the circumstances for which the sensed details provide the background. Frederic Moreau, whose *sentimental education* course we track, liked the environment these simple objects created:

«*La salle, qu'un parloir moyen âge, était tendue de cuir battu; une étagère hollandaise se dressait devant un râtelier de chibouques; et, autour de la table, les verres de Bohême, diversement colorés faisant au milieu des fleurs et des fruits comme une illumination dans une jardin.*
«*Il eut à choisir entre dix espèces de moutard. Il mangea du daspachio, du cari, du gingembre, des merles de Corse, des lasagnes romaines; etc. etc.*» [p.80-81] ["The walls of the room were covered with *cuir battu* like a middle age hall; a Dutch shelf stood in front of a rack of Turkish pipes; and, around the table, Bohemian crystal glasses of various colours, placed among fruit plates and flower pots, created the illusion of an illuminated garden."

"He had to choose between ten kinds of mustard. He ate gazpacho, curry, ginger, Corsican blackbirds, Roman lasagna; etc. etc."]

And one knows, feels, that the taste of all these delicacies, such as e.g. the *daspachio*, was much better than their spelling. Also their description appears to be just *le charme apparent, copiable, des êtres*, but the context gives a character description, as in the case of madame Verdurin. Here it is the occasion to reveal yet another, in itself minimal trait of character of Flaubert's Arnoux, the host. The description of objects is the *cadre* for a characterization:

«*Arnoux se piquait effectivement de bien recevoir. Il courtisait en vue des comestibles les conducteurs de malle-poste, et il était lié avec des cuisiniers de grands maisons qui lui communiquait des sauces.*» [p.81] ["Arnoux made a point of well entertaining. He courted post-coach drivers to find out about various comestibles and befriended the cooks of distinguished households who gave him their sauce recipes."]

It took a lot more details to characterize the Verdurins. Blame it on the Goncourts.

Recovering from Doubts

During his trip to Paris, Marcel, sitting in his compartment, remembers sadly:

"*la pensée de mon absence de dons littéraires, que j'avais cru découvrir jadis du côté de Guermantes ... cette pensée qui ne m'était pas depuis bien longtemps revenue à l'esprit, me frappa de nouveau et avec une force plus lamentable que jamais.*» [p.242] ["the idea of my lack of gift for literature which I thought to have discovered long ago by the side of the Guermantes ... This belief, which did not come back to my mind for a long time, hit me once again and more grievously than ever."]

It was on this trip when the crowd of impressions thronging through the coach window and asking to be recorded, interpreted and returned in literary expression, that Marcel was forced to consider once again his tormenting obsession. The description of their slipping into his mind is itself an introductory exercise in Marcel's literary recovery, a trial to break through the limits of naturalistic expression. But the recounting of the parade of impressions does not yet succeed without being overshadowed by melancholy observations about his lack of literary talent. Marcel shall be relieved of this pessimistic mood much later when he will discover, following a chain of accidental events, that he is indeed equipped with the means by which to regain that lost time. Yet it is clear by now, in spite of his transitional gloom, that the problem is not really the lack of talent but the inability, or not yet discovered ability, to push the mastery of the Word beyond that which can be achieved by simple, well controlled naturalistic techniques. Pursuing his progress in "*Le temps retrouvé*" we can also realize how far he went, how far one may generally go along that particular track, and what it means to transcend naturalistic "imitation". We shall start with a sample of travel impressions where descriptive precision is still the relevant technique, though not satisfying Marcel. The first:

«*C'était, je me rappelle, à un arrêt du train en plain campagne. Le soleil éclairait jusqu'à la moitié de leur tronc une ligne d'arbres qui suivait la voie du chemin de fer. 'Arbres, pensai-je, vous n'avez plus rien à me dire, mon coeur refroidi ne vous entend plus. Je suis pourtant ici en plain nature, eh bien, c'est avec froideur, avec ennui que mes yeux constatent la ligne qui sépare votre front lumineux de votre tronc d'ombre. Si j'ai jamais pu me croire poète, je sais maintenant que je ne le suis pas'.*» (p.242-243) ["This happened, as I recall, during a train-stop in open country. The sun cast its light down to the middle of the trunk of trees lined up along the rail track. 'Trees, I mused, you have nothing to tell me anymore, since my cold heart no longer understands you. I am here in the midst of nature, yet my eyes assess only with coldness and boredom the line which divides your luminous forehead from your shady trunk. If I ever thought of myself as a poet, now I know that I am not one."]

Was this really so? If we pick out the melancholy remarks we could get a fine description of those trees, with no word changed, only the phrase rearranged. We could then write:

«*Le soléil, éclairant jusqu'à la moitié une ligne d'arbres qui suivait la voie du chemin de fer, séparait leur front lumineux de leur tronc d'ombre*».

But then these observations would be diluted in the brine of sorrowful resignation. And so it continued throughout the journey:

«*Un peu plus tard j'avais vu avec la même indifférence les lentilles d'or et d'orange dont il [le Soleil] criblait les fenêtres d'une maison; et enfin comme l'heure avait avancé, j'avais vu une autre maison qui semblait construite en une substance d'un rose assez étrange.*» [p.243])
["A little later, I have looked with the same indifference upon the patches of gold and orange which [the sun] painted upon the windows of a house; and finally, as the hours went by, I noticed another house which seemed to have been built of a rather strange pinkish material."]

Assessments made with cool indifference. So we are assured. But do *we* read them with cool indifference? It is something we cannot state *a priori*. And the mood or state of mind of the poet is also indifferent to us, because between his emotional condition and our reception of its emanation are only the words he devises. Yet the apparently dull impression of the sun-lit trees along the railroad, or of the frolicking colors on the windows of "passing" houses, returned in a cool description, may end up as a joyous picture of a summer afternoon. The whole is as if Monet would have painted an ugly monster in the middle of his "*Impressions*".

The problem of Marcel was, so it seems, not the lack of talent but the limits of what is objectively possible by means of verbal expression. We can quite clearly realize this by reading the following passages, again filled with impressionist light:

«*Si j'avais vraiment une âme d'artiste quel plaisir n'éprouverai-je pas devant ... ces petites fleurs de talus qui se haussent presque jusqu'au marchepied du wagon, dont je pourrais compter les pétales*». [p.243]
["If I really had the soul of an artist, what a pleasure would I experience seeing ... these little flowers on the bank stretching themselves

almost to the height of the railcar steps, so that I could count their petals."]

But he claims not to have *"une âme d'artiste"*, wherefore:

«*je me garderais bien de décrire la couleur [de ces petites fleurs] comme feraient tant bons lettrés car peut-on espérer transmettre au lecteur un plaisir qu'on n'a pas ressenti*» [p.243]
["I would refrain from doing what many a fine man of letters would have done, namely to describe the color [of these little flowers], for can one hope to convey to the reader a joy one does not feel?"]

It is like a tiny monster of Hyeronimus Bosch slipping into a beautiful flower covered landscape of Whistler, Proust's beloved Whistler. The monster is the doubt about the ability to communicate a unique experiences: how can it happen by means of words?

In a way it already happened. It is perfect. Except that, so far, it is not what the poet can do beyond the art of the painter. And it is the limits of the painter the poet has to break through. So far it didn't happen.

We may see the difference by comparing with how Flaubert was handling the views and impressions of a traveler from a moving craft. It is in the *"Éducation sentimentale"* where Frédéric Moreau, brand new *baccalaureus*, aboard the *Ville de Montereau* on the river Seine, contemplates the view unfolding as the boat leaves the *quai Saint Bernard* of Paris. The recording is precise in descriptive detail, not yielding to the whimsical impression. We first notice

«*les deux berges, peuplées de magasins, de chantiers et d'usines, filèrent comme deux larges rubans que l'on déroule.*» [p.37] ["the two embankments, along which warehouses, building sites and factories lined up as two large unwinding tapes."]

This recording neither excludes nor diminishes here the value of the metaphor but the mental picture we get is common to most of us, easy to be intuited. No difficulty is or should be encountered when details of the picture, such as those unfolding *rubans* met by the traveler's eyes, are to be communicated:

«*A travers le brouillard, il contemplait des clochers, des édifices dont il ne savait pas les noms; puis il embrassa, dans un dernier coup d'oeil, l'île Saint Louis, la Cité, Notre-Dame, et bientôt, Paris disparaissant, il poussa un grand soupir.*» (p.37) ["Through the fog he surveyed bell towers and buildings he couldn't name; then he embraced with one last glimpse the isle of Saint Louis, the Cité, the Notre-Dame and finally, while Paris vanished from his sight, he released a deep sigh."]

We have here once more a factual enumeration with just a simple, casual, mention of a subjective state, the sigh, of which we have not to be told explicitly how melancholic it was, since the suggestion of a farewell by the metaphor of the unfolding ribbons helped us get into the desired mood. The rigorous material description does *not* lock out the intimate. The trick of such description, the simple order in which the items seen are catalogued, will enlist the empathy also of those readers who haven't yet released a big nostalgic sigh when seeing, from train or plane, "*Paris disparaissant*".

These were the pictures covered by the eyes of a sad young traveler who, being very poor, couldn't afford to stay in Paris. But he was a contemporary of the birth of a new (physical) view of the world which at some stage of its development was to be called impressionism. The moving picture of the river offered from the boat was also compatible with this emerging view:

«*La rivière était bordée par des grèves de sable. On rencontrait des trains de bois qui se mettaient à onduler sous les remous des vagues, ou bien, dans un bateau sans voiles, un homme assis pêchait; puis les brumes errantes se fondirent, le soleil parut, la colline qui suivait à droite le cours de la Seine peu à peu s'abaissa, et il en surgit une autre, plus proche, sur la rive opposée.*» (p.38) ["The river was flanked by sand banks. One could see floats of wood undulating while stirred by the waves, or again, a man, sitting in boat without sails, fishing; then the erring fog patches dissipated, the sun appeared, the hills which followed on the right side the Seine's course diminished slowly-slowly, while another hill, a much closer one, surfaced on the opposite shore."]

The other traveler, Marcel, heading for Paris, cast his very similarly cultivated gaze upon his physical surroundings. What made him suffer was his inability to pull together all these "cool" assessments of his eyes, which learned all the lessons taught from Corot to Whistler (and, why to deny it? - all the lessons advanced by the naturalists), into a system pivoting a story or the description of a character. The moving-landscape description of Flaubert supplied the frame for Fréderic Moreau's moral growing-up. The descriptive fragments clustering in Marcel's mind would not, yet, make for as much.

> «*Peut-être dans la nouvelle partie de ma vie, si desséchée qui s'ouvre, les hommes pourraient-ils m'inspirer ce que ne me dit plus la nature. Mais les années ou j'aurais peut-être été capable de la chanter ne reviendront jamais.*» [p. 243] ["Perhaps in that new, however dull phase of my life which begins now, people might be able to enkindle in me what nature doesn't offer me anymore. But the years when I might have been able to sing the charms of nature will never return."]

These years did never return, indeed. However, their memory has been captured and returned in the novel cycle, though not by abandoning the description techniques of those so bitterly criticized craftsmen of the 19th century French novel; not by breaking the mirror "imitating" physically perceivable things. The enormous efforts of Proust to transcend their method, ended up in its perfect employment rather than its defeat and abandonment. It was by the integral sum of the art as naturally developed from Balzac through Stendhal (highly esteemed by Proust as the master of the "*roman d'idée*) to Flaubert - mainly! - that he found and brought back that "*temps perdu*". The time-honored methods were not abandoned, however, interesting technical additions are to be reported. Yet not before trying to scratch off the somewhat oversize "price tag" stuck to the precious merchandise - after having studied it for the method's sake!

The Accident of Discovery

Marcel returns to Paris to start a "new life" while trying to convince himself that he is cool, composed, indifferent to art and literature. The only trouble is that experiences once nestled as memories in the human mind, will continue their nagging existence. Marcel remembers. He recalls being "annoyed" the day before when, traveling through countrysides *"réputées les plus belles en France"*, he thought to be unable to give a description, worthy of a poet, of the line separating light and shadow on trees. Nevertheless, the irritating episode did not prevent him to continue delving in his memory in search of something which might prove worthy of yet another literary trial. Venice comes to his mind, but the colorful memory flashes are dismissed - with annoyance - because his mood associated them with the idea of picture postcards, the paragons of standardized, i.e. not *poetic*, souvenirs. Now that he felt again like abandoning the hope of ever becoming a poet or author, life seemed to offer him new joys, the delights of relaxed acceptance of everyday pleasures, the bliss of one who doesn't expect anything and thus can have only pleasant surprises. It was in this mood that he went, after arriving to Paris, to the morning reception of Mme de Guermantes. Entering the courtyard of the Hôtel de Guermantes, scared by an incoming carriage, and jumping aside

> «*je reculai assez pour buter malgré moi contre les pavés assez mal équarris derrière lesquels était une remise. Mais au moment où me remettant d'aplomb, je posai mon pied sur un pavé qui était un peu moins élevé que le précédent, tout mon découragement s'évanouit devant la même félicité qu'à diverses époques de ma vie m'avaient donnée la vue d'arbres que j'avais cru reconnaître dans une promenade en voiture autour de Balbec, la vue des clochers de Martinville, la saveur d'une madeleine trempée dans une infusion ...*» (p.256) "I jumped backwards so that, unawares, I stumbled against the curb in front of the coachhouse. But when instantly regaining my balance and stepping on a slightly lower laying pavement, all my discouragement dissipated being overcome by the same blissful emotion which I experienced at other occasions when I believed to have recognized some trees during a coach drive around Balbec, or the belfries of Martinville, or the taste of a madeleine dipped in tea."]

This turned out to be a decisive accident and therefore calling for closer scrutiny. We are told about an occurrence, similar to others in the past, which prompted an untold sensation of rapture. Three phases of the process are to be distinguished here. *First*, there is an accidental occurrence which brings up the memory of past happiness. *Second,* the pleasant memory takes hold of the writer's mood, lifting him above the current state of philosophical resignation. So we are told. We have to believe it because, unless we had ourselves similar experiences or revelations, we have nothing but the word of him who tells the story. So far there is nothing in this story which could enlist our empathy. We have to wait awhile for that. The sentiment of felicity-brought- back was the same as in the celebrated instance of the *madeleine* cookie or, more importantly, experienced

«*sur deux dalles inégales du baptistère de Saint Marc.*» (p.257) ["on two unequal slabs of stone facing St. Marc's baptistery."]

in Venice, the difference being only the efficient cause which brought it about and images associated with it in memory. But we have now a *third* phase in this process of recognition: Marcel arrives to the decision that he must find out how and why these states of mind are generated. In other words, we are back to square one: how to find the personal and intimate in something which may be described in words only in its material, commonly perceivable manifestations, and then how to translate it, nevertheless, in words for the reader's benefit?

But can we ever know the cause of such recognition? What we know with certainty is how the fact itself ended up in the novel, namely in the manner of the good old 19th century French novel which did not require a cumbersome "price tag". The plus in descriptive art may have been learned outside literature. The poetic competition, sometimes with Turner, sometimes with Monet, then again with Whistler, is successfully pursued, and "will" come up in the beautiful description of Venice in "*La fugitive*", which we have read "earlier". Here is just a sample:

«*... tandis que la gondole pour nous ramener remontait le Grand Canal, nous regardions la file des palais entre lesquels nous passions refléter la lumière et l'heure sur leurs flancs rosés, et changer avec elles, moins à la façon d'habitations privées et de monuments célèbres que comme une chaîne de falaises de marbre au pied de laquelle on va le soir se promener en barque dans un chenal pour voir le soleil se coucher ... Mais en même temps ... comme nous eussions fait à Paris sur les boulevards,* *dans les Champs-Élysées, au Bois, dans toute large avenue à la mode, nous croisions dans la lumière poudroyante du soir les femmes les plus élégantes, presque toutes étrangères, qui, mollement appuyées sur les coussins de leur équipage flottant, prenaient la file, s'arrêtaient devant un palais où elles avaient une amie à aller voir ...»* [La Fugitive, p.286-287] ["While returning in the gondola along the Canal Grande, we contemplated the line of palaces between which we passed as the glare of their pink flanks changed with the light and the hour, appearing not so much as private habitations or famous monuments, but rather as a row of marble cliffs on the foot of which, at evening, one promenades in a boat to see the sunset ... But at the same time ... just as it might have happened on the Paris boulevards, on the Champs-Élysées, in the Bois (de Boulogne), or along any of the large fashionable avenues, we passed in the powdery light of dusk, the most elegant women, almost all foreigners, softly leaning against the cushions of their floating coaches, lining-up when stopping at some palace where they went to visit a friend ..."]

This may be, so we may guess, the section which Giorgio Bassani (in "*Parole Preparate*") mentions as "*la perfetta pagina di Proust sul Canal Grande, bella, fresca e leggera come un Monet*". But the praise is followed with a dismissal: "it isn't worth reading it". Why? This is not clearly stated in the nebulous argument. But for us, to be sure, it is perfect, beautiful and fresh, as well as *leggera*, and it is worthy to be read and occasionally reread as there is no reason to avoid a beautiful canvas of Monet. Or Turner, or Whistler. There is only one trouble with it: it does not, as it is claimed, break with the naturalist method *in principle*; it is only better - *una perfetta pagina* - than most of them could have produced. And it is comparable with only the other impressions flashing through the novel, which were recorded by eyes, no doubt, schooled on the images discovered by the painters of the age, such as in the *Le Coté des Guermantes I*:

«... plus tard, à Venise, bien après le coucher du soleil, quand il semble qu'il fasse tout à fait nuit, j'ai vu, grâce à l'écho invisible pourtant d'une dernière note de lumière indéfiniment tenue sur les canaux comme par l'effet de quelque pédale optique, les reflets des palais déroulés comme

à tout jamais en velours plus noir sur le gris crépuscule des eaux.» (Guermantes I. p.222) ["Later in Venice, well after sunset, when it seemed to be late night already, I saw, thanks to a barely discernable reverberation of light vaguely descending upon the canals, as if produced by some optical device, the velvety black reflection of the palaces spread-out as if forever upon the grey of the twilight."]

We may now ask ourselves: is it really so that the

«bronze sur lequel des pétales en cuivre rougeâtre sembleraient être la vivante effeuillaison de la fleur»

at Mme. Verdurin's table, meant to be some caricature of *"Goncourism"*, is a conveyer of impressions of a lesser rank than that "azur profond" of which Marcel records that

«enivrait mes yeux, des impression de fraîcheur, d'éblouissante lumière tournoyaient près de moi»?

Hardly. The gap separating the sensorial and *the reader's* emotion couldn't be bridged over by spangling the story and description with, however cleverly formulated, theoretical instructions about how "really" we ought to feel. We know, of course, as Proust so beautifully says, that

«le geste le plus insignifiant que nous avons fait ... portait sur lui le reflet de choses qui logiquement ne tenaient pas à lui». ["any, however insignificant gesture we have made ... carries upon it the reflection of things with which it is in no logical connection."]

But then how do you mirror back those reflections? There may be many ways, yet Proust, *the poet Proust*, has chosen the naturalistic-to-impressionistic arrangements by the methods perfected in the days of Flaubert (and fed on experiences with Monet, Whistler etc.) with "suggestive" verbiage added, of the kind which would dignify the best of symbolists. And so did *Proust the novelist*.

Readers, such as the one writing these notes, have also their locked receptacles of past (reading!) experiences which may be abruptly clacked open by some sympathetic contact. Thus, whenever reading in the critical literature some comparison between Proust and Flaubert, another association, namely between Tolstoy and Flaubert made by Matthew Arnold, comes to mind. He writes about Flaubert, apropos Madame Bovary, that:

> "He is cruel, with the cruelty of petrified feeling, to his poor heroine; he pursues her without pity or pause, as with malignity; he is harder upon her himself than any reader even, I think, will be inclined to be."

- while Tolstoy reveals compassion and understanding for (and in) his heroes/heroines. In the case of Proust, instead, "cruelty" is mitigated by para-philosophical tidbits and disquisitions. Not always very happy ones. But then, is this all that different from what he deemed to be "vulgarity" in Balzac? The prolific "price tag", may indeed attenuate "cruelness", but does not really testify against the achievements of the 19-th century novel.

Theoretical Excursus

The set of above displayed quotations may still require a short theoretical stocktaking if this essay is to transcend - as it intends to - the plain status of a reader's record. The purpose here is to point out what a friendly reader should not miss in order to be able to fully enjoy Proust. (This, of course, is once again, just a communication from another reader.)

What is that which makes *description* in Proust different from the naturalists? The simple affixing of appealing words on the thing to be described wouldn't do the trick. The fact is that Proust's descriptions, say of "nature", are not plain poetic imitation. It is rather imitation of an already existing imitation on which the writer's eyes are schooled, and the reader's are assumed to have done the same. Whenever Marcel beholds something, he is not simply and only recording and reporting it with the stage-directing techniques of naturalists, but he associates the registered external thing(s) with what he learned from several painters. Every image observed is viewed through the lens of a painter who has reproduced something alike. So whenever a reader happens to make a similar association, being aware of the existence of such in the work, he will receive more than from a simple description. Take an example, other then the above, and others more often quoted ones:

> *"Le jour gris tombant comme une pluie fine, tissait sans arrêt de trans-*
> *parents filets dans lesquels les promeneurs dominicaux semblaient s'ar-*
> *genter"* (Guermantes, II, p.91) ["The murky day, descending as a
> fine drizzle, continuously created transparent nets in which the
> Sunday strollers seemed to reflect a silvery glare."]

What do you *think* when you are said about those leisurely *promeneurs dominicaux* that they *semblaient s'argenter* [or "reflect a silvery glare"]? Any number of things, including nothing. The latter case is possible but you will certainly be losing a lot. Yet there is no rule of translation. However, there are possible association. Thus, when you have seen in the Louvre that *Souvenirs de Mortefontaine* or that other Corot landscape in the Frick Museum on the Fifth Avenue, New York, then you may get an inkling of how people or things may *s'argenter* without precise verbal instruction. This is a bit different from when the poet composes his own images to appeal to your own plain optical experience:

> «*Les rideaux de tulle de la fenêtre, vaporeux et friables ... avaient ce*
> *même mélange de douceur et de cassant qu'ont les ailes de libellules et*
> *les verres de Venise*» (ibid.) ["The tulle curtains on the windows,
> vaporous and friable ... displayed the same mixture of sweetness
> and fragility as the wings of dragon flies and Venetian glass."]

In all cases quoted, a complete comprehension of the written text requires the reader to have *seen* something before *reading* the clear text. This claim is a variation of the thesis following from Philostrat's "Travels of Apollonius of Tyana" and which is useful to quote, once again, in this context. We recall the traveler's discussion with Damis, his disciple, in which a distinction is made between imitating with the skill of the artist and that of the mind alone, even when the imitator is not endowed with "delineative faculty". We learn that

> "... those who look at works of painting and drawing require a mi-
> metic faculty; for no one could appreciate or admire a picture of

a horse or of a bull, unless he had formed an idea of the creature represented." [This is discussed in more detail in 'Introduction I' to these essays.]

By extension of this line of reasoning we may say that if you read about anything described, you need to have prior knowledge of what that thing is; if you read that the *promeneurs ... semblaient s'argenter*, you need to have had yourself once the impression of some things "silvering themselves". And Corot may have offered you samples.

The value of an imitation is thus to be judged according to the ability of the viewer to do "the same" as the artist, but only in thought. And this opportunity may be granted to the reader also by those whom we call naturalists, but in a limited fashion. This should be clarified in only a few words.

We may distinguish between two kinds of metaphors, typical for two very different approaches to literature. The first kind can be accessed by any and every reader. The metaphors here meant are easy to comprehend by anybody because the two objects meant to be paragons of one another are known to all. Thus when a poet, any poet, claims that the lips of his beloved lady are like rosebuds burst into flower, then this will be understood by anybody who has ever seen roses and lips. It will also be easy to associate the blueness of her eyes with the skies of France. But naturalists wouldn't very often succeed, even when using metaphors of this "first kind", to raise in the reader such sympathetic emotions as when Proust described his Marcel's much admired Duchess:

> "*ses yeux, où était captif comme dans un tableau le ciel bleu d'une après-midi de France, largement découvert, baigné de lumière même quand elle ne brillait pas*" (Guermants, I, p.290) ["her eyes which captured, as if in a painting the blue of an open, fair, afternoon sky in France saturated with light even when not radiating."]

For the second class of metaphors, however, it will not be sufficient for the reader to be familiar with the world he experienced. He will have to have *experienced the mediated experience* of somebody else, such as a painter, as in the earlier quoted examples. This is a major specialty of Proust and makes part of his work's enjoyment a function of other, contemporary, artistic achievements. - And after Marcel's rapturous illumination, this type of descriptions sifted through the nine volume narration.

(An humble advice to the reader: Read again the boat scene in Flaubert's *"Éducation sentimentale"* and keep it in mind when comparing it to the sailing experience on the *Canal Grande*. And then try to find in a museum or in books with reproductions of the mentioned painters, to have an additional illustration of the argument here advanced.)

Doubts Defeated

Thus an accident in the courtyard of the Hôtel de Guermantes engendered new confidence. It lent the poet determination, leading to the firm decision that every experience to be made henceforth will be looked upon as raw material to be shaped into a work of literary art by the awakened creative will. Encounters and conversations in the Past, accumulated and sedimented in a so far passive memory, will be treated as an archeological site to be excavated for its literary potential, as a source of the Time-to-be. An example of such a treasure is the gallery of personages who "will" be written about (and whom we already know) in the nine volumes of the recovered time's prehistory. Each of these personages, or the ones they remind us, appears in this last volume, that receptacle of past history as experienced by Marcel, who will reconsider it presently, and write about them what we already have read...

> «*Plus d'une des personnes que cette matinée réunissait ou dont elle m'évoquait le souvenir par les aspects qu'elle avait tour à tour présentés pour moi, par les circonstances différentes, opposées, d'où elle avait, les unes après les autres, surgi devant moi, faisait ressortir les aspects variés de ma vie, les différences de perspective, comme un accident de terrain, colline ou château, qui apparaît tantôt à droit, tantôt à gauche, semble d'abord dominer une forêt, ensuite sortir d'une vallée, et révèle ainsi au voyageur des changements d'orientation et des différences d'altitude dans la route qu'il suit.*» (p.375) "More than one of the people present this morning at the party, or people whose memory this reunion just evoked, according to the various aspects by which they revealed themselves one after another when appearing in front of me in different, or even opposite circumstances, made reappear the

various aspects of my life and its differences of perspective. It was as if various features of a landscape, a hill, a castle, were popping up now on the right, now on the left, at first appearing to dominate a forest, then emerging from a valley, revealing to the wayfarer changes in direction or differences of altitude along his way."]

How pleasantly it reads! (I mean the original). But when we come down to the substance of the story, Marcel's world of the beautiful and execrable is pictured with the best late 19th century art. This would be our *first impression* before we arrive to the fundamentally **NEW** in it - which comes through at the second reading, as will be argued. Until then it is *only* better, richer, denser, and sometimes even more dramatic than the best of naturalists, Flaubert, has ever produced.

Narration, Description and Structure.

To appease the displeasure of Proust enthusiasts, who will perceive much of what was so far said as sacrilegious, some remarks may be added in anticipation of the subsequent discussion. This is a bit against the practice of orderly conceptual analysis. But devotees, when so well justified in their allegiance as in the case of this great author, are to be forgiven and helped along with a concise anticipatory *précis* of excursive nature. It should be thus stressed that so far only those particulars of the work have been, and will be for a few more pages, discussed, which apply to the construction material of Proustian poetry, but not its structure. The masterly new and personal comes through in the structure of the novel as a whole. Still dwelling on the "brick" and the "mortar", each and every one of the seven novels can be classed as a last affirmation of the great 19th century French novel. And I feel the pleasure that un-repenting heretics might have felt, screaming their truth in the face of the inquisitor, when saying: Proust is the greatest master of the techniques developed by the naturalists; he not only added luster and glamour to this particular way of writing, but used it to reveal more about the human beast than anyone of his predecessors. Since beyond the cool and limited technical virtuosity of Flaubert (not to speak of Zola), Proust pushed this art to the very last limits of its potential. There was no way to get farther than Proust did: taking the same person(s), the same experience from as many angles as accessible by the techniques of the 19th century novelists, among whom he is probably closest to Balzac (a comparison he may not have taken as a compliment).

When an art reaches its limits, in the sense that it has used up all instruments it could develop - does it not mean that it is over with it? Certainly not. There will always be stories to be told, and the writer may choose any of the fully developed methods up to their respective limits. And, of course, he may discover new devices of representation to be fused with the inherited ones. Thus, while the method will no more be a new one, the story could still be very good.

Essay and Aphorism in Novelistic Disguise

The development of the art of narration, and its auxiliary, the art of description, pursue many parallel roads. None is endless: every type of storytelling arrives, sooner or later, to a point where it turns out that its means have been exhausted. The end of one road is, naturally, not *the* End itself for the parable. New roads are opened, yet, eventually, they also will reach an end somewhere at the edge of a cliff below which gapes the infinitely deep precipice of Nonsense. It threatens to swallow anyone who pushed by the urge of verbal expression loses control of his rhetoric balance. Proust may not have searched from the beginning for new ways. He first walked the last extension of the road leading from Balzac (of whom he was not particularly enthusiastic) to Flaubert (whom he didn't like very much either), and past it, to the point where it seemed that the technique of realist narration and naturalist elaboration, even if employed with maximum virtuosity, as he did, could be improved only with some of that glamour he so subtly and movingly translated into beautiful French from the paintings of contemporary artists. Marcel (either of them) knew about these limits and succeeded, sometimes with difficulty, to keep his balance: the urge translated into poetic will and controlled by rhetoric discipline has found its fulfillment in the poetry of confessions. *Mimesis* by confession?

This is what it was in the beginning when, as the first reading of the work reveals, memories of a long past were recovered by being transformed into a story rich in implications and ramifications. But the difficulty of translating *all* the most intimate memories into words to be communicated to the reader, haunted the enterprise all along on the way to completion. Remember this:

«*le geste le plus insignifiant que nous avons fait ... portait sur lui le reflet des choses qui logiquement ne tenaient pas de lui*». ["any, however insignificant gesture we have made ... carries upon it the reflection of things with which it had no logical connection."]

Yet all a story is able to verbally communicate to the reader is the "insignificant gesture" in conjunction with the "logically separated object". But then how to bring about that *reflet* which makes for the uniqueness characterizing the connection between the *geste* and the *objet*? Doesn't art mean the transformation of this unique reflection into the reader's own experience? But here the Word runs into difficulties. It would be only the arrangement, the succession, the connection and interaction of the *verbally expressible and describable* which might generate empathy and reliving in the reader. [To the reader: please compare once again the Flaubert and Proust version of travel emotions]

The characters of the tale will have to declare themselves; the metaphors of their experience may help us along. So Proust introduces the *metaphors of experience*, repeated in numerous variants so as to conjure the reader's empathy. However, beyond these metaphors, and often using them as disguise, a new form of *essay* is slipped between the pages of the narration, sometimes blocking its free flow, without being fully elaborated on its own. The parable and its metaphors yield to the theoretical "price tag". True, this intrusive editing exercise abides by the essential principle underlying the essays of Montaigne, the founder of the genre, that it be a form of honest confession, purposing the transmission of past experiences to those who will come. Only Montaigne developed a terse and disciplined form of such restatements and knew were to stop:

«*Que si j'eusse esté entre ces nations qu'on dict vivre encore sous la douce liberté des premiers loix de nature, je t'assure que je m'y fusse très-volontiers peint tout entier, et tout nud.*» (*Au lecteur*) ["If I were among those nations of which it is said that they are still living according to the sweet freedom granted by the first laws of nature, I can assure you that I would freely paint over my whole naked body." ("To the reader")]

- which he did not. He did not over-paint anything, recommending himself to the reader rather by the ideas he discussed. Proust tried to do the same. He dissertates about the art of reliving, and his discourse remains often a flow of confessions in essayistic terms, and not a new way of narration. What he says about past experiences is, of course, very often, perfectly, and beautifully, suggestive:

«... le geste, l'acte le plus simple reste enfermé comme dans mille vases clos, dont chacun serait rempli de choses d'une couleur, d'une odeur, d'une température absolument différentes; sans compter que ces vases disposés sur toute la hauteur de nos années pendant lesquelles nous n'avons cessé de changer, fut ce seulement de rêve et de pensée, sont situés à des altitudes bien diverses, et nous donnent la sensation d'atmosphères singulièrement variées.» (p.260) [«... the simplest gesture or deed remains encased as in thousands of sealed receptacles, of which each is filled with things of absolutely different color, scent or temperature; not to speak that the receptacles, ranged at different heights, according to our years during which we never stopped changing, even if only in our dreams or way of thinking, convey us the impression of various unique atmospheres.»]

This is a set of fine metaphors - metaphors because they don't *state* anything - about our memory's storage system. We enjoy such an image for its own beauty; if picked out from the whole and edited into a volume of aphorisms it could likely be read, as good para-poetry, for its pre-philosophical suggestions. But a novel, flooded with such, will not be the proof of its art transcending the "naturalists". If they prove anything it is that the *storyteller* needs to look for a new line, parallel and not continuing that which achieved its success in the 19th century, if he wants to be *different*. Now, it is not mandatory at all to be different - except when one makes a claim of being such by criticizing the very art one employs. Even if with great mastery!

The resistance of the words to translate experiences, unique, intimate experiences, "was" particularly painfully felt "later" when Marcel recounts what happened at *"Le coté des Guermantes"*. The big fuss about the importance of names in Proust's work should not mislead us about the plain fact, also plainly recognized in the novel, that names may signify a lot to Marcel or anyone of us, in a strictly subjective sense, but are unable to communicate anything to a second person such as a reader. We read (*Le coté des Guermantes* I) that

> «... *une sensation d'autrefois ... permette à notre mémoire de nous faire entendre ce nom [un nom] avec le timbre particulier qu'il avait alors pour nos oreilles.*» (Guermantes I, p.70) ["... a sensation from the past ... permits our memory to hear that name in the particular timbre with which it was received then by our ears."]

Such we too may have experienced, but then there is nothing we can do about it: pronouncing the name is no literary communication, just as *stating* to have had the same experience later in the courtyard of the Guermantes as in Venice, wouldn't communicate anything of this experience's directness and intimacy. What remains is a metaphor for experiences of any kind, including those associated with names. Names are just another memory awakening signal along with optical or mechanical accidents. Their significance, the significance of a name, any name *in general*, can be suggested by a metaphor. But its *uniqueness*, if ever communicated, can be conveyed only by empathy-generating narration. It strikes us beautiful when we read:

> «*Et le nom de Guermantes d'alors est aussi comme un de ces petits ballons dans lesquels on a enfermé de l'oxygène ou un autre gaz: quand j'arrive à le crever, à en faire sortir ce qu'il contient, je respire l'air de Combray de cette année-la ...*» (p.70)
> ["And the name *de Guermantes* of erstwhile is like one of those little balloons filled with oxygen or some other gas: when I manage to pierce it to discharge its content, I breathe the air of Combray of that year..."]

But we, the readers, will have to go five volumes back - or four ahead - to *respire* the air of Combray through the respective description and narration thereby making redundant any lengthy philosophizing about names in this novelistic context. If it was gotten right, as it was indeed, then the verbal effusion about its remembrance - *and no remembrance can be imitated*! - is not a new style, but a burden on another well proven one.

The entire work of Proust, if read with the awareness of this problem, will appear as a composite of two major distinguishable elements. The first is the recounting of the struggle of a young author to transform a host of anecdotic episodes, unified by a stream of memories, into a sequence of narrations with psychological relevance. The second is an attempt to mould the myriads of aphoristic crumbs into some philosophical consistency by sticking them to a narration. The former was a great success, yielding some of our century's worthiest stories about morally not all that worthy people, including *a singular achievement: the story of its own genesis.* The second, a failure, if the philosophical purpose is considered, though celebrated in countless nonsensical panegyrics. Yet it is saved by its piecemeal poetic-suggestive beauty. (E.g. the description of the numerous time-indexed memory receptacles of one and the same *geste* or *acte plus simple.*) I do firmly believe that Proust, who was a very odd yet also a very intelligent person, realized full well the contrast and invented the volume, "*Le temps retrouvé*", to justify it and make the two ingredients of the nine volumes compatible with each other through the mediation of the hero's mind. And being aware of all this we are able to appreciate an ever beautiful story and an ensemble of fine *excursi* constituting good reading on their own. Yet it remains true that storytelling does not seem to be able to go beyond its limits with the listing of occurrences of subjective, incommunicable experiences.

ESSAY NO.12
The Modern Novel on Trial

- Of Kafka's *Der Prozess* -

'Sei nicht übereilt', sagte der Geistliche, 'übernimm nicht die fre-
mde Meinung ungeprüft. Ich habe dir die Geschichte im Wortlaut
der Schrift erzählt. Von Täuschung steht nichts darin'.[Don't
hurry to espouse untested a foreign opinion, said the priest.
I told you the story according to the letter of the Scripture.
There is no mention about deception in it.]

One of the things often said about Kafka is that so much has been said about
him that not much remains to be said. And after this has been said, explicitly
or just by implication, many go about to complete what still seems to have
remained unsaid. However, whatever has been said and written about Kafka
is in most cases, partly or totally, in violation of the principle quoted in the
motto to this essay. Maybe I will succeed to be, at least in part, different.

The motto repeats the words of the *Geistlicher*, or "the priest", in the novel's ninth chapter and is quoted here meaning to imply an obligation for the
writer of this essay: work out your ideas strictly respecting the text proper;
respect that what is in it; try to avoid the traps of hermeneutics. And when
this is done, be honest about what you remain with. How much and what can
a reader afford by way of interpretation? You may read incomplete statements
within a story which then can be filled in with a variety of compatible statements. Filling in the open spaces in the structure of a story with logically compatible statements is legitimate; looking for hidden meanings, hidden that is

by the author, should not be this reader's business. Various "fillings in" may, of course, yield alternative meanings, yet each ought still to be compatible with as much of the story as told. And should we still remain dissatisfied with what we get thereby, "hidden meanings", that is hidden by the author, should still not be our business. After all why assume that the author plays hide-and-seek with the reader? He may, but I don't play along. And before entering into the exercise of re-reading the proposed novel, the following should be kept in mind:

- There could be a difference between what the author might have wanted to say which, however, he didn't say straight, and the associations the reader makes after or while reading. This should be discussed later in some detail.

- The question to be studied here is not what made the author write his story, but rather why is a reader impressed by it. If it is the case. This is not the same question than engaging in hermeneutic exegesis. The book, the story, the characters in the story exist just as the reader. Reading is a relationship between the reader and the literary work. As written!

It may not yet follow from these summary remarks where this discussion should lead. Neither can it be made clear without a short and precise review of "The Trial". Therefore, this analysis should begin with a simple summary of the "story", stressing that which lends itself to a meaningful restatement of what is actually in it. Every other aspect of analysis should follow this restatement. Important: the restatement will be understood only by those who already read the novel, also keeping it handy while perusing this essay. I really mean it: keep the book handy; if possible the German original. As for the English version of the subsequent quotations: don't blame any on the so far published translations.

The subsequent abstract has the purpose to recapitulate sections which I, the writer of these notes, believe to be essential for understanding the particulars of Kafka's novel. The main ideas proposed will be repeated several times within this essay in order to introduce in sequence alternative yet complementary approaches to the text. The repetitions may seem boring, and they might sometimes be indeed. Yet they cannot be avoided. *Der Prozess*, as all writings of Kafka, is fundamentally deviating from everything we knew until him as a *novel*. So we will have to put it on *trial*. And though the trial procedure may not be always entertaining, it is hoped to be enlightening also with the help of the boring repetitions. The rehearsal of the story will have, naturally, a subjective part to it: it is *the choice of accents* on various sections and also on the terminology employed by Kafka, for which this writer is responsible.

(1) The Review of the Story

The "authority"'s men are in the apartment of Josef K. to arrest him. The opening phrase is the introduction into a mystery yet also the basic assumption for a solution, if any, to it. It reads:

> "*Jemand musste Josef K. verleumdet haben, denn ohne das er etwas böses getan hätte, wurde er eines Morgens verhaftet.*" [p.259] [Somebody must have calumniated Josef K., because one morning he was arrested without having done anything wrong.]

Being arrested means being subject to a legal act. But one is normally arrested on the basis of either a *denunciation* or a *suspicion*. Yet we know nothing about either a denunciation or a specific suspicion. It was a *Verleumdung*, a calumny or slander or defamation, which lead to Josef K.'s, a bank employee of medium rank, arrest, and not an *Anzeige* (denunciation) by somebody or the *Verdacht* (suspicion) of the "authority". But was it an arrest in the legal sense of the word? Just as there was no denunciation for any specific act so there was no arrest in the legal sense: nothing happened of what the reader or Josef K. normally associate with the act of detention or of taking in custody for which the English word "arrest" or the German word "*Verhaftung*" is used. This is what K., who continued to go freely about after his "arrest", didn't quite understand. Yet we, the readers, should keep in mind that the "arrest" in case is based on a *slander*, not a *denunciation* assuming the breaking of the law in a positive sense. It is important for everything what follows in the novel.

While the arrestors were present, K.'s landlady, *Frau* Grubach, wanted to come into his room, but was prevented by one of the "guards", *Wächter*. Why? "Because you are arrested" was the terse answer given to a puzzled K's question. Did they have such a right? The purportedly "defamed" or "calumniated" or "slandered", and then "arrested" had his doubts:

> "*Hier sind meine Legitimationspapiere, zeigen Sie mir jetzt die ihrigen und vor allem den Verhaftbefehl.*" [p.262] ["Here are my

identification papers, now show me yours', and first of all the arrest warrant."]

He asked for a *Verhaftbefehl*, an arrest warrant, which is the official confirmation of any arrest. Normally. But this "arrest" was quite unusual and K.'s request was frustrated. It certainly was by no means something which the reader associates with what could happen to anybody within any society in which a modicum of legality prevails. This was obvious to K. who evaluated his situation in a few clear statements:

> "... *die Sache [kann] auch nicht viel Wichtigkeit haben. Ich folgere das daraus, das ich angeklagt bin, aber nicht die geringste Schuld auffinden kann, wegen deren man mich anklagen könnte. Aber auch das ist nebensächlich, die Hauptfrage ist, von wem bin ich angeklagt?"* [p.267]
> ["... the matter cannot have much importance. This I conclude from the fact that I am charged, yet I cannot find the least of guilt for which one might charge me. But even this is only of secondary importance. The main question is: who accuses [charges] me?"]

So neither K. nor the reader knows *why* and *by whom* is he subjected to something which in the story is called an arrest. Indeed, we don't even know what he is accused of, rightly or wrongly, or whether he is accused of anything at all. K. just assumed that there might be an accusation because he, like all of us, associate such with an act called "arrest". Nor do we or K. know anything of what the calumny might have been. And for the subsequent reading and discussion you may retain the following section from the above quotation of K.'s words: "This I conclude from the fact that I am charged, yet I cannot find the least of guilt for which one might charge me." Did K. already assume that it is he himself who has to provide a confession of a not-yet-specified guilt for which he was "arrested"? Because otherwise he might have said: "This I conclude from the fact that I am charged, yet I still don't know why, since you didn't tell me." Neither did the arrestors say too much. A mysterious "supervisor" of the mysterious "authority" answered to K's question that

> "*Ich kann Ihnen auch durchaus nicht sagen, das sie angeklagt sind oder vielmehr, ich weiss nicht, ob sie es sind. Sie sind verhaftet, das ist richtig,*

mehr weiss ich nicht." [p.268] ["I cannot tell you exactly that you are charged; I don't know whether you are [charged]. You are arrested, that is true, [but] I don't know more than that."]

And he serves K. also with an advice:

"*... denken sie weniger an uns und an das, was mit ihnen geschehen wird, denken sie lieber mehr an sich.*" (ibid.) ["... think less about us and on what might happen to you, better think of yourself."]

So, analyze yourself, your behavior, your past? What does this really mean? At least, it by no means contradicts the advice. It is perfectly logically compatible with it. Since, what else can we conclude from all this? Nothing much, indeed. K. is in a state of limbo just as the reader. The reader, just as K. himself may also be puzzled by the difference, implied in the supervisor's advice, between *not* thinking about what might happen to him and yet thinking of himself. The one thing we know is our and K's uneasiness with the environment in which the story unfolds. Nobody actually *accuses* K; he is just *suspected of being accused* of something, having been, probably, *calumniated* or *slandered*. The consequences are not yet very clear. Nor the accusations, if any. Are we entitled to look for analogous situations in life or literature? We are. But not yet. We still have to carefully rehearse the story *im Wortlaut der Schrift* or, according to the letter of the "Scripture", never forgetting that *von Täuschung steht nichts darin* or that "nothing is said in it about deception". And once again something you may commit to your memory for later consideration: in the world in which all this happens *legal* arrests are not operated without charges, otherwise K. wouldn't imply right at the beginning that he is charged. But this may than be something different than the legal arrest which exists also in K's society. It must be some parallel order of things asserting itself within that very same society.

So K. was remanded - but not "in custody" - for investigation. But he could continue his professional activity. Thus the arrested K. was supposed to go to work as usual. The "supervisor" made this clear to him:

"*Sie haben mich missverstanden. Sie sind verhaftet, gewiss, aber das soll sie nicht hindern Ihren Beruf zu erfüllen*". [p.270] ["You misunderstood me. You are arrested, of course, but this should not prevent you from performing your duties."] - But don't forget, just by the way, that *"Ihren Beruf zu erfüllen"* could be also translated as "live-up to your calling". Or destiny? Sorry, this is too much guessing. I apologize.

Moreover, three junior colleagues of K. were at hand to go with him to the Bank. It was said that their presence may make things inconspicuous. So K. went to work, yet later he was at home again, as usual.

The reader is presently in the middle of the story. A witness in the centre of it. Everybody else, that is the characters of the story, seem to be going along with the "official" suspicion. If suspicion it is. So are the folks in the neighborhood as well as K.'s landlady *Frau* Grubach. She spied around, as a good landlady should, eavesdropped, talked to the *"Wächter"* or "supervisor", and then said later to K.:

> *"Es kommt mir wie etwas Gelehrtes vor, das ich zwar nicht verstehe, das man aber auch nicht verstehen muss."* [p.274] ["It appears to me like something scholarly, something I don't understand and what one doesn't have to understand either."]

The simple woman thought that one should better keep one's nose out of what is not one's own business. And then there is a neighbor, *Fräulein* Bürstner. She is also suspected, but only by *Frau* Grubach, of a much too easygoing sexual life. K. defends Miss Bürstner, yet he is lectured by the landlady about the need for the "cleanliness" of her boarding house or pension. (p.274-275)

Later K. provokes *Fräulein* Bürstner to a conversation enquiring about what she might think of his guilt. She did not know more then K. or us, but then, if somebody is suspected, it must be something to it:

> *"'Nun, schuldlos' sagte das Fräulein, 'ich will nicht gleich ein vielleicht folgenschweres Urteil aussprechen, auch kenne ich sie doch nicht, es muss doch schon ein schwerer Verbrecher sein, dem man gleich eine Untersuchungskommission auf den Leib schickt. Da sie aber doch frei sind - ich schliesse wenigstens aus Ihrer Ruhe, dass sie nicht aus dem Gefängnis entlaufen sind - so können Sie doch kein solches Verbrechen*

begangen haben.'" [p.279] ["Well, guiltless, said the *Fräulein*, I wouldn't like to pronounce right away a foreboding verdict, and I also don't [really] know you. But he must be a hardened criminal whom they send a Commission of Enquiry on his back. Yet given that you are still free - since I assume from your calm that you did not escape from prison - you may not have perpetrated such a serious crime."]

Question: what made *Fräulein* Bürstner believe that it is a "Commission of Enquiry" which is involved with K.?

Now, K. wants to get friendly with Miss Bürstner. She is interested in legal matters and wishes to improve her knowledge. She might have succeeded. If so, she certainly was way ahead of all readers. And then:

"K. war telephonisch verständigt worden, dass am nächsten Sonntag eine kleine Untersuchung in seiner Angelegenheit stattfinden würde. Man machte ihn darauf aufmerksam, dass diese Untersuchungen regelmässig, wenn auch nicht jede Woche, so doch häufiger einander folgen würden." [p.283] ["K. was informed by telephone that next Sunday a short inquest in his case would take place. He was warned that such inquests will now follow regularly and, even if not every week, still more frequently."]

Hence it is a systematic and recurring *Untersuchung* or inquest. So *Fräulein* Bürstner knew something, it may indeed have been a Commission of Enquiry. Take notice that the first session was tentatively scheduled for a Sunday. K. was permitted to pick some other day or even night. After all he could have had some objection against a Sunday. Only he? Did the judges or commission members never go to church? Well, K. complied with the summons. It was not easy to find the court where the *Untersuchung* or inquest purportedly took place, because no exact address was given to him. (Could such a strange "court" reside anywhere or everywhere, being in session at anytime? Even at night?) Yet he chanced upon it while first erring in a poor neighborhood. It was a spooky place and so was the public attending the trials, disposed in the room according to some arcane principle in "left" and "right" sections. Then, who knows why, the judge leading the inquest (*Untersuchungsrichter* or investigating magistrate) took K. for a house-painter which prompted our hero to thus characterize the situation:

> "*Ihre Frage, Herr Untersuchungsrichter, ob ich Zimmermaler bin - vielmer sie haben gar nicht gefragt, sondern es mir auf den Kopf zugesagt -, ist bezeichnend für die ganze Art des Verfahrens, das gegen mich geführt wird. Sie könnene einwenden, das es ja überhaupt kein Verfahren ist. Sie haben sehr recht, denn es ist ja nur ein Verfahren wenn ich es als solches anerkenne. Aber ich erkenne es also für den Augenbick jetzt an, aus Mitleid gewissermasen.*"[p.291] ["Your question judge, whether I am a house painter - in fact you never asked me, just declared me to be one - is characteristic for the entire trial conducted against me. You may object that this is in fact no trial at all. You are right, since it is a trial only if I take it as such. And for the moment I accept it as such, out of compassion as it were."]

Can this be read just as an episode of no consequence? May be, though it seems that the possibility of a house painter being in the same "accused" position as a junior bank executive was not unthinkable to the judge. Indeed, did this have to be a story of a bank executive or could it have been also of a house-painter? Of what we know so far there seems to be no difference. But we now continue to read and, who knows, we may find out why K. had to be a bank employee. Just recall the house-painter episode while continuing to read.

Important for the understanding of the story: it is nowhere said in the text but it wouldn't contradict it either if we, the readers, would assume that the entire action is meant to provoke a self-search by K.. We recall, of course that he was earlier given the advice to "think of yourself" rather than what may happen to him. Is he expected to find himself guilty? Does such enquiry of the reader not contradict the aforementioned principle of strictly respecting the *Wortlaut der Schrift*, or the letter of the "Scripture"? No. We do not have to interpret or re-interpret anything actually written. We just try out a conditional "fill in" of some apparently empty spots in the story. Because the *Verfahren*, the procedure, against K., which is one if he recognizes it as such, makes sense only in the case he were to discover his own presumed guilt of something yet to be specified. He may ignore all this, as he did so far. But he cannot continue forever like this because he is *Verhaftet*. Just like Job who also thought he was innocent but having been afflicted had no choice but to examine himself, even though headstrongly denying any wrongdoing.

To recapitulate, the following strange things happened so far:

- We have an *arrest*, but nobody was actually *arrested* - unless somebody takes it for such;

- No *guilt* is specified, indeed we are told right at the beginning that a person was arrested *ohne das er etwas böses getan hätte,* or without having done anything wrong. Yet he may still consider himself guilty. By implication of course, i.e. by defending himself; because there is *no charge* or *Anklage.* Once you defend yourself you may, unwittingly, regard yourself as being charged for some guilt.

- A trial is said to have started, but there is *no trial procedure* - unless all this maneuvering is taken by somebody as such. The mentioned *Untersuchung,* or inquest, was in the best case just an *Untersuchung,* or investigation, of something unspecified, but not a trial.

Yet K. takes everything "as such" while purporting not to. Out of "compassion" for the Court, as he says. And because he professes to stand up for others in similar situations:

"*... was mir geschehen ist, ist ja nur ein einzelner Fall und als solcher nicht wichtig, da ich es nicht schwer nehme, aber es ist ein Zeichen eines Verfahrens, wie es gegen viele geübt wird. Für diese stehe ich hier ein, nicht für mich.*" [p.292]
["... whatever happened to me, is only a single instance and as such of no importance, since I don't take it seriously. Yet it is characteristic of a procedure directed against many. And I stand up for all those [others]."]

So he accepts, implicitly, and without admitting it, a guilt of which he doesn't know anything, by standing-up against the unspecified or suspected accusations. But many are in the same boots. Probably also house painters? - He further characterizes the system:

> *"Und der Sinn dieser Organisation, meine Herren? Er besteht darin,*
> *dass unschuldige Personen verhaftet werden und gegen sie ein sinnloses*
> *und meistens, wie in meinem Fall, ergebnisloses Verfahren eingeleitet*
> *wird."* [p.295] ["And the purpose of this organization, gentlemen?
> It consists in having innocent people arrested and initiating a
> meaningless procedure against them which is, in most cases, just as
> in mine, also without any conclusion."]

In fact, once again, nobody is arrested formally; K., as anybody else, can escape. But he does not. He recognizes the "meaningless" authority by fighting it or, more precisely, by just talking back. And everybody else goes along with it. Also K.'s uncle. The latter invites him to come to the country to avoid *temporarily*(!) the Authority. This is possible because in the country its agents will have more trouble to find and torment K., though it is not clear why. But no total escape is recommended by the uncle even though this appears to be so easy. [p.335] It seems that the uncle knows something that K. and the rest of us don't:

> *"Willst du den Prozess verlieren? Weisst du, was das bedeutet? Das be-*
> *deutet, das du einfach gestrichen wirst. Und das die ganze Verwandschaft*
> *mitgerissen oder wenigstens bis auf den Boden gedemütigt wird. Josef,*
> *nimm dich zusammen. Deine Gleichgültigkeit bringt mich um den*
> *Verstand.* [p.336] ["Do you want to lose the Trial? Do you know
> what this means? This means that you will be simply blotted out.
> And that the whole family will be dragged along [with you] or at
> least deeply humiliated. Josef, pull yourself together. Your indiffer-
> ence makes me crazy."]

So what is the potential sentence in that "trial" of undefined nature and form? The answer is: *"das du einfach gestrichen wirst"* or that "you will be blotted out" (or deleted or erased or obliterated). Some translators make their life easy by interpreting *gestrichen* as "ruined". This is absolutely incorrect. There are several words in German for "being ruined", and there was no reason for the author not to use either of them had he meant that or only that. But it is certainly comfortable for the reader who may have been excused for not asking: deleted wherefrom? He will now be deprived of this comfort. So the question is indeed: deleted wherefrom? Keep guessing, but do not communicate your guesses, *yet!*, because they are only yours, the reader's.

Yet K. does not accept the "escape" to the country because

> "*Das würde Flucht und Schuldbewustsein bedeuten. Überdies bin ich hier zwar mehr verfolgt, kann aber auch selbst die Sache mehr betreiben.*" [p.336] ["that would be [equivalent to] flight and imply a guilty conscience. And though here [i.e. in the city] I am more harassed, I can also better pursue the case myself."]

The uncle agrees and takes him in his auto:

> "*Wir fahren jetzt zum Advokaten Huld*" [p.337] "We now go to Huld, the attorney"

who is an expert in such matters. And is also called *Huld* i.e. grace.

> "*Er hat als Verteitiger und Armenadvokat einen bedeutenden Ruf.*" ["He has a considerable reputation as a defence attorney and a lawyer of the poor."]

Huld knew about K.'s case from courthouse rumors but he happened to be sick and in bed, yet still quite talkative, while being cared for by the nurse Leni. She may have had some mysterious affairs of her own because, all of a sudden, some *Kanzleidirektor*, or office executive, cropped-up in a dark corner of the room. He was trying to hide when K. and his uncle unexpectedly arrived. K. thought that he may have seen the man during one of the inquest proceedings. So: *they* [who?] were all over the place.

Then, while in the study of the lawyer, K. and Leni engaged in a little flirting. On the wall of the study there was a portrait of yet another *Untersuchungsrichter* who, according to Leni, showed more impressive on the canvas then in life. And just by the way: has anybody ever seen the portrait of a judge or even only an *Untersuchungsrichter* hanging on the wall of a lawyer's office? One thing is quite clear, namely that the word "judge" by which we designate persons of a specific position, is used here for something quite different. But let us continue with the rehearsal. Now Leni volunteered with an advice:

"Machen sie doch bei nächster Gelegenheit das Geständniss. Erst dann ist die Möglichkeit zu entschlüpfen gegeben, erst dann." [p.345]
["Make that confession on the next occasion. Then, and only then, will there be an opportunity to slip out."]

Attention! She says *"**das** Geständniss"* or "**the/that** confession", not "***ein** Geständniss"* or "**a** confession". So they didn't quite expect just any confession but a specific one. Or this seems to be the public's perception. In spite of this K., being convinced of his innocence [of what?], considers to write some memorandum completed with his *curriculum vitae* recording all his more significant acts in life. Since he quite obviously did not know what to confess. So let "them" pick out something what they might understand as guilt. It is to be seen whether they can discover some guilt in it. K. believes that

"Die Vorteile einer solchen Verteitigungsschrift gegenüber der blossen Verteitigung durch den übrigens auch sonst nicht einwandfreien Advokaten waren zweifellos. K. wusste ja gar nicht, was der Advokat unternahm; viel war es jedenfalls nicht, schon einen Monat lang hatte er ihn nicht mehr zu sich berufen ... Vor allem hatte er ihn fast gar nicht ausgefragt. Und hier war doch so viel zu fragen. Fragen war die Hauptsache." [p.349]
["The advantages of such a defense-memorandum, when compared to those of a simple defense conducted by an otherwise anything but impeccable lawyer, were beyond question. After all K. didn't even know what the lawyer was undertaking in his case; it could hardly have been a lot since he [the lawyer] failed to call him for a whole month ... And most importantly he never questioned him. And there were so many questions to be asked. After all questioning was the main thing."]

Let it be clear: a *complete* autobiography of a person is to contain everything that person ever did, consequently those who possess some criterion/criteria of choice will be able to pick out something which reveals guilt or innocence. Since K. is convinced of his innocence yet has also a perfect memory [which we have just "filled in"], the *curriculum vitae* will not hide anything. Therefore it, attached to the memorandum, has clear advantages over the lawyer's services.

Otherwise it seems - once again *it seems* - that the *Advokat* has not to defend him but to find out about his guilt. We still don't know what it was. [It may lead us a little too far when we conjecture that the lawyer is to help K. discover something which is deemed to be guilt, or *the* guilt in the view of the "authority", and then help the accused to find extenuating circumstances rather than deny any culpability. Not that we haven't ever heard of such, but it is not according to the *Wortlaut der Schrift*. So let us get freed from such conjectures and follow again the text.] In the given situation it is enough for the Court to believe that you are guilty, only the guilt has to be *ex post* found. And K. was looking to find something to prove his innocence as opposed to the unspecified guilt. Because:

> "*Das Verfahren ist nämlich im allgemeinen nicht nur vor der Öffentlichkeit geheim, sondern auch vor dem Angeglakgten.*" [p.351] ["The procedure is not only kept secret from the public, but also from the accused."]

What is kept secret is *the procedure*; not the fact that such one exists. Only the way it is pursued remains a mystery. And it is kept secret "also from the accused". Accused? We know K. is arrested, he was earlier told by a supervisor that he may not even be accused. However it may be, various reactions are possible or compatible. Thus we also know that

> "*jeder Angeklagte, selbst ganz einfältige Leute, gleich beim allerersten Eintritt in den Prozess an Verbesserungsvorschläge zu denken anfangen und damit oft Zeit und Kraft verschwenden, die anders viel besser verwendet werden könnten.*" [p.355] ["every defendant, even very simple people, would start thinking on some improvement proposals right after their first involvement in the trial, thereby wasting time end energy which could otherwise be much better used."]

They try to "improve" though without knowing what they have to improve on. K. attempts to resist. His purpose may have been suggested by the circumstances, namely:

> "*Einzusehen versuchen, dass dieser grosse Gerichtsorganismus gewissermassen ewig in der Schwebe bleibt und dass man zwar, wenn*

man auf seinem Platz selbständig etwas ändert den Boden unter den Füssen sich wegnimmt ..." [p.355]
["To try to understand that this big judicial organization will remain, to some extent, permanently in suspense, and that if one were to change something in one's position, that would result in loosing the ground under one's feet."] - Of course, *Schweben* translates correctly as *hovering*. But the English phrase would rather require the definition of that over which something is hovering. Therefore *suspense* was chosen; not "delicate balance" as in some translations which does away with everything which is hovering in this novel.

However, for now he has no choice but to go along with the trial. Remember? - at the beginning there was an *arrest*. But there was no *detention*. K. didn't even have the chance to escape, since you can escape only when you are detained. Then there was a trial which never came to a resolution because there was no clear accusation. It had to come from somewhere, but it did not come, and:

> *"... er hatte kaum mehr die Wahl, den Prozess anzunehmen oder abzulehnen, er stand mitten darin und musste sich wehren."* [p.360] ["he had hardly anymore a choice between going along with the trial or reject it, [since] he stood in the middle of it and had to defend himself."]

Once again the text *may* betray something: K. had *kaum mehr die Wahl* or "hardly anymore a choice". *Kaum mehr* - hardly anymore! It implies, if anything, that such a choice may have existed or at least was perceived to have existed before, yet has been forfeited, perhaps unwittingly. Therefore K. thought it necessary to produce a Memorandum. Whatever that meant, it turned out that the most unlikely people were informed about his case and exhibited some willingness to help. With advices! But we are not told that they doubted K.'s guilt! Thus a business partner of the bank, the *Fabrikant*, unannounced, came to offer him a new connection. It was a portrait painter called Titorelli who earlier informed the *Fabrikant* about K.'s case. The painter knew about it because, as it turned out, his livelihood depended mainly on his work for *das Gericht*, the Court. The Court, not just any Court. Otherwise, he completed his budget by peddling with small paintings and thus getting acquainted with various people. The *Fabrikant* was one of them telling Josef K. that:

> "*Er kommt schon seit Jahren von Zeit zu Zeit in mein Büro und bringt kleine Bilder mit, für die ich ihm - er ist fast ein Bettler - immer eine Art Almosen gebe.*" [p.368] "For many years, he comes from time to time to my office bringing with him small paintings, for which - he is almost like a beggar - I give him some alms."]

This is how Titorelli also peddled the news from The Court, including those about K. And so K. was introduced to the portray painter of the judges by the *Fabrikant*. In the conversation with Titorelli K. claimed his innocence, also realizing that:

> "*'Es kommt auf viele Feinheiten an, in denen sich das Gericht verliert. Zum Schluss aber zieht es von irgendwoher, wo ursprünglich gar nichts gewesen ist, eine grosse Schuld hervor. ... Darin stimmen aber alle überein, das leichtsinnige Anklagen nicht erhoben werden und dass das Gericht, wenn es einmal anklagt, fest von der Schuld des Angeklagten überzeugt ist und von dieser Überzeugung nur schwer abgebracht werden kann.' 'Schwer?' fragte der Maler und warf eine Hand in die Höhe. 'Niemals ist das Gericht davon abzubringen. Wenn ich hier alle Richter nebeneinander auf eine Leinwand male und Sie werden sich vor dieser Leinwand verteitigen, so werden Sie mehr Erfolg haben als vor dem wirklichen Gericht'*" [p.379-380] ["It depends on many subtleties with which the Court gets mixed up. And at the end, they will pull forth a major guilt from where there was no such at the beginning ... Yet they all [those who have some knowledge about the Court] agree on one thing, that charges are not laid in a haphazard fashion and when once the Court lays a charge, it is firmly convinced of the defendant's guilt and it will be difficult to make it reverse its opinion. 'Difficult?' asked the painter while lifting one hand in the air. 'Never is the Court to abandon that opinion. Were I now to paint on a canvas all the judges, side by side, while you were to defend yourself facing this painting, then you would certainly be more successful than standing before the real-world Court.'"]

K. finds out from Titorelli that there are two classes of judges, belonging to a lower and, respectively to a higher, very recondite, difficult to approach, court. There are also two modes of defense. The one is relatively easy and depends on the disposition of lower ranking judges Titorelli's clients. It means that if the accused manages to propitiate the judges then the charges may be dropped. More exactly[?] the judges have the power to "free the defendant from the accusation" (*von deer Anlagen loszulösen*). But

> "*wenn Sie auf diese Weise freigesprochen werden, sind sie für den Augenblick der Anklage entzogen, aber sie schwebt auch weiterhin über Ihnen und kann, sobald nur der höhere Befehl kommt, sofort in Wirkung treten.*" [p. 388] ["being acquitted in this fashion, they [the accused] are relieved for the moment from any accusation which, however, will continue to hover over their head and may become effective as soon as a dictate from higher places arrives."]

Hence freeing the defendant from the accusation is a temporary matter. It is called "*scheinbarer Freispruch*" or "delusive acquittal". Because the trial may start anew at any time. And even when once again an "acquittal" is achieved, the trial may start again, and again, and again. Forever - if the defendant is lucky. Otherwise he may end-up badly. In any case the accusation will still hover (*schweben*) above his head.

There is, however, another avenue, that of getting to the higher court or judges. Here the process of the trial consists in dragging it on forever. No *scheinbarer Freispruch*! But an everlasting effort, if the relevant judges are appropriately cultivated. From all this the following is essential:

> "'*Beide Methoden haben das Gemeinsame, das sie eine Verurteilung des Angeklagten verhindern.' 'Sie verhindern aber auch die wirkliche Freisprechung' sagte K. leise, als schäme er sich, das erkannt zu haben. 'Sie haben den Kern der Sache erfasst.'*" [p.390] ["'Both methods have in common that they prevented a conviction of the defendant.' 'However, they also prevent a real acquittal' said K. quietly, as if embarrassed for having recognized this. 'You have grasped the gist of the matter.'"]

No real acquittal is possible. (Of course it would also be difficult to acquit somebody from a guilt which has never been specified. But then it may be, sometimes, a temporary relief from the compulsion of searching for guilt.) Maybe no use for the *Advokat* either. K. decides to *kündig*, or fire, him. But yet again, he first pays him a visit. K. rings the bell. Nobody answers right away. Certainly not Leni. But then a man in *negligé* appears who, peeking through the peep-hole before opening the door, tells somebody inside that "it is him". Important detail not to be overlooked: K. doesn't know the fellow who, however, recognizes him. K. is known by most everybody ever since there is a *Verfahren* against him. It also appears that the man is Leni's lover. Block, as the fellow is called, tells that he also has some legal business, though K. and the reader wonder why he and Leni have to be in negligé. Further, they converse about the "group" of those who have to do with the Court. So, once again, there is a *group* of individuals - some section of society? - who are in a situation akin to K.'s. Yet they arrive to the conclusion that everybody is on his own. No "common cause". According to Block:

> "*Wenn manchmal in einer Gruppe der Glaube an ein gemeinsames Intersee auftaucht, so erweist er sich bald als ein Irrtum. Gemeinsam lässt sich gegen das Gericht nichts durchsetzen, nur ein einzelner erre-icht manchmal etwas im geheimen; erst wenn es erreicht ist, erfahren es die anderen; keiner weiss, wie es geschehen ist. Es gibt also keine Gemeinsamkeit ...*" [p.401] ["Whenever the belief in a collective interest wells-up among a group of individuals, this soon will prove itself to be an error. Nothing can be achieved collectively against the Court. Only an isolated individual may, sometimes, accomplish something in secret. And only after this is achieved, will the others find out about it, while nobody will learn about how it actually happened. Hence, there is no such thing as a common cause."]

As for the formalities of the procedure it is now even more obscure than ever before: it turns out that

> "*keiner hat die Festsetzung der Hauptverhandlung verlangt oder durchgesetzt...*" [p.403] ["no one had asked or imposed a date for a court hearing"]

How useful are lawyers in such cases? Are there some more powerful lawyers who may also be more reliable than the one in the story, i.e. lawyers specialized in cases where the role of a lawyer is not defined? They must be of a very strange kind. But then Block advises against them:

> *"Lassen Sie sich lieber nicht dazu verführen. Wer die grossen Advokaten sind, weiss ich nicht, und zu ihnen kommen kann man wohl gar nicht. Ich kenne keinen Fall, von dem sich mit bestimmtheit sagen liesse, das sie eingegriffen hätten. Manchen verteitigen sie, aber durch eigenen Willen kann man das nicht erreichen, sie verteitigen nur den, den sie verteitigen wollen."* [p.404] ["Better don't let yourself be mislead into this. I don't know who those great lawyers are, and then one may not even come close to them. I don't know of any case in which one could say with certainty that they have intervened. They do defend some, but this cannot be obtained by one's own intervention. They defend only him whom they want to defend."]

Neither did the pettifogger recommended by his uncle lead K. any farther. K. thought that by employing a lawyer he will ease the burden on his shoulders. Yet exactly the contrary happened. [p.410]

Then came the visit of an Italian client of the bank. The guest was supposed to be shown around by K. who also brushed up his basic Italian knowledge for the occasion. The visit to the city's famous cathedral was considered a must. By whom? By the management of the Bank. Because for the reader the significance of this visit consists in the fact that the Italian guest was late at the rendezvous, so that K. got the opportunity to get involved in a new adventure *in* the cathedral. Attention: the house painter could not have been involved in such an adventure. House painters do not receive distinguished foreign guests and are seldom proficient in foreign languages to be brushed up. So, whatever happened so far could have happened also to any house painter, junior bank executive, taxi driver or university professor. But for what was to happen from this point on, at most the university professor could have qualified, apart from Josef K.

Thus the reader will meet K. inside the *Dom* where he noticed that the sexton, walking around in the side-aisle, was watching him. The sexton was not really hiding, but kept moving while pointing out something to K. It was a little chancel in the wings, and then a larger one. Finally a priest appeared.

"Der Geistliche gab sich einen kleinen Aufschwung und stieg mit kurzen, schnellen Schritten die Kanzel hinauf. Sollte wirklich eine Predigt beginnen? ... Aber konnte den wirklich gepredigt werden? Konnte K. allein die Gemeinde darstellen?" [p.428] ["The priest hurried up the stairs of the chancel with short and swift steps. Was he really to start a sermon? ... But was it really possible to give now a sermon? Could K. represent by himself an entire congregation?"]

K. believed that the *Geistlicher* went up only to put out the light. But no, at some moment he addressed him directly as *Josef K.!*. This is an abridged, yet *verbatim* reproduction of the conversation between G. (*der Geistliche*) and K.:

G. *"Ich habe dich hierher rufen lassen um mit dir zu sprechen."*
"Weisst du, dass dein Prozess schlecht steht? ... Ich fürchte es wird schlecht enden. Man hält dich für schuldig. Dein Prozess wird vieleicht über ein niedriges Gericht gar nicht hinauskommen. Man hält wenigstens vorläufig deine Schuld für erwiesen."
K. *"Ich bin aber nicht schuldig, es ist ein Irrtum. Wie kann denn ein Mensch überhaupt schuldig sein? Wir sind doch alle Menschen, einer wie der andere."*
G. *"Das ist richtig, aber so pflegen die Schuldigen zu reden."*
K. «*Hast du ein Vorurteil gegen mich?*»
"G. Ich habe kein Vorurteil gegen dich ... Du missverstehst die Tatsachen, das Urteil kommt nicht mit einemmal, das Verfahren geht allmählich ins Urteil über."
G. *"... Du suchst zu viel fremde Hilfe, und besonders bei Frauen."* [p.430-431]

[G. "I called you here to talk to you. Do you know that your trial is in bad state? ... I am afraid that it will have a bad end. They consider you guilty. May be your trial will never get beyond a lower court. At least for now, they hold your guilt for proven."
K. "But I am not guilty, this is an error. How can a man be guilty anyway? Aren't we all, one like the other, human beings?"
G. "This is true, yet it is the guilty who speak like this."
K. "Are you prejudiced against me?"

G. "I am not biased against you ... You misunderstand the facts, the verdict does not come at once, it is the procedure that transmutes gradually into a verdict." - [Does this not fit the character of a court system of which we already know to be *ewig in der Schwebe*? - T.S.] ... G. "You are seeking too much help from strangers, and particularly from women."]

Well, well, K. had his weaknesses. Yet K. still believed that the preacher or priest or chaplain, or whatever your translator may call him, was honestly on his side and that he were able to help him in some fashion,

"nicht etwa wie der Prozess zu beeinflussen war, sondern wie man aus dem Prozess ausbrechen, wie man ihn umgehen, wie man auserhalb des Prozesses leben könnte." [p.432] ["not how to influence the trial, but how to break out from it, how to bypass it, how to live outside this trial."]

The reader may not have noticed at first reading a small detail but which is to be retained in memory because possibly useful when considering the argument in the next sections of this essay. It is important to recall all the time of the reading the possibility of "living outside the trial". Not winning or losing it, just living outside it. How to get around it? Is that the Law?

Now the *Geistlicher* was indeed friendly. He subsequently tried to explain the "Law" to K. As the story advances we encounter more and more often the term Court - *Gericht* - **court,** as well as *Gesetz* - law, and less often that of the *Behörde* - authority. Why? The text does not say anything about this change in frequency. But the priest thinks that K. deceives himself about the Court, and implicitly about the Law. So he goes about to explain the Law by a parable. It is not of his invention. Rather it is part of the *"einleitenden Schriften zum Gesetz"* or the "introductory text[s] or scripture[s] to the Law". Yet another difference from what we may think to be a *law*. This one is introduced by a parable. Laws, in our common perception, are supposed to be unambiguous. Parables seldom are. A parable is something of an empty form which we may fill with things of our own perception, which happen to be perceived to match that form. But this should be discussed a bit later. Here we first rehearse that parable, the *Türhüterlegende* or the legend of the gatekeeper, recalling also the conclusion of him who tells the story:

> *"Ich habe dir die Geschichte im Wortlaut der Schrift erzählt. Von Täuschung steht nichts darin".* [p.436] "I told you the story according to the letter of the Scripture. Yet nothing is said in it about deception."

So let us believe that nobody wants to deceive either K. or the reader. But then we also have to carefully "listen". We did this when we read the book so that here we shall only mark down a few points needed to continue the discussion of *what is written*! First we are told:

> *"Vor dem Gesetz steht ein Türhüter."* [p.432] "In front of the Law a gatekeeper is posted."

So, please, do your best to stick with the *Wortlaut* and nothing else. You will not be accused by anybody of fanciful hermeneutics when concluding that the *Law* has a physically specified abode which also has a *Gate*. As far as the *litera* goes. We don't yet wander any farther. Now we find out in sequence that a man from the country arrives to the Gate and asks the *Türhüter*, the gatekeeper, for admission. He is told that this may be possible sometime later, not yet. It certainly proves, once again, that the Law of this story is physically localized. Yet do not try to find out "what the author wanted to say", because there is no reason to assume that he submitted to you a riddle. He just told you a story, several stories within a larger one. So it is we, the readers, who may be enlightened by *our* associations, not *his*, of which we know nothing. But we are not yet as far as making associations. What we know is that there is something called the Law which is physically localized and has a Gate through which you may enter *to the Law* if permitted by a gatekeeper. Recall your text: the Gate is always open, only admission is not always permitted by the guard. Or is it? The man from the country tried to peek through the Gate behind the guard, who was amused by this and told him in a friendly manner:

> *"Wenn es dich so lockt, versuche es doch, trotz meinem Verbot hineinzugehen. Merke aber: Ich bin mächtig. Und ich bin nur ein*

Türhüter. Von Saal zu Saal stehen aber Türhüter, einer mächtiger als der andere. Schon den Anblick des dritten kann nicht einmal ich mehr vertragen." [p.433] ["If you are tempted to enter, try it against my forbiddance. However, remember the following: I am powerful, though I am only a gatekeeper. But inside, from hall to hall, there are other gatekeepers, one mightier than the other. Even to me the sight of the third one is already unbearable."]

Not much of an encouragement. Certainly not for our man who thought - don't we? - that

"das Gesetz soll doch jedem und immer zugänglich sein." ["everybody should always have access to the Law."]

What remained to be done? The man from the country decided to stay on. And while he was waiting the reader could ask himself: is it the Law, the *positive Law*, or is it rather *Justice* which was meant by the author? Since Justice being a more general, or rather a hazy notion, we may be inclined to associate it with some "physical" concepts such as "access". But we should abandon this for the moment because it is not according to the *Wortlaut der Schrift*. - So the man tarried. For years! And even bribed the guard who accepted the gifts *"damit du nicht glaubst etwas verseumt zu haben"* - "so that you shouldn't think to have missed out on something". Good fellow that gatekeeper, indeed. And the man from the country lingered for years, until his supplies were exhausted - he must have had quite a lot with him - and approached the end of his days. Yet he would still have liked to have an explanation; how come that nobody else asked permission to enter when we know that everybody "dies for the Law"? (Would Justice not still be a better term than Law?) And here is the answer:

"Hier konnte niemand sonst Einlass erhalten, denn dieser Eingang war nur für dich bestimmt." [p.434] ["Nobody else could have been granted entrance here, since this entrance was meant only for you."]

So the man was lost. He didn't achieve to *enter* the Law, he didn't get Justice. Is the burden of the parable a metaphor of K.'s case? We are entitled to think as much even though the *Geistlicher* was not explicit. As for interpretations, we are warned several times against such. We will have to accept temporarily that

> *"Richtiges Auffassen einer Sache und Missverstehen der gleichen Sache schliessen sich nicht vollständig aus."* [p.435] ["understanding correctly or misunderstanding the same thing do not completely exclude one-another."]

And, of course:

> *"Die Schrift ist unveränderlich, und die Meinungen sind oft nur ein Ausdruck der verzweiflung darüber."* [p.437] ["The Scripture/Script is unchangeable, and [the various] opinions are often only an expression of despair about it."]

This remains so even if we consider the *Türhüter* himself to be in a worse predicament than the man from the country. And why did the *Geistlicher* tell him this story? His confession at the end of Chapter Nine is explanatory of the *why* but not of the story's *what*. And this is it:

> *"Das Gericht will nichts von dir. Es nimmt dich auf, wenn du kommst, und es entlässt, wenn du gehst."* [p.440] ["The Court does not want anything from you. It grants you admission when you come and releases you when you go."]

Thus there is a *Behörde* (authority) to which a *Gericht* (tribunal) belongs, meant to apply *das Gesetz* (the Law) preserved behind a *Tor* (gate). The same *Behörde* orders arrests. Of whom? May be of those who have no courage to "come" so they be admitted by the *Gericht* which sometimes seems to be synonymous with the *Gesetz*? Let's settle for a compromise: the *Gericht* in the novel of K. is possibly the *Gesetz* in the parable of the *Türhüter*. And now, to get to the *Gericht* in the "real" world, or to the *Gesetz* in the parable, is utterly difficult because of the horrifying array of guards or gatekeepers. The "message" would then be that those who don't take the risks will fare like K. who was cruelly executed by the agents of the *Behörde*. With no sentence pronounced in a court of law. The agents took him to an abandoned quarry outside the city. On the edges of the quarry there was a house and a man in a window appeared to show some signs of despair.

> *"Wer war es? Ein Freund? Ein guter Mensch? Einer der teilnahm? Einer der helfen wollte? War es ein einzellner? Waren es alle? War noch hilfe?"* [p.444] ["Who was it? A friend? A good man? One who had compassion? One who wanted to help? Was he alone? Were they all like him? Is there still some [hope of] relief?"]

Hardly. But questions remained:

> *"Gab es noch Einwende die man vergessen hatte? Gewiss gab es solche. Die Logik ist zwar unerschütterlich, aber einem Menschen, der leben will, widersteht sie nicht. Wo war der Richter, den er nie gesehen hatte? Wo war das hohe Gericht, bis zu dem er nie gekommen war?"* [p.444] ["Are there still arguments forgotten? There must have been such, for sure. Logic is, of course, unshakeable, but it does not resist a man who wants to live. Where was the Judge whom he never saw? Where was that high Court to which he never came?"]

No answer. And K. was cruelly executed. There was no answer in the story. Can we find one?

(2) Possibilities and Limits of Interpretation.

The story, the text of *The Trial* is obviously puzzling. I will address here the puzzle while trying to keep my partiality for classical writing under control, which, of course, is much more difficult than just putting the book away half-read. I will start with a few simple assessments about the text proper, the mode of its composition. Repetitions will have to be accepted because they are inevitable.

The first thing to strike the reader is the plain character, the apparent precision of phrases. We don't find anything conventionally "literary" about them. Seldom are metaphors thrust upon the reader. Much, though not all of the text reads as a report in *Protokolsätze*, to fall back on Witgenstein's terminology.

But are those *Protokolsätze*, clear, unambiguous statements about matters of fact as they seem to be when we relax our critical urges? We read, e.g. that Josef K. was *verhaftet* i.e. arrested. This is a simple assessment. Or is it? When we or anybody else but Kafka say "K. was arrested", we think to have made an assessment about a fact. And we all associate this with exactly the same thing. It has little to do with our belief about the guilt or innocence of the person arrested. It, the arrest, may not be true, it may not have happened at all, but then we know exactly what that is what did not happen. So we have a simple phrase to which we would not be inclined to associate anything allegorical. But then it turns out that it is not factual either. Certainly not by our, universally adopted, usage of the language. Any language.

Then there is another class of "factual" statements which carry a vague hint of being allegorical, only the reader doesn't find out what they are allegorical about and so may still accept them as factual. What is the *actual* fact they are related to? Let me elaborate on an example already mentioned in the previous section. The uncle tells K. that he may be *gestrichen,* for which the English "blotted out" may not be the happiest translation. It may be also translated as erased, or deleted, or eradicated or obliterated. Not *ruined*! Now the precondition of being *gestrichen*, if literally meant, is that one should first be, allegorically or actually, recorded somewhere wherefrom to be *gestrichen* or erased. Is it a real or allegorical list, a real or allegorical register, or any other form of really or allegorically *written* evidence? But where is that evidence? Who keeps it? Does it exist at all, even in an allegory? And, most importantly, what are you deprived off when being *gestrichen* or blotted out? One thing is absolutely clear: just as being "arrested", being "blotted out" in that novel cannot be related to anything with which we associate such in regular speech.

Thus we have a non-"literary" text full with purportedly factual assessments, yet we do not, because we cannot, connect them to some facts or objects the language of which they seem to use. And yet we realize that the text is eerie. The impression is ghostly, spooky, weird. What exactly do these words mean? Do they mean anything? It was just said that much of the story appears to be presented in phrases worthy of a dry official document, yet we also realize that it is eerie. At least for some readers. It means, probably, that the reader associates what he reads with something which is not in the text proper. Meant being here the reader who is not yet "guided" by scholarly interpreters. The latter will try to translate the eeriness into words of explanation. These words are in most cases components of anything but *Protokolsätze*. But then, their meaning may also be questionable. They will not be taken on here. The purity of the text will be respected by trying *not to reduce* it to some meaning purportedly underlying it. An attempt will be made rather to *connect* the written text to the reader's own associations or "streams of thought". One particular reader's, such as the one's who writes these lines. And certainly not the author's possible associations, whichever they may be, absent from the text and kept from the *Wortlaut der Schrift*. However, the reader cannot keep at bay his own associations. They are descending upon him.

To keep clean of the arbitrary, the subsequent exercise will respect the principles on which these essays are based, and which have been outlined in **Introduction I and II**. These principles will be reiterated here in a simplified form and adapted to the discussion of this particular novel; mainly because the novel lends itself to interpretative distortions as well as to the demonstration of the fallacious character of such. Two rules should be set down concerning what I view as *permissible and non-permissible associations*. These two rules are most obvious and most important:

(1) Explanations to references within the text of the work assuming, sometimes mistakenly, every reader's knowledge of certain facts, are of the *permissible* category. These are not to be considered text falsifying. Therefore their detection to help pursue the reading is perfectly legitimate. It does not "interpret" the text. E.g. if a text mentions, and the reader hasn't heard of "Napoleon" or "Heisenberg's uncertainty principle", then the editor is entitled to add an explanatory footnote, or if failing to do so the critic may step in for him. Not many such cases will occur in the subsequent discussion, but they had to be mentioned to stress the difference between legitimate and illegitimate interference with the author.

(2) Biographical references are of the *non-permissible* category. We, the readers, do not know, should not know, anything about the life of the author. Or whatever we know we have to forget when reading. We know the text. Hence any biographical interpretation is illegitimate. Why? Because it may be useful to the author's shrink or relevant to such subject as "how novels come about". But the novel

or any literary work as given has to stand for itself when facing the reader. It has to be relevant to the reader.

Yet I cannot abstain from making a few comments on the existing explications of Kafka. Very short ones! Mostly to bracket them off. And then back to the *Trial - Prozess*.

There are a few widely held and variously commented wholesale judgments about the work of Kafka. I mean here the favorable ones. Their wide acceptance should not necessarily mean that they are "stereotypes", a word which in current usage means distortion by simplification. Though general statements are always simplifications, unable to carry more than a meaningful statement can anyway, we should not dismiss them out of hand. We can sympathize, even if not always agree, with things said purposing to free the critic and the reader from the pressing urge to express, by the means of the spoken/written *verbum*, the impression made by Kafka's major works. (Don't forget that while sometimes such formulations have no other purpose then to justify some, not necessarily meritorious theory, they are also very often the result of what in Hermann Broch's language would be the honest search for *"das Wort befreiend aus der Ruchlosigkeit des Unzulänglichen"* or" the word liberating from the infamy of inadequacy". Now try to translate this in factual statements. With a little effort you may be able.)

There are two most frequently, implicitly or explicitly propounded theses which, as simple formulations go, have the purpose of suggesting some orientation for interpretative empathy. One such explication, trying to come to grips with the bizarreness and eeriness in the *Prozess*, would outline something about prophecies of totalitarianism, and trying, probably not without good reason, to pick exemplary elements as metaphors of instants of the infamy of the twentieth century. One can, of course, freely choose passages in the *Prozess* serving as anecdotally quotable metaphors of whatever happened in the World throughout the twentieth century. But does this justify calling the "Trial" a prophecy? Just imagine somebody who might have read the novel over the shoulder of the author at the time when he was setting his words on paper. Would that person have made any metaphoric association between the mentioned passages and some future development of the kind they were supposed to be prophetic about? So the author is not likely to have implied *them* either. If *here and in this particular case* we are entitled to second-guess the author it is only to find out that there must be something else to be considered. And if we were to have to do here with some prophecy then it is such in a very roundabout fashion. The way "roundabout" is essential. So we should do this in sequence.

The other thesis, more muddled, claims that Kafka's novel is a parable of the modern man's alienation. This may not be all that bad a characterization if universal fuzziness would not prevail about what is after all that something man is alienated from, how and why. I do not claim that nothing can be used of the hundreds of analyses available, even if many of these serve more often as ideological promotion rather than a critical key to the intellectual pleasure of reading and analyzing. Yet I will avoid, as far as possible, to take issue with any of these writings which I disagree (or, for that matter, sometimes agree) with, and will try out my own interpretation. Yet the "possible" might have some limits, set also by temper.

(3) Associations: the Reader's Freedom

I start with the threatened repetition and reformulation of what was said in section (2) about the language of "The Trial", this time as the start for an alternative line of discussion.

Unlike when reading a story or a novel in what we may call the classical vein, the reader of The Trial can seldom associate the nonmaterial concepts employed in the discourse of Kafka with anything of his, the reader's, own experience. By *material concepts* I understand designators of things we may perceive. In the "Trial", words designating a wall, a window, a table, an auto or a cathedral, are used in the same way as anybody else would. But nonmaterial, i.e. abstract concepts employed in the *Prozess* cannot be associated in an obvious fashion to what anybody understands to be an arrest, an indictment, an "authority", a court, etc. in any political order. The court session in Chapter 2 can be viewed as such by material association, though not the "Court" itself. While the "arrest" is not an arrest proper because K. remains free, the trial in Chapter 2 has some characteristics of any real world trial, each taken separately: judges on the bench, public in the courtroom, etc. Only it is bizarre, but not incomprehensible as most everything what lead to it. And the reader continues to read because he wants to find out "where is all this leading?"

So the reader is uneasy. He looks for an explanation of his uneasiness and not for K's guilt, since the latter cannot be assessed. Thus, perhaps, the simple fact that K. is under some *unspecified accusation* yet subject to *very specific harassment,* may bring up thoughts in the memory of the reader concerning similar situations. The oft mentioned political associations are not unjustified in the sense that nobody has a complete control over his thoughts. There are controllable thoughts, such as an orderly logical or, also, un-logical or fallacious consecution. But then there are thoughts which just come upon us, sometimes provoked by memories. Memories of experiences but also memories of past readings. One may recall the classical case of an afflicted man, punished, though firmly convinced of his innocence: Job. But from the Book of Job the reader finds out about the cause of his affliction; it is not guilt of any kind, it is rather an experiment, decided in Heaven, meant to test Job's faith and to counter the Adversary's allegations. And Job was finally rewarded for his undue sufferings. But in the case of Josef K. we are not informed about the sources of his tribulations. Therefore, unlike in the case of a first reader of the book of Job, we are totally uncertain and at the mercy of our "streams of thoughts". The common feature between the Book of Job and the *Prozess* is the "trial" (not necessarily in a court of law!) of a man who *may be* perceived to be innocent. By *us,* the readers. May be. But then we have the human environment in which the man on trial is living: neighbors and relatives, lawyers and officials in the case of K., and the three, later four friends in the case of Job. [And I don't exactly know why, but the three colleagues from the bank where Josef K. works intrude in my thinking, even though they are not as talkative as the friends of Job.] Can we make associations? We know that both Job *and* K. consider themselves innocent but this is not the opinion of those in their surroundings. Nobody wants to believe an afflicted person to be innocent, especially not when he is already "tried". We hear Eliphaz of Teyman say to Job:

"4.7. Remember, I pray thee, who ever
perished, being innocent?

"4.8. According as I have seen, they that plow iniquity,
and sow mischief, reap the same.

"5.6. For affliction cometh not fourth from the dust,
Neither does trouble spring out from the ground;"

These are the non-comforting words of a "friend" of Job. If it sounds familiar it may be because you also recall the earlier quoted opinions of *Fräulein* Bürstner, representative of most everybody else's opinion about K's "Trial":

> "*'Nun, schuldlos' sagte das Fräulein, 'ich will* nicht gleich ein vielleicht folgenschweres Urteil aussprechen, auch kenne ich sie doch nicht, es uss doch schon ein schwerer Verbrecher sein, dem man gleich eine Untersuchungskommission auf den *Leib schickt*." [p.279] ["Well, guiltless, said the *Fräulein*, I wouldn't like to pronounce right away a foreboding verdict, and I also don't [really] know you. But he must be a hardened criminal whom they send a Commission of Enquiry on his back."]

But also Josef K. realizes the inevitable. We recall him having said to the painter Titorelli:

> "*Darin stimmen aber alle überein, das* leichtsinnige Anklagen nicht erhoben werden und dass das Gericht, wenn es einmal anklagt, fest von der Schuld des Angeklagten überzeugt ist und von dieser Überzeugung nur schwer abgebracht *werden kann*." [378-379] ["Yet they all [those who have some knowledge about the Court] agree on one thing, namely that charges are not laid in a haphazard fashion and that once the Court is firmly convinced of the defendant's guilt it will be difficult to make it reverse its opinion.]

And K. asserts his innocence all the time, especially in his long speech in the Court in Chapter 2. He does exactly what Job decided to do:

"7.11. Therefore I will not refrain my mouth;
I will speak in the anguish of my spirit;
I will complain in the bitterness of my soul."

K. is also recalcitrant and does not seem to recognize any guilt. To a very unnerved uncle he says:

"Ich dachte ... dass du dem Ganzen noch weniger Bedeutung beimessen würdest als ich, und jetz nimmst du es selber so schwer." [p.335] ["I thought ... that you would grant the matter even less importance than I do, and now you yourself take it so seriously."]

The uncle seems to see K. behaving like the assumed sinner in the Bible who says

"'I shall have peace, though I shall walk in stubbornness of my heart - that the watered be swept away with the dry'"? [Deut. XXIX, 18]

But then we also read about that same sinner that

"...the anger of the Lord and his jealousy shall be kindled against that man, and all the curse that is written in this book shall lie upon him, and *the Lord shall blot out his name from under the Heaven.*" [Deut. XXIX, 19]

This may be what the uncle knows when he reacts to K.'s apparent stubbornness:

"Weisst du, was das bedeutet? Das bedeutet, das du einfach gestrichen wirst." "Do you know what this means? This means that you will be simply blotted out."

Gestrichen - erased, or blotted out. Moreover, everybody close to the sinner may suffer because of that closeness, yet without guilt: "the watered be swept away with the dry". Or otherwise stated:

"... das die ganze Verwandschaft mittgerissen oder wenigstens bis auf den Boden gedemütigt wird. Josef, nimm dich zusammen. Deine Gleichgültigkeit bringt mich um den Verstand." [p.336] ["... that the

whole family will be dragged along or at least deeply humiliated. Josef, pull yourself together. Your indifference drives me crazy."]

K. doesn't seem to have much understanding for the idea of the kind of Justice which is behind his prosecution, whatever that is, therefore he is served by the *Geistlicher* with the *Türhüterlegende* or "The priest behind the gatekeeper legend". Attention! It is that very same *Geistlicher* who was quoted to be so very concerned with respecting the *written* word, the *Wortlaut der Schrift*. But, in fact, it is not he who invented the legend. It is rather an explanation meant to help K. avoid some misunderstanding or *Täuschung* about him, the *Geistlicher*. And right "in the introductory passages to the Law we read about the Deception" (*"in den einleitenden Schriften zum Gesetz heisst es von der Täuschung"*) something what turns out to be a legend. So we find out that the Law itself operates with parables, because factual statements would not suffice. The parable itself is "factual" in its formulation. And it is now Chapter 9 in which for the first time "literature" slips into the report which so far was edited mostly in what appear to be *Protokolsätze*.

We find out that it is about a gate behind which the Law resides. We don't know how to correctly translate the meaning of this metaphor. It is the metaphor of what? Has such been used before? Yes, countless times. The Hebrew *Shaareh Tzedek*, the Gate of Righteousness or of Justice, is a common notion in the Hebrew lore. Several synagogues, and even some hospitals, carry this name. We know about it from Psalm 118:

> "19. Open to me the gates of righteousness;
> I will enter into them, I will give thanks to the Lord.
> This is the gate of the Lord;
> The righteous shall enter it."

The term *Tzedek* is alternatively used for Justice and Righteousness, sometimes also for "good deed" in Biblical, Talmudic and modern spoken Hebrew.

Did the author know about it? Irrelevant! What the author wanted to say is said in the text. The reader *may* make associations. Is it not arbitrary? A literary work is an imitation, in the Aristotelian sense of the word, of a fact or an experience. Simple statements, however, are limited in their ability to render the contents of an experience. Still, they may be able to reproduce the image of material things and connections in which the experience comes about thus helping the reader to mentally "imitate" the experience. Yet when this is not possible then metaphors and parables may be helpful in bringing about the same. Now, several authors may have the same experience and thus chance upon the same metaphors. The parallel, which is no "interpretation" but an association, may then open the reader's way to further associations. If, however, he is discreet, he will keep for himself the associations that occur to him further. Except when such occur to the prophet:

"Open you the gates,
That righteous people that keep faith may enter it." [Isaiah, XXVI, 2]

If they are ready to. The "man from the country" in this parable was not. (And just by the way of another association: was the "man from the country" an *am-haaretz,* or as it might have been more familiar at the café frequented by Kafka in the *Dlouha ulica* in Prague, an *am-hooretz*? Sorry, I slipped into the sin of second guessing the author. Withdrawn.) So the man from the country just faced a gate behind which seemingly unsolved mysteries were kept. Indeed many more gates after gates create a puzzling labyrinth. We remember what the gatekeeper said to the man from the country:

"*Wenn es dich so lockt, versuche es doch, trotz meinem Verbot hineinzugehen. Merke aber: Ich bin mächtig. Und ich bin nur ein Türhüter. Von Saal zu Saal stehen aber Türhüter, einer mächtiger als der andere. Schon den Anblick des dritten kann nicht einmal ich mehr vertragen.*" [p.433] ["If you are tempted to enter, try it against my forbiddance. However, remember the following: I am powerful, though I am only a gatekeeper. But inside, from hall to hall, there are other gatekeepers, one mightier than the other. Even to me the sight of already the third one is unbearable."]

The gatekeepers create an enormous difficulty even for the most adventurous and brave. Because if it were only the multitude of gates, and no watchmen, some solution may still exist as we can find out from the *Midrash Rabbah* [MR]. A legend in it is often quoted as an allegory of the Law - the Torah. The following parable is attributed to Rabbi Nahman:

"Imagine a large palace with many doors, so that whoever entered therein lost his way. What did a certain wise man do? He took a ball of cord and tied it near the door. Then all commenced to enter and go out by means of the clue."

The allegory is said at least three times, in slightly modified forms, first in the *Midrash* to Genesis XII and Job XXVI.14, as quoted above, and then to the Song of Songs where the idea is further developed in a way to generate associations relevant to this discussion. Here is the variant:

"Said R. Nahman: Imagine a large palace with many doors, so that whoever entered could not find his way back to the door, till one clever person came and took a coil of string and hung it up on the way to the door, so that all went in and out by means of the coil. So till Solomon arose no one was able to understand properly the words of the Torah, but as soon as Solomon arose all began to comprehend the Torah.(Quoted from the *Midrash Rabbah* to the Song of Songs. - MR-I,1.8)

Solomon was wise and also lucky. This was not given to every king or leader. Their power could have been limited. So was Moses'. He could not cross the Jordan "to see the good land that is beyond" (Deut. III, 23), because his mission was over.

"This can be compared to a king who had a favorite, who had the power to appoint generals, governors, and commanders-in-chief. Later, the people saw him entreating the gatekeeper to let him enter the palace, and he would not permit him. Everyone was amazed at this and said, 'yesterday he was appointing generals, governors, and commanders-in-chief and now he in vain begs the gatekeeper to let him enter the palace'".(*Madras Rabbi* II,3. to Deuteronomy III, 23.)

What is the difference between the two kings? Solomon didn't encounter any watchman, but the other king, *any* other king, had to face a gatekeeper. He/they tried to entreat him, just as the "man from the country" tried to bribe him. To no avail. The "gate" is not to be crossed by everybody. Some are kept out.

Josef K. did not understand that particular Law, *das Gesetz*, the one that seems to have had application in his case. So the *Geistlicher* treated him with a parable. How much did K. get out of it? And the reader? What we find are like-sounding literary precedents. But then: what about the answer? Do we really, did K. really search for it? We try to understand the parable and suspect(!) it to be an allegory. Of what? Well, we just search for other allegories because when we categorically state that "it is the allegory of X", then we may be asked why is the X not being made explicit. If we were able to do that, would we need the allegory or the parable in the first place? What is the Law by which some may be saved and others, such as K., doomed?

The parable does not specify everything. It keeps open ... the gate. Yet another gate. We may walk in with our understanding, but there is no unique such. If it were, we would not use allegory conveying parables, and the *Prozess* as an open parable would not have been written. So we just multiply the parables, as others did before:

> "So proceeding from one thing to another, from one parable (*mashal*) to another, Solomon penetrated the innermost meaning of the Torah ... Our Rabbis say: Let not the parable be lightly esteemed in your eyes, since by means of the parable a man can master the words of the Torah. ... So the parable should not be lightly esteemed in your eyes, since by means of the parable a man arrives at the true meaning of the words of the Torah." (Again *Shir Ha-Shirim Rabbah*, I,1.8.)

Now the Rabbis, such as the earlier mentioned Rabbi Nahman (he died in 320 C.E.), tell us that the *litera*, if not explicit, can be enlightened by the *allegoria*. (Though they didn't use the Latin terms I borrowed from a famous saying of Augustin of Dacia who lived about one thousand year later.) Why? Probably because the *litera* cannot state everything. There is a plus for which we are searching. Wittgenstein concluded his treatise on the principles of logic and philosophy with the following recommendation:

> "Whereof one cannot speak, one must be silent."

Yet he may have had an inkling that being "silent" will not really liberate us from the "*Ruchlosigkeit des Unzulänglichen*" (Broch), since his Tractatus Logico-Philosophicus is not loath of using metaphors. These metaphors were meant to supplement what the plain philosophical statements, those which *we can speak of*, may not have completely conveyed. Therefore we may rather say: Whereof one cannot speak *meaningfully* one may say or read(!) parables, i.e. parables conveying allegories and using metaphors. And then how far can we go interpreting the *Prozess*? Well, we may do it by "proceeding from one thing to another, from one parable to another". And we may as well start again with the Book of Job.

So we may start anew. But in the book of Job we can clearly distinguish three parts, namely

(1) The decision in Heaven about Job to be tried, i.e. tested. So we know why he is/will be tested/afflicted.

(2) The story of the trial or test of Job.

(3) Job's redemption.

This is, after all, a complete outline for the plan of a literary *trial* or *test* of a human's value and valor. Josef K. was also tested. With a difference. In the case of the Book of Job, the main character of the story ignored the cause of the trial. But the reader was informed right from the beginning. In Kafka's Trial neither the main character in the story nor the reader learn about the origin of K.'s misadventure. His story may be an empty form in which so many similar trials may fit, with a variety of root causes. And it may not be one man's trial. The reader may have had experiences which he associates with his reading. Maybe K. is only a representative case for something more general. It is about life under only half-specified accusations. Against such there is no defense in a court of law for the simple reason that it is indeed only half-, or un-specified. Yet many defend themselves against it:

> "*jeder Angeklagte, selbst ganz einfältige* Leute, gleich beim allerersten Eintritt in den Prozess an Verbesserungsvorschläge zu denken anfangen und damit oft Zeit und Kraft verschwenden, die anders viel

besser *verwendet werden könnten.*" [p.355] ["every defendant, even very simple people, would start thinking on some improvement proposals right after their first involvement in the trial, thereby wasting time and energy which could otherwise be much better used."]

Indeed, they want to improve. To improve what? The alternative is to think of some form of collective defense. But then

"Wenn manchmal in einer Gruppe der Glaube an ein gemeinsames Intersse auftaucht, so erweist er sich bald als ein Irrtum. Gemeinsam lässt sich gegen das Gericht nichts durchsetzen, nur ein einzelner erreicht manchmal etwas im geheimen; erst wenn es erreicht ist, erfahren es die anderen; keiner weiss, wie es geschehen ist. Es gibt also keine Gemeinsamkeit ..." [p.401] ["Whenever the belief in a collective interest wells-up among a group of individuals, this soon will prove itself to be an error. Nothing can be achieved collectively against the Court. Only an isolated individual may, sometimes, accomplish something in secret. And only after this happens, will the others find out about it, while nobody will learn about how it actually happened. Hence, there is no such thing as a common cause."]

And why should life, over which unspecified accusations are hovering, end in such a horrible death? No explicit answer to this question can be found in the story of Josef K. Yet we cannot give up looking for one.

A parable is a form in which the reader fits his own experience. And there are many who could make sense of *Der Prozess.* There are many who have memories to associate with the Trial parable. But this is by no means simple and straightforward. The novel in case, unlike the more familiar classical novel, is something we may call an empty form. What is that *empty form*? Instead of a definition, yet another parable may help to get through yet another gate behind which *one* possible understanding of a new novel resides. And while it is very unlikely that the professional litterateur will approach with much sympathy or knowledge that gate, it is much more likely that among the general readers there will be many who are in the possession of an entry ticket. This is thus not the gate to the Law or Justice. It is the gate of understanding. One of the gates of the many. And the reader may try to get access to it with the help of a

(4) Mathematical Parable

about yet another gate. This time about a gate in ancient Athens on which it was written:

ΜΗΔΕΙΣ ΑΓΕΟΜΕΤΡΗΤΟΣ ΕΙΣΙΤΟ.

Plato thought that nobody ignorant of geometry should get beyond the gate of his school. And he meant by *geometry* not only and not simply the surveyor's art, but rather the art of logically rigorous consecution, the paragon of logic's successful application. And the thus shown respect for careful thinking could justify anybody who forgives Plato, and his master Socrates, for quite a few logical fallacies. I mean some of those fallacies which are the delight of so many who are actually αγεωμετριτωσ and who also indulge in misinterpreting works of literature. Now, the platonic prohibition could have a wider application. Geometry is just a branch of that much larger field of knowledge called mathematics. Yet it is still the paragon of correct reasoning wherefore some, who care to be consistent, still endeavour, even if not always successfully and/ or avowedly, to reason *ordine geometrico*. Or ordine matematico. This being, of course, a metaphor. Now, these sciences may also offer something in addition to logical rigor. They could offer metaphors and allegories to help us understand what plain words do not or cannot directly convey. For example, by using a mathematical-geometric example we may understand something of what is that "filling in" of the empty spaces in an "open novel", such as Kafka's Trial. There is, however, a little problem: a minimum of geometry and algebra is required to cross the gate. The first(!) gate. Because there are many. But the humble gatekeeper at the first gate, though himself frightened by some of those stern and lofty others guarding the following entries, will generously provide an example which may grant entry also to the reader of *Der Prozess*.

Take as an example a randomly chosen number, say number '72'. It is the one which follows '71' in the array of natural numbers, and precedes '73'. But this number may "come about" in an infinite variety of ways. It may have many stories. For instance by some addition or subtraction such as 2+70, 34+38,

81-9, 20+15+37, etc., etc. ... etc. The result is always 72, but the story is quite different in every instance. A more interesting case would be to consider: $2 \cdot 6^2 = 72$. This is a different story but also completely told. No mystery hiding behind it. And what about an example from the border area between algebra and calculus? We could say $2 \cdot x^2 = 72$. Is this any different from what was given earlier? Well, it is not straightforward because it requires to be solved, and we will find out that $x=6$. We do this sometimes when reading a story. Or *the author* when he is writing it. In the development of the story we are lead to the solution of some mystery, an "unknown". In very simplistic stories, and there are lots of such, you may have no trouble guessing that "x", while hardly getting any smarter. - We may add now a further complication to the above relationship such that it becomes: $2 \cdot x^2 = y$. There is no unique solution to this. In fact it is not something to be solved, it is rather the map of an infinity of possibilities for which we have learned to construct a graph. A graph for a *parabola of second degree*, that is. Not "everything is possible", though the possibilities are infinite. Because permitted is just as much as can be fitted within the form of the function defined by some pivotal numbers, namely the coefficient 2 and the power 2. And yet there is an infinity of pairs (x, y) which satisfy the frame-formula $2 \cdot x^2 = y$ not to be trespassed. If it is given, we may play around by fitting in the numbers. As mentioned above, the formula is that of a *parabola*. One shouldn't rush to the conclusion that this is meant now to be the parable we are discussing. The etymological connection exists, but it is of no direct interest to this argument. Of interest is the fact that it, or its more general form $a \cdot x = y$, can be "filled-in" in a variety of ways. It is not yet a story. But is it just the empty paper? Hardly, because it already has a *form*. Countless other empty forms can be contrived. By adopting the convention whereby the "given" values in such a form[ula] are taken from the first letters of the Latin alphabet while the "unknown" values are indicated by the last ones, we may construct any number of empty forms, such as: (1) $ax+by=z$, or (2) $ax+by=c$, or (3) $ax+by+z/c=d$ ... etc., etc. Still, we are almost as if on the "empty paper". The "storyteller" may start out by giving specific values to the as, the bs, the cs, etc. at the beginning, keeping for a while the reader in suspense about how the other values, the xs, ys, zs, etc., will be filled in. Because the above aligned forms or formulae do not have unique solutions. There is an infinity of such for each of them. They are solved in classical, and good, "storytelling" by one or another array of compatible numbers being filled-in as the story goes on. And at the end the suspense will be over because nothing will remain empty when the symbols become numbers. If, however, the "author" chooses to leave something open, it is the "reader" who will have to make compatible substitutions. The trouble is that very often the substitutions are made rather arbitrarily and the "equation" will have a fallacious resolution offered by the critic or the careless reader. And I am afraid that among the former the αγεωμετρητωι are much more numerous than among the latter. - (The reader could, of course, expand the algebraic metaphor to equation systems. Thus we may have, as in most above quoted examples, under-specified systems in which the "storyteller" may substitute arbitrary values yet compatible with the *given* frame. Arbitrarily chosen yet compatible with the form-frame: this is essential to the manner we may fill-in the emptiness. And, may be, the reader may construct additional equations to make the system completely specified. But be careful: the additional equations have to be compatible with the already existing ones. Don't dabble with the pre-given frame! It *is* the *Wortlaut der Schrift.*)

Before returning to the Kafka novel by employing the above introduced notions, a short listing of their possible uses should be given:

- Of course, this is a metaphor of that something which is behind the gate of understanding in the "mathematical parable". But novels don't have mathematical solutions; yet the mathematical notions of above will bring the approach closer to logical compatibility by warning us about the possible connections between *given frames and the values/stories to be filled-in.*

- Beware of those who change the *litera* i.e. the Latin letter-values already given at the beginning, or the frame form[ula] proper.

- The legitimate parable has a similar form[ula] to suggest the possible ways of solving when there is no unique solution. Since there are cases when some of the a, b, etc. numbers are not specified. Here parables may also help. But how to substitute?

- Thus in *Der Prozess* some pivotal values, required to solve the problem, are missing. E.g. not only the "unknowns" are unknown but neither are some of the "givens" given. It looks as if like this:

$$ax+5y+8z=d$$

So we now come back to the story. There is a trial against K. But we have no specific accusations. In fact the accusations would be a given constant in a classical story. Or: K. is afflicted by the harassment of the "authority". It doesn't look very frightening at the beginning, but we don't know why. In classical stories we know it. We also know it in the case of Job.

One more repetition to see what is in the frame and what can be compatibly filled in. Consider the schema of any real world variety of a trial or even show trial in a totalitarian society. First let us define the point of view of an Authority (not an "Authority") in any real-world society. The phases should be the following:

(1) Suspicion and/or denunciation.

(2) Arrest.

(3)

   (3a) Detention or

   (3b) release on bail.

    If (3a) then

   (4a) Arraignment, charge or indictment.

    If (3b) then

   (4b) Inquest or inquiry or probe or investigation or whatever you may call it.

(5) Trial.

(6) Sentence:

   (6a) Conviction.

   (6b) Acquittal.

(7) In case 6a: Execution of sentence.

In the text of any trial's story offered to the reader, some of the above phases may be skipped by the author. How much is the freedom of the reader to substitute? From the discussion in previous sections the reader may now check the above list to see what he may count on. For K., however, there are two aspects to this whole story, an objective and a subjective one. As far as the objective aspect is concerned: (2) is symbolic and (3a) or (3b) did not come up at all. But the most important thing is (4) and (5), which appear in a fuzzy fashion and this is at the origin of K.'s trials and tribulations.

Since none of the formal aspects of a real-world trial comes up, we are entitled to suspect a parable. But parables have structures deemed to be *parallels* of what they are supposed to be parables of. So we are in trouble. The story impresses (some of) us, yet we don't know why? Is it a thriller to be solved? A mystery? Before continuing, it is important to explain why the answer to this question is in the negative: it is no thriller, thrilled though we may be. There are essential differences between "The Trial" and any thriller or mystery story of any brow height. To be specific, we may distinguish two types of suspense stories/plays. There are those where the reader knows at the beginning, or is helped to find out early, about what the *crime* is, or that there is a crime to *be specified*. And then there are those in which the *criminal* is early specified. In the first case the *suspense* offering the thrill to the reader/spectator consists in the process of discovering the criminal. It can be by a peripeteia as so often from "Oedipus the King" to some of the good stories of Georges Simenon. In the second case the reader's anxious expectation is addressed to the process of finding the proof. Once again it is the ancients who could teach us best about this, but also Hercule Poirot may occasionally step-in offering free tuition. Important: the knowledge of either the crime or the criminal has to give the solid frame of a story in which the author has to fit in, stepwise, the values for the unknowns as *compatible with the frame*. Now, in our novel, we neither know the crime nor is the "criminal" a criminal without the crime specified. But he is arrested or rather "arrested", which means harassed in a most outlandish manner. Vague insinuations of an unspecified guilt are called prosecution. This is the fuzzy frame.

All considered, this is a novel from which the solid frame is missing. Yet we read it. We read it like an un-precise poem which stirs our mood or feelings, for reasons we cannot specify. We then try associations such as those with earlier readings, as quoted in previous sections. Then associations of experiences in life. There are countless. But just try the following without being able to avoid, once again, some repetitions. Neither some widely spread conclusions. Only this time the conclusion will come about by filling in one of the possible "unknowns"; they will not be guesses but an array of developments consistent with the frame story. Also an allegory.

Think again of a man who *seems to be* accused of an unspecified guilt. Not even his accusers bother to be specific:

> *"Ich kann Ihnen auch durchaus nicht sagen, das sie angeklagt sind oder vielmehr, ich weiss nicht, ob sie es sind. Sie sind verhaftet, das ist richtig, mehr weiss ich nicht."* [p.268] ["I cannot tell you exactly that you are charged; I don't know whether you are [charged]. You are arrested, that is true, [but] more I don't know."]

Then, the arrested person realizes that he is by far not the only one to be in this predicament. Maybe even house painters could be in the same situation. And our man makes it clear that

> *"... was mir geschehen ist, ist ja nur ein einzelner Fall und als solcher nicht wichtig, da ich es nicht schwer nehme, aber es ist ein Zeichen eines Verfahrens, wie es gegen viele geübt wird. Für diese stehe ich hier ein, nicht für mich."* [p.292] ["... whatever happened to me, is only a single instance and as such of no importance, since I don't take it seriously. Yet it is characteristic of a procedure directed against many. And I stand up for all those [others]."]

Many of those "many" search for that guilt while denying having any such. And, just in case, they also try to improve as

> *"jeder Angeklagte, selbst ganz einfältige Leute, gleich beim allerersten Eintritt in den Prozess an Verbesserungsvorschläge zu denken anfangen und damit oft Zeit und Kraft verschwenden, die anders viel besser verwendet werden könnten."* [p.355] ["every defendant, even very simple people, would start thinking of some improvement proposals right after their first involvement in the trial, thereby wasting time end energy which could otherwise be much better used."]

They may try to defend themselves collectively against any abuses. But what are the abuses? We are not told and are free to make any compatible(!!!)

substitution. Neither had K. any idea of his guilt, and was never to find out because his never really held trial ended with execution. He tried alone, as many, and as felt to be the proper way by somebody who thought to provide a friendly advice:

> "*Wenn manchmal in einer Gruppe der Glaube an ein gemeinsames Intersee auftaucht, so erweist er sich bald als ein Irrtum. Gemeinsam lässt sich gegen das Gericht nichts durchsetzen, nur ein einzelner erreicht manchmal etwas im geheimen; erst wenn es erreicht ist, erfahren es die anderen; keiner weiss, wie es geschehen ist. Es gibt also keine Gemeinsamkeit ...*" [p.401] ["Whenever the belief in a collective interest wells-up among a group of individuals, this soon will prove itself to be an error. Nothing can be achieved collectively against the Court. Only an isolated individual may, sometimes, accomplish something in secret. And only after this is achieved, will the others find out about it, while nobody will find out how it actually happened. Hence, there is no such thing as common cause."]

Is the society postulated by the story very different from what we think to be "normal"? Not all the way. Because all the characteristics of a society of law are also postulated. Josef K. knows about such things as arrest warrants, courts of law, charges etc., in the "normal" fashion. What happened struck him as a deviation from the "normal". All the "trial" happened *parallel* to what is normal. *Not instead of it but by the side of it*! Even the judges were assumed to be aware of all this. At least by Josef K. When characterizing the court procedure he said to the judge:

> "*Sie könnene einwenden, das es ja überhaupt kein Verfahren ist. Sie haben sehr recht, denn es ist ja nur ein Verfahren wenn ich es als solches anerkenne.*" [p.291] [" You may object that this is in fact no trial at all. You are right, since it is a trial only if I take it as such."]

No judge contradicted him. Indeed, the one who conducted the *Untersuchung*, the inquest, was quite embarrassed. And the public was in a tense expectation. But then, they were not among those against whom a *Verfahren* was undertaken, whether they were bank executives or house painters. Yet we find out something very important about them: they had some badges on their collars.

> *"Alle hatten diese Abzeichen, soweit man sehen konnte. Alle gehörten zueinander, die scheinbaren Parteien rechts und links, und als er sich plötzlich umdrehte, sah er die gleichen Abzeichen am Kragen des Untersuchungsrichters, der, die Hände im Schoss ruhig hinuntersah."* [p.296] ["They all had these badges, as far as one could see. They all belonged together, these purported parties of the left and right, and as he (Josef K.) instantly turned around, he saw the same badges on the collar of the instruction judge who looked down on them with his hands on his lap."]

So they had something in common with the judges and all the officials of the "authority": they wore the same badges signifying a community of purpose! Was everything undertaken by a coalition so far tolerated by the legal system? It certainly didn't show any sign of resistance. Josef K. had earlier expressed his own judgment about how the real system may be affected by the parallel one:

> «*Wie liesse sich bei dieser Sinnlosigkeit des Ganzen die schlimmste Korruption der Beamtenschaft vermeiden.?*» [p.295] ["How could then the worst corruption of civil servants be avoided in this meaningless situation?"]

Well, it was not. The "parallel" system prevailed:

> *"Darum suchen die Wächter den Verhafteten die Kleider vom Leib zu stehlen, darum brechen Aufseher in fremden Wohnungen ein, darum sollen Unschuldige, statt verhört, lieber vor ganzen Versamlungen entwürdigt werden."* [p.295] ["Therefore snatch the guardsmen the clothes from the body of the arrested, therefore break the supervisors into peoples' homes, therefore are the innocent, instead of being questioned, rather humiliated in front of an assembly."]

And those affected by a *Verfahren*/Procedure? Few of them contemplated resistance. They thought of improving or *proving themselves* "thereby wasting time and energy which could otherwise [have] be[en] much better used". And "everybody else", a third category, those without badges, who were not accused? They were either like *Fräulein* Bürstner giving some dubious credit to the prosecution, or the likewise puzzled landlady of Josef K. who preferred to be concerned with her tenant's morality, or the neighbors silently peeking from behind curtains, or the desperate man in the window at the sight of K.'s execution. None was *willingly* doing the job of the "authority". Lack of any will was enough for such. And Titorelli? Who knows, he may also have been provided later with a badge and gotten high up in the "authority". After all it would not have been the only instance in history when a fellow peddling bad little paintings in coffee houses gets way ahead. All of them were there; well before those things happened with which some associate developments in the story of Josef K. Yet it is undeniable that it was their behavior which helped those with the badges to open yet another gate. It was a gate through which could walk many of those who tried to "improve", thereby "wasting time end energy which could otherwise [have] be[en] much better used". Atop that gate they could read "*Arbeit macht frei*".

The author may never have thought of such. He may just have fitted in a value compatible with the story's equation when subjecting K. to a cruel execution. Yet he gave the picture of the "parallel" system. And what would the reader have found in the story had he read it in the early 1920s? He may, just may have done the same thing as quoted above. He may have picked out of *Der Prozess,* a story compatible with it all, with no deviation from the *Wortlaut der Schrift,* a story which lead to the horrible end of K. And he may hardly have had an explanation if not taking it as a parable of "a group" of individuals with unspecified, or only half specified accusations permanently hovering over their heads, individuals who also "would start thinking on some improvement ... thereby wasting time and energy which could otherwise be much better used". Because no matter how you twist the story to fill in for unknown values, few other varieties, if any, could be pulled out to explain the doomsday atmosphere of this poetic work. The conclusion may not be the only one, but it is compatible with the *Wortlaut der Schrift*. In the story proper the variety of conclusions is limited. And in real life? What, if some may attempt *not* to waste "time and energy" on offering themselves as "improved" to their accusers, realizing that "time and energy ... could ... be much better used"? Wouldn't they run the risk of being equated by some subtle litterateurs to the executioners of Josef K.?

Appendix to
The Modern Novel on Trial

- Of Kafka's *Der Prozess* -

Another Summary

This should be yet another discussion, a summarizing one, of the relationship between the text and the reader's reception. Meant is the reader who carefully considers the following three things: (1) the *Wortlaut der Schrift*; (2) whatever may be logically compatible with and deducible from the *Schrift* whenever it is not explicit about something; and (3) the plausible classification of the associations he makes while reading. This will be yet another recapitulation, however, when compared to the discussion in the main essay, it will partially change the order of presentation. This change of order is meant to be also a change in emphasis or accent. The here postulated reader knows also the mentioned essay but will avoid explaining anything in the text by using Kafka-biographical references.

The *Wortlaut der Schrift* was given a lot of attention in the essay but will be addressed again here. Very shortly! Yet it is absolutely necessary. So we have a society in which a number of things happen and which are designated with terms familiar to the reader. But while the terms or expressions are from our common vocabulary, it turns out that they are used to designate something different from that. Thus the author calls *arrest* something which is different from what the expression normally denotes; he implies the existence of an *authority*, some undefined entity which has only a very spurious resemblance to anything of this kind within any legal system; relates about a *court* or a *tribunal* the working of which is regulated by totally unidentifiable rules, though judge it does, and all this within a *trial* or *Prozess* in which no clear indictment is formulated, the "arrested" and "accused" defendant having no idea against what to defend himself; etc., etc. At some point we even read that

> *"keiner hat die Festsetzung der Hauptverhandlung verlangt oder durchgesetzt..."* [p.403] ["no one had asked or imposed a date for a court hearing"]

Does a society exist which lives and functions under such "laws"? Well, it may exist, but this is not the one in which Josef K. lived until the "trial" began, and when he was *arrested, prosecuted, tried,* and finally *actually executed* in the curious way we know. How do we know that this is not the established law in the society in which K. lives? Careful reading will show us that apart from what happened to the novel's main character (and less explicitly to others as well, such as perhaps a certain house painter), the very same terms listed above also designate exactly the same thing as *we* would understand. Josef K. knows about such things as *arrest warrants* which he asks his arresters to produce; he also knows that they have to have *identification papers* if they want to arrest him in the normal, legal fashion; he is aware of the fact that a court and a trial has to function, by and large, as we know it when we use the words *trial* and *court*. While facing his "judges", Josef K. makes no secret of this and no judge makes even an attempt to counter his opinion. The difference between a lawyer in a normal legal system and those within the *Prozess* is also perfectly well known to everybody in the novel and comes through in their thoughts and conversations.

All this is not interpretation or alternative "reading". It is written in the novel in which all the characters are living in a society in which there are courts, judges, wise, silly or unjust ones, authorities, etc. etc., according to the notions we have of such. Yet it is equally clearly shown that a *Prozess* is going on, *within the same society* but *outside and parallel to the existing established legal order* - which exists! - and that it is promoted by an undefined authority. It is likely that most readers are aware of this, yet it may also be the case that many are not considering *the permanence or duration of the parallelism between the two "systems"* within the same fictional society. The "second order", within which Josef K.'s *trial* proceeds, is different and outside the legal, institutional one. (And if I am using too many quotation marks, it is because our vocabulary is not fashioned to express in precisely definable terms things for which also Kafka had to resort to a quotation-mark terminology. Even if the quotation marks were missing from the print.)

But the "second order" exists though it is not shown to have any legally established foundation, yet the established legal system doesn't do anything to counter the "parallel" one, to oppose it in a definite, determined fashion. Further, the story reveals the existence of clearly definable groups within that society according to how they relate to the "trial". And it may just be said, *per tangentam*, that this typology would have required a little more attention in the critical literature than it actually received. Thus we first have the class of those who stand openly behind the purported authority which ordered the "arrest" and "trial" of Josef K. They have not been identified initially but they show up at the "trial", in the "court". They don't do very much, but demonstrate their attachment to the authority by wearing the same badges as the judges. They *belong*; they are distinguished from those who don't wear badges, from those who *don't belong*. So it is they who are the basis of the harassment. Still: harassment for what? We still don't know. And then, there is the class of those who are, were, or will be accused, for that unspecified, remaining to be unspecified, reason. Their harassment implies that they are "accused". One of them is likely a house painter. But there are many more. Some, indeed many of these others, try to "improve" themselves, though they haven't been told what exactly to improve. They understand that some people, followers of an "authority" to be reckoned with, consider them guilty of something. Those who imply their guilt are, of course, the badge wearers and the "court" they back. But not only they. There is a third class of individuals (a majority?) most of whom do not accuse directly or explicitly either Josef K. or anybody else, some(!) of whom may have mixed feelings about the whole "prosecution", yet who do not oppose it. And they do not show any opposition even though they know, just as Josef K., that within the institutionally established legal system, in order to be *arrested* an arrest warrant has to be produced; that in order to be *tried* an accusation has to be spelled out; etc. etc. They are aware of the *parallel system* and some, though not wearing badges, go along with it.

This is the story's frame definition. Should we call it a sociological frame? And Josef K.'s tragedy unfolds within this frame. In Greek tragedies the hero falls while trying to oppose or avoid the will of the gods. Josef. K. was condemned while he tried, in vain, to oppose the *parallel order* emerging within some "normal" society. And all the others? Were *Fräulein* Bürstner, K.'s land-lady, the neighbors peeking through their window curtains, etc. willingly par-ticipating in this? Not *willingly*. They were *lacking the will* to ask any questions and thus go to the bottom of things. And the "lawyers" were just taking ad-vantage of the emerging parallel system and, of course, posting the pictures of "judges". As for K.'s uncle, he tried to improve himself and his nephew hoping that thereby they will be saved from being *gestrichen*, blotted out. As for how the "improvers" fared, nothing is told in the *Schrift* proper.

Missing from the novel are the specifics of the second order system, the parallel one. We know *some* of its manifestations, but nothing more is indi-cated. Now think of a reader in whose life experience things of this kind hap-pened. There were many "second systems" in history which functioned like this and some may feel empathy with the story - and Josef K. To use again the terms of the mathematical metaphor discussed in the essay, several human experiences could be those *variables* which are compatible with the workings of the "second system's" *known* frame. The story as told fits many different ex-periences which, however, function like the one defined by the *Authority* and its badge wearing followers. You read it as a poem. Not a hermetic one though. Except for those who cannot associate any life experience with the novel. Nothing wrong with that. Bad is when all this is talked away by disregarding that framework which is exactly according to the *Wortlaut der Schrift*.

But there is a second layer of associations, and these are given by literary precedents. So the reader may now go back to the third section of the essay and consider its examples. There parables are recalled which refer to the pos-sibilities of searching, finding or missing the Truth. Or the Law. But these are only associations made by the reader in his, respectful, freedom. Remains to see what function the gatekeeper's story has in the whole recite. If anything, it is about the tragedy of the lone fighter. What is avoided is the fact that with K.'s execution the "parallels" actually met; the one became the other. So it hap-pened often in the real world, though the author hardly could have imagined it as bad as it happened to be after his death.

And just an additional question: was the insertion of the gatekeeper leg-end absolutely necessary from the point of view of the novel's economy? The question is open and doesn't really need an answer. It may be - just *may be!* - that Kafka believed that his readers are able of some associations we made in the essay. We could, of course, imagine an alternative way of presentation. Just think of the possibility that the guest of the bank whom Josef K. was supposed to meet at the cathedral had not been an Italian. Had he been a German or a Swiss then he would have arrived on time at the *rendezvous*, thereby depriving the *Geistlicher* of the opportunity to tell his story. The novel would still have made the same sense as the one suggested, only the critics may have had, perhaps, some more opportunity to disregard the *Wortlaut der Schrift*.

BIBLIOGRAPHIC NOTES

These are the sources of the various quotations included in the essays.

In all the essays in which they appear, quotations from Greek Classics are taken from editions easily accessible to the reader. Only when these "popular" editions were deemed to be of questionable quality have I used the Harvard (or Harvard-Heinemann) editions. In

Introduction I and II I used

- for Plato's "Republic" the 1982 edition of the Bollingen Series LXXI, Princeton University Press;

- for the "Poetics" of Aristotle, the Butcher translation available in many editions, as well as on the "web". This edition is also used in other essays of this collection;

- for "The Life of Apolonius of Tyana" by Philostratos, the translation by Charles P. Wels in the Stanford University Publication Series, 1923;

- for the "Encomium of Helen" by Gorgias of Leontini, the translation of D.N. MacDowel in Bristol Classical Press, 1982.

Essay No.1

For all quotations from Shakespeare, the Act, Scene and verse numbers are indicated as used in most editions. I used mainly "The Arden Shakespeare" edition. The sources of other quotations in this essay are indicated in the text.

Essay No.2

All quotations from Gogol are according to the English translation of Andrew R.MacAndrew, Signet Classics, 1961. Quotations from Chekhov's *The Steppe* are according to the English translation of Constance Garnett available in various editions and also on GOOGLE. Quotations from various other authors are translated by the author of this essay.

Essay No.3

The quotations from Sophocles' *Oedipus* are from the Harvard-Heinemann edition, translation by F. Storr. All other quotations are in the authors' language. For Shakespeare, once again, "The Arden Shakespeare" was used. Quotations from Dryden's *An Essay of Dramatic Poesy* are according to the text included in the series "English Critical Essays", Oxford University Press, 1922.

Essay No.4

The quotations from Balzac are according to several easily accessible editions. For *Gobseck*, GF FLAMARION, 1984; for *Splendeurs et miseres des courtisans* [SM], GF FLAMARION, 1968; for *Illusions perdues* [IP], Livres de Poches 1983.

Essay No.5

All Chekhov quotations are according to the translation of Avraham Yarmolinsky included in the "Portable Chekhov", Viking Press, NY. 1947.

Essay No.6

All quotations are in the translation of the author of this essay.

Essay No.7

All quotations from Joyce's Ulysses are according to the Penguin Modern Classics, 1986 edition. See also the "Notes" at the end of the essay.

Essay No.8

All quotations from Joyce's Ulysses are according to the Penguin Modern Classics, 1986 edition. This author's remarks to some of the quotations are in square brackets.

Essay No.9

All quotations are translated by the author of this essay and are based on the following original editions: for *Die Unbekannte Groesse* by Hermann Broch, Suhrkamp edition, 1977; for all Robert Musil quotations the *"Gesammelte Werke"*, *Rohwolt Verlag* edition, 1978.

Essay No.10

All quotations from *Der Mann ohne Eigenschaften* are translated from the easily accessible *Rowohlt Verlag*, Hamburg, 1952, edition. Other quotations are translated from the nine volumes *"Gesammelte Werke"* of Robert Musil in the *Rowohlt Verlag* 1978 edition. The first five volumes of this edition are also *Der Mann ohne Eigenschaften* and are continuously paginated. Volume numbers are given only for the other quoted writings in the essay.

Essay No.11

All quotations are from the handy "seven books in ten volumes" edition of Proust's novel, GF-Flammarion, 1986. The Flaubert quotations are likewise from the respective GF-Flammarion volumes.

Essay No.12

All quotations are according to *"Franz Kafka:Die Romane"*, S.Fischer Verlag, 1976.

Made in the USA
Lexington, KY
20 April 2014